Evolution of the Game

A Chronicle of American Football

By

FRANK FRANCISCO

Copyright © 2016 Frank Francisco

All rights reserved.

ISBN: 1495963845
ISBN 13:9781495963841

For my boys:

Jeff, Jim, Jaxson, Brandon, & Colin

"Perfection is not attainable, but if we chase perfection, we can catch excellence." - Vince Lombardi

Table of Contents

Chapter 1	Origins of the Game	1
Chapter 2	The Game in America	4
Chapter 3	Changes in the Game	16
Chapter 4	Dodging the Mass Formation Rule	31
Chapter 5	Saving the Game	60
Chapter 6	Outcry Brings More Changes	84
Chapter 7	The "Aerial Circus"	111
Chapter 8	The Game Opens up	120
Chapter 9	Innovations Abound	149
Chapter 10	A Growth in Defensive Tactics	170
Chapter 11	Development of the Contemporary Game	195
Chapter 12	The Option Dominates	213
Chapter 13	Changes in the Passing Game	232
Chapter 14	Adjustments	252
Chapter 15	A New Game	271
Chapter 16	Into the Twenty-first Century	298
	Index	326

Preface

There have been numerous texts and articles written about American Football. For the most part, the writings have focused on individual players, the history of specific teams and college programs, or critical events in the history of the game. Probably the two most comprehensive works on the development of the game are Allison Danzig's *The History of American Football*, Prentice Hall, 1956 and David Nelson's *Anatomy of a Game: Football, the Rules and the Men Who Made the Game.*, University of Delaware Press, 1994. What follows is an attempt to show the why, when, and how the game developed. We have made every effort to provide an accurate account of the way the game of football has evolved. By definition evolution is a process, a gradual development of something, especially from a simple to a more complex form. In studying the game of football, there is no simple timeline. It is often hard to identify the initial use a particular formation or play. Often several changes take place simultaneously. For that reason, it may seem that events are out of order or, at times, repeated.

There is a vast amount of information available depicting a wide array of offensive and defensive advances in the game. Deciding what information to include in the text was challenging. The author has drawn information from a bibliography of over one hundred and thirty books, numerous websites, individual college archives, newspaper articles, AFCA Manuals, and the author's notes from many years of coaching clinics and college campus visits. Multiple sources have recognized each of the innovations discussed in this book as having been essential to the advancement of America's favorite game.

Acknowledgements

The inspiration for this text came from the many players and coaches with whom I have had the privilege to work.

When the people around you have high expectations, it raises your own performance. It. is especially true in the coaching profession. In my forty-three years of coaching, I have had the pleasure of working with many exceptional coaches with high expectations. I am grateful for their support, assistance, and friendship. It was an honor working with such outstanding people.

I would especially like to thank Joe Rinaldo, who introduced me to the game of football and unknowingly inspired me to become a teacher and coach. Dick Wood gave me my first job. One could not ask for a better individual to have as a mentor. I also want to say a special thank you to Tom Murray, Joe Susan, Rich Alercio, and Marc Anderson, who, at different times in my career, provided me with exceptional guidance, inspiration, motivation, and friendship. These men all possessed a common attitude. Good coaching is good teaching - nothing else. If I have been able to pass that thought on, to even one other coach, my career has been a success.

Understanding the Diagrams

Offensive Player

Offensive Center

Defensive Player
- Nose tackle — **N**
- Defensive Tackle — **T**
- Defensive End — **E**
- Linebacker — **LB** or **L** or **B** or **F** or **Q**
- Pass Defenders — **C** or **S** or **SS** or **N** or **H** or **Q**
- Defender (general) — **V** or **X**

Path of a player on a shift

Path of a player before snap

Line of ball movement

Running path of a player

Path of a ball carrier

Defensive Pass Zone

CHAPTER ONE

Origins of the Game

(478 BC - 1862)

Ancient Games

Long before there was the no-huddle, offense, before there was the Nickel defense, and before there was the zone blitz, there was the Chinese game of Tsu Chu (cuju). Military manuals dating to 2000BC indicate that Chinese soldiers used Tsu Chu, played with a stuffed leather ball using the feet, as a physical activity. According to Chinese legend the founder of the Han Dynasty, Liu Bang, was a big fan of the game and had a unique field built near the Palace where he invited skilled players to play. However even before the Military Manuals, Chinese legend maintains the game may have gone back as far as 5000BCE.

Some claim that the real forerunner of American football may have been the games of Episkyros and Harpastron played by the ancient Greeks. The purpose of those games was to move a ball across a goal line. Scoring could be done by kicking, throwing, or running with the ball.

The literature of the time contains vivid accounts of the games. They were rough games with fierce tackling. The name Harpaston (meaning forward pass or forward pass game) evolved from the Greek word, Harpazein -- meaning to throw forward. The ancient Greeks competed in the game on a rectangular field with regular sidelines, a goal line, and a centerline (similar to the soccer mid-line). They used forward passing to move the ball. Primarily men and sometimes women played the game. Regardless of their gender, the Greeks usually performed nude. [1]

Passages in the Bible and literature such as the Odyssey verify that the Greeks played a game with a ball as long ago as 750 BC. At some time during the succeeding 250 years, in addition to Epikoinos and Harpaston, the Greek games of Phenindra, Episkyros, appeared. There are aspects of all these games that are similar to modern Rugby.

Around 500 BC, changes in the styles of play and various other developments took place as the game spread to other nations in Europe. The Lacedaemonians played the game under the name Epicyrus, and about 300 BC the Romans popularized the game under the name of Harpastum. Soldiers played it as recreation. It is the same game that the Romans would later call Follis and Calcio. [2]

At least concerning football, the Nordic races benefited from the invasion of Britain by the Romans. The game spread rapidly among the Jutes, Angles, Saxons, Vikings, and Danes after the Romans overcame them.

In 28 BC, Augustus Caesar modified the game to a more severe contest to help train his soldiers. He later banned it because he thought it was too kind-hearted a method of training for his troops.

For nearly a thousand years following the birth of Christianity, the game gradually faded in all but the Nordic countries and the British Isles. In England, it was undergoing a steady growth. A succession of English rulers, including Edward II through Henry VII, all banned the game at one time or another for various reasons. During the regimes of both Queen Elizabeth and James I, the game of "football" was re-established.

The primary place of popularity was in the English prep schools such as Eton, Harrow, Rugby, Winchester, and Charterhouse. Also during the fifteenth century, the Italians revived the game of Calcio. [3]

There is evidence that football played an important part in England during the 12th century. The English holiday "Shrove Tuesday" became a whole day of football. They suspended business and citizens turned out for the afternoon game. Frequently several hundred men took part in the games. Town challenged town or parish confronted parish. Play began midway between the two places, and the game could last for hours until one side kicked the ball into the other's province or until darkness called a halt. Some say that "Shrove Tuesday" may have originated as early as 217 AD when the English of Chester formed a flying wedge and rushed the Roman legions out of the town. [4]

In King Lear, Shakespeare refers to the game of football. In Scene IV of Act I the king says to Oswald, who is General's steward, "Do you bandy looks with me, you rascal?" Oswald replies, "I'll not be struck, me lord." After that the Earl of Kent interposes, "Nor tripped neither, you base football player," as he upsets Oswald by tripping him.

The Game of Football

Throughout the world, there are many games called, "Football." Most Western versions of football originated in England. There were several different games as early as the 12th century. The original games seem to have been similar to the traditional "mob football" played in England at the time. Several English monarchs attempted to put an end to the games because they felt it took interest away from the sport of archery, a key to their military success. By the midpoint of the 19th century, football was played in two different forms. These two sports are still popular today. Those two games are rugby and The Football Association Game. The three letters, s-o-c in Association is the source of the word soccer. In rugby, players run with the ball and there is tackling. Our modern American football, almost certainly, evolved out of these two sports. [5]

There are, essentially, five distinct varieties of the game of football played throughout the world today. They all have a foundation rooted in the ancient early games. The first of these, which we in America call "soccer," was probably the original game. Most of the nations of the world know it as football. The second is Gaelic Football and is the national football game in Ireland. The third form of the game is rugby, getting its name from the English secondary school Rugby. Australian Rules football, the fourth variety, is a variation of the English game and played, almost exclusively, in Australia. The fifth type is our own game of American Football (also played in Canada with slightly different rules). Of the five modern-day games, American Football probably has the least use of the foot as an integral part.

The Turn to Rugby:

It is interesting to follow the game as it evolved through the ages.

A popular theory is that an accident created the game of Rugby. In 1823, the famous English Rugby School had very strict rules requiring that all games at the school end promptly with the five o'clock ringing of the bell. William Webb Ellis, a young student at the Rugby School, had the ball kicked at him just as the bell began to ring. As a substitute for trapping the ball with his foot and taking a free kick, Ellis caught the ball and put it under his arm. He proceeded to run toward the goal, in an attempt to score before that fifth stroke sounded. His teammates and opponents watched in disbelief as he made that final score. His actions were bemoaned as unfair and unbecoming the behavior of an English gentleman. However, with the passage of time, students in pick-up games started incorporating running with the ball as part of their matches. Alas, the game of Rugby was founded.

There were now two games of football in England. There was one game in which the ball was only kicked and another where carrying the ball was permissible. For some years, the rules of that second game were very flexible and agreed upon just before the start of each match.

London Football Association

In 1862, the London Football Association adopted rules of a game very similar to the current game of soccer. Nine years later the Rugby Football Union adopted formal rules for the Rugby game.

---

[1]. *Ancient Ball Games: The Mediterranean*, Posted on Dec. 23, 2012 by Admin http://expertfootball.com/wp/ball-games-mediterranean/
[2] Allison Danzig, *The History of American Football*, (Englewood Cliff, N.J.: Prentice Hal 1956),p. 3-4.
[3] Allison Danzig, *The History of American Football*, (Englewood Cliff, N.J.: Prentice Hal 1956),p. 3-4.
[4] DaGrosa, John *Functional Football*, (Philadelphia & London: W.B. Saunders Co., Pub.,1936), p.18
[5] Yost, Fielding, *Football for Player and Spectator*, (Ann Arbor Michigan, The Ann Arbor Press, 1905), p. i

Chapter TWO

The Game in America

(1820 – 1888)

Football in America

As far back as colonial times, there is evidence that some form of football was part of the American life. It was a rough game with few rules, with an indefinite number of players on each side, and little team play. It consisted of a mass of players kicking a blown-up bladder toward their opponent's goal. Strategy and tactics were not essential elements of the game. In the 19th century, the games remained largely unorganized. However, intramural games of football were seen on college campuses. Each school played their own variety of football with rules that often changed from time to time. There were times they might change in the midst of the game. Under the best of circumstances, it was a "mob" style game.

It was in 1827 that Harvard began a tradition of the freshman and sophomore classes playing each other on the first Monday of the school year. Later they called it "Bloody Monday." They played by rules similar to rules being used at Princeton.

By 1840, each school had rules of the game. Scheduled contests took place within the schools. Amherst, Brown and Yale were all playing some form of football. The games consisted of kicking, pushing, punching, and outright fighting; of course all within the rules. [6]

Although Dartmouth published official rules for a game they called "Old Division Football" in 1871, there is evidence the Dartmouth game dates back to at least the 1830s. They were "mob" style games, with massive numbers of players attempting to move the ball into a goal area. They used any means necessary to achieve the feat. The rules were simple, and violence and injury were common.

Harvard & Yale Ban Football

In 1851, Yale began a similar tradition to Harvard's "Bloody Monday". The violence of these mob-style games led the administration and faculty of both schools to voice their disapproval loudly. Finally, in 1858, the Yale games came to a stop. The city of New Haven refused to allow the use of the town green for such brutality. At Harvard, the game was so brutal the faculty brought a halt to Bloody Monday in 1860. [7]

While colleges were outlawing the game, it was growing in popularity in a number of the east coast prep schools. They began to use manufactured inflatable balls in 1855. These balls were much more consistent in shape than the handmade balls of earlier times. It helped to make kicking and carrying the ball easier. There was organized football "games" between secondary schools sooner than intercollegiate games. In 1860, Boston Latin, Roxbury High School, Dorchester High School, Boston English, and The Dixwell School, all in Massachusetts, were playing a form of football against each other.

The "Boston Game"

Two general types of football developed: "kicking" games and "running" (or "carrying") games.[8] In 1862, a group of men, led by Gerrit Smith, wanted to play a hybrid of the two varieties. They formed The Oneida Football Club and created a new style of the game known as the "Boston Game." The club played their "Boston game" on Boston Commons. Although they played among themselves, they eventually helped organize a team of non-members and played a game against them in November 1863. The Oneidas won easily. However, the game caught the attention of the press and the "Boston Game" continued to spread throughout the 1860s.[9] Oneida was undefeated and unscored upon from 1862 to 1865.

In Canada a "running game", resembling rugby and similar to the "Boston Game", was created by the Montreal Football Club in 1868.[10] It is significant because Harvard would later find this game more to their liking and schedule games with the Canadian teams.

Princeton vs. Rutgers: 1869

During the Civil War, fewer students were attending the colleges and it curtailed the play of football at that level. With so much violence throughout the country, it did not seem too sensible to play the game.

Some colleges restored the game by the late 1860s. Yale, Princeton, Rutgers, and Brown all started playing, a "kicking" games during this time. By 1867, Princeton established rules based on those of the English Football Association. Around the same time, Rutgers formed rules very similar to those used by Princeton.[11]

It was on November 6, 1869, at Rutgers' College Field in New Brunswick, New Jersey that the first intercollegiate game took place. Lore has it that the game was a continuation of a long battle for a Revolutionary War cannon that George Washington had captured from Lord Howe in the Battle of Princeton during the War for Independence. The troops initially placed the gun on the Princeton campus, but the two schools had a tradition of stealing the cannon from each other. Princeton had put an abrupt end to the annual struggle for the cannon by embedding it in concrete on the Princeton campus sometime around 1840. It did not stop the Rutgers undergraduates from trying to move it.

The first game called for twenty-five players to a team. Players advanced the ball only by kicking or butting it with the head. Players could not run with the ball. There were no "free kicks" allowed (a concession by Princeton) and no mounting of the ball to kick it (a concession by Rutgers). The goal posts were twenty-five feet wide, and six goals were necessary to win a game. Although the players wore no uniforms, the Rutgers team did wear scarlet turbans.

Rutgers scored the first goal, and they went on to win the game by a score of six to four.

From the very first game, there was enthusiasm and passion by the fans from each school. It was during this first game that the Princeton students provided the first college cheer. Legend has it that the Princeton students had taken it from a song the soldiers of the Seventh Regiment of New York sang as the unit was mobilizing in Princeton for the war in April of 1861. [12]

The two teams met a week later at Princeton. They used the Princeton rules with one significant difference being awarding of a "free kick" to any player who caught the ball on the fly). Princeton won that game eight to zero. [13]

The Growth of the Game:

The game of American Football grew rapidly during the next quarter-century. In 1870, Columbia University joined Princeton and Rutgers in intercollegiate play. Cornell formed a Football Association that same year. Also, at Yale, the students once again began playing on the New Haven green.

By 1871, Harvard started to play by rules different from the Princeton Football Association rules. They preferred the "Boston Game"; a combination of the rules of rugby and soccer that was being played by the Oneidas. A player could catch and run with the ball. It was not just a kicking game. The "Boston Game" was much closer to Rugby and quite different from the games played at Princeton, Rutgers, Columbia, and Yale. Harvard was not a part of that early competition. [14]

The first evidence of paying customers witnessing a contest was the 1872 game between Yale and Columbia. An estimated crowd of four thousand spectators paid twenty-five cents each to watch Yale defeat Columbia 3-0. [15]

A Common Set of Rules

On October 19, 1873, representatives from Yale, Columbia, Princeton, and Rutgers met at the Fifth Avenue Hotel in New York City for the purpose of creating the first comprehensive set of intercollegiate football rules. Before this, the home team usually dictated playing the game by their particular regulations. They created a list of rules, based more on soccer than on rugby that was to be used for intercollegiate football games. These rules were essentially the London Football Association rules with accommodations for the Princeton, Columbia, and Yale Associations. One major revision was the reduction of participants from twenty-five per team to twenty. [16] Harvard intrigued more with the "Boston Game" refused to attend this rules conference and continued to play under its set of rules [17]

First International Game

The first international football game took place in New Haven, Conn. in 1873 between Yale and the Eton Players, a visiting team of Englishmen. According to Yale history, the rules of the game were much closer to soccer than football. Some rules modifications were necessary, yet Yale history has it that they played under rules that were much closer to soccer than football. One significant adjustment, requested by the English, was reducing the number of players to eleven on a side. It proved to create a more open game and converted Yale to arguing for eleven man sides in intercollegiate play.[18]

Harvard-McGill

Harvard's voluntary absence from the 1873 Fifth Avenue Hotel Meeting in New York precluded them from scheduling games against other American universities. Instead, they agreed to play McGill University, from Montreal, in two contests. The McGill team traveled to Cambridge, Massachusetts for the game.[19] One cannot dismiss the considerable significance of the McGill University (Montreal, Canada) and Harvard series played on May 14, of 1874. McGill played Canadian Rugby and Harvard, of course, was still playing the "Boston Game". They played the first game with Harvard's rules, which permitted rushing (running with the ball), as well as tackling. Harvard won that contest three goals to zero. McGill's modified Rugby rules were in effect for the second game. These were different in several ways. It was predominately a kicking game using an oblong sphere as opposed to a round ball. Touchdowns, as well as goals, counted in the scoring. Dropkicking was allowed, there were such rules as 'off-sides,' 'free kicks', and 'putouts' that are common to the game of Rugby. Harvard quickly learned the game and won three touchdowns to zero. The Harvard students thoroughly enjoyed the rugby game and its use of the try, which American football did not use. The try would eventually evolve into the score known as a touchdown. In late 1874, the Harvard team went to Montréal to play McGill and won by three tries. A year later, on June 4, 1875, Harvard confronted Tufts University in a game using rules similar to the McGill/Harvard contest. Tufts won that game 1-0.[20]

"Concessionary Rules": Harvard vs. Yale

In 1875, representatives from Harvard and Yale met in Springfield, Mass. so that the two schools could engage in the game of football. They agreed upon a set of game guidelines that they called, the "Concessionary Rules." That first contest, known as "The Game," (the annual contest between Harvard and Yale) took place on November 13, 1875.[21] They permitted running with the ball and tackling. Touchdowns, as in British Rugby, affected the score only by allowing a try for goal. Yale also compromised by playing fifteen men to a side as opposed to their favored eleven. This game was, also, the first documented game where college players wore uniforms. The Harvard students wore crimson shirts, stockings, and knee breeches while Yale donned yellow caps with blue shirts and dark pants.[22] Although Yale was totally overwhelmed by this new form of the game, they thoroughly enjoyed playing the game by the "Concessionary Rules". Over two thousand spectators attended this encounter, paying an admission price of fifty cents. Among the spectators were two Princeton men, W. Earle Dodge and Jotham Potter, who returned to old Nassau with the idea of converting Princeton Football to these new rules. After much discussion with their fellow students, Dodge and Potter convinced the Princetonians to adopt the Rugby-like rules.

In the 1944 Football Guide Alonzo Stagg wrote about a conversation he had with Eugene Baker the Yale captain of 1876.

> "From Mr. Baker's conversation I would judge that the 1876 line-up consisted of six linemen, or 'rushers,' as they were then called. These formed the forward wall of the 'scrummage' (changed to "scrimmage' in 1880) with a corresponding line-up of opponents opposite. Outside and behind the rushers hovered two quarterbacks, called 'half tends,' watching for the ball to come out of the struggling mass of forwards. The ball was put in play, except for the opening kick-off, by a scrummage by placing it on the ground between the two rush lines, and each line endeavored to work the ball back with their feet to the half tends.] There were three other backs called 'tends," corresponding, only playing deeper, to our halfbacks and fullback. Both sides were alert to get the ball when it came out of the scrummage. The first man to get it tossed it back or out for the run or the kick. If run with, the runner was always alert to throwing the ball to a teammate behind him when tackled. Much more often, the strategy was to kick the ball. It was preferred by the rushers, who usually were out of the play when the ball was carried." [23]

Figure 1

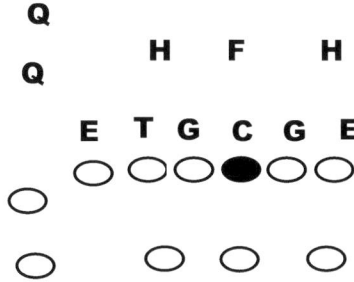

Figure 1 – Scrummage Formation

In that, same guide Stagg quotes the great Walter Camp regarding the 1876 Yale vs. Harvard contest in which Camp played as a freshman. "Within ten minutes the differences between the two teams were most unmistakably shown. Harvard was far more systematic and skillful. They played an intelligent passing game (not forward passing - only back) and our men seemed like snapping wolves in their vain attempts to catch the runner and ball together, for we had no notion of that style of play." [24]

Camp's observations are significant for two reasons. First, it suggested the introduction of tactics and strategy in the game. Equally important, is the fact that these observations are an indication of Camp's insight into what had to be changed. Walter Camp was to go on to become the most influential person in American Football for the next fifty years. As Chairman of the Rules Committee, he was primarily responsible for the movement of football away from Rugby and into the game that we know today. The game was to evolve from a contest dominated by kicking the ball and shuttling the ball laterally to the game that today thrills millions of people each year. It has evolved into a game with the technical proficiency of eleven men performing intricately designed plays. The plays are run from numerous formations that are conceived to confound ingeniously designed defenses.

The Intercollegiate Football Association

Having been impressed with the game between Harvard and Yale the previous year, Earle Dodge and Jonathan Potter of Princeton led the way in organizing a meeting to draft a standard set of rules for the game. Representatives from Harvard, Yale, Princeton and Columbia met at the Massasoit House in Springfield, Massachusetts on November 23, 1876. The particular purpose was to adopt a uniform system of rules and to form an Intercollegiate Football Association. This meeting resulted in a compromise of the Rugby Union Code with "The Concessionary Rules"; especially regarding scoring. One significant difference was the establishment of a kicked goal as a touchdown being the primary means of scoring. This change would later be adopted by rugby itself favoring the try as the primary scoring event. The compromise read, "A match shall be decided by a majority of touchdowns. A goal shall be equal to four touchdowns, but in the case of a tie, a goal kicked from a touchdown shall take precedence over four touchdowns." [25]

The playing time of a game consisted of two forty-five minute halves, with a ten-minute intermission at the end of the first half. The size of the field was established at one hundred and forty yards by seventy yards. They discarded the round ball for a more egg-shaped oblong. Each game would have a referee and two judges as officials (a judge from each team). In games prior to this, the team captains decided all disputes. The number of players was set at fifteen, although Yale still argued vehemently for their preference of eleven men to a side. Because of this disagreement, Yale refused to join the association, but they did send representatives to all the meetings. The meeting ended with a list of sixty-one rules. Today the game still employs twenty-two of those rules. [26]

With the advent of a standard set of rules, the game began to spread throughout the northeast. We should note, by 1878, there is evidence that the game was moving south. They were playing the game at both Washington and Lee and the Virginia Military Institute. In 1881, Michigan came east to play Harvard, Princeton, and Yale. No one envisioned that the game would spread at such a rapid pace and certainly, no one could have dreamed of the influence the game would have on the nation.

Even though Yale was not yet a member of the Intercollegiate Football Association, Walter Camp became a regular at the Massasoit House conventions. He took part in debating changes in the rules. It was not a surprise when, at the first meeting he attended, he suggested reducing the number of players from fifteen to eleven. With Camp arguing relentlessly, the group still rejected the proposal. Yale finally joined the Intercollegiate Football Association in 1879. Camp finally prevailed in the fight to get the number of players reduced to eleven, and the eleven-man rule went into effect in 1880. It was only the first of a multitude of recommendations for change that Camp would make over the next forty-seven years to earn him the title of "The Father of Football." He arguably had more to do with the development of the game than any other person.

There was a reduction in the size of the playing field. They changed the one-hundred and forty by seventy-yard field to one-hundred and ten by fifty-three yards. The new rules placed a stripe from sideline to sideline twenty-five yards from each goal line. Also, they now kicked-off from the center of the field.[27]

Introduction of Blocking

The first indication of the brutality that would dominate the game was the introduction of interference or what we commonly ball blocking today. Credit is given to Princeton as being the first to use blocking. In 1879, they delegated two men to run directly alongside the ball carrier in the Harvard game. Although this was a direct violation of the rules at that time, the referee of that game was Walter Camp of Yale. He did little to stop the Princeton scheme. As might be expected, and as it still happens with coaches today, successful innovations are quickly imitated. Yale, under Camp's leadership, used a similar action in games of their own later in that season. In the beginning, "interference" took the shape of teammates just running along with the ball carrier with their arms extended. They did not aggressively chase would-be tacklers, but merely impeded their pathway to the ball. It would be eight years before the group would attempt to prohibit blocking.

Establishing a "Line of Scrimmage"

Of equal or greater importance, however, was the rule adopted in 1880 for putting the ball in play. They abandoned the Rugby "scrummage" or "scrum" for a new system. The rules of 1876 did not call for any limit to the number of times a team could put the ball in play before having to give possession to their opponents. Before this time, kicking was the dominant means of scoring and punting the ball was a common method of moving the ball. With all the kicking, there was a natural change in possession. Following the rules of 1876, a team in possession could "scrimmage" or run play after play without moving the ball and without scoring. They kicked the ball as often as they carried it, often kicking it on the run. Frequently both the linemen and the backs spread themselves throughout the field.

Once again, Walter Camp of Yale proposed a change. He recommended a "line of scrimmage" to replace the scramble for a loose ball. The new rule provided that clear possession of the ball be given to one team at a time. The new law read, "A scrimmage takes place when the holder of the ball puts it on the ground before him and puts it in play while on-side, either by kicking the ball or by snapping it back with the foot. The man who first receives the ball from the snap-back shall be called the quarterback and shall not rush forward with the ball under penalty of foul." [28]

This new rule changed the game dramatically in that the previous method of starting play allowed each team equal opportunity to take control. The new rule established the principle of possession. The team putting the ball in play, knowing that they had possession, could now employ a strategy. They could now make plans in advance of the snap, on how to move the ball toward the goal. Many believe that this promoted the first use of the Punt formation offense. Later changes made it possible to snap the ball with the hands, either through the air or by a direct hand-to-hand pass.

There were several immediate outcomes of the scrimmage rule change. Harvard employed a system that presented seven men on the scrimmage line, three halfbacks, and one fullback. The halfbacks would alternate as the quarterback. *Figure 2*

Figure 2 The Harvard Formation

Princeton placed six men on the line, one at quarterback, two at halfback, and two at fullback *Figure 3*

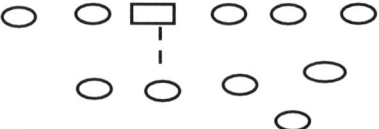

Figure 3 The Princeton Formation

Walter Camp's approach at Yale, and the one that eventually gained the most popularity was to stand seven men on the scrimmage line, one at quarterback, two at halfback, and one at fullback. *Figure 4* The Yale formation was the forerunner of the modern T-Formation. However, the method of putting the ball in play was quite different. Until the turn of the century, they referred to this formation as the "Regular" formation.

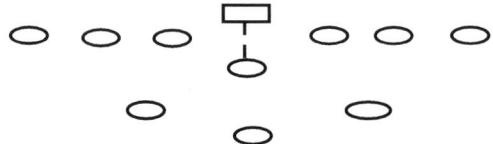

Figure 4 the Yale Formation: The Forerunner of the Modern "T" Formation

Although Camp's new scrimmage rules revolutionized the game, the changes were not always as intended. In a noteworthy move, Princeton used the scrimmage play to slow the game, making slow progress towards the end zone moving only a short distance on each down. Rather than increasing scoring, which had been Camp's intent, teams took advantage of the new rule to maintain control of the ball for the entire game, resulting in sluggish contests with little excitement.[29] Christy Walsh's *Intercollegiate Football* stated,

> "In the Princeton-Yale game of 1880 the Princeton captain, Francis Loney, decided not to kick but to hold the ball indefinitely, in order to force the game to end in a draw, which it did. It was the next year Princeton planned that if they won the toss, they would take the ball and scrimmage continually without kicking. This is exactly what happened. Princeton opened the game with the ball, executed scrimmage after scrimmage throughout the first half without releasing the ball and without scoring. Yale, having the right to open play in the second half, also adopted the 'block game' and scrimmaged throughout the second half, also without releasing the ball and without scoring. This type of tactics disgusted spectators."[30]

1881 Field Size

1881 brought another change in the size of the field to its present dimensions of 120 by 53 1/3 yards (109.7 by 48.8 meters).

Creating the "Five Yard Rule"

According to Parke Davis, "The chief result from the enacting of the 5-yard rule was to stimulate the study and development of the strategy of the game. A significant change in the composition of football elevens, the passing of the light, agile men of the seventies and the coming of the mighty young giants date from this period. In 1882, an unusually heavy team represented Yale for the times. Princeton possessed the ball first, abandoning the predominating offense; kicking and developing the play by short, hard rushes. So successful was this system that the following year it was imitated by nearly all the colleges, and thus came into vogue the modern running attack."[31]

One cannot doubt the impact that the down-and-distance rules, along with the creation of the line of scrimmage, had on the American game of football. It transformed it from a variation of rugby or soccer into the sport we know today.

Naming of the Positions

Late in the 1870s, Yale had labeled the line positions as well as the backs. They displayed little imagination in making the designations. Who was the man who stood on the end of the line? Surprisingly they called him "the end." The second man in on the line was called the "next to end." The man placed next to the center was the "next to center", and, of course, the center was the "center". The center, at that time, passed the ball back to the quarterback with his foot and the primary job of the "next to center" was to assist the center or brace him if necessary. Because he protected the center, the "next to center" quickly became the "guard". Conversely, the defensive lineman who lined up across from the "next to end" was in an excellent position to make many tackles. Consequently, they referred to him as the "tackler" or "tackle". With the advent of the line of scrimmage, these terms became more significant.

Rules Conventions

Walter Camp suggested several significant rule changes that helped in the evolution of American football. At the Intercollegiate Rules Convention of 1883, Camp presented the following scoring system: "safety, 1 point; touchdown, 2 points; a goal from a try, 4 points; a goal from the field, 5 points." [32] In 1884, the system of scoring was altered again with a touchdown counting as 4 points, the goal after a touchdown, 2 points; and the safety 2 points.

At the Rules Convention of 1885, Walter Camp first introduced to the Rules Committee the concept of a neutral zone between the two opposing lines. They did not make this change until much later. [33]

In 1887, the playing time was settled on as two 45-minute halves. Also in 1887, two paid officials, a referee, and an umpire, were to preside over each game. [34]

The Tackling Rule

From 1876, tackling of the ball carrier had been restricted to contact above the waist as was permissible in the old Rugby Union Code. The method of play resulting from above the waist tackling was an open and spread out game. Both the offensive and defensive linemen started each play from an upright or semi-upright position and would pull, push, twist, and, in general, proceed to fistfight with each other. Consequently, when running with the ball the backs ran wide around the end or they kicked with much more frequency than they plunged into the middle of the formation.

In the Rules Convention of 1888 Walter Camp introduced, and successfully lead the way for the enactment of a new rule about tackling. It was one more development in generating greater brutality in the game. Camp's new rule permitted tackling as low as the knees. There was also an attempt to remedy the blocking violation when in 1888 a rule was passed which prohibited blocking 'with extended arms'. However, to the innovative football mind, implied in that well-meaning proclamation was that blocking with the body was, therefore, legitimate. The new rules were to have a far-reaching and much greater impact than anyone had anticipated. With the use of dynamic interference would come two decades of brutal fighting that will almost destroy the game.

As often happens when new rules are initiated, there were unconstructive unintended consequences. The new rule necessitated that the backs be protected from defenders diving at their legs. The result was a tightening of the formations by bringing the linemen in close together and often almost shoulder to shoulder. The backs then aligned in a position behind this tightly massed line. Where once the backs were far out and the line of scrimmage stretched from sideline to sideline, open field running all but disappeared. Teams began to rely on large amounts of interference, revolving wedges, tandems, guards back, tackle tandems and some other inventive attacks, which would characterize football for the next decade.

---

[6] Meacham, Scott, (2020). *Old Division Football, The Indigenous Mob Soccer of Dartmouth College* (pdf), dartmo.com. Retrieved 2007-05-16.

[7] Professional Football Researchers Association, *No Christian End!. The Journey to Camp: The Origins of American Football to 1769. To Camp.* Retrieved 2007-05-16 http://www.profootballresearchers.org/Articles/.pdf

[8] Professional Football Researchers Association, No_Christian_End *No Christian End!. The Journey to Camp: The Origins of American Football to 1769.* Retrieved 2007-05-16 http://www.profootballresearchers.org/Articles/No_Christian_End.pdf

[9] Allaway, Roger, (2001). *"Were the Oneidas playing soccer or not?"*. The USA Soccer History Archives. Dave Litterer. Retrieved on 2007-05-15. http://www.bigsoccer.com/soccer/roger-allaway/2011/12/05/who-were-and-werent-the-oneidas/

[10] *"The History of American Football"*. The History of Sports. Saperecom (2007). Retrieved on 2007-05-15. http://en.wikipedia.org/wiki/History_of_American_football

[11] Danzig, *The History of American Football*, p.7

[12] Danzig, *The History of American Football*, p.8

[13] Davis, The [13] *"The History of American Football"*. The History of Sports. Saperecom (2007). Retrieved on 2007-05-15. http://en.wikipedia.org/wiki/History_of_American_football
American Intercollegiate Game, p. 50

[14] Professional Football Researchers Association, *No Christian End!. The Journey to Camp: The Origins of American Football to 1769.* Retrieved 2007-05-16 http://www.profootballresearchers.org/Articles/No_Christian_End.pdf

[15] Danzig, *The History of American Football*, p.8

[16] Timeline created by mahooty in History *The Development of American Football*, http://www.timetoast.com/timelines/the-development-of-american-football

[17] Cohan, Tim, *The Yale Football Story*, (New York, NY, G.P. Putnam's Sons, New York, 1951), p 369

[18] Boyles, Bob, and Paul Guido, *College Football Encyclopedia*, (Skyhorse Publishing, New York, NY, 1947), p 14.

[19] Professional Football Researchers Association, *No Christian End!. The Journey to Camp: The Origins of American Football to 1769.* Retrieved 2007-05-16 http://www.profootballresearchers.org/Articles/No_Christian_End.pdf

[20] Sweene, Paul, *Tufts-Harvard* first game story breaks nationally, http://asc.tufts.edu/athletics/menFootball/press/2004-2005/firstgamebuzz....html

[21] Professional Football Researchers Association, *No Christian End!. The Journey to Camp: The Origins of American Football to 1769.* Retrieved 2007-05-16 http://www.profootballresearchers.org/Articles/No_Christian_End.pdf

[22] Danzig, *The History of American Football*, p 10.

[23] Danzig, *The History of American Football*, from Amos Alonzo Stagg, 1944 Football Guide.

[24] Danzig, *The History of American Football*, from Amos Alonzo Stagg., 1944 Football Guide.

[25] Danzig, *History of American Football*, p.10 from Parke Davis, Football Guide, 1926

[26] David Nelson, *Football Principles and Play*, (New York, NY, The Ronald Press Co., 1962), p.33-34

[27] Danzig, Allison, *Oh How They Played the Game: The Early Days of Football and the Heroes Who Made It Great*, (New York, NY," Macmillan, 1971) p.16

[28] Danzig, *Oh How They Played The Game* p. 18.

[29] Professional Football Researchers Association Camp and His Followers: American Football 1876–1889 *The Journey to Camp: The Origins of American Football to 1889*.. Retrieved on 2007-05-16.

[30] Danzig, *The History of American Football*, p16 , from Walsh, Christy, Intercollegiate Football

[31] Danzig, *The History of American Football*, p16

[32] Danzig, *The History of American Football*, p.17

[33] Allison Danzig, *Oh How they Played the Game*, 1971, p.20.

[34] Danzig, *The History of American Football*, p.17

CHAPTER THREE

Changes in the Game

(1888 – 1889)

The Princeton "V Trick"

Although the "wedge" or "V trick" was first used during the 1884 season, it was not until 1888 that there was extensive use of the play. Although Princeton is credited with first use of the wedge, some say Lehigh also used it at about the same time. You must understand that at the time, all teams made use of a loophole in the rule that required a team to kickoff. The rule did not specify that the opposing team receive the ball. There was a common tactic of employing the "inch kick". The kicker made the short kick to himself and then hand the ball back to a teammate. Thus, the kicking team retained possession of the ball. Park Davis in his book *Intercollegiate Football* described Princeton's first use of the play.

"Princeton was not making any headway against Penn in running a halfback behind seven men charging abreast down the field. It occurred to (Richard) Hodge to form the seven men into a solid V-shaped mass, with the runner inside and the apex forward." The Princeton players formed themselves into a mass of the shape of the letter V, solidified by men inside the jaws and all locking their arms around one another. The runner was inside, just behind the man in the apex. The ball went into play and away went the wedge of men, their legs churning in unison like the wheels of a locomotive.

"The play was very much a success and Princeton scored a touchdown. However, the play was considered a temporary makeshift and was abandoned until four years later when it was brought out at the start of the second half of the 1988 Yale game. The revived practice was adopted by nearly every team as the standard opening play, and it remained the formal opening play for four years."[35] *See Figure 5.*

Stagg described the Princeton "V Trick", and the way he taught it to his team, in the following way:

> "To send the wedge straight down the field from the center, the men form in the positions shown, as closely and firmly bound together as possible.
>
> "At the signal C puts the ball in play by touching it with his foot, and passes it back to QB, who is immediately behind him, ready to receive it. As the ball is put in play, the entire wedge rushes forward in a compact mass, preserving its formation, and endeavors by mere force of weight and momentum to advance the ball as far as possible straight towards the opponent's goal" [36]

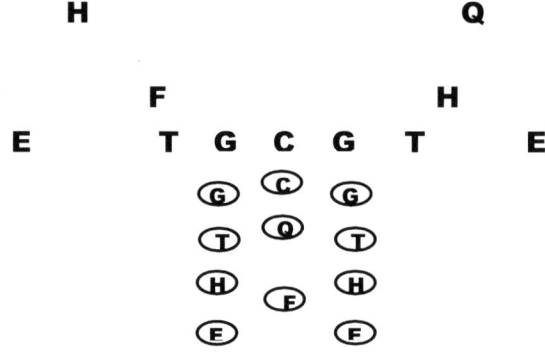

Figure 5 The Princeton V-Trick or Wedge V-Trick.

The Yale Wedge

Later in 1888, Alonzo Stagg of Yale introduced the concept of having two outrunners. They would run ahead of the wedge and block the defensive center and guard to the side that the offense wished the runner to go.

Stagg described how he moved from using the Princeton Wedge to one of his own design, the Yale Wedge. *Figure 6*

> "This wedge differs in one very important respect from the preceding (Princeton Wedge). Instead of being a part of the wedge formation, the guards are placed "outside" of the wedge directly abreast of C.
>
> "The instant the ball is put in play, LG and RG spring forward in advance of the wedge, and meet the opposing guard and center midway between the wedge and the point from which their opponents start." [37]

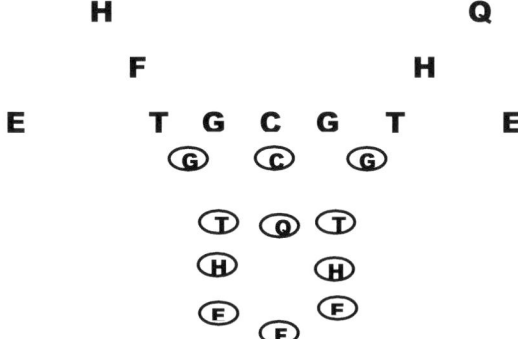

Figure 6 the Yale Wedge

Boxing the Tackle

When not utilizing their powerful "wedge", Princeton initiated a strategy where they would put two blockers on the defensive tackle. Both the tackle and the end would block him. Between the two of them, they would "box" the defender and drive him back and toward the sideline. This would open up huge holes in the defensive line for the ball carrier to run through. This strategy was especially effective against the 7-1 defense, also called the "Seven Diamond" defense. "Boxing the tackle" was the phrase they used to describe this blocking strategy.

See Figure 7.

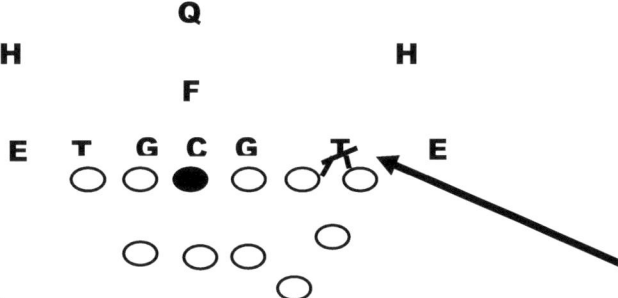

Figure 7 Boxing the tackle

Pulling the Guards

Many claim that in the following year, 1889, Pudge Heffelfinger of Yale, under the instruction of Walter Camp, began the practice of "pulling" out to lead end runs from his guard position. However, Parke Davis maintains that George Woodruff, later to coach at Penn, actually was the first to pull linemen to lead the ball carrier in 1886.[38] *See Figure 8*

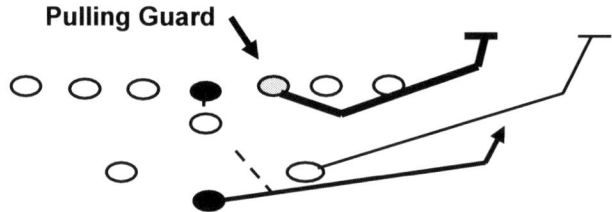

Figure 8 - Yale's Use of the Pulling Guard, 1889

1889 was also the year that Walter Camp came up with an innovation that would have a considerable impact on the game. Near the end of the decade, Camp began to have his center bend over the ball and snap it to the quarterback by bouncing it back. [39]

In an attempt to bring the physical aspects of the game under control, in 1889, the officials used whistles and stopwatches. [40]

Defending the Mass Plays

Defenses were finding it extremely difficult attempting to survive the mass plays that resulted from the use of interference and tackling below the waist.

The defense adopted by most teams to stop this play was to run forward with the first defenders diving at the feet of the players forming the wedge. The intent was for the first line of defenders to take the wedge down so that the second wave of defenders could get to the ball carrier. It was not unlike the military maneuvers typical during that time.

Stagg and the Mass Momentum Plays

He created the huddle, the direct pass from center, the lateral, the backfield shift, and cross-blocking. He introduced wind sprints. He was the first to put numbers on uniforms. He was using the 7-2-2 defense as early as 1890. Amongst other things, he was the first or one of the first to introduce the quick kick. He added the spiral snap, the Statue of Liberty play, the T-Formation, the forward pass, the man in motion, and the unbalanced line. That early innovator was Amos Alonzo Stagg. He was influential in the growth and development of the modern game of football. However, one of his first creations was the first step in a movement that almost destroyed the game in its early stages. His "ends back" plays are said to be the first of the momentum plays; begun in 1890-91. The mass momentum plays almost killed football.

Ends Back

While coaching at the Springfield, Massachusetts YMCA College Amos Alonzo Stagg created the "ends back" formation. This was a condensed structure with the ends placed in the backfield. From this alignment, he used the Ends as both ball carriers and lead blockers. The ends also acted as 'pushers' on plays over the center or guards.[41] The formation is shown in *Figure 9*.

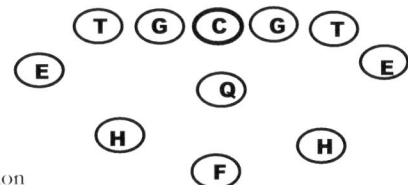

Figure 9 Ends Back Formation

In a letter written to Allison Danzig dated March 18, 1952, Stagg provides his own description of his invention.

"In 1890, when as a student, I was given permission to organize a team at Springfield (referring to Springfield College in Mass., previously International YMCA College); I created a new system of play by playing both ends behind the line. Previously the ends always played on the line of scrimmage. I used the ends: (1) as effective runners with the ball off tackle and around end. (2) For blocking and interference purposes (a) on mass plays on tackle by the fullback and by the off halfback, (b) on mass plays on center by the fullback, (c) on off-tackle drives by the off halfback, (d) on around-end runs by the off halfback. (3) Also, I devised several new crisscross plays in which the ends participated."[42]

At first glance, the relationship between the tackles and the ends in their "back" position appears to be very similar to the relationship of Warner's wingback and end in his future "Double Wing". However, the same type of double-team block on the defensive tackle which we will see later is to make Warner's formation so famous and influential was not used by Stagg. Later, Princeton used this same formation to produce a very successful season in 1893.

Several of Stagg's more popular plays, from the Ends Back formation, are shown in the following. *Figures 10-14*

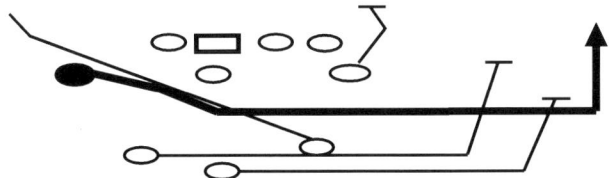

Figure 10 The "End Around" Play from the Ends Back Formation

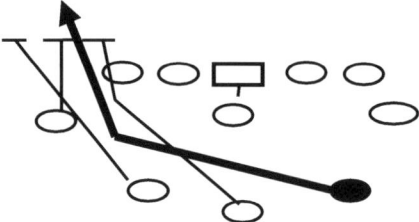

Figure 11 The Halfback Off-Tackle Drive

Figure 12 The Mass Play on Center by the Fullback

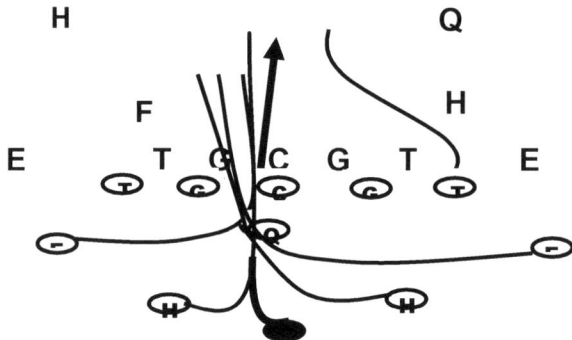

Figure 13 Full Back Buck from Ends Back Formation

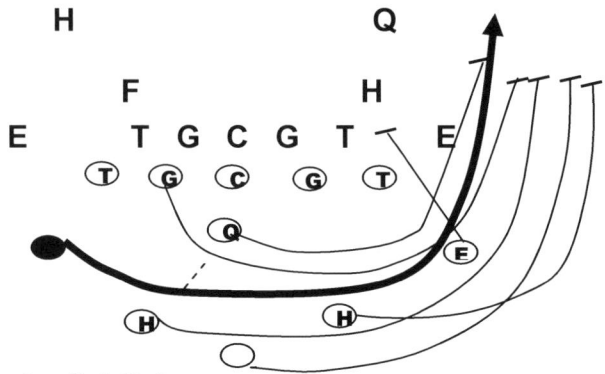

Figure 14 Left End Sweep from Ends Back

Stagg described some other varieties of his innovations of the "ends back."

(1) "Halfback criss-cross with the end, which ran around the opposite end."

NOTE: This is the first documented use of the play we now know as a reverse.

(2) "Fullback crisscrosses with the end, which ran around the opposite end."

(3) "End crisscrosses with other end, which ran around the opposite end."

(4) "Double pass from end to fullback in a run around the opposite end." [43]

7 Box Defense

Stagg is also credited with devising, what was then, a unique defense for his "Ends Back". By keeping seven men in the line, keeping two linebackers and two deep defenders created a 7-2-2. This defense became the "Seven Box" *See Figure 15.*

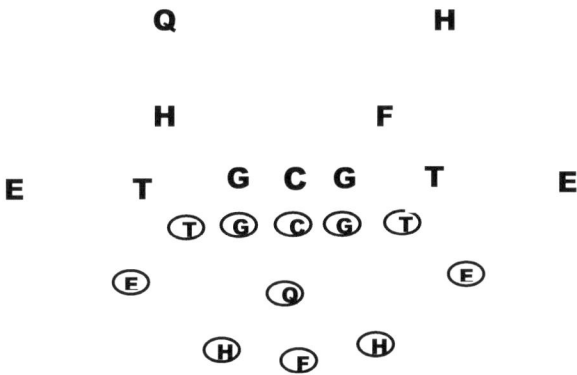

Figure 15 the Seven-Box Defense [44]

Many teams later used this defense vs. the Penn "Guards Back" formation

It is crucial to remember that the forward pass was still not legal during this era of mass formations. There was little deception. Defenses were as brutal and brainless as the offenses. Defensive linemen aligned in a semi-erect or crouched stance. The offensive and defensive lines stood opposite each other in, what amounted to, hand-to-hand combat. Only after battling and attempting to maul the player opposite them did defensive lineman try to get free to pursue the ball carrier. Battles that today might lead to an arrest were crucial for survival.

Stopping the Ends Back

In 1893, at both Chicago under Stagg and Princeton under Phil King there developed another defense meant to stop the "ends back" offense. The defensive backs aligned close to the line of scrimmage creating, what amounted to, a nine-man line. The line's job was to smash the interference. For the most part, it was the job of the fullback (playing as a linebacker) and quarterback to stop the running attack.[45]

Figure 16

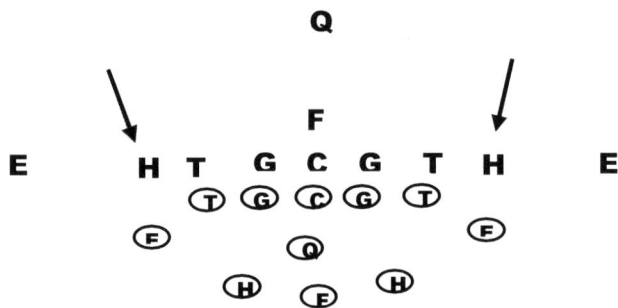

Figure 16 Halfbacks "Up" vs. the Ends Back Formation

The "Turtleback Play"

Because there was still no rule regulating the number of men a team must put on the line of scrimmage to begin each play, teams started to bunch their line. They placed a larger number of players in the backfield. On the snap of the ball, all would rush toward one defender, usually an unsuspecting defensive guard or tackle.

Stagg once again demonstrated his genius, in developing the "Turtleback Play". See *Figure 17*

As described by Stagg himself in a letter to Allison Danzig, "On all line play between the tackles and the fullback, both ends preceded the fullback while both halfbacks pushed the fullback and helped him hold his feet. In the evolution of that formation in 1890 and 1891, the attack gradually worked out into a revolving oval, with one end and the quarterback pushing the halfback when he carried the ball on a close revolving formation around tackle. This was the beginning of the mass play known as the turtleback."[46]

"Pa" Corbin, a Yale captain in 1888, described the play as he saw it in the Springfield YMCA versus Harvard game in 1891:

"Ten men formed in a mass with their bodies bent over, forming a 'turtle back,' several yards behind the center of the field. The ball was snapped back and disappeared into the middle of the mass. Soon all but one of the bunch started toward the side of the field in what appeared to be a flying wedge … with one man somewhat bent over and apparently carrying the ball and nearly the entire Harvard team in pursuit. A minute later an unnoticed man on the ground, who all the time had the ball concealed under him, got up and ran down the other side of the field for a touchdown." [47]

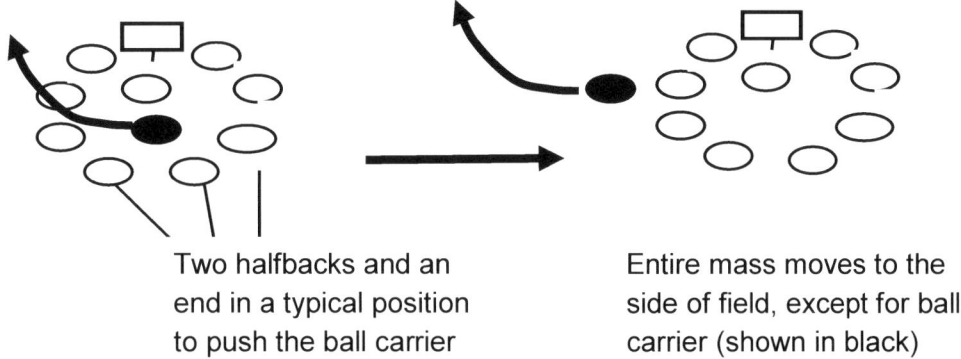

Two halfbacks and an end in a typical position to push the ball carrier

Entire mass moves to the side of field, except for ball carrier (shown in black)

Figure 17 The "Turtle Back" Play

Although Amos Alonzo Stagg credits himself as the first to use the "turtleback play in 1888, some historians credit Harvard with the first use of the turtleback as early as 1883.[48]

The "Flying Wedge"

One of the legendary plays in football, the "Flying Wedge" was the creation of the 1892 Harvard team. The "Flying Wedge" was one of the most brutal plays in football.

In *"Intercollegiate Football"*, Parke Davis talks about the play created by Harvard student Lorin F. Deland,

"Deland had not been a football player, but he was a chess expert and a student of military tactics. As he saw the rugged old Princeton wedge start with the 'touch-off' of the ball and plow its ponderous way down the field, he conceived the stupendous idea of starting the wedge before the ball was in play and thus obtaining a motion of 20 or 25 yards before it struck its opponent's momentum. Harvard leaders were captivated, and they practiced this great maneuver secretly in the summer of 1892 on a farm where the Harvard team assembled. Finally perfected, it was reserved for Yale." [49]

Yale and Harvard have traditionally met on the last Saturday before Thanksgiving. That Saturday fell on Nov. 19th in 1892. Having practiced the "Flying Wedge" all summer, Harvard had decided they would introduce the play against Yale. They waited until the opening of the second half to spring the surprise on their archrival. Unaware, Yale lined up across the field as was typical for the kickoff. They were prepared for the standard wedge or "V" from a standing start. There are many descriptions of what happened next. According to Parke Davis,

"Without putting the ball in play, Trafford (the Harvard Center) waved his hand and the two sections came swiftly forward in lock step, converging toward Trafford and gather tremendous momentum as they ran. Just as they reached Trafford, the latter put the ball in play and disappeared with the mass of men, thus launching against the Yale men standing still in their tracks the famous flying wedge, the invention of Lorin F. DeLand. Fearlessly Yale's rush-line leaped against the mass finally pulling to pieces and brings down the run on their 25-yard line. No play ever has been devised so spectacular and sensational as this one. It not only was the feature of the game, although the contest eventually was won by Yale, but it was the most discussed topic by the country at large for many days and the central subject of football for several years. To-day the episode is preserved by the passage of the word, "the flying wedge," from a technical term of football to a standard phrase in the English language." [50]

There were varying accounts of that first play. They were not all in harmony. However, there was a consensus of all those who saw that first "flying wedge" that the new maneuver was a truly a historic, brutal, and outstanding innovation.

Said the Boston Herald the next day, "It was a play that sent the football men who were spectators into raptures." [51]

A year later, the New York Times was still lauding the play. "What a grand play! A half ton of bone and muscle coming into collision with a man weighing 160 or 170 pounds. A surgeon is called upon to attend the wounded player, and the game continues with renewed brutality." [52]

From Amos Alonzo Stagg, "the most spectacular single formation ever." [53] Parke Davis, a player at Princeton, and renowned football historian, "no play has ever been devised so spectacular and sensational as the flying wedge." [54]

The Journal of Sports History Describes the play, in detail, the following way, "Harvard captain Bernie Trafford initiated the play with the remainder of the Harvard team located a number of yards behind the ball that lay at mid- field. Five of Harvard's heaviest men were located some 20 to 30 yards behind the ball at about a 45-degree angle to the sideline and in line with the ball. This quintet was led by William H. Lewis the first African-American to be chosen a Walter Camp all-American football player. Opposite Lewis and his slower but the heavier group were four of the faster men. They were located somewhat closer to but on the other side of, the ball. They, too, angled from the sideline toward the ball. Art Brewer, a fast and shifty freshman halfback, was located between the two halves of the wedge, ready to receive the ball from Trafford. Upon the captain's signal, the heaviest men began a sprint toward Trafford, while the faster men on the other side came toward them to create a wedge-like formation. As Trafford picked up the ball, the two lines met just beyond him and directed their three-quarter ton of massed momentum toward one man on the opposing line who would catch the brunt of their attack; that is, Harvard's objective was to mass all their effort at Yale's Alex Wallis, located toward the end of Yale's right side, and to literally mow him down. Brewer, who was trailing the wedge at top speed, was expected to find a hole created by the flying bodies and break through to the rear of the Yale defense as Napoleon would have it, for a large gain or possible touchdown." [55]

Figure 18

By 1893, everyone was using the flying wedge. To prevent the wedge from being penetrated players resorted to all sorts of tricks. John Heisman is quoted in Frank Menke's Encyclopedia of Sports 1953. "Some backs had leather straps, like valise handles, sewed or riveted on the shoulders of the jackets and on the hips of their trouser, so as to offer good handholds for their teammates." [56]

The forward pass was still illegal and with only five yards needed for a first down in three attempts, the inventive flying wedge play quickly became the focal point of offensive strategy.

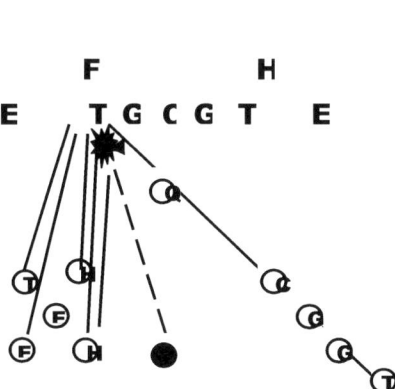

Figure 18 Harvard's Flying Wedge

Stagg, in his book "*Scientific and Practical Treatise on American Football*" described how he taught the player assignments of the Harvard wedge. Refer to figure 18.

"QB stands with the ball in the center of the field. F stands from five to ten yards behind QB and a little to the right. The remainder of the team is divided in two sections.

"Section No.1 is composed of the heaviest men in the line and is drawn up from twenty to thirty yards from the center, back and to the right, facing QB.

"Section No.2 is composed of the lighter and swifter men, drawn up five or ten yards back and to the left of QB.

"Section No.1 has the "right of way" the other regulating their play to its speed.

"At a signal from QB, section No.1 dashes forward at utmost speed passing close in front of QB.

"At the same moment FB and section No.2 advance, timing their speed to No.1. Just before the sections reach the line QB puts the ball in play, and as they come together in a flying wedge and aim at the opposing defensive tackle, or straight down the field, passes to F and dashes forward with the wedge.

"A slight opening is left in front of QB to draw in the opposing tackle. As the opposing defensive tackle dives into the wedge, LH and QB take him. RE and LE swing out to the left to block opposing right defensive end. At the same moment, right halfback puts on utmost speed and darts through the opening between left halfback and RE.

Note: The arrangement of the men is arbitrary. The wedge may be directed against any point desired. The strength lies in the fact that the men are under full headway before the ball is put in play." [57]

Development of Flying Wedge Strategy

Expanded coaching staffs allowed the better teams to employ specialized position coaches. The strategic progress of college football rested with these mentors in devising new possibilities for organized plays and arranging them in a well-organized series as Harvard, Yale, and Princeton were doing. Harvard's dangerous flying wedge quickly became the standard opening play for teams all across the country. Stagg implied the need for more development when he wrote in 1927,

"The Deland invention probably was the most spectacular single formation ever opened as a surprise package. It was a great play when perfectly executed, but, demanding the exact coordination of eleven men, extremely difficult to execute properly." [58]

As with all innovations in football, new forms of the play emerged. It was no longer a tactic used solely when teams lined up for kickoffs. In fact, Lorin Deland prepared 60 new momentum plays in the off-season, plus a counter-play for each of the new offensive formations for Harvard to run from the line of scrimmage. [59]

Attempting to Defend the "Flying Wedge"

As is always the case, soon after the use of the offensive maneuver, there was a defensive scheme to stop the brutal display of the flying wedge. Yale, at times, just avoided a massive collision. Rather than charging its men to meet the converging wedge the men in blue sweaters stood aside, let the opponent's interference run through, and then tackled the unprotected ball carrier. Harvard opted for a more unconventional defensive method. Aligning five yards behind the line of scrimmage, the Crimson defenders began their own assault the instant Yale shot forward. The disastrous result: 22 men in a big heap, bodies bruised and bones were broken. [60]

In reality, no one came up with a solution to the "flying wedge" that could overcome the plays dominance of the game. It was all but impossible to break up a mass formation play without terrible harm to some players.

Danzig, in *The History of American Football*, describes what it was like to play in those days. "In the push- pull days of football, the days of close-order mass plays, when there was no forward pass to reckon with and little deception, the defense was as elemental as the offense. Lineman stood erect or crouched, hand fought their way to get at the ball carrier, and chased the play as it developed. A lineman had to be good with his hands and fists on both defense and offense. Actions that might lead to expulsion today were a necessary part of the game. It was no brawl, but a man had to be rough and ready and protect himself. "With no pass to guard against, the backs had only to support the line in crashing through wedges and breaking up momentum mass plays. The defense amounted to a nine-man line, with the fullback in the backer-up spot and the safety deeper. Linemen and Backs could both commit themselves to stopping the running attack without reservations." [61]

"Flying Wedge" is Outlawed

As the use of mass momentum plays increased so did the deaths on the football field. Simple physics will tell you that the greater the mass and greater energy an object has, the more difficult it will be to stop. It would eventually take a rules revision to slow down the play. This play, which used the principle of mass momentum to great advantage, was as deadly as it was efficient and they would outlaw the play after only two seasons. Even most of those who espoused the play had to admit it was not only dangerous but also unsportsmanlike.

Not all agreed, however. Penn's George Woodruff's thoughts were rather than limit mass momentum plays; they must address the habit of players acting as "babies" on the field. "There should be less delay of game, less sponging during a game, less fuss about injuries already received" Woodruff is quoted. "If the hurt is great the player should leave the field; if small he should smile and play harder." [62]

At the time, Walter Camp contended that aspects of the English game of rugby, from which American football had evolved, be brought back to prevent college football from destroying itself. As a result, he suggested several solutions for the flying wedge dilemma. First, football could return to the time when interferers or blockers leading the ball carrier were illegal. Second, if the rules mandated a long kick or lateral pass on the third and final down, it would open up the game and there would be fewer mass plays. Third, he argued that the distance needed for a first down be extended to 10 yards; or a team might be required to advance the ball at least 15 yards to either side of the original ball marking, thus promoting a more open game with end runs. Finally, Camp suggested the possibility of prohibiting offensive players from changing positions before the snap of the ball, consequently limiting the number of blockers for the ball carrier.[63]

At the October meeting of the 1893 Intercollegiate Football Association, no action was taken on the legality of mass plays. The two most significant rule changes were, first, that each game was to have two judges and a referee. The referees were to be alumni of the respective schools. The second change mandated that a kicking team could not deliberately miss a field goal.

In December of 1893, the IFA met a second time. There was no action taken regarding mass plays. However, they did strengthen the rules relative to fouls. Note, Harvard had withdrawn from IFA in 1889; Penn had withdrawn earlier in 1893. Only Yale and Princeton remained with the IFA. In reality, they did not have any rulemaking authority.

On February 3, 1894, representatives of Harvard, Yale, Princeton, and Penn, along with members of the University Athletic Club of New York, met with the intent of forming a new rules committee. They wisely invited Professor Paul Dashiell of United States Naval Academy to provide direction. Dashiell was considered the leading football official of the time and was highly respected by all of the representatives of the attending schools. The Intercollegiate Rules Committee consisting of Princeton, Yale, Harvard, and Penn. replaced the Intercollegiate Football Association, of which only Princeton and Yale were still members. However, at this meeting in 1894 there were no significant changes to the rules. The offense could still place seven men in motion. Still, the defense had to wait at the line of scrimmage for this mass to attack them.[64]

Because of the lack of action taken by the new committee, there were shouts for reform. Camp as secretary of the rules committee sent letters to former players to question them about injuries and the game's brutality. The poll concluded that charges by the critics of the game, were exaggerated and accusations subsided. Camp was no fool. He knew who to ask when the good name of the game was at stake.[65] Stated the New York Times of Camp's position on reform,

> "The conservative Camp, Yale's athletic advisor for nearly a half-century and sometimes head football coach became the reluctant reformer. He was, indeed, more interested at first in creating a 'fair catch' rule to protect the punt receiver than in abolishing the flying wedge." [66]

In May of 1894, The Intercollegiate Rules Committee met for the second time. It was decided that the officials, umpire, referee, and linesman would all be delegated specific duties within the game. They reduced the playing time of the game from 90 minutes to 70 minutes, with two 35-minute halves. However, the two most significant rule changes were:

Rule #4- "In all cases where the rules provide for a kick, the ball must actually be kicked the distance of at least ten yards into the opponents' territory unless stopped by the opponents."

NOTE: Later that year Stagg would be the first to circumvent this rule and utilize the Onside kick. Also, in that same year, Stagg was the first to use the "sleeper" play on the kickoff when he started the whole team running one way only to throw the ball to a back alone on the other side of the field where he could run for long distances before he risked disruption.[67]

The rule change that year that would have the greatest consequence was Rule# 8- "No momentum mass play shall be allowed. A momentum mass play is one in which more than three men start before the ball is put in play. Nor shall more than three men group for that purpose more than five yards back from the point where the ball is put in play." The Rugby kick-off was brought back. [68]

---

[35] Davis, *The American Intercollegiate Game,*. P 83

[36] Stagg, A. Alonzo, Henry L. Williams, *Scientific and Practical Treatise on AMERICAN FOOTBALL*, (New York, D. Appleton & Co., 1894), p.185

[37] Stagg, p. 187

[38] Danzig, *Oh How they Played the Game*, p. 120.

[39] Stagg, Alonzo. *1941 Football Guide.* (Danzig, p.22)

[40] Camp and His Followers: American Football 1876–1889". *The Journey to Camp: The Origins of American Football to 1889.* Professional Football Researchers Association. - Retrieved on 05,16, 2007

[41] Craig, John, *football-history-momentum--mass-plays* http://www.helium.com/items/950527-football-history-momentum--mass-plays - - retrieved Feb. 15, 2009

[42] Danzig, *The History of American Football* p. 23.

[43] Craig, *Football History: Momentum –mass plays*, http://www.helium.com/items/950527-football-history-momentum--mass-plays

[44] Danzig, *Oh How They Played The Game*, p. 57

[45] Danzig, *The History of American Football*, p.108

[46] Danzig, *The History of American Football*, p24

[47] Danzig, *The History of American Football*, p24

[48] Danzig, *Oh How They Played The Game*, p37

[49] Davis, Intercollegiate Football,*The History of American Footb*all, p. 24

[50] Davis, *The American Intercollegiate Game* p-94

[51] Boston Herald, 20 November 1892

[52] New York Times, 2 December 1893, p. 3.

[53] Amos Alonzo Stagg and Wesley W. Stout, *Touchdown!* (New York: Longsman, Green, 1927), p. 182

[54] Davis, Parke, *The American Intercollegiate Game*, p. 94.

[55] McQuilkin, Scott A. and Ronald A. Smith ,*The Rise and Fall of the Flying Wedge: Football's Most Controversial Play*, Journal of Sports History, Vol. 20, No.1 (spring 1993) p 58

[56] Danzig, *Oh How They Played The Game*, p.72

[57] Stagg, Henry L. Williams, *Scientific and Practical Treatise on American Football*, (New York, NY, D. Appleton and Co., 1894) p.197

[58] Stagg and Wesley W. Stout, *Touchdown!*, (New York: Longsman, Green, 1927), p. 182

[59] Outing, XXIII (October 1893), p. 1.

[60] New York Times, 1 October 1893, p. 4

[61] Danzig, *The History of American Football*, p. 108

[62] Walter Camp, *Football Facts and Figures*, p. 128

[63] Walter Camp, *The Current Criticism of Football*, Century Magazine, XLVII (February 1894),

[64] Nelson, *Anatomy of a Game*, p. 71

[65] Nelson, *Anatomy of a Game*, p. 72

[66] New York Times, 8 Feb. 1894

[67] Danzig, *Oh How They Played The Game*, p. 56

[68] Danzig, *The History of American Football*, p. 25.

CHAPTER FOUR

Dodging the Mass Formation Rules

(1890 - 1905)

Tackles Back:

After the flying wedge had been outlawed, new variations of the mass formations were conceived that were, even more, vicious and dangerous.

The 1894 season saw the introduction of two new mass formations. There is a dispute as to who actually created the "Tackles Back" formation. Amos Alonzo Stagg claimed in the Saturday Evening Post, "I originated the tackles back play that season (1894).[69] In a letter to Allison Danzig dated July 29, 1954, he states;" I first used the tackles back play in 1894 and drew back both tackles to serve as interference, particularly for the runs of the fullback. The tackles were placed one behind each guard about 2 to 2 ½ yards back. The fullback was located about 3 ½ - 4 yards back The attack went mostly inside the defensive tackles on either side of the line. Sometimes the halfback carried the ball. It made very substantial interference and the thought was a natural sequence of my developing the ends back play in 1890."[70] *Figure 19*

However, John McGovern who played at Minnesota at the time credits Dr. Harry Williams with creating the tackles back formation. In a letter to Allison Danzig, dated April 27, 1953, he claimed that Williams developed the tackles back while studying medicine in Philadelphia, Pennsylvania. Williams coached at the Penn Charter School and McGovern claims it was during that time that he developed the tackles back formation. The belief is that he then brought the creation to both Yale and later Minnesota.[71] They suggest he worked with Camp in perfecting the single tackle back formation. As we will see a little later, Camp will make a change in his use of this play in 1900.

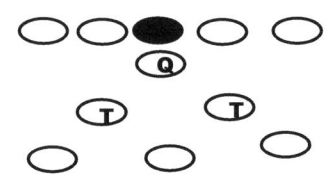

Figure 19 The Tackles Back Formation

Single Tackle Back

Walter Camp thought that aligning both tackles behind the guards created a front line that lacked length. With a single tackle back behind the guards, they still ran inside the defensive tackle on either side. *Figure 20.* Sometimes the halfback carried the ball allowing for the development of massive interference.

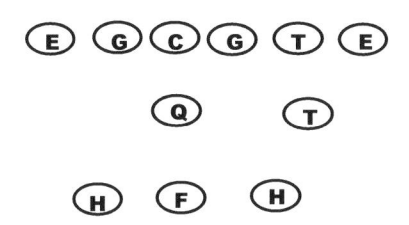

Figure 20 Single Tackle Back Formation: used by Camp & Williams

Some say the first use of the tackle back with a halfback up off the end of the line was by Penn. What we are sure of is that Camp and Williams both used single tackle back plays in the early 1890s. In his book *"Football for Player and Spectator"*, Fielding H. Yost gives some examples of plays from the "Tackle Back" formation and its variations. *Figures 21 - 26* [72]

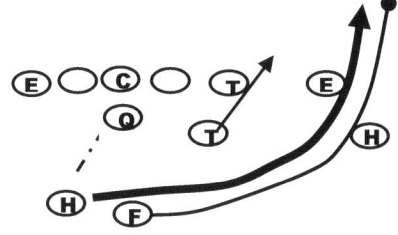

Figure 21 Tackles Back with the Halfback Up

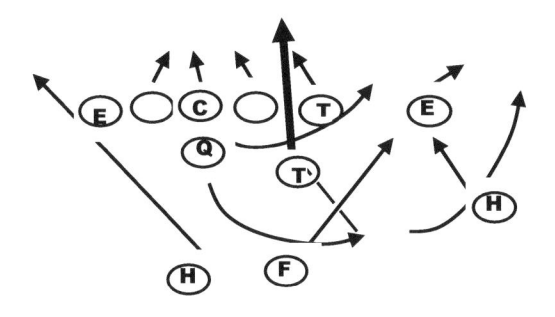

Figure 22 Tackle Back Formations - Tackle Straight Ahead

32

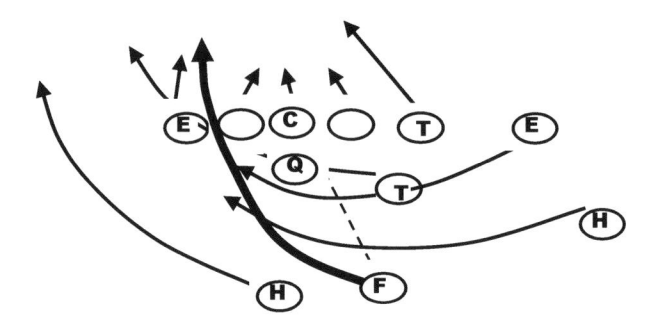

Figure 23 Tackle Back - Fullback Buck Over Left Guard. This play had outstanding success when opposing linemen were shifting to the right. [73]

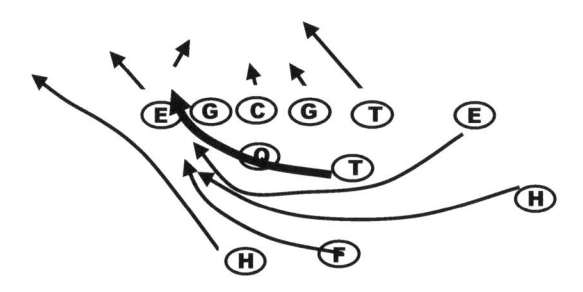

Figure 24 Tackle Back - Tackle Cross Buck. This play is useful especially when opponents are shifting to meet this formation. [74]

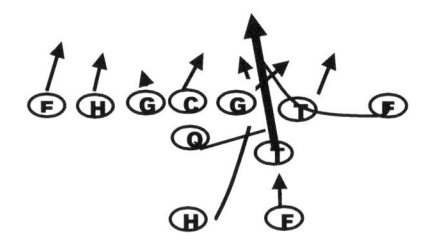

Figure 25 Tackle Back "Square" - Left Tackle Plunge Through Center. This is a close mass play. Execute slowly; all hold together. [75]

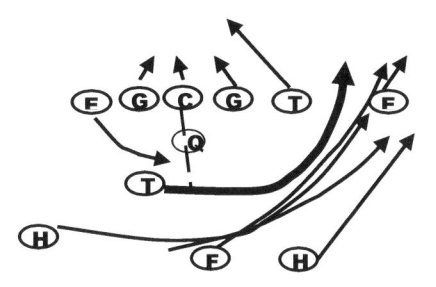

Figure 26 Tackle Straight Back Formation - Left Tackle Cross Buck. This play strikes on the strong side. The men should take their positions in the formation as they line up; not go to the regular formation and then shift. When the men are in position, they immediately execute the play.[76]

Guards Back

The second new formation of the 1894 season was the use of "Guards Back" created and used with immense success by George Woodruff at the University of Pennsylvania. See *figure 27*.   Woodruff was a firm believer that any offense should be physical, overpowering, and punishing in its treatment of the defense.   His formation had five men on the line of scrimmage and placed two guards 3 1/2 yards behind the line of scrimmage. The guards preceded the runner as he advanced.   This provided a great deal of power at the point of attack. John Minds, who played at Penn from 1894-1897, provides the following description for of the Penn offense at that time.

> "From 1894 to 1897 the regular offensive formation (at Penn) was a seven-man line, the quarterback directly behind center and backfield 4.5-5 yards from the line of scrimmage the Fullback being in the center of the trio. It was a form of the T formation. Sometimes we used a formation that became famous as the guards back formation. Penn first used the formation when Playing Princeton at the Trenton Fair Grounds in 1894. The field captain would call, 'Guards back, right', or 'Guards back, left.' They would take either position at a convenient distance to the right or left of the quarterback and slightly behind him. The tackles and ends would move in to take the vacant places, after which the signal for the play would be given; but the mere fact that the guards were right or left didn't mean the play would go in that direction. It might or might not. It might even be an end run play all the way around the opposite direction. It might go straight through the line or it might go off tackle. A guard might carry the ball or a backfield man might carry it. We even had an end carry the ball all the way around his opposite end. Where they went depended entirely on the judgment of the field captain. If he used constant line plunges, it was mass; if he used end plays or off-tackle plays, it was open. It just gave two additional men in the interference.

"Guards back wasn't always a mass play, as frequently charged against it. An open play could always come from it if the field captain so willed. This was not true of the old Turtleback formation or the revolving wedge formation, used by teams of other colleges. An open play could not develop from these formations." [77]

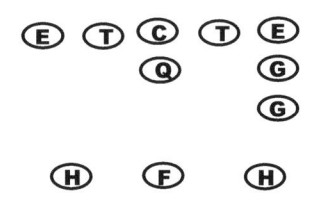

Figure 27 Guards Back Formation - Penn

Flying Interference

Another innovation used by Woodruff at Penn was the principle of "flying Interference". *Figure 28* [78]

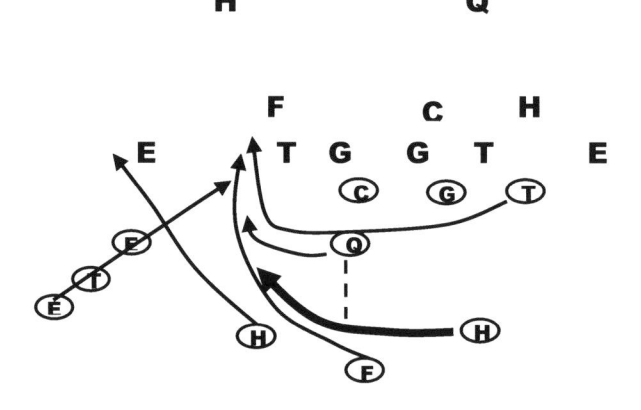

Figure 28 Halfback Around the Tackle with Flying Interference

Stagg's description of this play in his book *"Scientific and Practical Treatise on American Football"* provides an excellent account of the ferocity of the play.

"At a given signal, before the ball is snapped, RE, RT, LE withdraw to the left, from five to ten yards back from the line, and take a position directly behind one another, in readiness to start, as shown.

"At a nod from the captain RE, RT, LE start on the run. When RE has traversed half the distance to the rush line he shouts "Now!" and at the same instant the ball is snapped and the other players start forward as indicated.

"Re rushes directly into the opposing RG while LT and LE take the opposing RT and QB.

"FB precedes RH, who receives the ball, and RT follows behind, in the line indicated.

"The important feature of the play is that the ball be snapped before the flying interference reaches the line so that the runner with the ball will be able to follow directly in their rear." [79]

Teams that utilized these formations dominated play and virtually no one found an adequate field defense for them. Using the "Guards Back" formation Woodruff's Penn teams won 65 games and lost only 2 from 1894 – 1898. Woodruff took a "no holds barred" approach to the game and the Penn teams of that era played with a fierce lack of restraint.

Defending the New Formations

With no forward passes to contend with, defenses bunched up around the line of scrimmage. One of the more successful defenses used at the time was a variation of the 7-1 or "Seven Diamond" with the halfbacks each playing up behind the defensive tackles and the ends in a wide position. This placed 10 men on or near the line of scrimmage. With the snap of the ball, there was the creation of one large mass of players, many be who were maimed or injured. *Figure 29* [80]

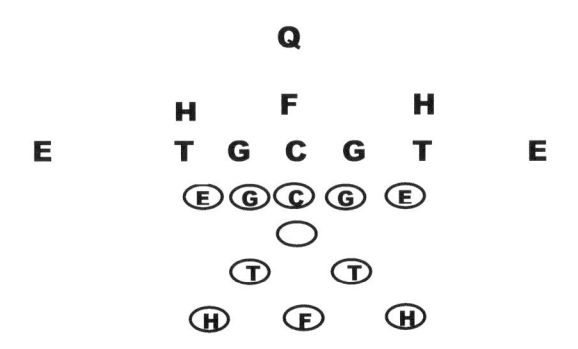

Figure 29 Seven Man Line (7 Diamond) Defense -To Stop the Tackles Back

Around 1894, George Woodruff, the creator of the "Guards Back" formation, created a defense that brought the defensive ends in closer to the ball. He had the tackles shoot across the line of scrimmage. They would then create havoc in the offensive backfield before the play could fully form. His intent here was to disrupt any buck play while still protecting any off-tackle play with the end. See *Figure 30*

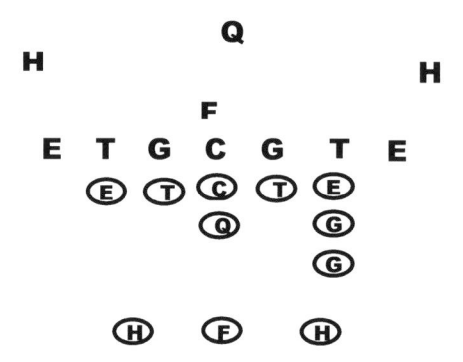

Figure 30 Woodruff's Ends In Defense

For years, the strategies of the other big four schools was to position their ends wide with the only responsibility being to tackle the ball carrier on any wide plays. At the very least, they were to turn the play into the center of the field. Shattering the play in the backfield often resulted in Woodruff's Ends In Defense turning the ball carrier outside, into a supporting halfback or forced out of bounds.

That same year Woodruff created an adjustment to his "Ends In" defense by bringing the halfbacks up to support the flank and have the ends crash hard. Some claim that Woodruff combined this maneuver with the "Seven Diamond" defense in an attempt to confound the offense completely. *Figure 31* [81]

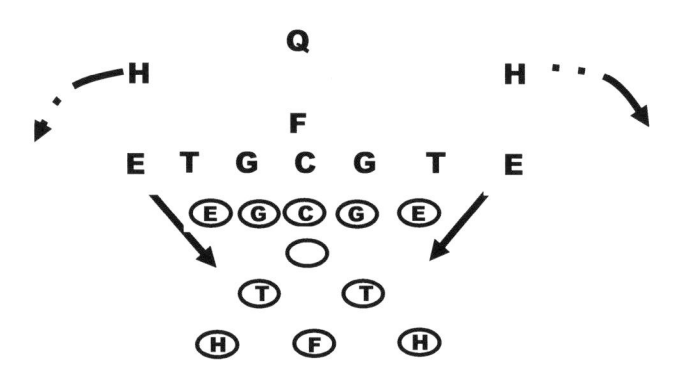

Figure 31 "Ends In" with Ends Crashing and Halfbacks Rotating Up

Another frequent adjustment to the mass offenses of time was to "over shift" the defense to the strength of the offense. *See Figure 32*

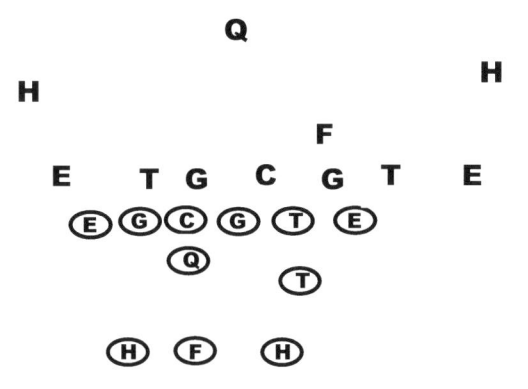

Figure 32 Over-shifted 7-1 Defense vs. Mass Formation

Amos Alonzo Stagg combated this defensive over-shift by pre-aligning each tackle back off the line of scrimmage behind their normal alignment position. Given a command, they would then take their position for the snap of the ball. This late alignment shift made it difficult for the defense to adjust. This was one of the first uses of the "line shift". *Figure-33*

Pre-alignment

Alignment after the Shift

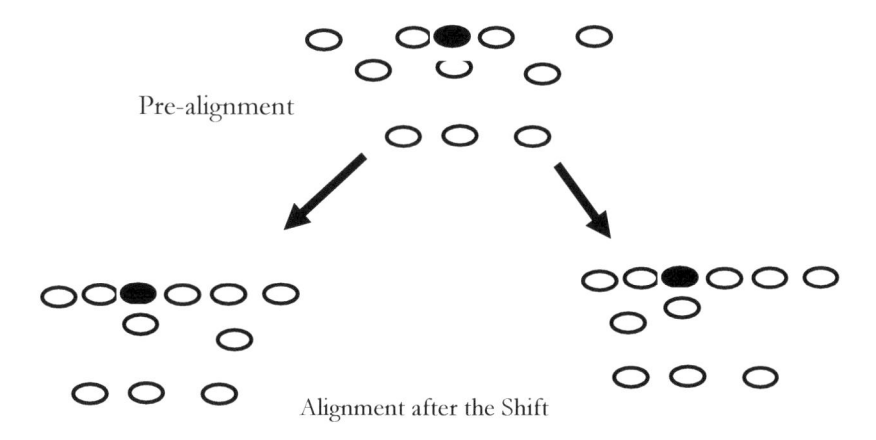

Figure 33 Two Examples of Stagg's Original "Line Shifts."

Disagreement over the Use of Mass Formation

The college presidents, the press, as well as the public, alleged that the "Ends Back," "Guards Back" and "Tackles Back" mass formations were all generating too much power. More importantly, they were creating far too many injuries. The game would not survive unless there were changes.

In March of 1895, the rules committee met to resolve the problem of brutality in the game. Yale and Princeton campaigned for the complete abolition of momentum mass play. The committee prohibited more than one man from starting before the snap and prohibited more than three players in a group behind the line. Cornell, Harvard, and Penn all adopted rules that had no restrictions behind the line of scrimmage. Of course, it was relatively easy to convince Penn to preserve the rules. George Woodruff, who was one of the leading advocates of the mass plays, coached Penn, and they were in the midst of a 26 game win streak using momentum mass plays.

During the 1895 season, teams had three choices of rules. The 1894 rules, the Princeton/Yale code, or the Cornell/Penn/Harvard rules.

Mid-Western Schools Define Their Own Rules

The presidents of Michigan, Minnesota, Illinois, Wisconsin, Northwestern, Purdue and Chicago met and held a rules conference of their own. They were unhappy with the void in leadership being displayed by the big four schools (Princeton, Penn, Harvard, Yale) and seized this opportunity to express some of their concerns about the game. Although everyone agreed on the set of rules, few followed them. The rules-making body that the mid-west schools launched would later become, the Big Ten Conference. There were several significant outcomes of those first meeting of the mid-western schools. They restricted transfers from participating in any games until they were students at their new school for 6 months. In addition, they restricted the participation of players who were delinquent in their studies. Also enacted were reforms relative to team training, and the agreement on a Freshman Ineligibility Rule, which restricted an athlete from playing in their first year and hence limited them to three years of actual playing time. Although no rules committee ever created an official statement, over the next decade Wesleyan, Amherst, and Williams all adopted the practice.

Freshmen Eligibility Rules

Harvard became the first "big-time" school to establish a freshman ineligibility rule in 1903. The result of Harvard introducing new freshmen rules was that many conferences and schools followed the same practice. The NCAA never formally established an association-wide policy on freshmen eligibility until 1968 when they declared freshmen eligible in all sports excepting football and basketball. In 1972, freshmen became eligible in both of those sports also.[82]

Hidden Ball Trick

It was in the 1895 season that John Heisman, coaching at Auburn, introduced "the hidden ball trick" during the Vanderbilt game. Edwin Pope in his book *"Football's Greatest Coaches,"* explained what took place,

"Once it was established that the ball could be easily and quickly concealed, they set up a formation to cover up the trick and draw opponents away from Tichenor so he could get free. Heisman decided to drop the guards back slightly, tackles still farther back, and the ends behind them. As they snapped the ball, a back was to jump forward and simulate taking it from quarterback Tichenor. At that moment, the entire team would form a circle and Tichenor would slip the ball into his jersey.

"Then he would drop to the ground and the team would swing out to the right en masse, leaving Tichenor prone as if K.O,'d in the jam. As soon as the mass moved away, Tichenor would jump up and skedaddle." *Figure 34* [83]

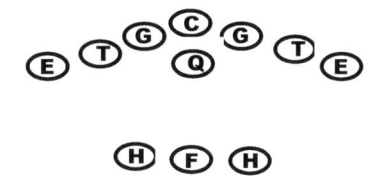

Figure 34 Formation Used for Heisman's "Hidden Ball Trick"   Note: Tichenor was the Q.

Short Punt

Stagg claims that he was the first to use both the "quick kick" and the Short Punt Formation in 1896. This formation positioned a back 5-6 yards behind the line of scrimmage. Later Fielding Yost of Michigan used this formation extensively with the ends split. In one form or another, almost every team in the country copied the short punt. *Figure 35*

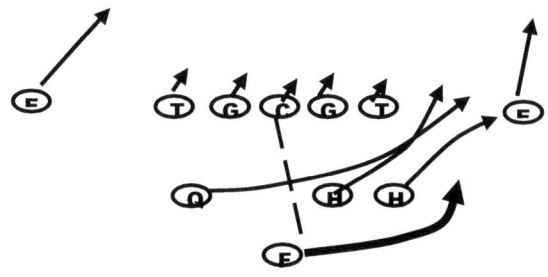

Figure 35 Yost's "Punt Formation Sweep."

Revolving Tandem

In 1896, Princeton introduced the "revolving tandem" devised by Philip King. "The play was executed by swinging one tackle and the halfbacks at the snap against the opposite tackle. This formed a wedge, the halfback carrying the ball propelled by Garret Cochran's strong arms. The play went through the line and over the defensive backs who vainly fell in front of the play to block it."[84] The purpose of this maneuver was to confuse the opponent as to who had the ball and to make it difficult to tackle the carrier as he revolved. This differed from the old Turtleback in that it spun rapidly not slowly as in the turtleback. The play did not catch on or become a favorite of many teams.

First Helmet

During the 1896 season, a player from Lafayette College wore a leather cap for protection. They described it as a "head harness" because he had persuaded a local harness maker to create it for him. The uniform of the day consisted of moleskin pants and a canvas jacket joined by a canvas belt.

1896 also saw the resurgence of the placekick.

Huddle

There is some dispute about who created the huddle. A Feb. 2, 2014 issue of The Week claims it was in the 1890s that Paul Hubbard, the quarterback for Gallaudet, a deaf college in Washington, D.C., had his offense form a tight circle so they could discuss plays without the other team seeing what they were signing. Danzig credits Stagg with using the huddle for the first time (at an indoor game).[85] Some say Bob Zuppke at the University of Illinois was the first to use the huddle, but not until 1921.

Direct Snap

Stagg was also the first to use the direct snap from center to a "deep" back. The center could now make a direct pass to the kicker who was usually 8-10 yards back. Before this time, the quarterback would receive the snap and would then lateral it back to the ball carrier or kicker. Some people argue that the first direct snap to a deep back was actually performed in 1895 by Walter Camp at Yale. Many others, such as Parke Davis, contend that George Woodruff at Penn was the first to introduce the direct snap a year later. Like so much in the game, there seems to be no definitive answer.

Rule Changes 1896-1897

In March of 1896, Led by Moffat of Princeton and Camp of Yale, a joint session of the two "rules" groups met. Of the rules agreed upon, the most significant change was Rule Change 5:

"No player of the side in possession of the ball shall take more than one step toward his opponents' goal before the ball is in play without coming to a full stop. At least five players shall be on the line of scrimmage when the ball is snapped. If six players are behind the line of scrimmage, then two of the said six players must be at least five yards behind the line or shall be outside the players on the end of the line." [86]

In February of 1897, the rules committee met and made some significant changes. (1) There were changes in the scoring by awarding 6 points for a touchdown (including point after). 5 points for a goal from a field kick, safety by opponent awarded 2 points, goal after a touchdown became 1 point   (2) They also stated that the center would be forbidden to feint before putting the ball in play in an attempt to draw the opponent offside.   (3) There was a change in the substitution rule so that another player at any time upon the captain's signal could substitute for a player. (Previously permission from the referee was necessary.)   (4) They placed limitations on the offense by proclaiming any player who received the ball from the snapper back could not carry the ball forward beyond the line of scrimmage unless he had regained it after having passed to another player. Schools in the south and mid-west continued to gain prominence and felt secure enough to create their own adjustments to the rules.

At the rules committee meeting in March of 1898, the most significant rule changes were about player conduct and personal fouls.

Shifts

It was only when the mass formation plays were outlawed that the actual benefits of the early shifts would appear. Although several shifts were introduced, the most notable was the Minnesota Shift, added after the turn of the century. The shift circumvented the new rules that prevented mass plays. The shift skirted the new regulations by having players pause ever so slightly; but not pause enough to stop them from using the momentum of the shift to propel them into the play. More on the Shifts later.

Use of Motion

During the 1898 season, Stagg began to use men in motion, that he called "flyers." Backs ran laterally or slightly back toward the sideline and, with the snap, the quarterback quickly threw the ball out to him.[87] *Figure 36*   More often than not, this motion was used as a decoy by the offense. These maneuvers forced the defense to adjust with a defender running outside with the "flier" or risk a long gain as the "flier" caught the ball and ran up the sideline. Of course, when the defense made that adjustment, Stagg would attack with the run in that area that defender vacated. Offensive coaches still use the same principle in attacking defenses. Stagg also had his quarterback sprint out behind his fullback and remaining halfback and then throw to the flier.

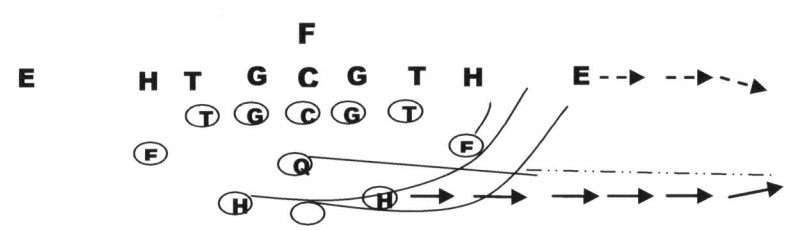

Figure 36 "Man in Motion or "Fliers" first used by Stagg

6-2-2-1 Defense: Over-Shift

In that same year (1898), Stagg pulled his defensive center out of the line of defense to create a 6-2-2-1. His use of this new tactic was to combat Penn's overpowering "Guards Back" formation. *Figure 37* The idea was for the Center (C) and Fullback (F) to push the guards in front of them through the line into the Penn backfield. Stagg also over shifted his Center and Fullback to the offensive strength. *Figure 38*

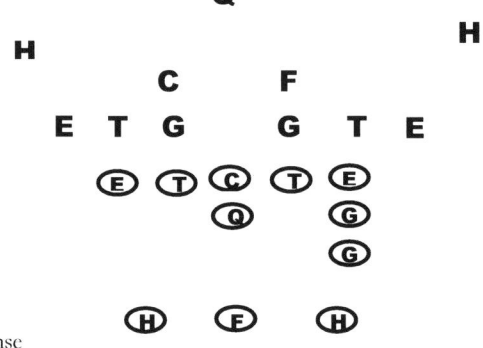

Figure 37 6-2-2-1 Defense

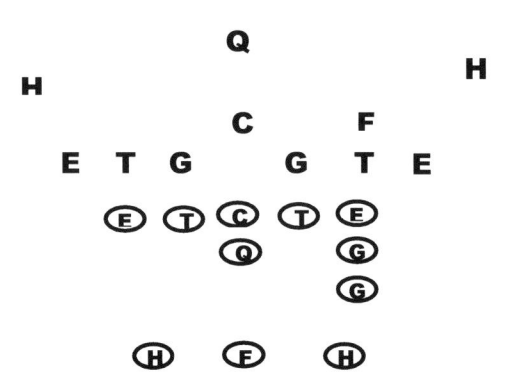

Figure 38 Stagg's "Over shifted" 6-2-2-1 Defense

7-3-1 Defense

Around the same time, Stagg devised another defensive move. He brought his halfbacks up as linebackers to create a 7-3-1 defense vs. the "Guards Back" formation.[88] *Figure 39*

Remember there was no forward pass to threaten the lone quarterback in the secondary. They positioned seven men on the line with a wing (halfback) behind each defensive tackle and the fullback behind the center. There were, essentially, ten men on the line of scrimmage.

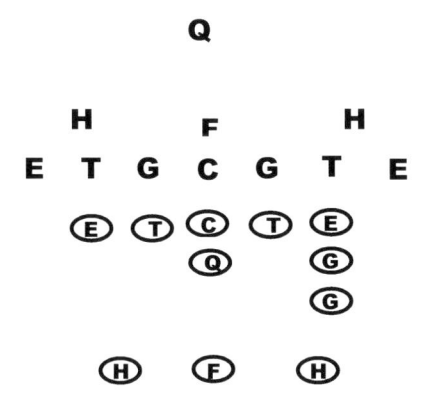

Figure 39 The 7-3-1 Defense vs. the "Guards Back."

Split Play

It was back around 1890 that Stagg first introduced the use of the split play. The quarterback turns his back to the line of scrimmage and pretends to hand the ball to one halfback. He gives the ball to the other halfback to plunge straight ahead through the tackle-end gap. He might also go through the tackle-guard gap. Another variation of the play was to give the ball to a halfback crossing to the opposite side of the line (dashed line). From this, Stagg would later create some pass plays after faking to the backs. A "play action" pass. *Figure 40*

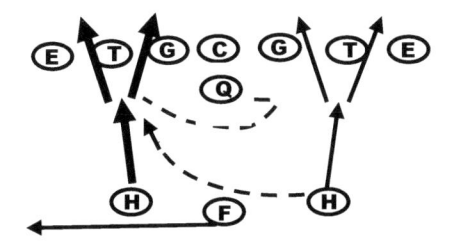

Figure 40 Stagg's Use of the "Split Play" The ball could be given to either of the halfbacks.

Split Cross Play

Still, another development by Stagg around that time was his split cross-buck plays that were a series of plays from "T" formation. He had the quarterback making pivots and feints to crossing backs before giving the ball to another back.[89] Although they were not true split buck plays, they were the precursor to the split buck plays. The "Split-T" coaches in the middle of the next century would use these same principles extensively. One can readily see how Stagg's thinking evolved. *Figure 41*

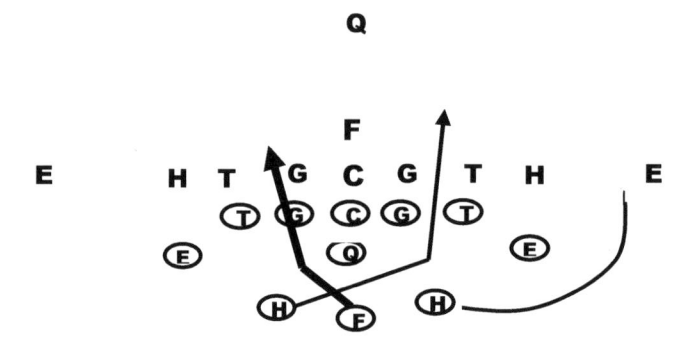

Figure 41 Basic Play in the "Split Buck" Series

Criss-Cross Play

Following are two criss-cross (split) plays taken from Stagg's 1894 book, "*Scientific and Practical Treatise on American Football*" that reveal the diversity of the series.[90] *Figures 42, 43*

Stagg described his Criss-Cross Play as follows,

"To send LE around the right end on a pass from RE, LE and RE both play in slightly while LE works back until he is nearly on a line with the half-backs.

RE and RH start toward the left the instant the ball is snapped, RH preceding and taking the first extra man in the line beyond the tackle.

RE receives the ball on a pass from QB, and running close in front of LE, passes him the ball and rushes on tin the opposing RE.

As RE reaches LE, FB, LH, and LG dash toward the right in the lines indicated.

FB takes the first extra man in the line beyond RT, LH runs directly for the opposing LE, and LG, preceding LE plays as shown in diagram twenty-five *See Figure 42*

QB blocks the first man through on the right-hand side of the center, if necessary, or plays as shown in diagram twenty-five LE, upon receiving the ball, starts toward the right at utmost speed, keeping just to the outside of LG. LT, RG, and RT play as shown in diagram twenty-five." [91]

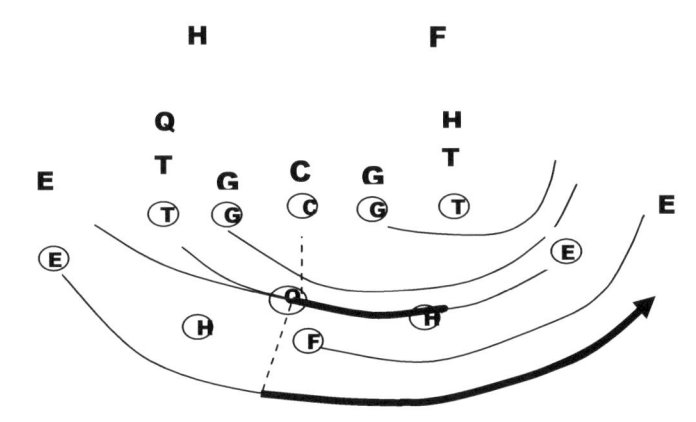

Figure 42 Basic Criss-Cross Play

Tackle Criss-Cross

Stagg's description of the Tackle Criss Cross;

"Tackle criss-crosses with the end in play around the opponent end.

To send RE around the left end on a pass from LT, before the ball is snapped RE works in and slightly back to RE.

As the ball is put in play LT leaves the line as shown in diagram seventeen, receives the ball, runs close in front of RE and gives him the ball as he passes. LT then runs around the opposing LE.

LH precedes LT, as does RH in diagram thirty-one.

As LT leaves the line, LE jumps in and takes the opposing tackle (as in diagram seventeen: from original text))

LG plays as shown in (diagram thirty: from original text).

RH starts forward in the line indicated as RE receives the ball, and precedes him around the left end, crossing in front of RG as the latter swings in behind the line." [92] *See Figure 43*

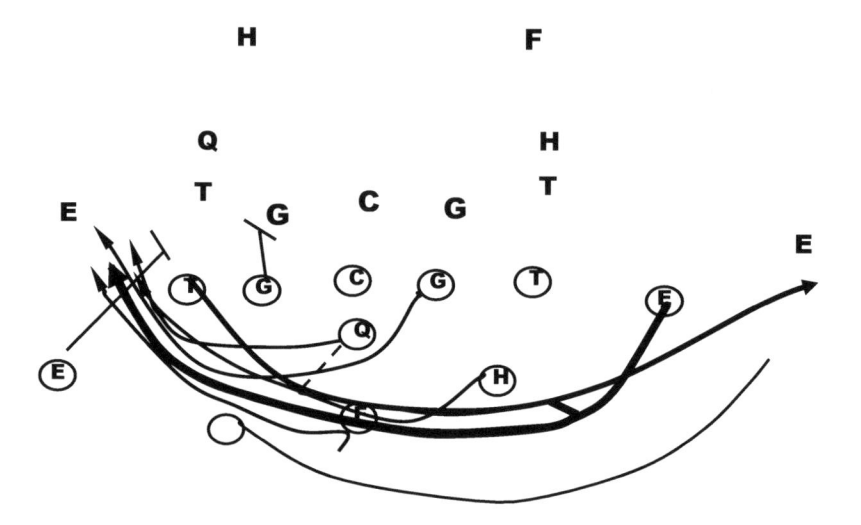

Figure 43 The Tackle Criss-Cross (Left Tackle carries the ball, gives to Right End on Sweep Left)

"Whoa Back" Shift

Also, in 1900, Amos Alonzo Stagg used a "shift" formation that he called the "Whoa back." One end would line up in front of the FB and one end would line up behind the FB. On the command "shift" one end would move to the Line of scrimmage outside the tackle (either right or left). Most often, the front end moved onto the line of scrimmage. The back end would be in a position to "push" the ball carrier. *Figure 44* This formation was disposed of in 1910 with the rule that required seven men on the line of scrimmage.

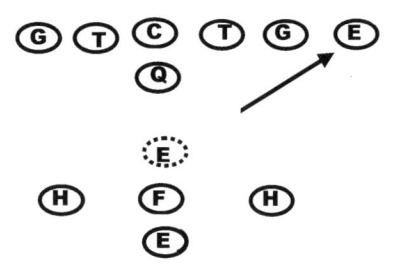

Figure 44 Warner's "Whoa-back" Shift

Slowing the Defensive Rush

As mentioned earlier, Camp in 1900 made a change in the Tackle Back that yielded big wins for Yale. Since the early days of the defensive game, linemen were taught to charge low and hard into the opponent's backfield. Camp reasoned that there had to be a way for the offense to take advantage to this unrestrained rush. He used the Tackle Back to encourage a defensive lineman to rush through thinking he was getting into Yale's backfield; only to watch as the Yale running back ran into the opponent's backfield unencumbered through the area he vacated. Yale would run up huge scores and produce victories over both Harvard and Princeton, their archrivals before anyone could devise a means of defending his new play. Of course, the way to defend the play was quite simple. Teams began to slow down the rush of their defensive line, especially the tackles. This defensive move, however, had its own drawbacks. Having one's defensive line sit back opened them to powerful, hard-hitting plays.

Northwestern Tandem

The "Northwestern Tandem" by C.M. Hollister was devised around the same time. At first glance, this looked very much like the "Full I" formation that would become popular much later in the century.[93] Of course, a significant difference was the exchange between the halfback and tackle. *Figure 45*

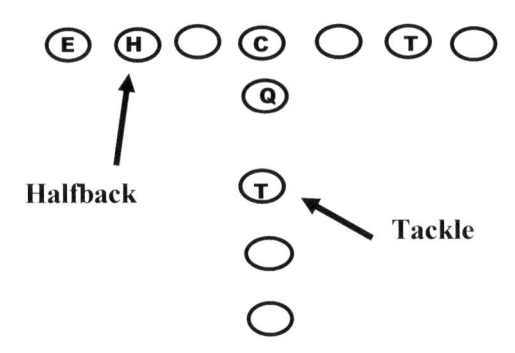

Figure 45 The Northwestern Tandem

Note the exchange between the left tackle and halfback

From this formation, Hollister could attack any point on the opponent's defensive line with equal force. Some further adjustments to this formation were known only as "divide." The offensive line would divide into two sections allowing the tackle in the backfield to move up and align on the line of scrimmage, the two backs aligning in tandem behind him.

Minnesota Shift

It was in 1903 or 1904 that Dr. Harry Williams introduced the "Minnesota Shift". As is usual in football history, there is some disagreement. Some say the "Minnesota Shift" did not appear until 1906. There was an article in the Associated Press in 1934 that made a claim that this shift first emerged at River Falls High School, Wisconsin around 1900 with J W T Ames as the coach. For the most part, the shift used an unbalanced line with two men on the short side. They also moved to a formation with only one man on the short side. Unlike some shifts that came later, the "Minnesota Shift" moved both the line and the backs. In a letter dated April 27, 1953, John McGovern, who played for Williams at Minnesota from 1908-1910, states,

> "On different plays, the backfield men ended up in different arrangements aft the shift. Dr. Williams also had a big shift with only one man on the short side, and on some plays, there were two shifts before the snap of the ball. The theory of the shift was to outflank the defense or, as I have heard, Dr. Williams express it, to get four men against three or five against four.
>
> "The great success of the formation resulted, I believe in the failure of the defense to shift sufficiently. These shifts took place quite rapidly, with just enough of a pause to satisfy the requirements of the rules on a complete stop. Plays were made to the short side, but the full possibilities and effectiveness of the short side play never reached the perfection to which Bernie Bierman brought it as an integral component of a shifting offense." [94] *Figure 46*

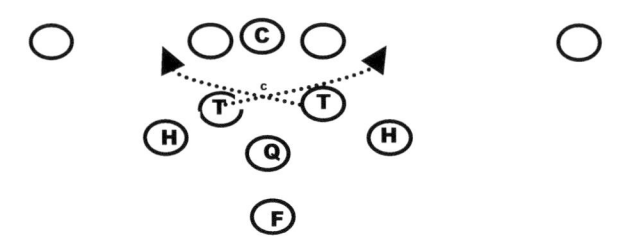

Figure 46 The Movement of the Tackles in the "Minnesota Shift." (the shift may end with both tackles aligned on the same side of the center) There were many different ways that the backs moved.

Defending the Shift

Robert Zuppke of Illinois, who was a big admirer of the shift, describes his 1916 unorthodox defense of the Minnesota Shift in this way; "I broke that up in 1916 by using an unusual defense. I made my tackles go wide with the Minnesota men (ends), sliding with them, and by lining up my three middlemen the same distance back from the line of scrimmage as Minnesota's tackles. My middlemen hopped into the line with their tackles, and we had forward momentum. Minnesota was caught flat-footed because of our unorthodox defensive maneuvers. I used an irregular pattern in my defensive secondary for this game. It resolved itself mainly into a 7-diamond." [95]

Unbalanced Line

It is a popular belief that Glenn "Pop" Warner created the unbalanced line in 1906. However, Stagg began experimenting with shifting a tackle from one side of the formation to the other to create an unbalanced line in 1902. [96] *Figure 47*

Stagg wrote, in 1932; "At the beginning of the century I was shifting linemen quickly from one side to the other for a quick attack, and in 1904 I sometimes used a backfield shift synchronously." He adds, "I started another type of backfield shift in 1910 on which the ball was snapped instantly without delay. This shift later received its most effective demonstration in the Notre Dame system under Harper and Rockne." [97]

Warner maintained his intent was to force defenses to adjust, since many defenses were beginning to over shift to the strength of the offensive formation. Putting both tackles on the same side of the line created confusion for defenses and they had to adjust their initial alignment. Also, because of the numbers advantage to one side of the center, an unbalanced formation created a more powerful blocking area for the offense. He forced the defense to spend valuable practice time preparing to adjust to an offensive scheme that he may or may not use. Indeed, in the ensuing years, "Pop" Warner drew on his own inventiveness and further developed the unbalanced line to create much more havoc for defenses.

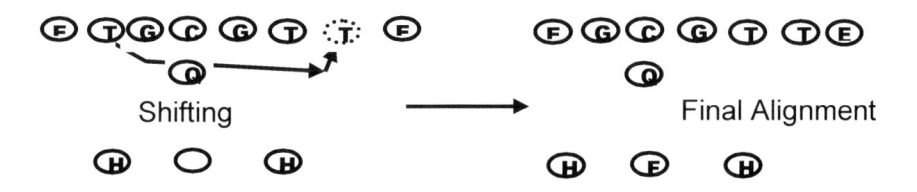

Figure 47 Shifting the line from Balanced to Unbalanced, 1902

Rule Changes to "Open" the Game

In spite of the numerous innovations, mass formations and vicious play still dominated the game. There was such a public clamor for change that the Rules Committee made a request for people with an interest in football to send suggestions for modifications for change.

There was unquestionably a widespread mood among the public for a more "open game." There were several significant rule changes made at the Rules Committee meeting in 1903. Among them were (1) a suggestion by Bert Walters, a former Harvard player, who introduced the idea of the present day neutral zone. In 1885, Walter Camp first introduced to the Rules Committee the concept of a neutral zone between the two opposing lines. It was not adopted at that time. (2) Between the 25-yard lines, the quarterback, or any other player receiving the ball directly from the snapper, was permitted to run with the ball. However, he must be 5 yards to the left or right from where the ball was snapped. Previously the quarterback could not advance the ball across the line of scrimmage. He had to pitch the ball to one of the others players while still in the backfield. They lined the field between the two 25 yard lines so that the players and officials could adequately judge the five-yard distance. The middle of the field now looked like a checkerboard instead of the old "gridiron" lines. (3) The team scored upon would now have the option of kicking off or receiving after their opponent scored. (4) Between the 25-yard lines, the offensive team now had to have seven men aligned on the line of scrimmage when they put the ball in play. Between the 25-yard line and goal line, it was only necessary to have five men on the line of scrimmage at the snap. [98]

Brutality Continues: 1904

The brutality of the mass plays continued into 1904. The same mass formations continued to dominate the game. The rules were once again changed. (1) There was a change in the rules that eliminated the mandatory seven offensive men on the line of scrimmage between the 25-yard lines. In its place, there was now a mandate that six men be on the line of scrimmage at all points on the field. (2) They reduced the value of a field goal from 5 to 4 points. For the first time, a touchdown was worth more than a goal from the field. Kicking would diminish and the game would change forever.

Backfield Shift

Stagg introduced the backfield shift. *Figure 48* The backfield shifts often were in combination with his earlier movements of the line shift. Just as with the line shifts, the backfield shifts placed the defense in a vulnerable position regarding an adjustment in their alignment.

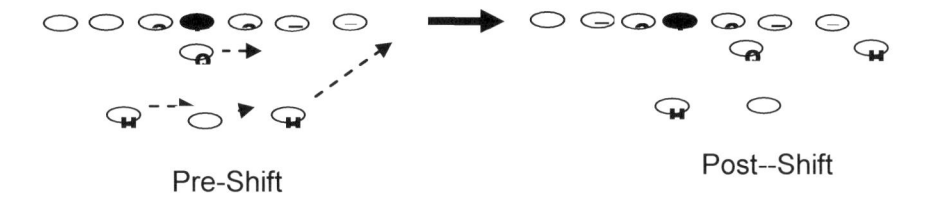

Figure 48 Shifting in the Backfield, 1904

According to a New York Times article published August 12, 1962, and written by Allison Danzig, Stagg also initiated a change in the quarterback's arrangement with the Center in 1904.[99] However, in a letter to a friend in 1949, Stagg states that he first used the new stance in 1894. For the first time, he had the quarterback stand directly behind the snapper in a semi-erect position with his hands under the center to receive the ball. He felt that the new stance saved time. The quarterback no longer had to rise from his stoop after having received the ball and that permitted the quarterback to use his body as well as his hands when taking the ball from the center. It allowed him to hide the ball as he turned his back to the defense adding to the deception of the play. It also gave the quarterback a better view of the defense before the snap.

Penn's "Roving Center" Defense

Penn introduced a significant change in their defense. They began to play with a "roving center". The defensive Center was free to line-up anywhere behind the defensive line. *Figure 49* Although most people regard Penn as the first to use the "roving center", Hugo Bezdek also claims credit for it.

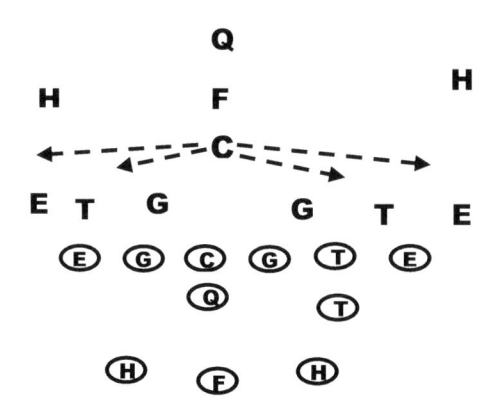

Defensive Center has freedom In his alignment

Figure 49 Penn's "Roving Center" Defense

Quarterback Sweep

Stagg introduced the quarterback keep sweep in 1905. The execution of the sweep was done with a pivot and fake to a diving back. The importance of this advancement is that it is the same concept used later in the 1940s with the Split T-formation.[100] *Figure 50*

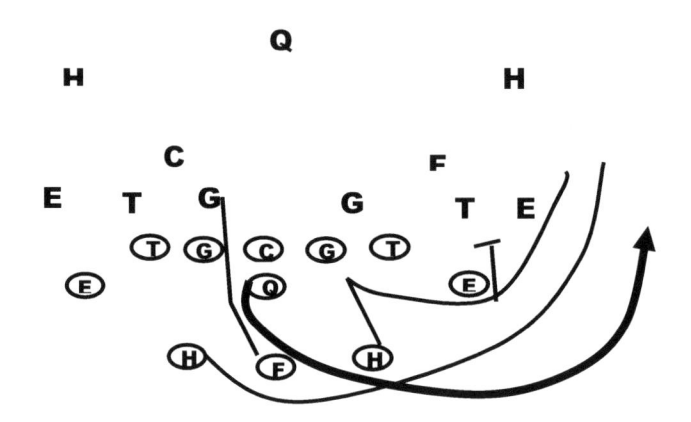

Figure 50 Stagg's Quarterback Keep Sweep play

Brutality Hits the Breaking Point

The problem of brutality reached the breaking point in 1905 when the number of reported deaths was 18. Additionally, there many were "severe" injuries. Newspaper editorials were calling for the abolition of football. Leading the movement was the Harvard President, Charles Eliot. He felt the game was lawless, encouraged brutality, and had an adverse influence on students. In midseason, President Teddy Roosevelt called representatives from Yale, Harvard, and Princeton to the White House. There are varying reports of the meeting. Some reports say Roosevelt told the delegates they must remove every objectionable feature of the game or it would be abolished. "Brutality and foul play should receive the same summary punishment given to a man who cheats at cards," Roosevelt said. Some say he called the meeting as a reaction to a head injury his own son had incurred at a Harvard practice. Still, others say that at the meeting he only said he loved the game, and he simply encouraged them to save the game by enacting some rule changes that would curb the violence.

No matter what his motivation, he had gotten the Rules Committee attention when no one else seemed able to do so. There was a resolve on the part of the President and the public, as well as the college administrators, to either change the character of the game or abolish play.

Before the next fall season began, there would be substantial changes in the game. Bill Reid, Harvard's coach, organized a meeting to establish a new rulemaking committee. It essentially was done to rival the older group controlled by Walter Camp. Reid formed the Intercollegiate Athletic Association (the forerunner to the NCAA). The new organization suggested 19 new rule changes. They discussed changing the yardage necessary for a first down from five yards to ten yards. They felt that the rule regarding the "neutral zone between the offensive and defensive lines be enforced. They considered having six men on the line at the time of the snap. They wanted to eliminate the flying wedge entirely. They agreed that the forward pass should be legalized with the intention of spreading the field.

"Hurry Up" Yost: Offense

No explanation of this period in football would be complete without mentioning Fielding "Hurry Up" Yost of Michigan. It was in 1901 that Michigan hired Yost. Unheard of at that time, he acquired a salary equal to a professor. From 1901 until 1905, Michigan went 56 games and did not lose. During that time, his teams scored 2326 points and there were only 40 scored against them.[101] The Michigan teams were renowned for their excellent conditioning and they played a fast-paced game. Yost's teams earned the nickname the "Point a Minute" offense. Yost often had his quarterback call the next play while getting up from the previous play. They often caught the defense misaligned or too tired to align properly. Opponents of today's "hurry up" offenses still seem to be having the same grievances.

His offense was an amalgamation of almost all the formations and plays that others were using. He ran from the T-Formation, Tackle Back, and Punt formation most frequently. However, there were some innovations that Yost introduced both in the plan of his offense and defense as well as a strategy. Yost put a great emphasis on the punting game and using the punt to gain field position for his offense. He was the first to use what we now refer to as the "Statue of Liberty "play. However, he ran it from a punt formation and fake punt. Below we show some diagrams from Yost's book *"Football for Player and Spectator"* that show some of the innovative aspects of Yost's teams.[102] *Figures 51-56*

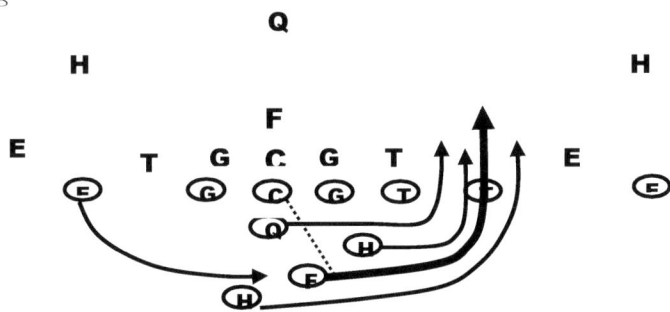

Figure 51 Tandem Tackle-Over Fullback Buck   Used when an opponent would over shift. Note the positioning of the backs.

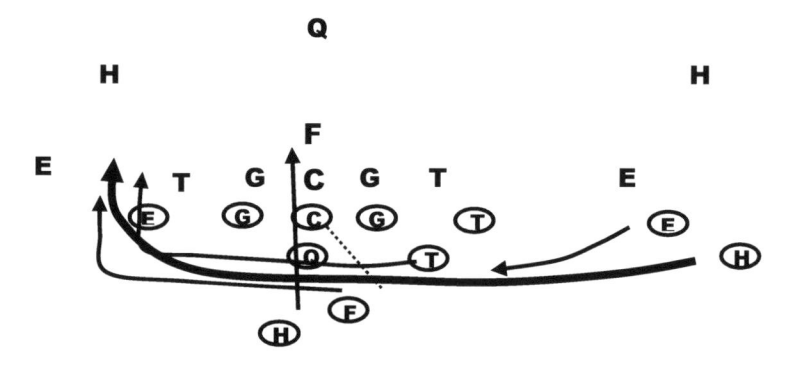

Figure 52 Tackle Back Formation.- Right Halfback Run Around Left End.

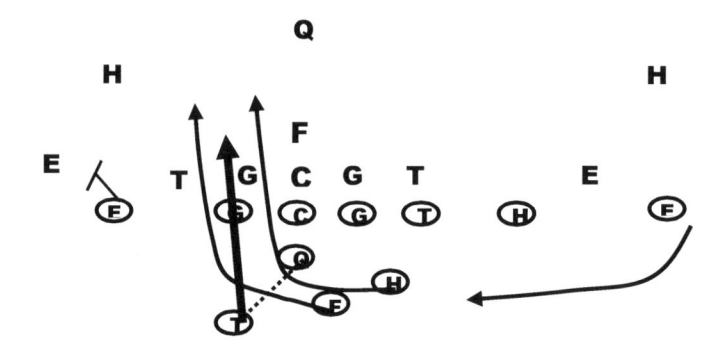

Figure 53 Tackle Straight Back. Left Tackle Straight Plunge. In this play the tackle bucks straight ahead over the position occupied by the left guard. Note position of Left Halfback, between right tackle and end.

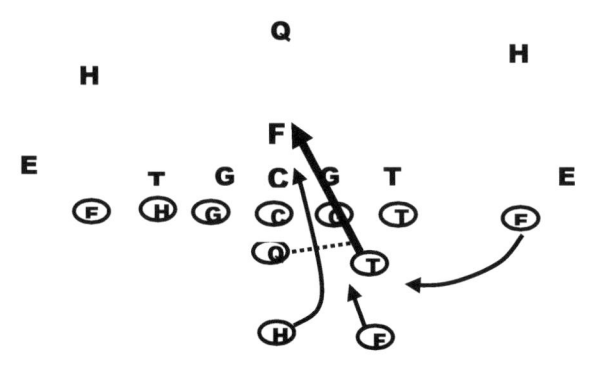

Figure 54 Tackle Back Square
        Left Tackle Plunge through Center. This is a close mass play.

55

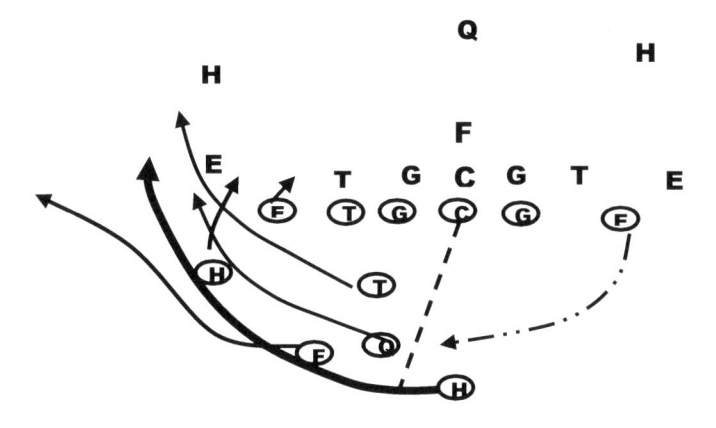

Figure 55 Direct Pass Formation: Right Half-Back Run Around Left End.
In this play, the halfback takes the ball on a direct pass from center.

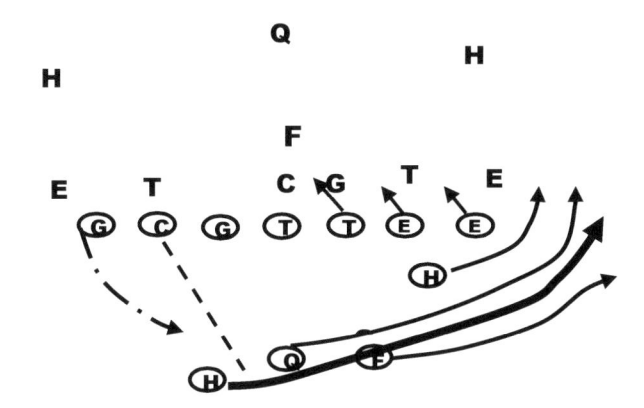

Figure 56 Wing Shift Formation: Direct Pass to Left Halfback.   Practically the entire team shifts and the success of the play will depend almost entirely on lining up quickly and starting the play immediately. Do not give opponents time to take in the situation thoroughly.

Defensive Adjustments

Yost discusses his Regular Defense the following way,

"The two ends should play close to the tackle, about three yards out; should charge ahead instantly with the snap of the ball, turning in quickly if the play is directed at the line, but keeping well outside of all opponents' interference

"The two tackles must play wide enough so that they cannot be easily boxed by the opposing ends, yet not so wide that they can be easily thrown out. Use hands freely. Remember the end is the dangerous man.

"The center should play a little higher and freer than either of the guards and he must be in a position to do tackling on either side of center, or in fact along the entire line.

"The three defensive backs must tackle everywhere. Wherever the runner is, there they must be.

"The defensive quarterback should judge his distance behind the line by the direction of the wind and the strength of the opposing kicker. He must never be drawn in too close." [103] *Figure 57*

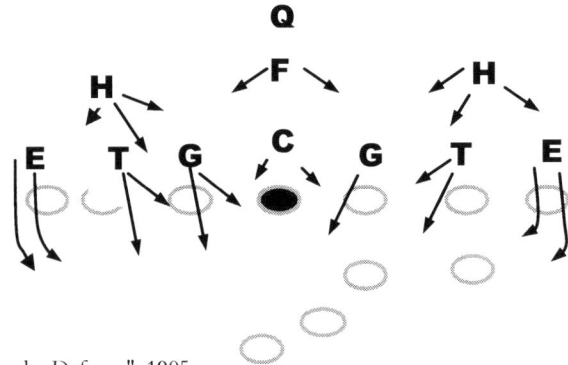

Figure 57 Yost's "Regular Defense", 1905

The Pennsylvania Defense

Below is Yost's illustration of, what was commonly called, the Pennsylvania defense. "The end, aligned very close to the tackle, was to oppose the offenses interference and break it up or to tackle the runner. They will meet the interference before it is under much headway and will often be successful in spoiling the play behind the line. If the ends do not tackle the runner, the runner will usually have little interference left and then can be grabbed easily by one of the defensive backs. The two tackles play wide. They are propelled inward toward the center by a shove from the defensive back.". [104] *Figure 58*

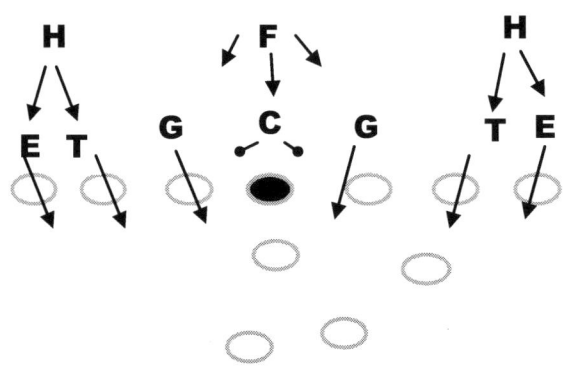

Figure 58 7-3-1 Defensive Formation - Ends In

The 8-2-1 Defense versus the Tackle-Back

Yost's explanation of the 8-2-1 defense "This formation is used to meet the various tackle-back plays and tackle over on the line plays. The halftone illustration on the opposite page shows the position the men should assume just before the opponents snap the ball. In the diagram above (the diagram is actually below in this book), the opposing center is shown so that the relative position of the defensive linemen is shown as compared with the offensive linemen; the entire line on defense is shifted a half a man to the right. The right halfback has gone up on the line with the right tackle. The defensive quarterback, which is being played by the full back, and the left half back have shifted their positions to the right. This would be the position taken by the team if the opposing side were using right tackle back or right tackle over on the line. The men would shift to just the opposite position should the opposing attack demand it."[105]

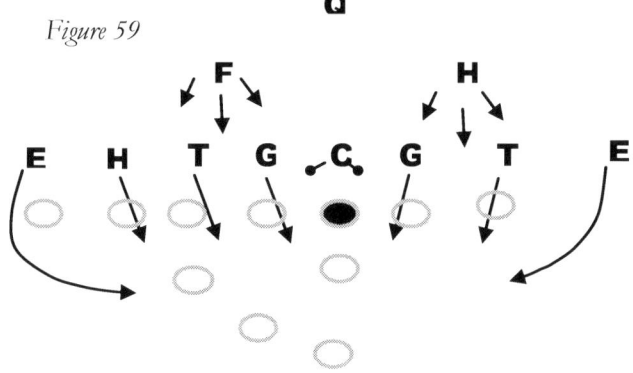

Figure 59

Figure 59 8-2-1 Defensive Formation: Line and Backfield Shift

---

[69] Saturday Evening Post October 23, 1926
[70] Danzig, *The History of American Football* p26
[71] Danzig, *The History of American Football* p26
[72] Yost, Fielding H., "Football for Player and Spectator," Ann Arbor, Mich., The Ann Arbor Press, 1905), p. 198
[73] Yost, *Football for Player and Spectator*, p.201
[74] Yost, *Football for Player and Spectator*, p. 202
[75] Yost, *Football for Player and Spectator*, p. 230
[76] Yost, *Football for Player and Spectator*, p. 239
[77] Danzig, *The History of American Football*, p. 25.

78 Stagg, Henry L. Williams, *Scientific and Practical Treatise on AMERICAN FOOTBALL*, (New York, D. Appleton & Co, 1894), p.194

79 Stagg *Scientific and Practical Treatise on AMERICAN FOOTBALL* p. 195

80 Danzig, *Oh How They Played The Game*, p.110

81 Danzig, *Oh How They Played The Game*, p.119

82 Zimbalist, Andrew, *The Bottom Line*, (Philadelphia, Temple University Press, 2006), p.232

83 Pope, Edwin, *Football's Greatest Coaches*, (Atlanta, Ga. Tupper and Love, Inc., 1955), p. 122-123

84 Nelson, p.79

85 Danzig, *Oh How They Played The Game*, p. 55

86 Nelson, p.77

87 Danzig, *Oh How They Played The Game*, p. 56

88 Danzig, *Oh How They Played The Game*, p. 57

89 Danzig, *Oh How They Played The Game*, p. 56

90 Stagg, Henry L. Williams, *Scientific and Practical Treatise on AMERICAN FOOTBALL*, p. 138

91 Stagg, Henry L. Williams, *Scientific and Practical Treatise on AMERICAN FOOTBALL*, p. 138

92 Stagg, *Scientific and Practical Treatise on AMERICAN FOOTBALL*, p 145

93 Yost, *Football for Player and Spectator*, (Ann Arbor, Michigan, Ann Arbor Press, 1905), p. 200

94 Danzig, *The History of American Football*, p. 65

95 Danzig, *The History of American Football*, p. 66

96 Wiley, Lee Umphlett, *Creating the Big Game: John W. Heisman and the Invention of American Football*, (West Port Ct., Greenwood Publishing Group, Inc. 1992) p. 74

97 Danzig, *The History of American Football*, p.59

98 Danzig, *Oh How They Played The Game*, p. 72

99 Danzig, *Oh How They Played The Game*, p. 56

100 Danzig, *Oh How They Played the Game*, p.56

101 Danzig, *Oh How They Played The Game*, p.131

102 Yost, *Football for Player and Spectator*, p.189-260

103 Yost, *Football for Player and Spectator*, p 255

104 Yost, *Football for Player and Spectator*, p 259

105 Yost, *Football for Player and Spectator*, p 257

CHAPTER FIVE

Saving the Game

(1906 – 1909)

Birth of the NCAA

As the sport became more popular and more schools began to field teams, more and more people viewed football as a moneymaking endeavor. With commercialization came the demands to win. There was also the issue of player safety. In short, many schools struggled with the same issues that schools are dealing with today

As previously stated, on October 9, 1905, President Theodore Roosevelt held a meeting at the White House of the head coaches and other representatives of the football powers—Harvard, Yale and Princeton. Roosevelt implored them to clean up the game, to rein in the violence and create a model for fair play. However, the 1905 football season resulted in 19 player deaths and 137 serious injuries.[106]

In December of 1905, thirteen schools met as the Rules Committee. This was the first of a series of meetings that would transform the old rules body from the Rules Committee to a new governing body. The new association, which consisted of sixty-two original members, was The Intercollegiate Athletic Association of the United States. Although lacking in both governing and decision-making powers, it was an attempt at the formation of regulations regarding the educational and competitive requirements for intercollegiate athletics. Although covering a number of sports, regulating football was its principle purpose.[107] Despite the change from student control to institutional oversight, the game remained under-regulated However; they did approve sweeping changes for the 1906 season.

In 1910, the Intercollegiate Athletics Association (IAA) would become the National Collegiate Athletic Association (NCAA).[108]

1906 Rules Changes

It certainly is not the intent here to focus on the rules or review all changes in the rules through the years. However, because of the importance of the 1906 changes and the manner in which these new regulations would alter the nature of the game, the complete list of rule changes in 1906 is detailed below. These rule changes attempted to rid the game of its brutality, spread out the action, make more efficient use of the officials, and make the game appealing to all concerned. These 1906 rules changes, along with the sixty-one original rules of 1876, have special import because of the big way in which they alter the makeup of the game. The legalization of the forward pass, although nothing, as we know it today, along with the ten-yard rule for a first down, was especially significant. Indeed, all historians agree that the 1906 changes were milestones in the evolution of the game and they moved football into the modern era. However, the next six years proved to be noteworthy in the way they enhance the game further.

You will see as the evolution of the game continues that it left much to the imagination of the resourceful and innovative coach. Taken from David M. Nelson's *"Anatomy of a Game"*, the 1906 rules read as follows,

Forward Pass: permitted behind the neutral zone as follows:

One forward pass shall be allowed to each scrimmage, provided such pass be made by a player who was behind the line of scrimmage when the ball was put in play, and provided the ball, after being passed forward, does not touch the ground before being touched by a player of either side.

Penalty: If a forward pass is made by a player who was not behind the line of scrimmage when the ball was put in play, the ball shall go to the opponents on the spot where the pass was made. If the ball, after being passed forward, touches the ground before being touched by a player of either side, it shall go to the opponents on the spot where the pass was made.

The pass may not be touched by a player who was on the line of scrimmage when the ball was put in play – except by either of the two men playing on the ends of the line.

Penalty: If a forward pass is unlawfully touched by a player who was on the line of scrimmage, or by any one of the players who was behind the line of scrimmage when the ball was put in play, it shall go to the opponents on the spot where the pass was made.

A forward pass over the line of scrimmage within the space of five yards on each side of the center shall be unlawful.

Penalty: If the ball is passed over the line of scrimmage within the space of five yards on each side of the center, it shall go to the opponents on the spot where the pass was made.

A forward pass is made by the side which did not put the ball in play in a scrimmage shall be unlawful.

Penalty: If a forward pass is made by the side which did not put the ball in play in a scrimmage, the ball shall go to the opponents on the spot where the pass was made.

A forward pass that crosses the goal line on the fly or bounces without touching a player of either side shall be declared a touchback for the defenders of the goal.

First down yardage: Increased to ten yards in three downs.

Onside kick and kicking game: A player of the kicking team becomes onside and may recover the ball as soon as it strikes the ground.

A kick that strikes the ground may not be kicked by either team.

A player attempting to make a fair catch must signal by raising his hand and arm clearly above his head.

The ball is dead when it strikes the ground from a kick across the goal line after touching the ground on the field of play.

The kicker in trying at goal by a placekick from a touchdown may touch or adjust the ball in the hands of the holder so long as the ball does not touch the ground.

Downing a runner: The runner is down when any part of his body except his foot or hand touches the ground while in the grasps of an opponent.

Personal fouls: These include, but are not limited to, striking with the fist or elbow, kneeing, kicking, meeting with the knee, and striking with locked hands by linemen breaking through. The runner may not be struck in the face with the heel of the hand by an opponent.

Penalty: Disqualification and fifteen yards.

Unnecessary roughness: Includes tripping, tackling out of bounds, piling up, hurdling, and other such acts.

Penalty: Fifteen yards.

Tripping is obstructing an opponent below the knee with the leg below the knee.

Hurdling in the open is jumping over or attempting to jump over an opponent who is still on his feet. Hurdling in the line is jumping over or attempting to jump over, a player on the line of scrimmage, with the feet or knees foremost, within the distance of five yards on either side of the point where the ball is put in play.

Tackling below knees: Prohibited but no penalty if the tackler makes contact above the knees and slides down.

Penalty: Five yards.

Unsportsmanlike conduct: Includes but is not limited to abusive and insulting language to opponents or officials.

Penalty: Disqualification

Neutral Zone and lines of scrimmage: Placed in rules.

The snapper is required to place the ball flat upon the ground with the long axis at right angles to the lines of scrimmage.

A player legally on the line of scrimmage must be within one foot of his line of scrimmage and may interlock legs only with the snapper.

The snapper may have a head, hand, or foot offside when snapping the ball and may not be interfered with.

At least six players are required on the offensive line: if there are more than six, the seventh must be outside the end player on the line.

No player of the middle five of the offensive line may drop back from the line unless he is five yards from the line of scrimmage and then only to kick the ball.

The term charging changed to "starting forward beyond the restraining line."

Holding:

The players of the side in possession may obstruct opponents with the body only, except the player running with the ball, who may ward off opponents with his hands and arms.

Holding is unlawful obstruction by the side in possession includes:

Grasping an opponent with the hands or arms.

Placing the hands upon an opponent to push him away from the play.
Circling in any degree any part of the opponent with the arms is prohibited.
Any use of the arms to lift an opponent in blocking.
Penalty: Fifteen yards
Note: The only allowable use of the arms in blocking or obstructing an opponent is with the arms close to the body.

Time Factors: Game shortened to sixty minutes from seventy, with two thirty-minute halves. Three time-outs per half, and a two-yard penalty for an extra timeout if the player does not leave the game.

Officials: Shall be a referee, two umpires, and a linesman, with the second umpire optional.

All officials are responsible for penalizing unnecessary roughness, unsportsmanlike conduct, and disqualification.

Penalties that carry the ball across the goal line are placed at the one-yard line instead of half the distance to the goal line.[109]

The rule changes did not eliminate football's dangers, but fatalities declined—to 11 per year in both 1906 and 1907—while injuries fell sharply. A spike in deaths in 1909 led to another round of reforms that further eased restrictions on the forward pass.[110]

The Forward Pass

Some claim that Yale used a forward pass in their game against Princeton in 1876.[111] Many John Heisman credit for the idea of the forward pass. There is evidence that he was intrigued with the idea when he saw an illegal forward pass thrown in the Georgia-North Caroline game in 1895.[112] The University of North Carolina used an illegal forward pass to defeat a University of Georgia team coached by "Pop Warner". John Heisman was a spectator at that game.[113]

However when it came to the change making the forward pass legal, the minutes of the Rules Committee indicate that four proposals for changing the forward passing rule were presented. Harry Williams, University of Minnesota; L.M. Dennis, Cornell; John Bell, Penn; and E.K. Hall of Dartmouth all made proposals regarding the forward pass. It indicates no proposal on the issue from Heisman.

In his history of the game, historian David Nelson deduced that the first forward passes were thrown on Christmas Day 1905. At that time, the forward pass rule had been passed but was not to take effect until the 1906 season. "Although Cochems was the premier passing coach during the first year of the rule, the first forward passes were thrown at the end of the 1905 season in a game between Fairmount and Washburn colleges in Kansas." According to Nelson, Washburn completed three passes, and Fairmount completed two.[114]

Most others also give St. Louis University, coached by Eddie Cochems, credit for throwing the first legal forward pass on September 5, 1906, in a game against Carroll College. Some credit Yale with the "first forward pass in a major game."

Others claim Paul Veeder threw a 40-yard completion in Yale's victory over Harvard in New Haven on November 24, 1906. However, that Yale/Harvard game was played three weeks after the St. Louis Carroll College game. [115]

In his book "*The Anatomy of a Game*", David Nelson wrote, "E. B. Cochems is to forward passing what the Wright brothers are to aviation and Thomas Edison is to the electric light."[116] Indeed, Cochems must be given credit as one of the first innovators in using the forward pass. Grantland Rice quotes "Pop" Warner as saying, "I don't think anyone knows who invented or first worked out the spiral pass. It was easy to see from the start that throwing a football end over end was not the best way. Many coaches and passers began experimenting with the spiral early in 1906." In 1952, Amos Alonzo Stagg thought that giving credit to any one particular coach with being the innovator of the forward pass would be difficult. "Stagg noted that he had Walter Eckersall working on pass plays and saw Pomeroy Sinnock of Illinois throw many passes in 1906. Stagg summed up his view as follows: "I have seen statements giving credit to certain people originating the forward pass. The fact is that all coaches were working on it. The first season, 1906, I personally had sixty-four different forward pass patterns." In 1954, Stagg disputed Cochems' claim to have invented the forward pass.[117] He claimed that in 1908 Hugo Bezdek, who would later gain fame as the Penn State coach, was the first to use the forward pass extensively while at Arkansas. However, there are numerous accounts of the use of the forward pass before 1908.

The Notre Dame-Army game of 1913 probably provided the greatest impetus for the growth of the forward pass. It was after that game that the use of the pass became widespread. In fact, for many, the Gus Dorais to Knute Rockne passing that led Notre Dame to their defeat of Army 35-13 was the start of the passing game.[118]

Unlike today, in 1906-09, a forward pass had to cross the line of scrimmage 5 yards out from the center. If a forward pass hit the ground untouched by any player, possession of the ball went to the team that had been playing defense. Also, remember that a forward pass thrown out of bounds gave possession to the opposing team. This encouraged many teams to throw deep out of bounds (coffin corner) on their final down. However, the elite Eastern teams did not embrace the new notion until late in the season when Yale beat Harvard with a forward pass that traveled 3 yards. It was caught on the 3-yard line and run in for a touchdown. Being used by one of the big four teams legitimized the pass in many eyes.

At the time, Glen "Pop" Warner put it this way, "It may be basketball but it's in the rules, so let's try it". [119] Warner agreed that the 1906 rule changes eliminated the old pushing and pulling of the ball carrier. The forward pass created what he called, "a way to scatter the defense" and force teams to defend the area well behind the line of scrimmage.[120]

Later in 1927, his opinion changed a bit. "The forward pass, a bastard offspring of real football, has come to be a very important and popular part of the game."[121]

Amos Alonzo Stagg claims to have had sixty-four different forward pass patterns in 1906. Writing about these passes he said, "The forward passes I originated in the first year the rule was in vogue practically cover in principle the whole field of forward passes allowable under the 1906 rules, as follows: (1) the quarterback running out from his position and making a running pass to the end or wingback. (2) The quarterback feinting to give the ball on a buck or split buck to one of the backs and then running back and throwing a forward pass to an end, (3) a running pass made to the end or wingback by the halfback. (4) A line shift in which everybody was over, excepting the guard and the pass was thrown to him. (5) a cross pass in which the ball is passed by the rear back to one of the halfbacks behind the end (wingback), who runs back and throws a forward pass. (96) Throwing a forward pass to a shoestring man (sleeper) far out near the sideline. (7) A forward pass to a single flanker. (8) A forward pass to a double flanker that is 20 or 25 yards out on either side. (9) A forward pass to one of two flankers several yards out on one side. The above forward pass evolutions combine every forward pass that I now think of, with the exception of: (1) a feint to forward pass followed by a run, which particular forward pass play originated for the Minnesota game in 1908, enabling Wally Steffen to run wild; and Chicago beat Minnesota, 29-0. (2) The criss-cross pass, which we sprang on Cornell in 1908. (3) The fake split buck pass, which I devised in 1910."[122]

The Button Hook Pass

By the luck of an accident in running for a pass, Knute Rockne made a genuine advancement in the passing game by running the first "button hook" pass route. He had fallen down while running out for a pass and quickly got to his feet and turned to face the quarterback. The defender, who had not fallen, kept running and was in no position to defend the pass. According to Gus Dorais, Rockne quickly came to realize that by making various "cuts" or quick changes in direction, as he ran he could create "pass Lanes." Previously receivers had generally just tried to outrun defenders. By taking advantage of the pass lanes receivers now ran routes that brought them open for a reception between defenders and not just beyond defenders.[123]

Screen Pass

It was in 1908 or 1909 that Bob Zuppke invented the screen pass at Muskegon HS. He would later develop it further while at the University Illinois. However, there are those who credit Bob Folwell at Washington and Jefferson College with perfecting the screen. In fact, many called it the Washington and Jefferson Screen.

Unintended Consequences of Forward Pass

Unfortunately, as is often the case, some unintended consequences of the new rule were neither anticipated nor beneficial to the purpose of the new game. In the early 1900s, the defenses crowded the line of scrimmage with linebackers and halfbacks aligned tight to stop the run. With the coming of the forward pass, halfbacks, and to a lesser extent the linebackers, were compelled to spread out and play deeper to protect against the possibility of a pass. It was not so much that teams were using the pass to a considerable degree; the principle value of the pass seemed to be in the fear of its use by the defensive team. The defensive tackle area, previously supported by the constricted play of the halfbacks, was weakened by their absence. Offensive teams began to return to a variety of adaptations of the mass plays that the legalization of the forward pass intended to avoid. Continuous massed attacks focused on the tackle area with impressive success.

Idaho Spread Formation

Idaho used a basic spread formation in 1907 from which they launched many and long passes. *Figure 60*

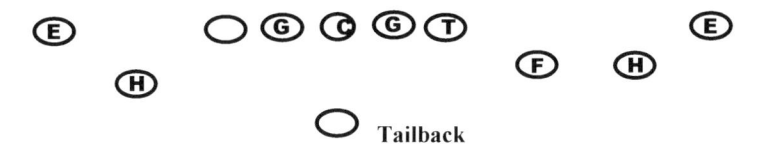

Figure 60 The Idaho Spread Formation

Percy Haughton

Although he began his coaching career at Cornell in 1899, Percy Haughton left coaching from 1900 until 1908 when he returned to coaching at Harvard, his alma mater. He contributed to several advances in the game around this time. Haughton created the modern coaching staff. At a time when most teams had just one coach, or at the most one assistant, Haughton had a backfield coach, a line coach, and an end coach, as well as coaches who worked with passers and kickers. The size of this staff allowed him to institute an extremely organized system of scouting his opponents. Using his large staff, he was able to schedule his practices to the minute, making the most efficient use of his practice time.

While most teams of the era emphasized power on offense, Haughton emphasized deception. He developed plays similar to those employed in the modern T-formation, with the quarterback often taking a direct snap from center, spinning, and faking or making handoffs to another back. The next four illustrations are from Haughton's book, "*Football and How To Watch It*", published in 1922. [124] See Figures 61-65

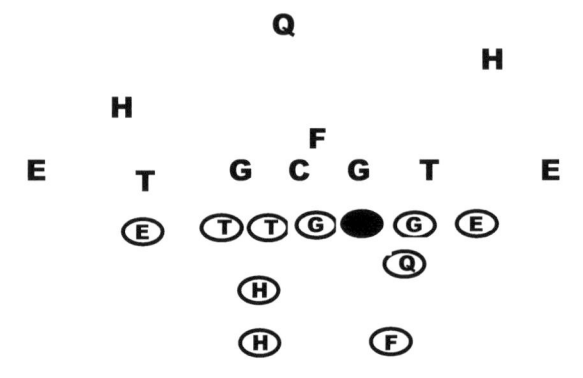

Figure 61 Haughton's "Close" Formation (shown as a left formation)

Above is Haughton's "Close" formation.[125] *Figures 61, Above*   His intention, were to attack all the primary points on the defensive line. The defense usually placed seven men on the line of scrimmage anticipating the power attack. The fullback (F) or linebacker over-shifted slightly to the strength of the formation to combat a run to the long side of the line.

Notice that the right defensive halfback, usually called a wingback back then, is positioned much closer to the line of scrimmage than the left halfback. That is because a massive running attack is more likely to come his way than the other.   This alignment is significant because it is the forerunner of the "rotated" or "tilted" defensive scheme that we will see later in the century to combat the T-formation.

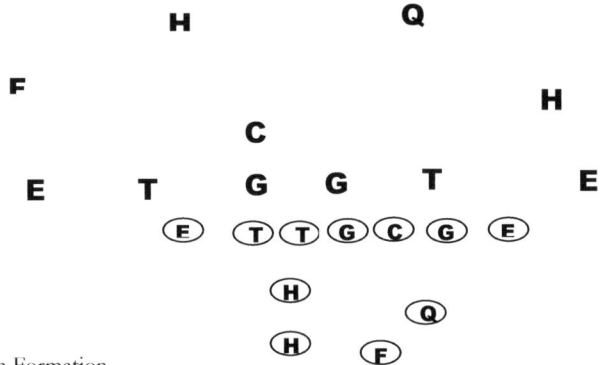

Figure 62 The Open Formation

The "Open" formation was often used for kicking (the way the diagram is drawn it appears he had a left-footed kicker). *Figure 62 Above* The defense, preparing for a possible kick, stretched itself vertically. From this formation, he also ran plunges, off-tackle slants, and sweeps. The sweep to both the long side and short side of the formation were both intimidating which is why you see the defense stretched horizontally putting them in a very vulnerable position. A defense can cope with being stretched one way or the other, but they have a problem when forced to stretch both ways. Most coaches tried to anticipate the play and align accordingly.

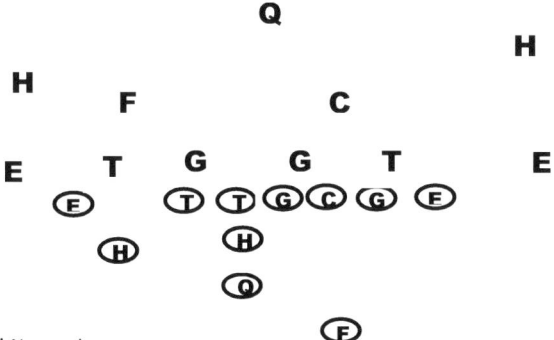

Figure 63 The "Loose" Formation

The primary objective in the "Loose" formation is to attempt to out-flank the defensive right tackle so that a long side sweep will be successful. Alternatively, to force him to widen with the halfback and end to the extent that it was possible to run a plunge or off-tackle slant can be run between him and the right defensive guard. An added threat to the defense is the alignment of the backs so that they can quickly get into pass patterns. This forced the defense to play with six linemen and withdraw the center to a linebacker position so that he can better support the weakened side of his defense. Notice also, the "tilted" defensive wingback. *Figure 63, Above*

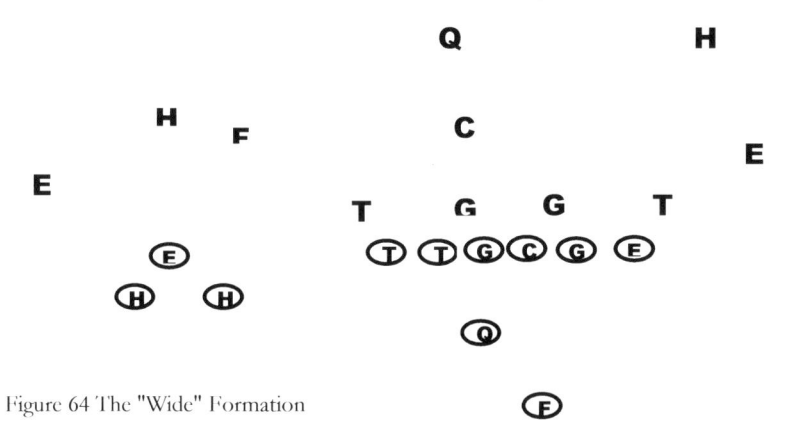

Figure 64 The "Wide" Formation

In the "Wide" formation, Haughton now has his offense aligned in a manner that allows little rushing strength of a plunging nature. The defense has dispersed in such a way that they have only left the two guards and two tackles to protect against the interior plunge. The remaining seven players are in a position to defend the pass. Both defensive ends have been placed in such a way that they will attempt to protect the flank against the run and be in a position to aid in the pass defense. The vulnerability of having an outside defender protecting against both the run and pass is something that offenses will exploit for the next fifty years. *Figure 64, Above*

Haughton demonstrated an unusual use of specialist players. In Harvard's 4-0 victory over Yale in 1908, Vic Kennard, who was put into the game for that one play, kicked the winning field goal. (A field goal was worth 4 points at that time.) Later he brought a player named Sprague into the game who sent a punt 60 yards from behind the Harvard goal line, keeping Yale out of scoring range.

Haughton often is given credit for inventing the mousetrap play, in which the offense allows a defensive player to cross the line of scrimmage only to be blocked from the side. *Figure 65* From the early 1880s, coaches taught their defenses to rush hard and low across the line of scrimmage. Against the mousetrap, this became a most significant drawback. When sportswriter Grantland Rice remarked to Haughton that Yale had massive, fast linemen, Houghton responded, "I only wish they were twice as fast. We'll let 'em through and then cut 'em down." Paul Brown further developed this concept and the "trap" became an integral part of the modern game.

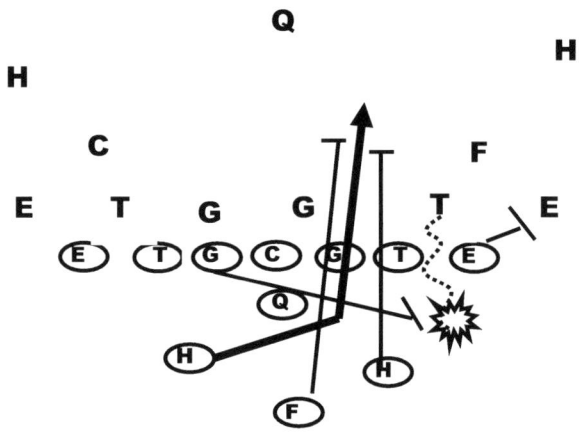

Figure 65 Haughton's "Mousetrap" Play

Double Pass

Amos Alonzo Stagg invented the double pass with the forward pass. This was the first double pass between a halfback and an end, followed by a forward pass by the end.

Glen "Pop" Warner's Swing Formations

We will discuss the many permutations of "Pop" Warner's wing formations as one element so that it is easier to follow the changes. One must remember that these adjustments took place over a number of years and with Warner coaching at several different colleges.

Although "Pop's" "Regular Formation" did not make use of flankers or men in motion as one might see in the modern "T" formation, a quick look at some of the plays he utilized will show both power and deception. He made ample use of criss-cross plays and pulling linemen leading the ball carrier. *See Figure 66*

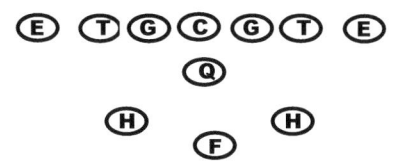

```
      E  T G C G T  E
            Q
         H     H
            F
```
Figure 66 Warner's "T" or Regular Formation

The Warner system includes many fakes and spins. Many of the plays include some passing of the ball or delays behind the line of scrimmage, with the intention of fooling the opposition into committing a charge in the wrong direction. This deception raises havoc with a line that tries to slice or follow the ball. However, it never deceives a line that charges straight across the line of scrimmage, regardless of where the ball is or what the players are doing.

Warner's wingback formations may have been the result of examining some previous offenses. In 1890 Stagg used an Ends Back-formation and 1893 Phil King used the Ends Back, positioning the ends two and a half yards behind the line of scrimmage. He stationed them outside the tackles and it looked much like the "Double Wing" formation that Warner would later use. The use of the unbalanced line by Percy Haughton at Harvard was probably the second influence. While playing at Cornell under Coach Marshall Newell in 1894, Warner likely experienced both the ends back formation and the unbalanced line.

The Z Formation or "Single Wing"

Many say that Warner's first use of the Single Wing was in 1906 at Carlisle. However, we must note that Warner was coaching at Cornell in 1906. He returned to Carlisle in 1907. Some say he did not employ the "single wing" until 1912. Warner's book "*A Course in Football for Players and Coaches*", published in 1908, mentions the Single Wing as well as the Regular Formation (or T-formation) in his discussions of offense. There is also an inconsistency regarding its first use because his explanation for why he made use of the formation, the abolishment of the mass formations. Changes in the rules abolishing the use of mass formations and guard/tackle back formations, especially those prohibiting aiding a runner by pushing and pulling, did not take effect until 1910. Up to the time of Warner's momentous advance, the fundamental design of offensive systems was to concentrate power in the backfield. Some mass plays had blockers ahead of or in tandem with the ball carrier. Other plays were from the wedge formations with blockers pushing the ball carrier from behind or pulling when in advance of him. Defensive tackles were difficult to keep out of the offensive backfield because they aligned outside the offensive end. It was difficult to block them effectively on wide plays. We have previously seen the precursor to Stagg's wing system in the "Ends Back" formation used by Stagg in the early 1900s as well as the unbalanced line implemented by Stagg.

There is no question that Carlisle defeated Army using the Single Wing in 1912. The Z formation referred to by Andy Kerr, a disciple of Warner's and coach at Washington and Jefferson and Colgate, was probably a precursor to Single Wing.

What everyone calls the "Single Wing" was, at first, called the "Z Formation" by "Pop" Warner himself. Because he used it early on with the Carlisle Indians and Jim Thorpe, this formation has also been referred to as the "Carlisle Formation". In a further conflict of terms, Warner refers to this formation as the A-Formation in his 1927 text *"Football For Coaches and Players"*. [126] *Figure 67*

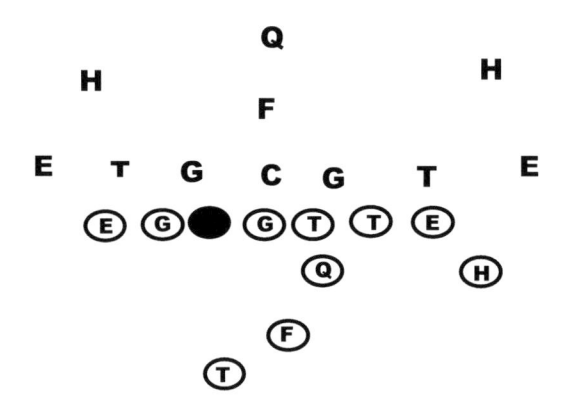

Figure 67 The "Z" Formation or "Single Wing"

Note in the above diagram the defensive alignment. It depicts a standard "Seven Diamond" defense with no adjustment to the unbalanced line or the fact that the backfield is aligning completely on the "long-side" of the formation. Although this was a typical defense versus the new formation, it allowed the Single Wing to apply an immense amount of power at the formation's strength, the long side of the unbalanced line. The formation was designed to double-team block at the point of attack. There were several ways they accomplished gaining the extra blockers. By alignment, the unbalanced line put extra linemen on one side of the center. The tight arrangement allowed guards, and sometimes tackles, to pull and lead the ball carrier. Also, with a "wingback" aligned outside the defensive tackle "Pop" could now double-team the tackle with his end and wingback and use lead blocks by his quarterback and fullback to overcome the defensive end.

Said the New York Herald Tribune of this new formation, "Pop Warner's principles of offensive line formation have been: (1) you must use an unbalanced line to cross-check effectively when running linemen pull out. (2) You must use a tight line from end to end, for you cannot safely pull interferers out of a line if spaces are left between men". [127]

Single Wing Plays

Below are some of Warner's basic plays from the "Single Wing". *Figures 68-70* The alignment of the tailback in the diagrams below differs slightly from what is shown above. He has moved the tailback slightly into a position behind the short side guard. Previously he aligned in a position between the guard and the center. By making this small adjustment, Warner was now able to pull the short side guard and get him in front of the ball carrier on plays to the long side of the formation.

Figure 68 The Fullback Buck

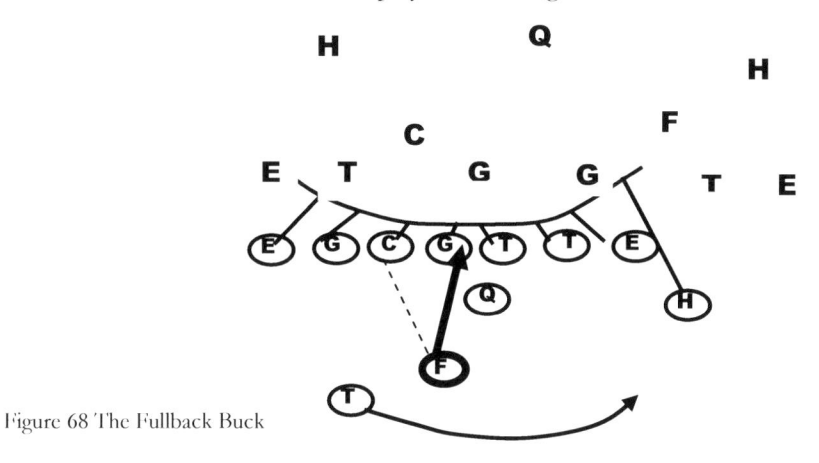

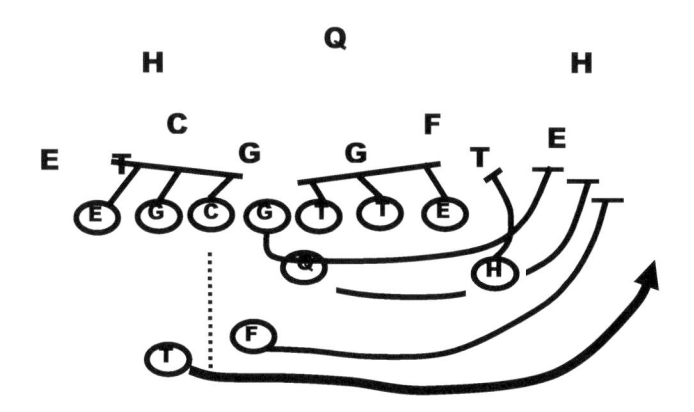

Figure 69 The Tailback Sweep

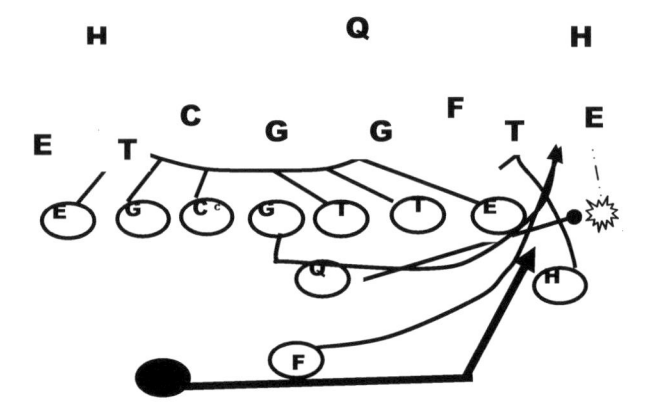

Figure 70 The Tailback Power Off-Tackle

Over-shifted Defense

At first, coaches began adjusting the defense by just widening the defenders on the long side of the formation. They reasoned that by expanding the end and fullback (linebacker to that side) they could keep the core defense intact to stop the fullback buck. The widened end would prevent the sweep, and the adjusted fullback (linebacker) would confound the off-tackle blocking. In general, it reduced the effect of running to the long side. *Figure 71*

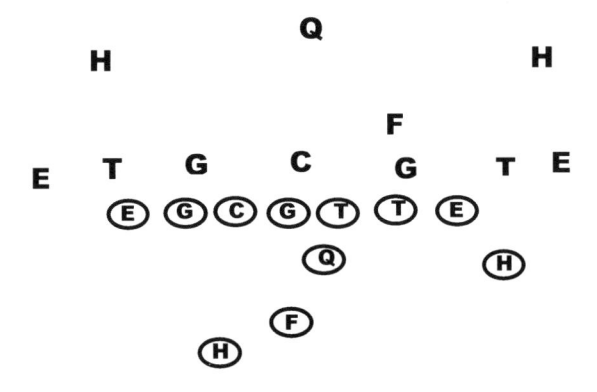

Figure 71 Over-Shifted 7-1-2-1 Defense: Bringing more defenders to the "Long Side."

The Single Wing's response to this adjustment was to run a crossbreed play the looked much like the sweep and off-tackle. They called it the "cut-back" play. If the defensive end and fullback (linebacker) widened to stop the apparent sweep, the tailback would cut back to the off-tackle area. If the defenders held their ground to stop what they thought might be an off-tackle run, the tailback would continue outside and run the sweep. *Figures 72, 73* The underlying concept of this attack is, in some ways, similar to today's "Zone" attack.

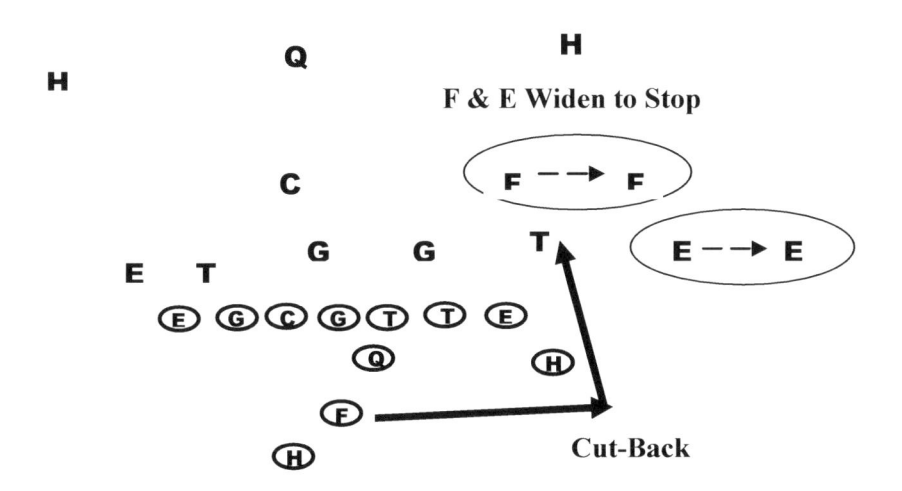

Figure 72 The Single Wing Cut-Back

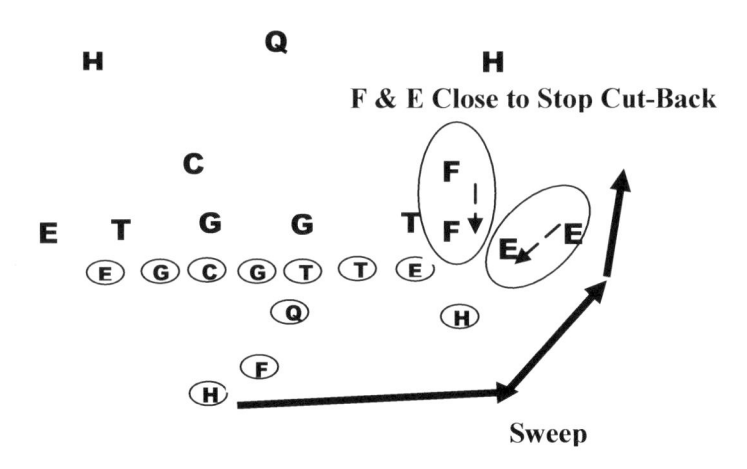

Figure 73 The Cut-Back Sweep

Another response to the over shifting defense, the single wing coaches developed many reverses to the short side. However, even the reverse plays had difficulty because the defensive tackle to the short side was difficult to block on any outside reverse. *See Figure 74*

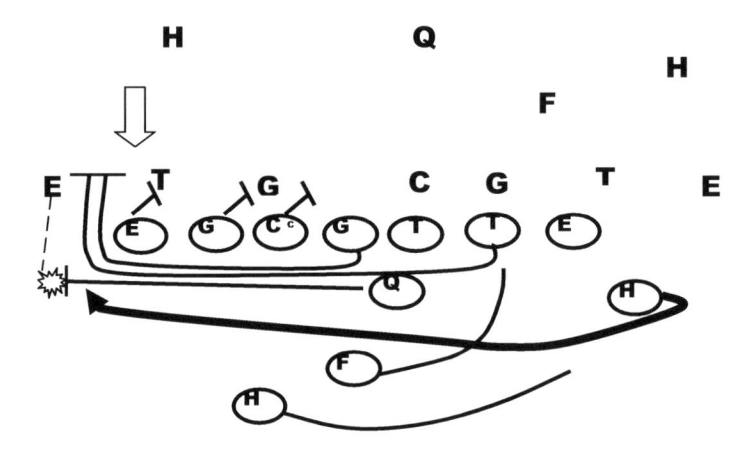

Figure 74 Wingback Inside Reverse

The A-Formation or "Double Wing"

The ultimate answer that Warner devised for the problematic over-shifted defensive adjustments to his new formation was to make a change that would reduce the value of the over-shifted defense and it would place a wingback in a position to block the defensive tackle to the short side. He could now run the reverses to the outside.

Many refer to the new formation he created in 1911, as the "A Formation" or "Double Wing". However, in his 1927 text, he referred to this as the "B Formation". *See Figure 75*

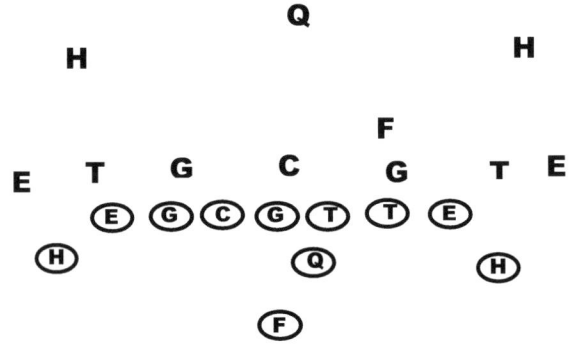

Figure 75 The Double Wing Formation

A separated unbalanced line characterized the "A" System. The objective of the offense was to provide power plays, speed, deception, and outstanding passing. The formation provided for good pass protection with four "quick" receivers. Because of the two wingbacks, there was a reasonable strength to both the short and long sides of the formation. It was strong off-tackle with good deception and the endless opportunity for laterals, reverses, and fakes. It was also a good formation to execute the quick kick that was widely used at that time. However when defensive coaches aligned their ends outside the wingbacks and crashed them hard, it made it difficult to run outside plays. Below are several examples of plays from the Double Wing Formation *Figures 76-81* [128.] Although it is not diagramed, it should be noted that the "spinner" series that was so popular with the Single Wing was also a popular series in the Double Wing. It is believed that the "Buck Lateral "series, shown in *Figure 9* above, very likely originated with the Double Wing. Andy Kerr, in a letter to Allison Danzig, said; "One of the advantages of the buck lateral series from the Double Wing is that the play may develop either to the right or to the left with equal effectiveness. In the buck lateral plays (plays mentioned above), the ball was not handled by the quarterback. The fullback passed the ball to a lineman, who in turn lateralled to one of the halfbacks. This provided our quarterback as an additional blocker. I have been informed by Tuss McLaughry, who was coaching Brown in 1931, that in the following year he used the buck lateral play to defeat Yale, 7-2." [129]

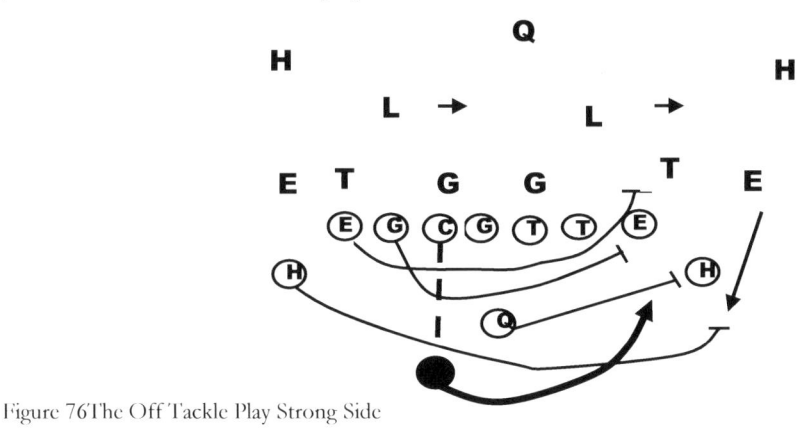

Figure 76 The Off Tackle Play Strong Side

Figure 77 Off-Tackle Play Short Side

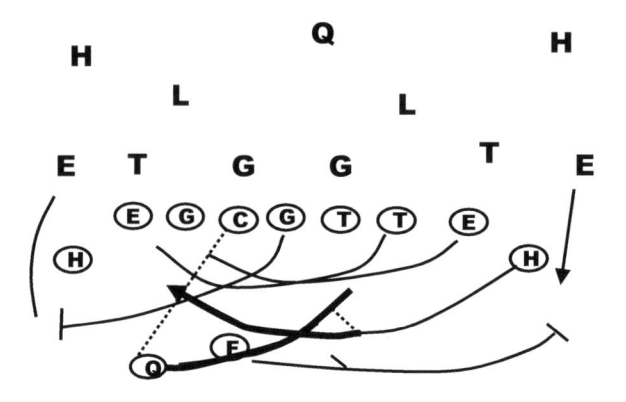

Figure 78 The Reverse Play

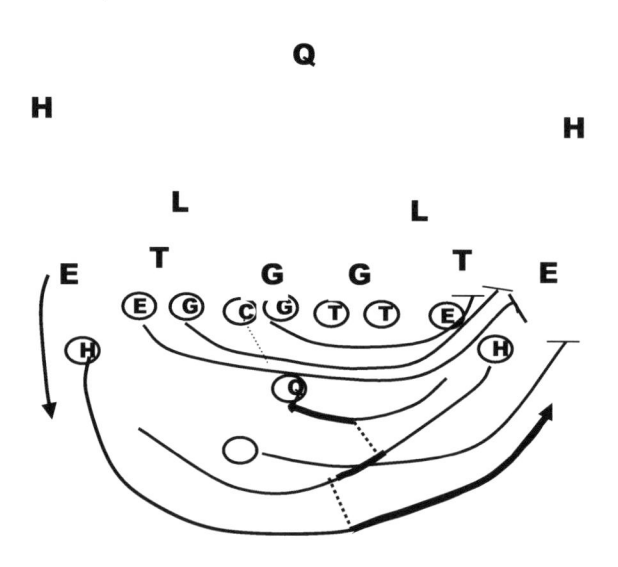

Figure 79 The Triple Pass Around End or "Double Reverse"

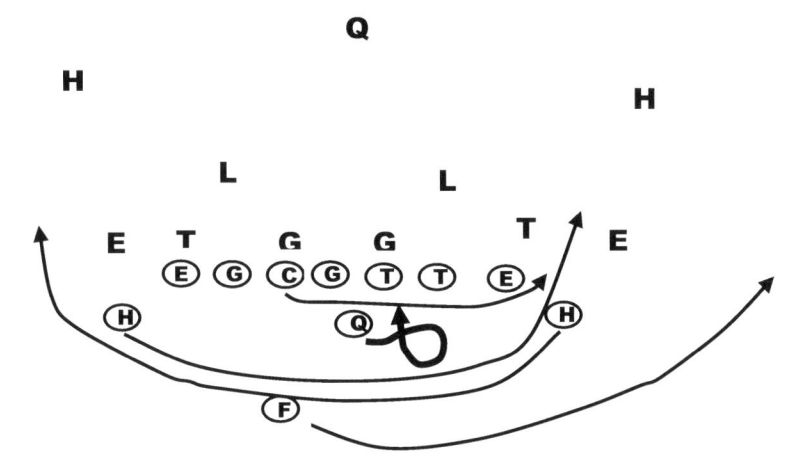

Figure 80 The Spin Play Straight Ahead with a fake Double Reverse

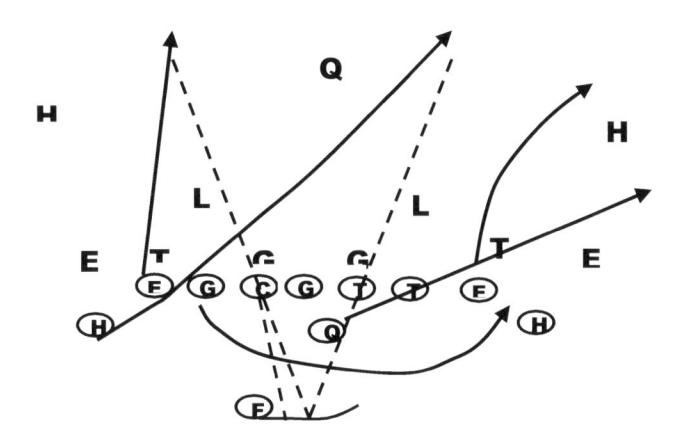

Figure 81 Long Pass Note: Ball snapped directly to the deep back. He then throws the long pass to either the end or the wingback. If "Q" plays the end, the ball is passed to the wing. If "Q" plays the wingback, the ball is thrown to the end.

Warner would often shift to the Double Wing from the Single Wing after the defense had completed their over shift. He shifted the Tailback to a position outside the end in a wingback position. This gave the formation as much strength to the short side as to the long side. Defenses could no longer over-shift. He also placed the quarterback between the two tackles; the wings are 1 X 1yard. The fullback aligned 3 ½-4 yards deep. Of course, to maximize the use of the formation one had to have a good fullback, as he was central to every play. Some people shifted the QB into a position closer to the center where he could receive the snap. At times "Pop" himself shifted the quarterback to a position behind the guard about 2 1/2 yards deep. Warner ran two basic series from the Double Wing. In the first series, the fullback either gives to a wing on a reverse or fakes to him and keeps the ball on a buck. *Figure 82* He may also fake to one wing and hands off to the other.

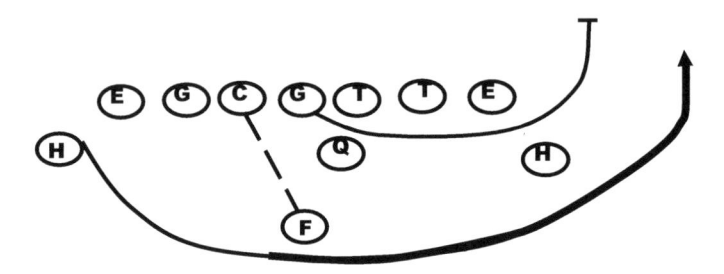

Figure 82 The Fullback can give the ball to the Halfback (H), as he does in this illustration or keep it himself on a line buck

A second key play in this series is the fullback making a full spin when faking to the wing and then keeping it. *Figure 83* When the defensive end is wide, he will run off-tackle, when the end crashes he will run wide. The fullback may also give the ball to either wing or fake a buck into the line between the tackles. The spin plays used not only straight blocking but also double-team blocking, and in 1918, Stagg would introduce cross-blocking (two offensive linemen crossing to block respective defensive linemen) into the blocking schemes. . The series has excellent deception.

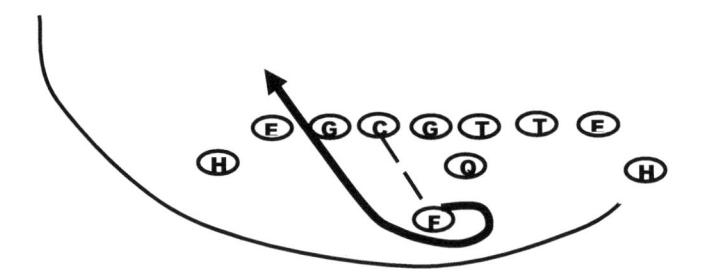

Figure 83 Fullback Buck after a full spin

Later the spinner series became part of the Single Wing using the tailback in place of one of the wingbacks. The series was highly developed by Bob Higgins at Penn State and Carl Snavely at Cornell and later at North Carolina.

The second series was sheer power with bucks by the fullback. *Figure 84* Also in this series, the fullback may give the ball to the quarterback, who may then give it to either wingback, keep the ball himself and run off tackle to the long side, or give the ball to the end for a short side end-around play. Snavely developed this deceptive concept. *Figure 85* This series also used trap blocking with the fullback bucks. Each of the series had some pass possibilities including the jump pass.

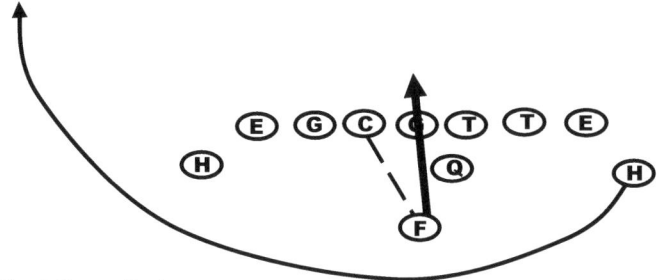

Figure 84 Fullback Power Buck

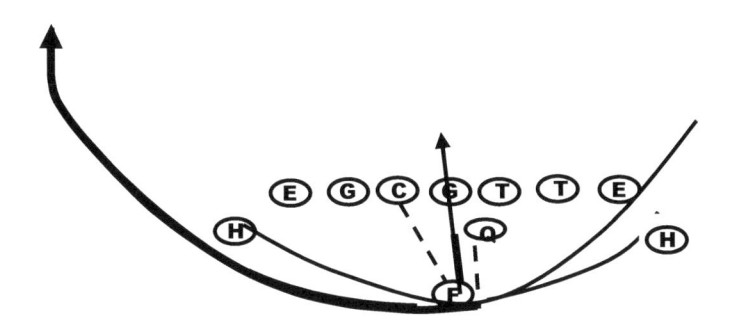

Figure 85 Fake fullback Power Buck and give to the Quarterback with a pitch to the Right Wing

The "B" Formation Double Wing:

The next generation of the Warner formations was what many have referred to as the "B Formation Double Wing". There is much confusion in how the "lettered" offensive formations were named. The only difference between the original Double wing formation and this new modification is the position of the fullback (F) and short-side end. The fullback became the "Triple Threat" back. The fullback is in a position 5 yards behind the line of scrimmage (LOS) where he was in a good position to run, pass or quick kick. The split of the short-side end placed him a better position as a pass receiver. *Figure 86*

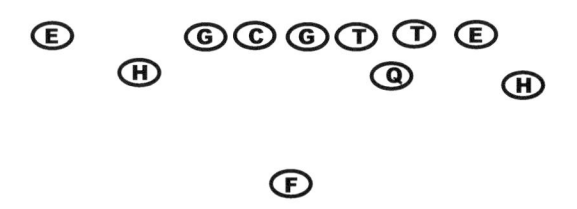

Figure 86 Double Wing with the Short-End split and the Fullback (today called a triple threat back or "tailback") aligned deeper

"C" Formation

The final transformation of the Warner formations is what has been commonly known as the" C Formation." *Figure 87* This formation may look surprisingly similar to today's spread formations. He split both ends. The quarterback was now placed in a position about 4 ½ yards from the line of scrimmage. Let us note however that, unlike today's spread formations, the quarterback was not the dominant passer and the position held by the fullback was where we often find today's quarterback. There was an interesting quote attributed to Andy Kerr speaking to the American Football Coaches Association in 1949 that has proven to be insightful.

> "In my opinion, the C is the best passing formation in football. It enables four men to go downfield quickly on all passes. For the defense, it presents the problem of covering passes against a single wing right and left at the same time. In my own experience, I have spent many hours trying to work out satisfactory defenses for passes from the double wing (C Formation). We believe this C Formation has great possibilities that as yet have not been fully explored, especially as regards to forward passing." Wow!

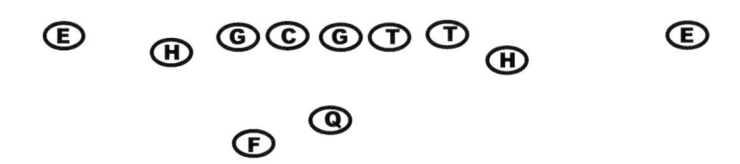

Figure 87 Warner's "C" Formation

Yost Six Man Line Defense

It was in 1908 that "Hurry Up' Yost made extensive use of the six-man line successfully. Later in the century, some coaches expressed the opinion that it was not because of any uniqueness that this defense had its success but rather because he was the only one using it as his primary defense at that time. *See Figure 88*

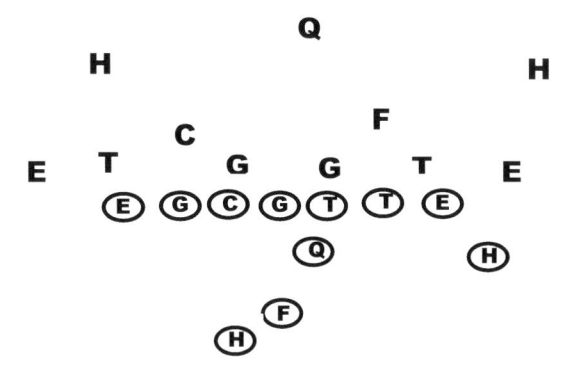

Figure 88 Yost's Six Man Line Defense

Violence Returns

In the season of 1909, the trend in the direction of a safer game was sharply changed. In a contest between Harvard and West Point, the Army captain, Eugene Byrne, who was fatigued by recurrent plays to his side of the line, died. In that same year, Earl Wilson of the Naval Academy, while attempting a flying tackle, was paralyzed and later died. At the University of Virginia, a halfback, Archer Christian, died after a game against Georgetown. "Does the public need any more proof," wrote the Washington Post, "that football is a brutal, savage, murderous sport?   Is it necessary to kill many more promising young men before the game is revised or stopped altogether?" [130]   Both Georgetown and Virginia suspended football for the remainder of the season.

Staggered by the death of one of his students, the University of Virginia's president, Eugene Alderman, who a decade earlier had declared, "I should rather see a boy of mine on the rush line fighting for his team than on the sideline smoking a cigarette," warned that the outcry was more than hysteria on the part of the press. Stanford's president referred to football as "Rugby's American pervert" and said that the "farce of football reform" that was slipped by the public in 1905 and 1906 was no longer acceptable.

---

[106] http://www.history.com/news/how-teddy-roosevelt-saved-football, September 6, 2012, *How Teddy Roosevelt Saved Football*. retrived Oct. 14, 2013.

[107] Danzig, *The History of American Football*, p.29

[108] Smith, Rodney, *A Brief History of the National Collegiate Athletic Association's Role in Regulating Intercollegiate Athletics*, 11 Marq.Sports L. Rev. 9 (2000) Available at: http://scholarship.law.marquette.edu/sportslaw/vol11/iss1/5

[109] Nelson, *Anatomy of a Game; Football, the rules, and the Men Who Made the Game*, p.123-125

[110] http://www.history.com/news/how-teddy-roosevelt-saved-football, September 6, 2012, *How Teddy Roosevelt Saved Football*. retrived Oct. 14, 2013.

[111] Wikipedia encyclopedia, *The Forward Pass*, http://en.wikipedia.org/wiki/Forward_pass

[112] Nelson, *Anatomy of a Game; Football, the rules, and the Men Who Made the Game*, p. 105

[113] *How-one-tar-heel-punter-killed-rugby-in-america* /http://www.davesfootballblog.com/post/2007/09/06/ accessed 03/17/09

[114] Nelson, *The Anatomy of a Game: Football, the Rules, and the Men Who Made the Game* p. 128.

[115] Nelson, *The Anatomy of a Game: Football, the Rules, and the Men Who Made the Game* p. 129

[116] Nelson, *The Anatomy of a Game: Football, the Rules, and the Men Who Made the Game* p. 128

[117] *The Forward Pass*, http://en.wikipedia.org/wiki/Forward_pas, 10/13/2013

[118] Danzig, *The History of American Football*, p.41

[119] Danzig, *The History of American Football*, p. 38

[120] Nelson, *The Anatomy of a Game: Football, the Rules, and the Men Who Made the Game*, p. 127

[121] Nelson, *The Anatomy of a Game: Football, the Rules, and the Men Who Made the Game*, p. 127

[122] Danzig, *The History of the Game*, p. 37

[123] Danzig, *The History of American Football*, p. 41

[124] Houghton, Percy, *Football and How to Watch It*, (Boston, Marshall Jones Co, 1922), p.46-52

[125] Haughton, *Football and How to Watch It*, (Boston, Marshall Jones Co, 1922), p.46-52

[126] Warner, Glen Scobey, *Football for Coaches and Players*, (Stanford University Press, 1927) p. 136

[127] Woodward, Stanley, New York Herald Tribune article, September 1939

[128] Warner, Glenn Scobey "Pop", *Football for Coaches and Players,* (Stanford CA, Stanford University Press, 1927), p 157-172

[129] Danzig, Allison, *History of American Football*, p. 108.

[130] *How brutal injuries plagued college football long before the ..*, http://www.nj.com/news/index.ssf/2013/12/how_brutal_injuries_plagued_college_foo (accessed September 22, 2015).

CHAPTER SIX

Public Outcry Brings More Changes

(1910 –1919)

1910 Rules Changes

When the committee convened to discuss revised rules, they voted on numerous sets of rules. It was apparent that the forward pass was the chief barrier to resolving the crisis. There was much haggling. Finally, the proceedings reached a pivotal moment. The opponents of the pass had accumulated enough votes to support a motion to limit its use to the area behind the line of scrimmage. While a three-man subcommittee put together a report, the two sides of the pass issue dug in. On the one hand were those who felt that the forward pass was ruining the game of football. Others subscribed to the theory that the forward pass was what the game needed to open play up and reduce the viciousness that closed and mass formations brought.

On May 13, 1910, the committee adopted the new rules; (1) seven men on the line of scrimmage, (2) no pushing or pulling, no interlocking interference (arms linked or hands on belts and uniforms), (3) crawling became a penalty, (4) an imaginary neutral zone of 12" was established between the two forward lines prior to the snap of the ball,(Note: this is a clarification of a previous rule) (5) four fifteen-minute quarters, (6) the first player to touch the ball could now cross the line of scrimmage at any point (previously they had to move horizontally for five yards before crossing the line of scrimmage. (7) The forward pass was narrowly saved, but with restrictions; a. the passer could throw the ball without moving 5 yards to the left or right of the center, b. Only players eligible to receive passes were the two players aligned on the end of the line of scrimmage and any back that aligned, at least, one yards behind the line of scrimmage, c. The passer must be 5 yards behind the line of scrimmage when the ball was thrown, d. No forward pass could be thrown beyond twenty yards behind the defensive line of scrimmage (the ball would be declared "dead" as soon as it passed twenty yards), e. within the legal pass zone no player on either side, while in the act of catching a forward pass, could not be tackled, thrown, pushed, pulled, shouldered, or straight-armed until they caught the ball and took more than one step in any direction. The final change required a player to tackle an opponent with at least one foot on the ground. The tackling requirement was a direct conflict with the wishes of Walter Camp, who was a very staunch supporter of the flying tackle. He had argued vociferously against the new rule. The rules eliminating the five-yard horizontal movement of a runner or passer marked the end of the checkerboard markings on the field. [131]

There was hope that the implementation of these rules would curtail the "Neanderthal football" of the past. It was to establish the groundwork for a sleeker, faster, wide-open game.

Even with the new pass rules, it would take a while before the actual benefits of the passing game were recognized. It would be in the South and Southwest, where schools were not as ingrained with the old power game as the tradition loaded Eastern schools, that the pass would be first used as a dominant weapon. Arkansas, under the leadership of Hugo Bezdek, who would later gain fame at Penn State, used a spread formation that put emphasis on the pass with much success.

Robert Zuppke: Pass Protection

Robert Zuppke at Illinois experimented with the new passing game. He discovered that he needed time and additional blocking protection to throw the ball vertically down the field. He introduced the concept of pass protection by dropping his guards back and running them in front of the quarterback to provide security for his passer. *Figure 89* He considered the line to be the essential element in winning football games. He stated; "The team that controls the first yard beyond the line of scrimmage, all other things being equal, should win." [132]

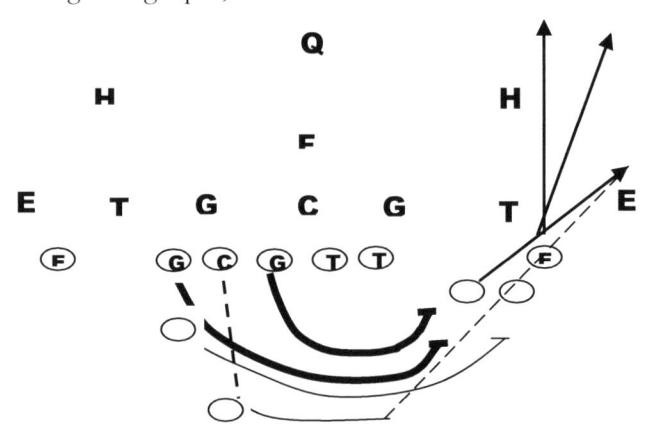

Figure 89 The Guards pulling to protect the passer

Zuppke is credited with many other football inventions and traditions, including his flea flicker.

The Shift

As was mentioned earlier, the design of shift plays was used to circumvent the mass momentum rule. John Heisman, who coached at Auburn, Clemson, Georgia Tech, and Penn, Washington & Jefferson, and Rice, began to utilize the shift. He lined up the whole line, except the center, behind the line of scrimmage with the backs lined in tandem at a right angle to the line of scrimmage then shifted.

Amos Alonzo Stagg, who most say was the first to introduce shifting around 1904, ran a backfield shift in 1910 snapping the ball "instantly without delay" to better exploit the momentum of their movement. Rockne credits this shift as the predecessor of the Notre Dame shift. Later Stagg would introduce several new shifts; "U Formation shift", "Shimmy Shift", "Whirlwind Shift" The extensive use of the shift will be discussed later in this chapter.

Defending the Passing Game

Also, in 1910 Zuppke introduced the first defensive adjustment to the passing game. When a pass was detected, his guards would drop back to help in the pass defense. *Figure 90*

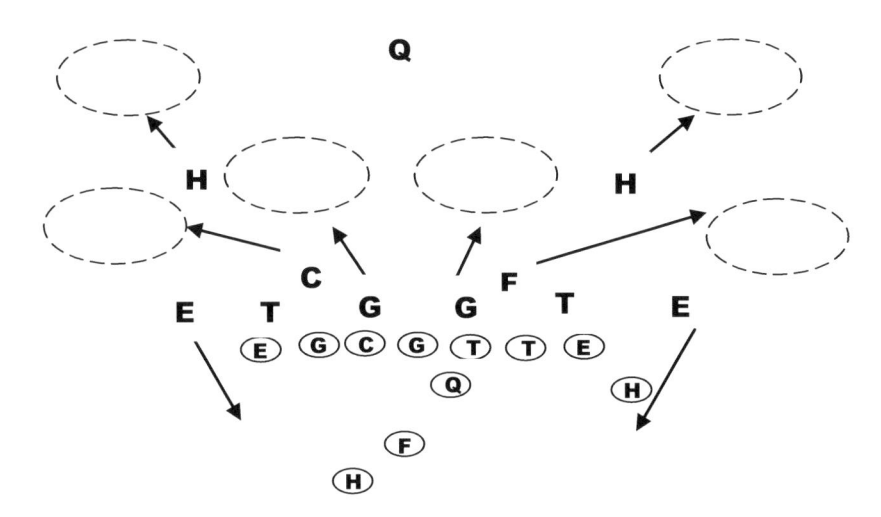

Figure 90 Zuppke's "Dropping Guards" into Pass Defense

Very cognizant of the passing game, Zuppke also had a rather unique defense vs. the spread formation. *See Figure 91* [133]

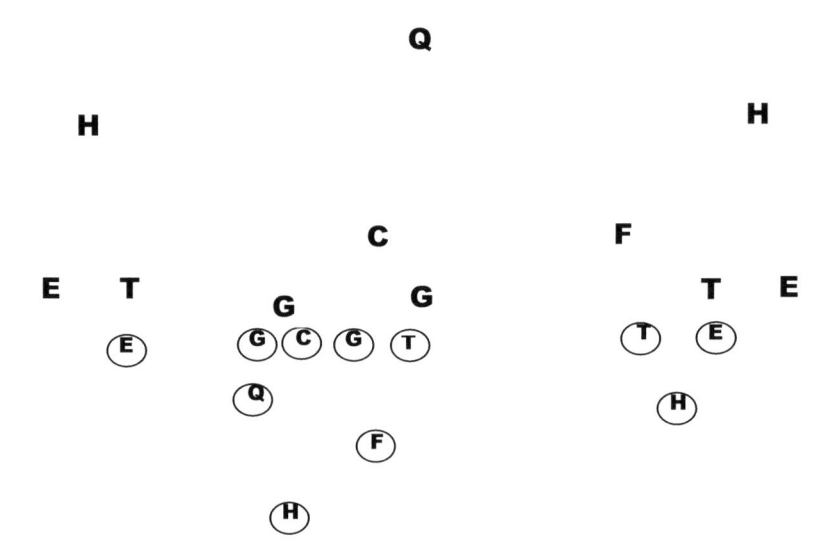

Figure 91 Zuppke's Defense versus the Spread Formation

Circumventing New Pass Rules

It was only a matter of time before someone would learn to evade some of the forward passing rules. It was in 1911 that the Wabash quarterback, "Skeets" Lambert, gave us the first instance of intentional grounding the ball to avoid a big loss. The trick was soon part of the Notre Dame offense also, but it was not until Army used it that it became a favorite tactic. The rules outlawed intentional grounding in 1914.

1911 was also the year that the rules committee added a fourth down to make ten yards, raised the value of the touchdown to six points, and reduced the field goal to three points. Although the pass still had to be thrown from five yards behind the line of scrimmage, the twenty-yard restriction on forward passes was eliminated. The field became 100 yards in length with two 10-yard end zones. Any pass caught in an end zone by an offensive player now resulted in a touchdown. With the lifting of the most restrictive rules, the forward pass quickly became a potent offensive weapon. It was fittingly illustrated by the brilliant performance of Knute Rockne and Gus Dorais in Notre Dame's 35-13 airborne upset of Army in 1913. The events of that game were probably the single factor that most influenced the expanded use of the forward pass.

"Cup" Defense

The "cup" defense came into being about this time. It was assignment football. As John DaGrosa describes it in his text *Functional Football*,

> "Individual line play without assigned territory as a responsibility is very poor line play because the players will follow the ball all the time, all being subject to deception by double-spinners, fake bucks, reverses,

etc., causing more than one defensive man to follow one man who may or may not have the ball. When a player is not responsible for any assigned territory, he will invariably take too many chances and will always have an "alibi" for those that failed. Individual play will also put a burden on the secondary.

"Each player on the defensive line is assigned a certain territory and told his responsibility in guarding it in relation to the strength of the offensive formation." [134]

Some consider this defense as being the forerunner of the "gap control" and slant and angle defenses that will be used later in the second half of the century They will severely slow offensive production. *Figures 92-94*

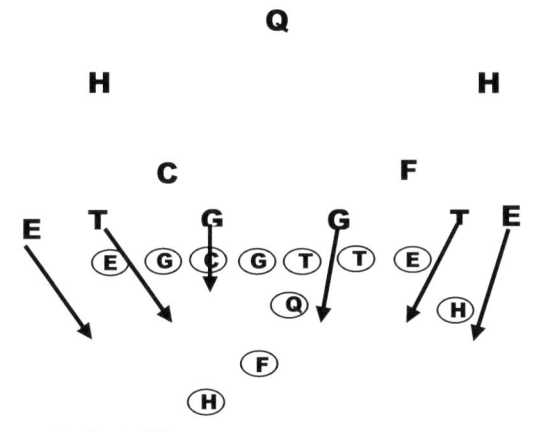

Figure 92 Cup Defense versus the Single Wing

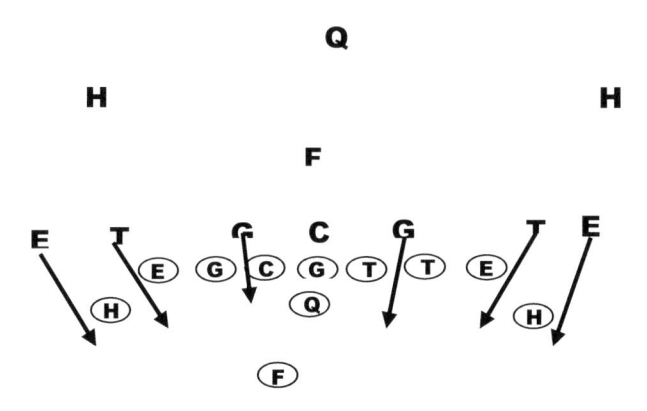

Figure 93 Cup Defense versus the Double Wing

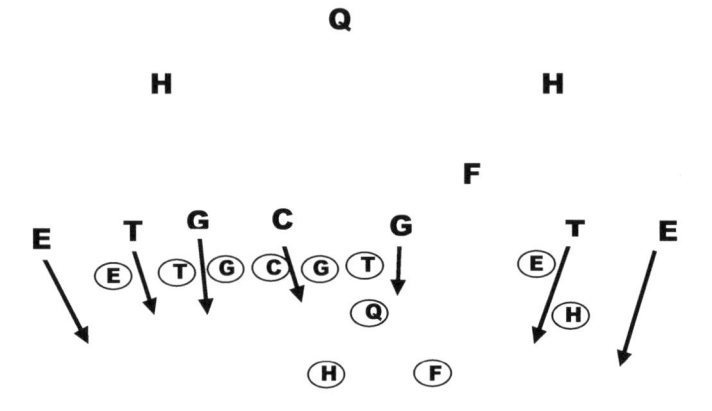

Figure 94 Cup Defense versus the Box Formation

The Cup Defense was used successfully to slow down Warner's Double Wing Reverse. *Figure 95* [135]

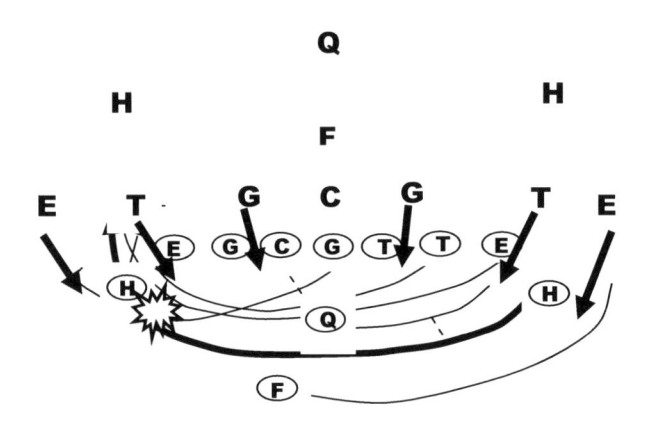

Figure 95 The Cup Defense vs. the Double Wing Reverse Play to the Short Side

1914 Rule Changes

1914 was another year when rule changes would have an enormous impact on the game. A forward pass going out of bounds after touching an eligible player would now go to the opponent. The kick-off after a touchback or safety is abolished and play now resumes with a scrimmage play from the 20 yd line. Intentional grounding of a forward pass becomes a 10-yard penalty. A new rule banned all persons from walking up and down the sideline. There was the return of the field judge as an official. Attempting to deceive an opponent by hiding on the sidelines is now unsportsmanlike conduct.

Bennie Owen

Bennie Owen became Oklahoma's coach in 1905. Owen learned the fast pace open game when playing for Fielding Yost at Kansas in 1899. He later joined Yost's coaching staff as an assistant at Michigan. He received a first-hand look at success being part of Yost's point-a-minute group in 1901 and 1902. During that time, Michigan scored over 600 points in both seasons. Although he spent twenty-two years as Oklahoma's coach, he first introduced his passing offense at Washburn College and Bethany College before going to Oklahoma.

Using the forward pass as the basis of his offense, his success was extraordinary. His 1908 team lost only one game. In 1910, they lost only two. The 1911 team was undefeated. Again, in 1913 he lost only two games. Following the 1913 season, Owen had to replace all of his starters. In desperation, he created what he called "a wide open, reckless game." [136] His 1914 team led all major colleges in scoring with 435 points and scored 25 touchdowns through the air while averaging more than 30 passes a game. His 1915 and 1918 teams were all victorious and his 1920 club was undefeated. Had they been playing in the northeast, they, most likely, would have been National Champions.

He utilized a long punt formation, using the direct pass for every play in his repertoire. With the forward pass being the major part of his offense, his passing yardage often surpassed the running yardage. Examples follow. *Figures 96-99* [137]

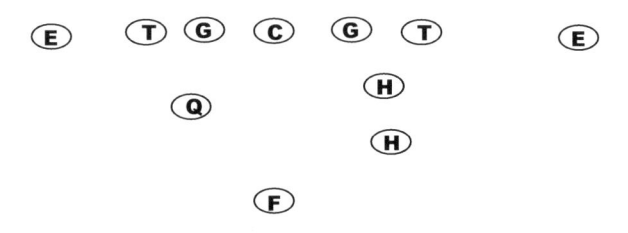

Figure 96 Long Punt Formation used by Owen at Oklahoma

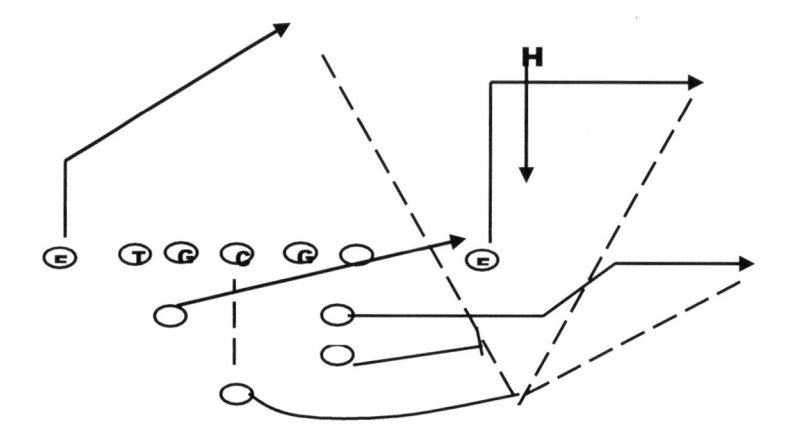

Figure 97 Pass used when the defensive left halfback is rushing down to stop the running plays. It was an excellent complement to his wide running plays

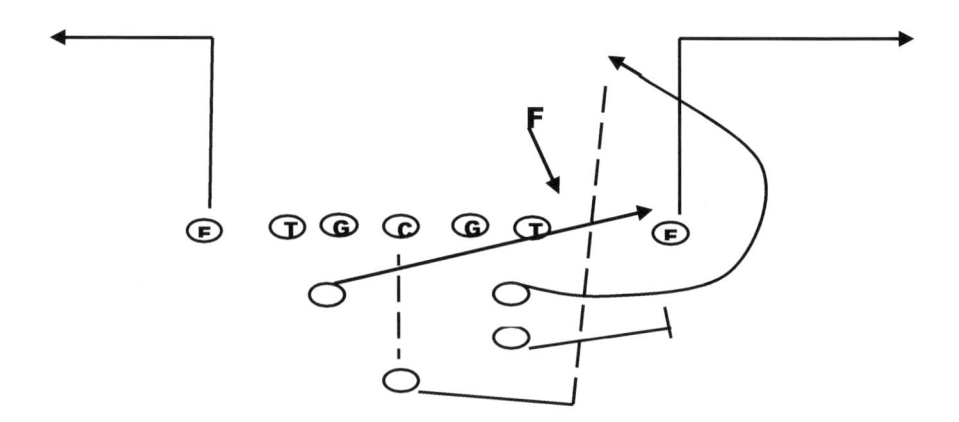

Figure 98 Pass used when the defensive fullback (linebacker F) is moving to stop the wide running plays

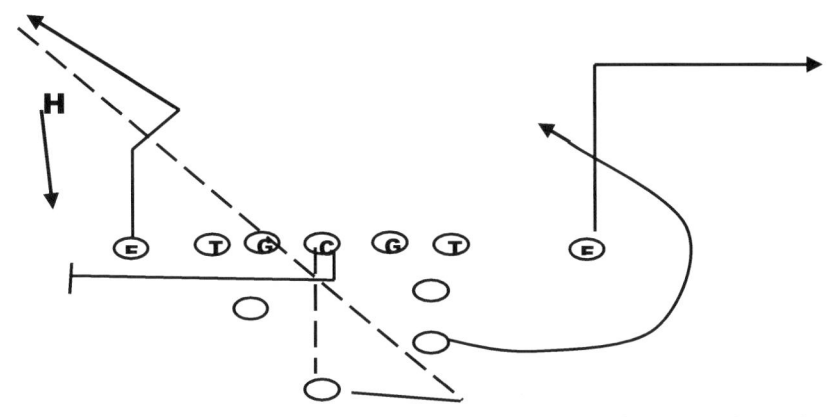

Figure 99 Play used when the defensive halfback is leaving his position and rushing to stop the running plays on his side. NOTE the "false" key created by having the center pull as if to lead block

Passing Emphasis Leads to Lack of Run Game

Although Oklahoma was undefeated and was gaining fame by using the forward pass as the major part of their offense, they began to have difficulty running the ball. That was especially true near their goal line. This will be a problem that plagues the predominantly passing teams for years to come. Owen quickly learned to use the run/pass option play, faking the pass and then running the ball. However, Stagg takes credit for the first use of the run/pass option in 1910. At another time, in his "*Scrapbook*", Stagg claims he used it as early as 1908. [138] Interestingly, the Run/Pass option is considered one of the newest things happening in football today.

Because of Owen's success against archrival Texas Tech, Tech also developed a high-level passing scheme.

5-3-2-1 Defense

Most people give Percy Haughton credit for being the first coach to use a five-man line and three linebackers. His teams were often undersized, and he felt the 5-3 defense, as was true of his offense, put a premium on speed. It is likely that he devised the 5-3-2-1 defense specifically for Yale's offensive lateral passing attack that Coach Frank Hinkey was using with much success at the time. *Figure 100*

Many think that Haughton was also the first to use a broad set of defensive signals, given to the other players by the center using numbers and hand signals. Using the five-man line, Haughton's Harvard system combined linemen stunts in ways previously unheard of. By playing with only five defensive linemen and three linebackers, there was always a linebacker to follow the backs and be in a spot to pursue them if a lateral pass came their way. Harvard taught the defenders to read offensive keys and respond quickly to a developing play. The apparent reason was to get their defenders to the point of attack quickly

In the next few years, the five-man line will be used by many other teams throughout the country, but almost exclusively as a "prevent defense" at the end of a game or half. It was not until 1923 that Ohio State under Doc Wilce used the defense throughout the game against Chicago. [139]

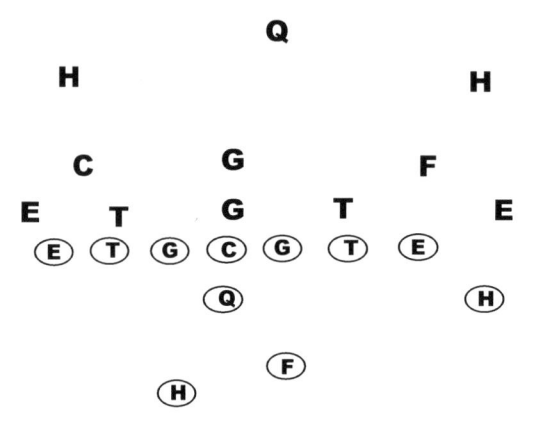

Figure 100 Harvard's 5-3-2-1 Defense

The Birth of the Pass Rush

In an attempt to slow the passing game, defenses began a hard rush on the passer to get to him before he was able to throw the ball. Said Ohio State coach J.W. Wilce; "Many teams assign six men or more to rush the passer and make him throw the ball before he is ready or before he can pick the proper receiver." [140]

Although we are not aware of who was the first to come up with the idea, we do know that it was around this time that defenses began to "double team" a good receiver.

Defenses Begin to Attack

Dick Harlow, with his groundbreaking ideas that were the foundation of the modern defenses, first came on the scene at Penn State. He later had success at Colgate, Western Maryland, and Harvard. Harlow approached defense with an attack mentality. Arthur Sampson, a longtime sports reporter for the Boston Herald, wrote,

> "Sometimes they deploy with six players on the line of scrimmage in Orthodox positions. Sometimes these linemen over-shift to the strong side. Sometimes they over shift to the weak side. Occasionally only five men are left on the line of scrimmage. Once in a while, seven take positions along the scrimmage line.
>
> "These various lineups are nothing more than a smoke screen, however. They don't mean a thing because when the ball is snapped the Harvard linemen seldom do an Orthodox job. Sometimes they charge straight ahead, but more often they loop or charge diagonally. Opposing linemen assigned to block men who line up in front of them discover they are nowhere to be found when the ball is put in play. Since the offensive linemen can't be in motion, they have to stay put and watch the players they are supposed to block slide laterally away from them toward other niches in the defense. It is very confusing to well-drilled operatives who

have spent hours and hours practicing certain definite blocks. It upsets the execution of the well-rehearsed plays.

"Not being able to locate the men they are supposed to take care of so confuses the offensive linemen that they frequently don't do anything at all. A vacillating football player is about as useful to an offense as a fine-tooth comb is to a bald-headed man." [141]

While at Harvard Harlow also began running double wingback plays from the single wing with much success. This offensive initiative caught on and numerous other coaches started to use it.

Punt, Pass, and a Prayer

It was only a matter of time before the pass-dominated offenses of the south and southwest came north. Robert Zuppke's 1916 Illinois team began to line up in a spread formation. His fast paced wide-open game became known as the "punt, pass, and a prayer" system of offense.

Below are some of the significant developments produced by Zuppke.[142]
Figures 101-106 Note the guards dropping off the line of scrimmage. As mentioned earlier, Zuppke first did this in 1910. In *Figure 102* note the similarity between this play and the "Bunch" passes that became fashionable in the 1990s and remain very popular today.

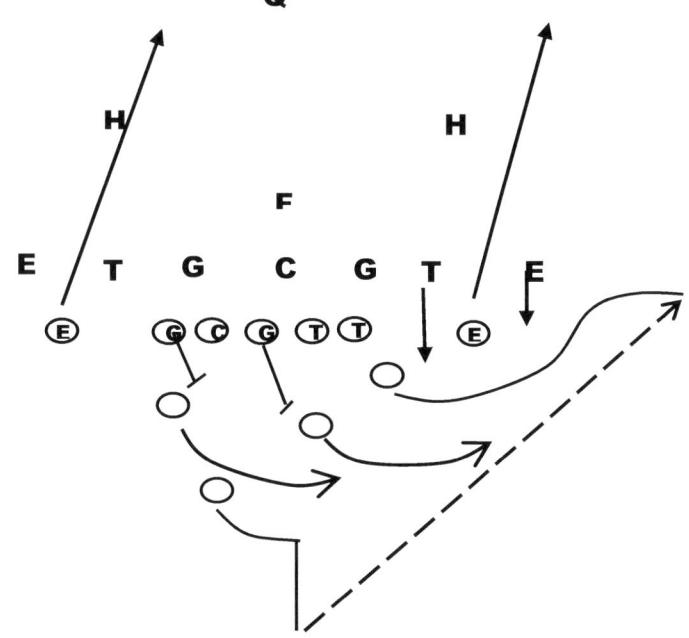

Figure 101 "Right end is a decoy to draw the defensive halfback deep and the wingback is the receiver in that flat". NOTE: He has a horizontal advantage on F, who is the defender responsible for defending him.

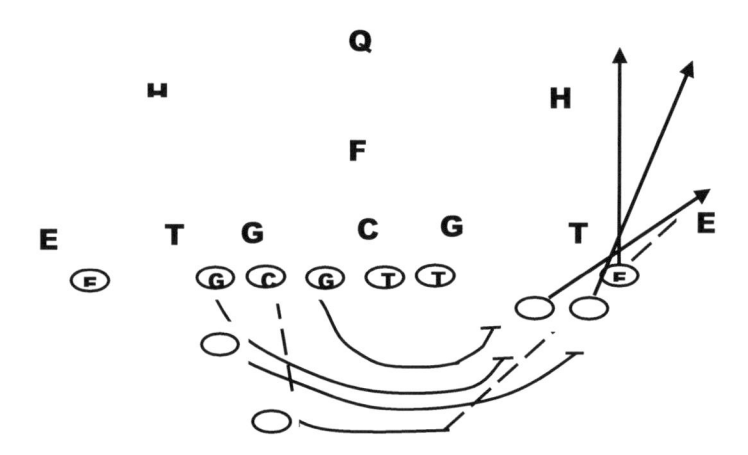

Figure 102 "Three eligible men run down the field in a group, with one of them designated by signal to receive. All three run toward the halfback, making it difficult for him to select the intended receiver and causing fatal hesitation" Note the similarity in the formation to today's "Bunch" formation.

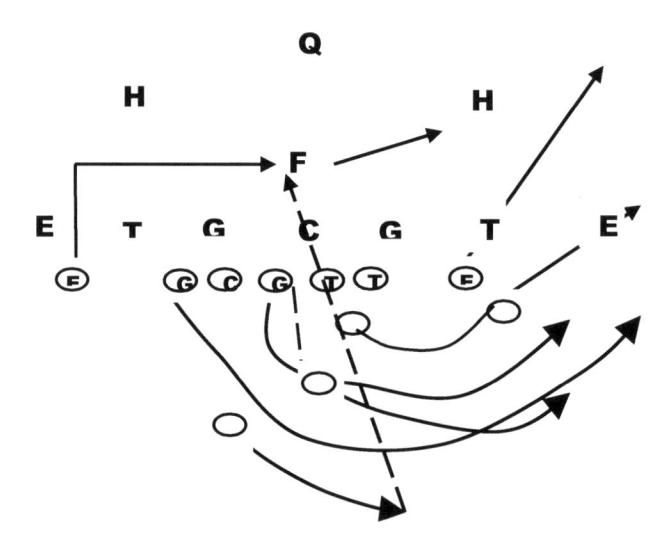

Figure 103 "The left end delays watching the opponent who is backing up the line (F), and then sneaks into the spot which the opponent vacates." Note that the guards are pulling and the backs leading to making the play appear like a run.

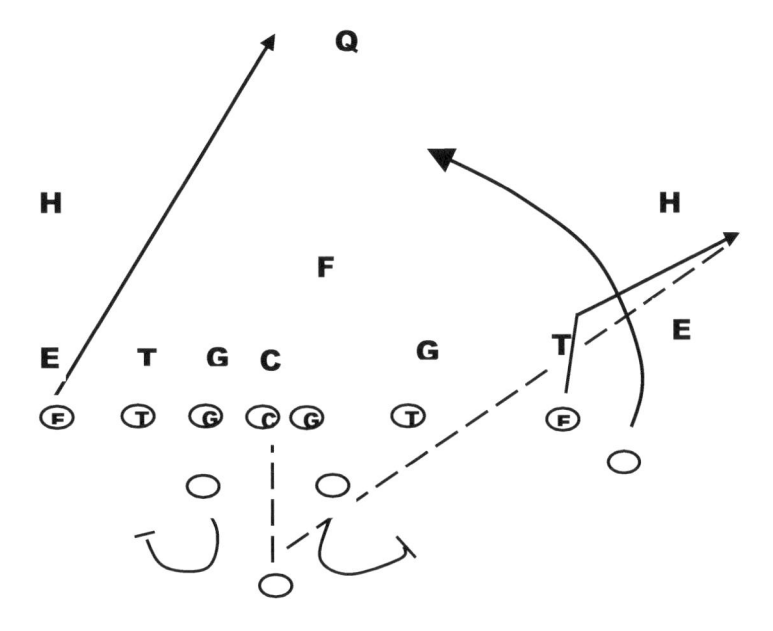

Figure 104 "'The receiver and decoy cross each other's path, starting together with the snap of the ball, or the decoy leads and the receiver delays his start." Note the similarity to today's play that offensive coaches call a "rub" play and defensive coaches call a "pick" play

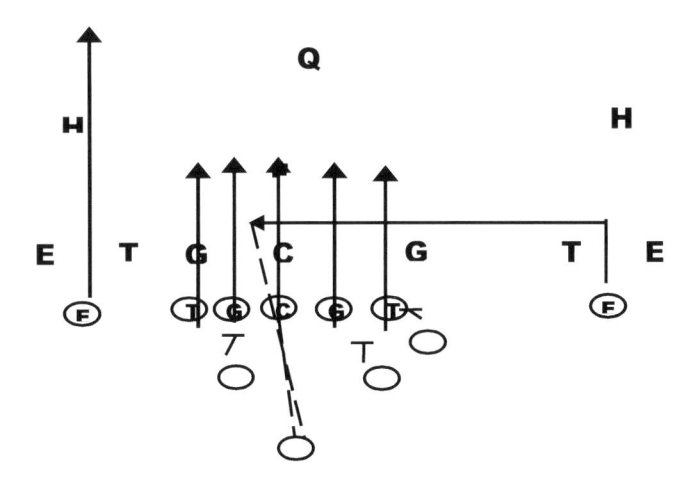

Figure 105 "Screen pass to the right end from punt formation"

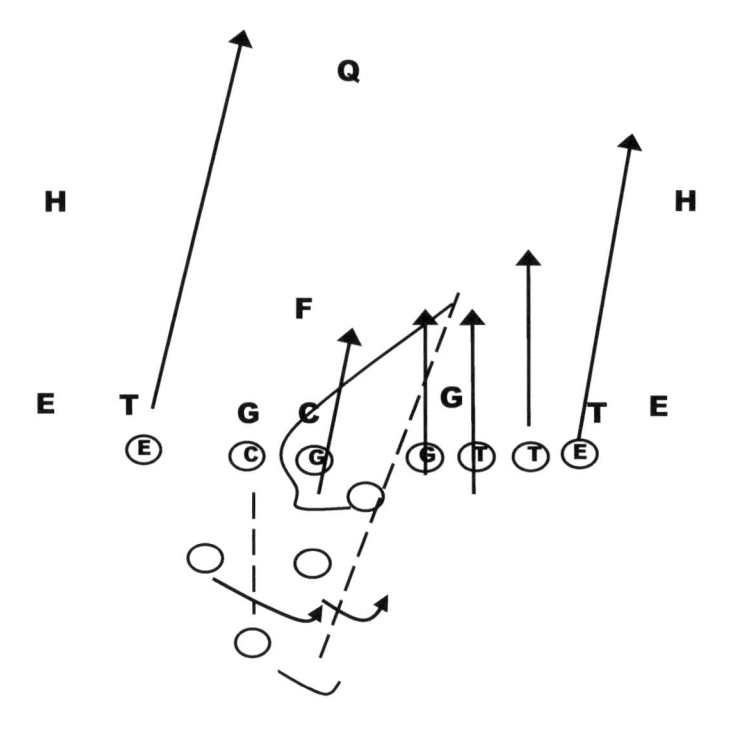

Figure 106 Illinois famous Screen Play - Used first versus Ohio State, 1921

It is worth mentioning that although not directly related to the clash between offense and defense, it was in 1913 that Amos Alonzo Stagg began to number his players. This would eventually have a significant influence on the strategy of the game as rule changes would ultimately prohibit coaches from interchanging players to various parts of the offensive formations as they once did. This inability to interchange players would have a profound influence on the use of the shift. However from 1915 – 1921 the shift became very popular.

The New Shift

A precursor to the true shift was "Pop" Warner's shift of years prior that consisted in simply having the linemen move to the right or left one man. At first "Pop's" innovation was very successful in spreading the defense. Defenses were hesitant to move and when they did, they shifted slowly. Although the use of both Warner's shift and the Heisman shift continued, the newer, more comprehensive, shifts proved to be more efficient.

The fundamental purpose of the line and back changes was to catch the defense in a sideways motion at the snap of the ball. A second purpose was to bring two strong linemen to the same side of the line to attack the defense. The third goal is that it enables an offense to hide their weaker players. Together the first and second objectives result in an "unbalanced" (more blockers to one side of the center than the other) formation. The shifting offenses may also end up in a balanced formation. Many coaches believe that the "balanced" line is the best method of attack. The early shift was called a "one-position" shift since only the linemen or only the backs moved from their pre-snap position to another just before the snap of the ball. *Figure 107* The newer variations, at times had all 11 players moving from their pre-snap positions to a new formation just before the snap. It became common to call these shifts "jump" shifts because it appeared the players were jumping from the first position into the second.

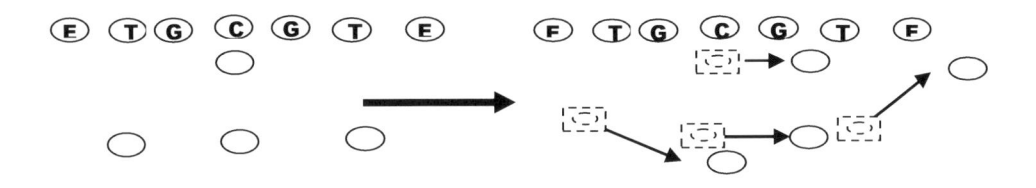

Figure 107 Typical "one Position Shift [143]

Minnesota Shift

Many think that the Minnesota shift was the invention of Dr. H.L. Williams while he was the Head Coach at the University of Minnesota. However, it was Bennie Bierman, a player of Williams and later an assistant coach, who further developed the shift and used it with remarkable success. We show the original Minnesota movement in *Figure 108*. Although we have shown only two pre "hep" alignments (initial position of the players), there were multiple starting positions. To add to the confusion of the defenders, the shifting teams often varied the time between the movement of the linemen and the movement of the backs.

Both Princeton and Yale made extensive use of the Minnesota shift, making their own unique adjustments [144]

Two Common "Pre-Hep" Positions

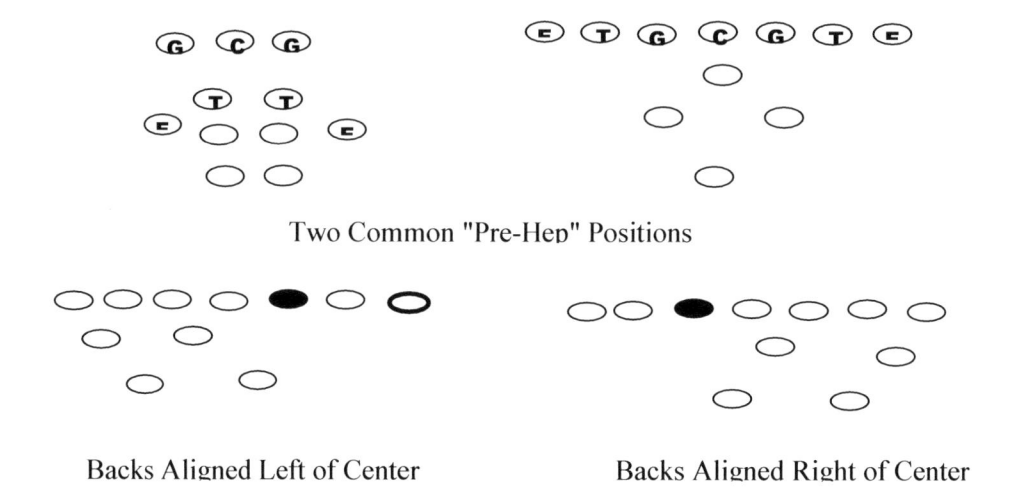

Backs Aligned Left of Center Backs Aligned Right of Center

Two Common "Post-Hep" Positions

Figure 108 The Minnesota Shift used by Bierman. From one of the two pre-set positions, the back eight players would deploy in a vast number of formation [145]

Howard Jones & USC

Howard Jones, who coached outstanding teams at both Iowa and The University of Southern California, began to use some unorthodox shifts. In 1921, he had 16 different shifts. By 1932, at USC, he had over 80 variations of shifts. For the most part, his players were interchangeable with tackles ending up in the backfield and backs ending up on the line. His theory was that because of the variety of shifts he employed, the defense, to protect itself, was forced to move with the shifters. When his players went unbalanced, the defense would move to an unbalanced alignment. However, they could not risk moving to an over shifted defense. He could now use his power plays to the long side of the formation because he had established leverage on the defense. His offensive formations were extremely complex in an attempt to confuse his opponent. He was able to provide both power and deception in his offense because, although the shifting was multifaceted, he kept his plays simple. Jones said of his shift,

> "Each season (at Southern California) I changed our attack slightly. One year the linemen first took their positions with their backs to their opponents. One year we line up three deep before the shift. Last year we went four deep, in parallel columns. These changes have

prevented the oppositions from spotting our principal men until the last possible moment and have thus increased our deception." [146]

Joe Glass, writing in 1933, said of Jones's shift,

"Probably a great deal of Southern California's tremendous success is due to its shifting line and backs, but that is only part of the story. Despite the confusing aspects of the shift, which comes after a huddle and is really two shifts, the plays employed by Howard Jones usually are extremely simple in their development. It is the simplicity of their plays, evolving from the complexities of the shift, which enables the Trojans to do things.

"It is a fact that many experienced football men do not fully understand the Southern California shift, and the huddle-and-shift employed by Jones has come to be called, in many quarters, the 'squirrel cage.' The shift is confusing to the opposition team because it is inclined to move with the shifters. Thus, it becomes unbalanced, and defensive leverage ceases to be the equal of offensive leverage. The advantage of a shifting offense must be reckoned largely upon its ability to unbalance and confuse the defense. The Southern California shift accomplishes this to an unusual degree because it enables men to be switched from one position to another with remarkable facility. A back may move into the line, an end may become a back." [147]

Lock Step Shift (Sing Sing Shift)

Little Center College brought the "Lock Step Shift" or "Sing Sing Shift" into prominence

The "U" Shift

Remember, Stagg was opposed to shifting for several reasons, that was until Notre Dame and Minnesota began to have success with it.

During this time, Stagg made use of three different shifts, "U Formation shift, "Shimmy shift", and "Whirlwind" Shift. The "U" shift is very similar to the Chicago formation. The linemen "hep" (shift) into the line on the first "hep", then remain stationary. The backs may remain stationary on the first "hep;" or may shift to some false position. On the second "hep", the backs will move into their position. . Together the line and backs will spring into action on the snap of the ball.   *See Figure 109*

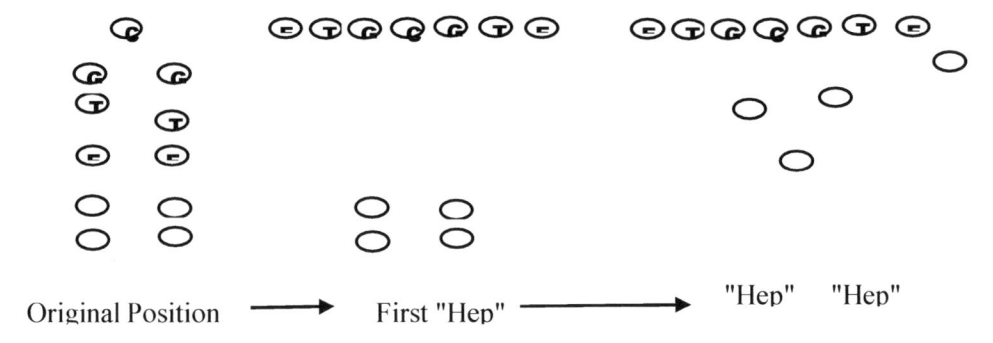

Figure 109 The "U" Shift

Following are several other significant shifts as depicted in Zuppke's book *"FOOTBALL Techniques and Tactics."*[148] *Figures 110-112*

The Illinois Shift

The shift below was first used by the University of Illinois and they had much success with it. The team will align as shown in position A below. On the first "hep" they will either snap the ball or shift into the alignment shown in position B. On the second "hep", they again might snap the ball or shift into position C. Given a third "hep", they may snap the ball or they may move into the alignment shown as position D. *Figure 110*

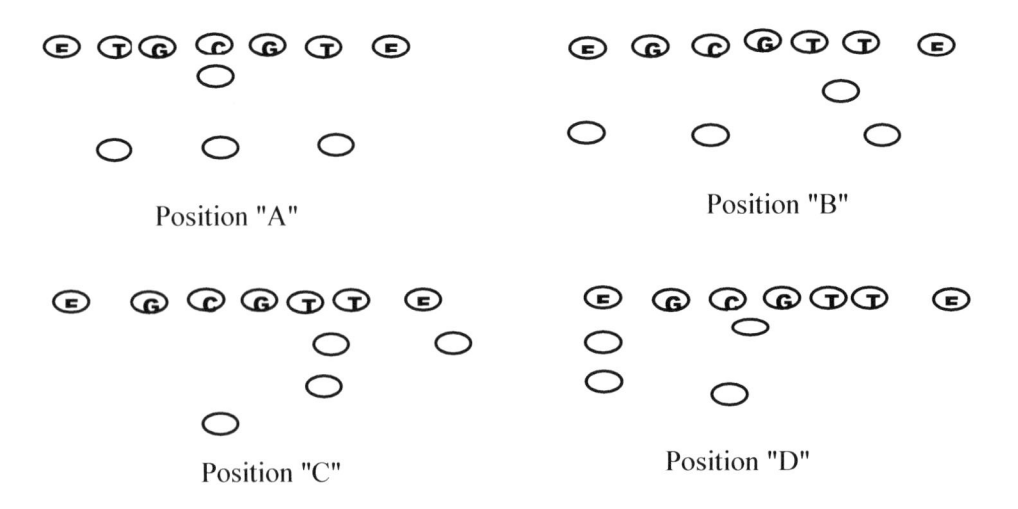

Position "A"

Position "B"

Position "C"

Position "D"

Figure 110 The Illinois Shift #1

Another Illinois shift that was used with great success is shown below. They aligned in an unusual formation, shown on the left, and from there shifted into the alignment shown on the right, below. There were multiple plays run from these formations. *Figure 111*

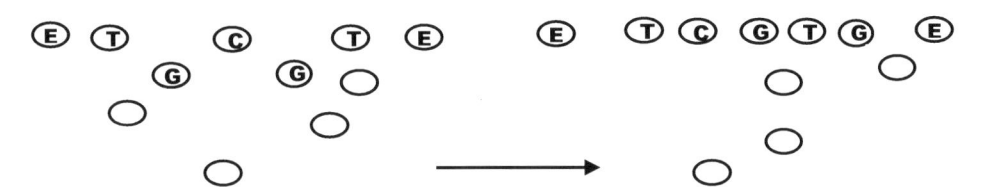

Figure 111 Illinois Shift #2

The Iowa Shift

Howard Jones used the shift shown below while he was at Iowa. The center and two tackles position themselves on the line of scrimmage. The fullback and deep back do not "hep". They will align in their final position from the start. On the "hep" the two guards will place themselves on the line of scrimmage, either both right, both left or one on either side of the center. The two backs who are shifting will assume their respective position in the formation. *Figure 112*

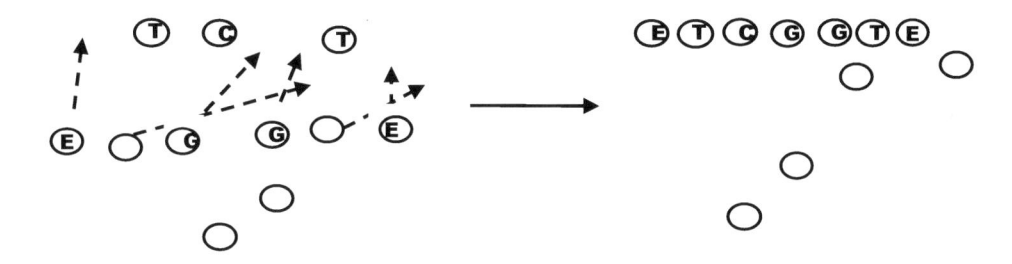

Figure 112 Iowa Shift. Shown is a typical pre-snap alignment with a shift to the Single Wing

The Notre Dame Shift

We have already referred to the 1913 use of the forward pass by Notre Dame's Dorais to Rockne to defeat Army 35-10 and bring the pass to the forefront of offensive football. Although it was nothing like the passing displays of today, it definitely was a signal that the game was moving from the old days. Gone was pushing, and pulling, it changed to a more open, more coordinated and skilled type of game cleverly designed and painstakingly perfected. There are some who claim that Notre Dame used the shift in that celebrated game. However, the famous Notre Dame shift was, most likely, not used against Army as some people claim. According to Jess Harper, they did not use the shift until later in the 1913 season.

There is some disagreement as to where the Notre Dame system and the Notre Dame shift were created. Some say Jack Marks brought it through Frank Cavanaugh at Dartmouth. Others, including Rockne himself, traced it back to Jess Harper, who played for Stagg at Chicago. Also, some claim that Stagg brought it with him from Yale. Rockne stated that Marks was the coach at Notre Dame before Harper and that, although Marks was a star at Dartmouth, he had left Dartmouth before Cavanaugh arrived. Knute Rockne asserts that he and Jess Harper discussed the shift on a train ride after a Notre Dame loss in 1913 and he credits himself for including the ends in on the shift.

In the Harvard A.A. News October 21, 1933, Dr. Edward Anderson gave the following description of the Notre Dame system. A coach at Holy Cross and Iowa, Anderson played for Rockne in 1918. "...Whenever someone chances to make mention of the Notre Dame System the first thought that arises in the mind of the listener is the shift. To be sure, the shift is one of the big factors of the style, but there are other equally important factors....

"Just where the shift originated will probably always be disputed to some extent... It is generally conceded that Jesse Harper, former head coach at South Band and now the director of athletics there, learned the idea of a backfield shift from Stagg. At any rate, the shift was in use at Notre Dame when Rockne played, and it was his development of it, and his additions to it when he returned as coach, that formed what is now known as the Notre Dame system. According to Knute Rockne, Jess Harper put the "Box Formation" in at Notre Dame in 1914. Gus Dorais, who played with Rockne and for Harper, claims they used the box prior to this time. Dorais claims that the "Box Formation itself was first used by Notre Dame in 1911. Dorais' claim is somewhat suspect because we know that Harper had played for Amos Alonzo Stagg at Chicago. It was while at Chicago that Harper became impressed with the shifting offense that he and Rockne would later refine into the famous Notre Dame shift- from the T-Formation to the box. Harper coached at Alma College (1906-07), and then at Wabash (1909-1912) until he accepted the head coaching post at Notre Dame in 1913.

"The Notre Dame Shift had a great advantage over the other shifts, especially the Minnesota Shift, in that Notre Dame could snap the ball from their T-Formation without a shift making it much more difficult for the defense to anticipate. The Minnesota shift could not. To help gain the same advantage as Notre Dame over the defense, Minnesota began to double shift.

"The purpose of the shift, in short, is deception and concentrated power. The idea is to get the right men in the right place at the right time and in so doing to throw the opposing players, the line especially, off balance. In the early days, there were many of the opinion that the shift was intended merely to beat the gun, to get off to a flying start without taking a penalty, an attempt to get the jump on the opposition. Some claimed the success of Notre Dame lay solely in the flying start.

"That myth is exploded by the Notre Dame record during the seasons of 1929 and 1930 when the Rockne Raiders went through both seasons without a defeat, even after the one-second rule had been placed on the shift. In the preseason rules, the shift was practically stopped to an ordinary formation, but that didn't cramp the Notre Dame offense in the least. They promptly had what were their two best years right after there went into effect the rule that was generally thought would stop them.

"The basic formation of the Notre Dame system is the balanced line and the backfield shifted from a T-formation. That is, the quarterback is directly in back of the center and the fullback is directly in back of the quarter and flanked by the halves. From this so-called T-Formation, the well-known shift is accomplished, and the success of the team depends on how it is accomplished. The most common shift is into a box formation, from which the opposing line is raked with spinners, reverses, crossbucks, and an occasional pass. The opposing line, unless it is exceptionally clever, is thrown off balance by the shift; and, more than that, cannot tell whether a center buck, a tackle slant or an end run will develop.

"The teams use their interference to get the ball-carrier by the line of scrimmage, and then, when he gets by, they let him make his own way. The Notre Dame teams have always done the opposite. They save their interference for the opposing backfield men, and, as a result, long runs are always in evidence when the team is in action. The Notre Dame system plays for the long runs while other colleges major in thrusts and short gains.

"The real reason for the success of the Notre Dame system is speed and perfection in the art of blocking. By speed, I don't mean merely the ability to run fast but shiftiness and general grace to perform a play not only with lightning speed but also with skill and coordination. The speed is necessary not only in the backfield but in the line as well. That is the reason why Notre Dame's lines often have contained men who were smaller and lighter that the average of other linemen. That is the reason why there have been stars like Bert Metzger. If a man is big and fast so much the better. If he is just big, his place is filled by a man who can get around with more speed although he is a good deal lighter. The art of blocking was always considered necessary by Rockne, and consequently by his pupils who coach at so many American colleges today. The idea is not just to knock a man down but to do it in the right way. The blocker edges him away from the play, and at the same time, the blocker must keep his feet because in the Notre Dame system a man is not designated to take out a certain opponent and let it go at that. He is ordered to follow up his first block by heading into the opponent's secondary and getting as many more as he can. This is responsible for so many long-gaining plays.

"Someone once said, 'Nothing great can be achieved without enthusiasm' and that applies to football…. For the enthusiasm for football at Notre Dame has been tremendous through this decade of success for her varsity teams. Basically, enthusiasm is the secret of the Notre Dame system."[149]

Notre Dame dominated the headlines and the college football world in 1918 under the innovative coaching of Knute Rockne. The following are from Knute Rockne's *"Coaching"*, first published in 1925. Shown first is an example of his shift [150] He describes how he divided his Notre Dame formations into four primary formations, with a brief explanation of what was done from each.[151] *Figures 113-117*

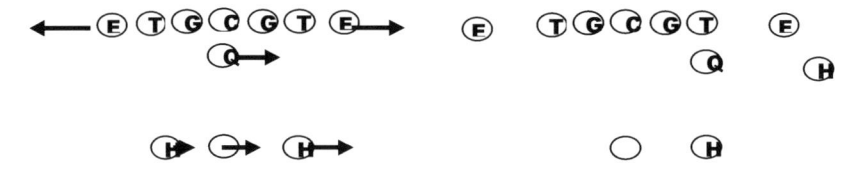

From "T-Formation"   To "Box Formation."

Figure 113 The Notre Dame Shift

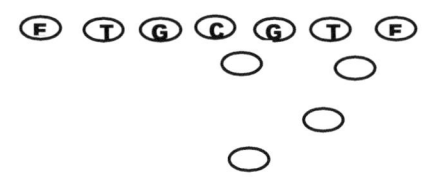

Figure 114 The Notre Dame Close Formation. "The Close formation (quarterback handling the ball, ends in close, backs in close). This formation stresses thrust plays."

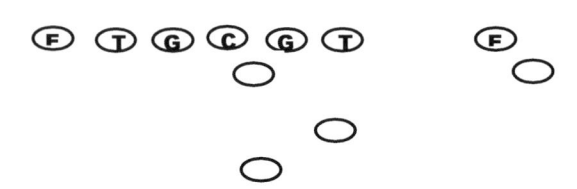

Figure 115 The Notre Dame Open Formation. "Open formation (direct pass to the quarterback, ends flanking tackles, backs a little wider apart). This formation stresses flank plays."

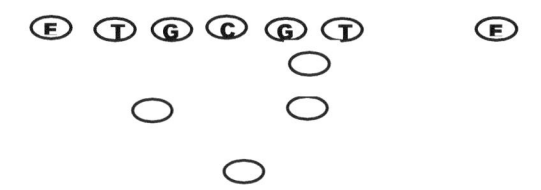

Figure 116 The Norte Dame Punt Formation. "Punt formation (man back about ten yards should be a triple threat). This formation stresses the kick."

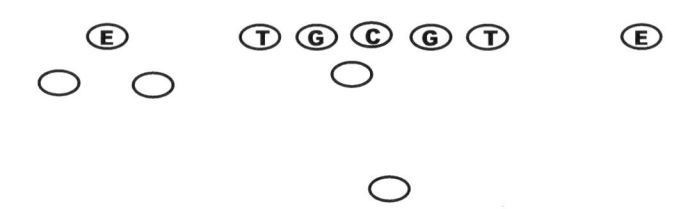

Figure 117 The Notre Dame Spread Formation. "Spread formation (ends and backs spread over a wide area-sometimes also linemen. This formation stresses forward passing" Dorias) (Rockne, Vol IV, No 2)

Defending the Notre Dame Shift

Stagg devised a defense for the Notre Dame shift. He lined both his defensive tackles off the line of scrimmage. After the shift, the defensive tackle to the strong side stayed off the line of scrimmage making it difficult for the offensive end to block him. This became a standard defensive maneuver for many teams. Tom Landry of the Dallas Cowboys would use a very similar plan many years later in his "Flex Defense". Stagg called his defense the "Butterfly Defense" *Figure 118*

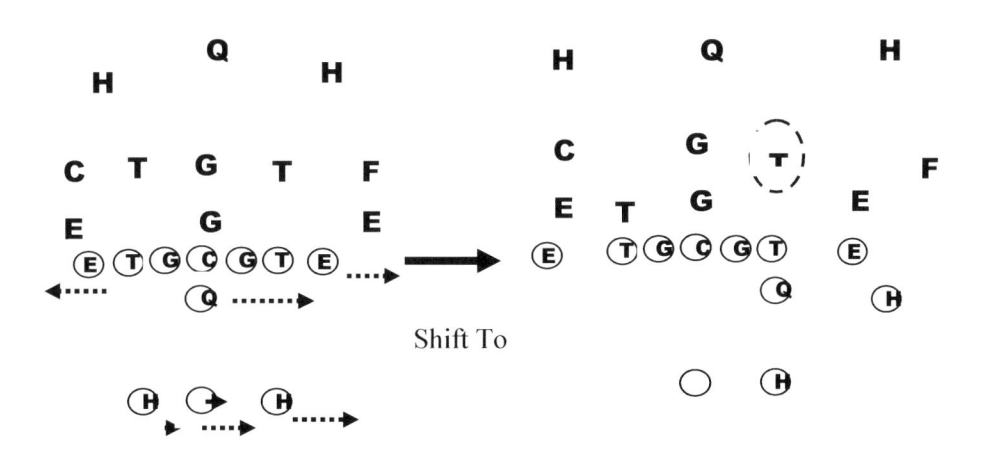

Shift To

Figure 118 "Butterfly Defense" devised by Stag for Notre Dame Shift

Spread Punt

Stagg, at Chicago, used the Spread Punt through 1932. *Figure 119* [152] However, some credit James McCurdy with having used it at Springfield College some time before 1916. There are also claims that Lebanon Valley College used it in 1913, 1914 under Coach Roy J. Geyer using Carl Snavely, who would later become a very successful coach in his own right, as the kicker.

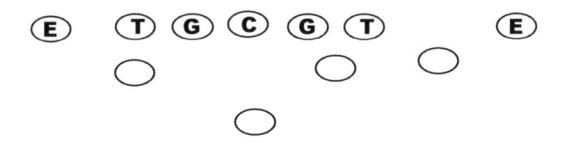

Figure 119 The Spread Punt Formation. Similar to that used by Amos Alonzo Stagg

The Pennsylvania Defense

The Pennsylvania style of defense got its name because the University of Pennsylvania initially used it. However, some other teams in the East also used it extensively. In this defense, the guards, tackles, and ends played wider than usual. They charged hard into spaces or gaps and attempted to push everything towards the middle. The defensive linemen charged hard using their bodies and shoulders. The center and the fullback looked for the hole that the running back would run through. The theory of this defense is that the defensive line will fill all the gaps and the ball carrier will come through free and alone without any blockers in front of him. He can then be picked off and tackled easily by the two secondary men. [153] *Figure 120*

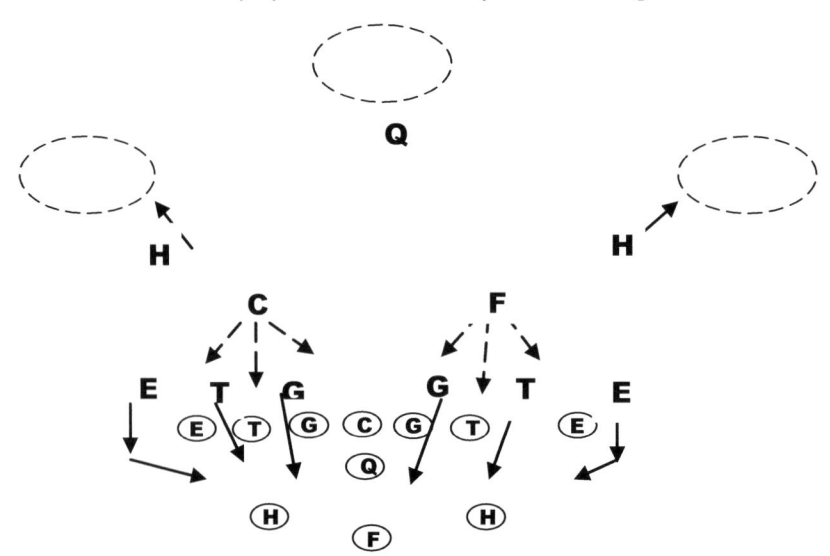

Figure 120 The Pennsylvania Defense

Stopping the Single Wing with the 5 man line

Around this same time, Andy Kerr at Colgate began using the 5-man line versus the Single Wing formation. Kerr, known as a defensive innovator, devised a unique short side defense, versus the Single Wing. He began to line up his short side defensive tackle over the offensive end with the defensive end on that side aligned just outside. On the snap of the ball, the defensive end slanted hard into the backfield and the defensive tackle delayed the offensive end and covered the flat if a pass appeared. This maneuver allowed him to play the long side defensive halfback closer to the line of scrimmage to help stop the run.

The short-side halfback could play deeper because he knew he had help in the flat. The safety (Q) could cheat over slightly to the long side. *Figure 121*

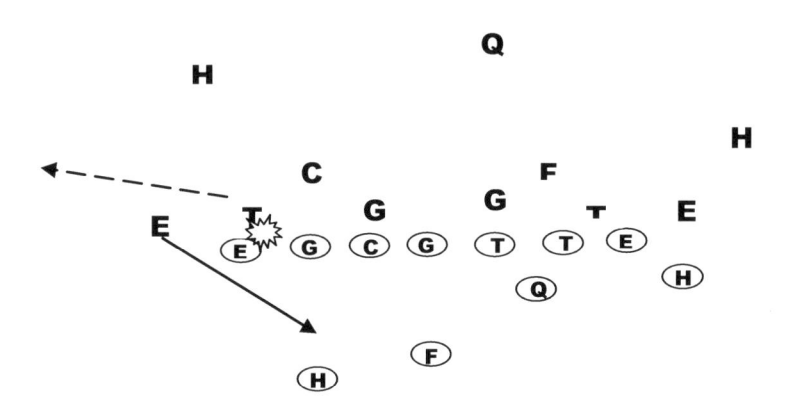

Figure 121 Andy Kerr's Colgate adjustment in stopping the Single Wing

6-2 Spot Defense

Glenn Killinger, in his book "*Football*", 1939 discusses a "special" defense for those teams running the single wing who both pass and run successfully. The 6-2 Spot Defense places a defender between the linebackers and the secondary defenders. The "Spot" defender attempted to read the offensive backfield play. He determined if it was a run or a pass and then reacted as a third linebacker to a run or a third defensive back if it is a pass. This defensive maneuver was, in effect, a precursor to the popular "Robber" defensive secondary scheme used today. *See Figure 122*

Stagg claims to be the first to use this defense. [154]

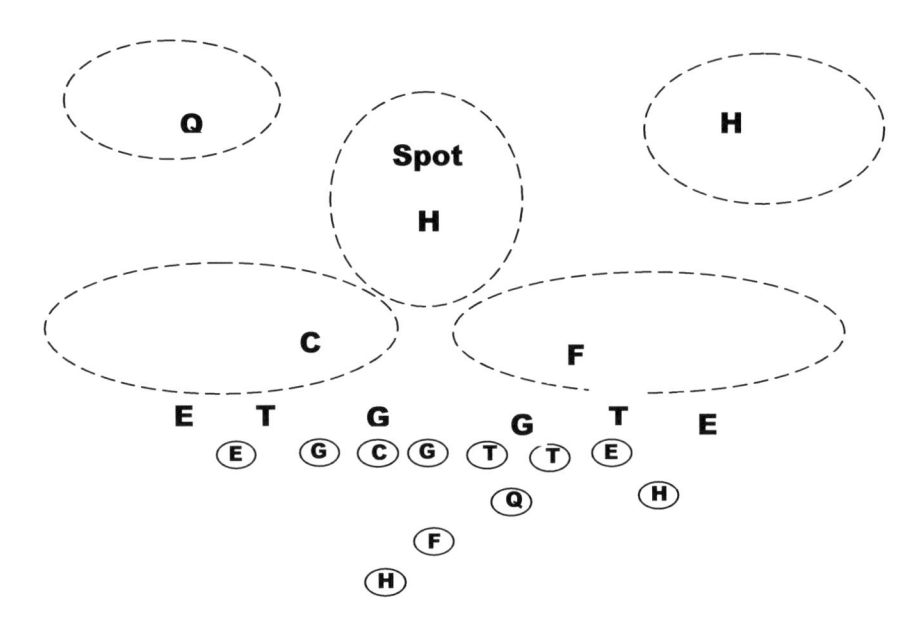

Figure 122 The 6-2 "Spot" Defense

6-2-2-1 Defense

Once again, in the 1920s, the 6-2-2-1 defense gained support. Although used just after the turn of the century, the 6-2-2-1 had fallen out of favor because it was thought to be less successful against the run. Bernie Bierman, at Michigan, ran the six when almost everyone else was using the 7-2. It protected against the long pass much better than the 7-2-2 defense, especially down the middle. *Figure 123*

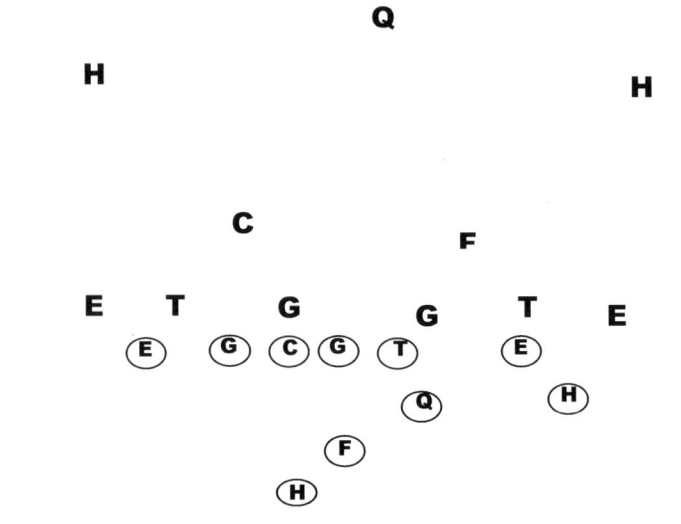

Figure 123 Reintroduced 6-2-2-1 Defense

131 Nelson, David. *The Anatomy of a Game: Football, the Rules, and the Men who Made the Game*,(Associated University Press, Cranbury, NJ), 1994. p. 144-147

132 Zuppe, Robert, *Football Technique and Tactics*, (Champaign, Illinois, Baily and Himes, Pub., 1924) p. 70

133 Zuppe p. 121

134 DaGrosa, John, *Functional Football*, (Philadelphia and London,W.B. Saunders Co.1936), p. 149-150

135 Warner, Glenn. *Football for Coaches and Players*. (Glenn Scobey Warner, Stanford University, CA),1927. p. 162

136 http://digital.libraries.ou.edu/*sooner*/articles/p12-14_1946v18n11_OCR.pdf, downloaded 04/21/09

137 Bachman, Charles W., *A Manual of Football for High School Coaches*, (Manhattan,Kansas, Dept. of Industrial Journalism and Printing Kansas State College1926), p. 148-150

138 Danzig, *Histoy of American Football*, p. 44

139 Danzig, *The History of American Football*, p. 110

140 Wilce, J.W., *Football How to Play It and How to Understand It*, (New York: Charles Scribner's Sons, 1924), p. 161.

141 Sampson, Arthur, The Boston Herald, October 27, 1941.

142 Zuppke, *FOOTBALL Techniques and Tactics*, (Champaign, Ill. Bailey and Himes Pub., 1924), p. 165-183.

143 Zuppke,, p. 206

144 Reed, Herbert H., *Football for Public and Player*. (New York: Frederick A. Stokes Co, 1913), p.155

145 Pittsburgh Press, *Famous Football Plays*, November 11, 1932 http://news.google.com/newspapers?nid=1144&dat=19321111&id=OPkaAAAAIBAJ&sjid=Y0sEAAAAIBAJ&pg=6040,5441136

146 Danzig, Allison, *History of American Football*, p. 68

147 Danzig, Allison, *History of American Football*, p. 68-69

148 Zuppke, *FOOTBALL Techniques and Tactics*, p.206-208

149 Danzig, The *History of American* Football, p. 63.

150 Rockne, *Coaching, The Way of the Winner*, (The Devin-Adair Co., New York, 1925) pp. 83

151 Rockne, pp. 22-23.

152 Rockne, p 69 (1919, 1920s decade: from the Rockne book. From page 69).

153 Rockne, , *Coaching, The Way of the Winner* (The Devin-Adair Co., New York, 1925) p.69

154 Danzig, *Oh How they Played the Game*, p. 57.

CHAPTER SEVEN

The "Aerial Circus"

(1920 –1929)

Ray Morrison: SMU Spread Offense

Ray Morrison became the first Head Coach at Southern Methodist University in 1915. After a dismal 2-13 first season, he left for the Army. Morrison returned to SMU as the freshmen coach in 1920 and became the head coach again in 1922. He installed a new spread offense passing game and was 6-3 in 1922 and undefeated in 1923. SMU began to dominate the southwest with his new "Aerial Circus" offense. At Texas A&M, Dana Bible won four championships ('19, '21,'25, '27) using the wide open spread passing game. The Southwest made the rest of the country aware of the spread formation passing game. They were throwing the ball all over the field using spread formations that had players positioned from sideline--to sideline. Two typical spread formations.[155] *Figure 124, 125*

Figure 124 Early Spread Formation

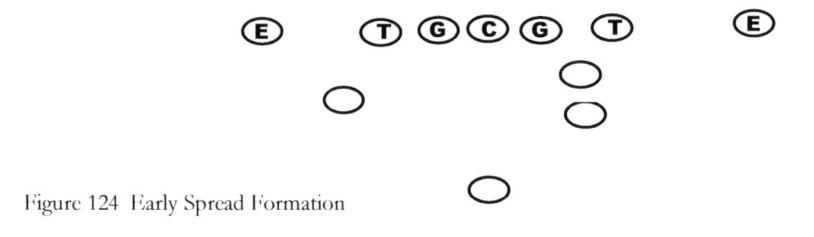

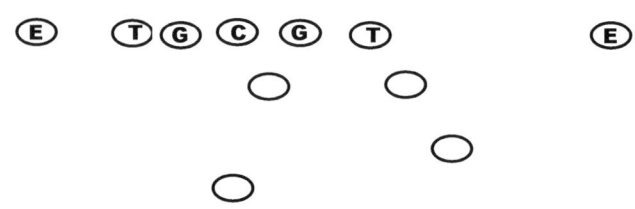

Figure 125 Early Spread Formation

The "Y" Formation

Morrison also introduced a Y- Formation, placing both the quarterback and the fullback in a position where a direct snap to either of them was possible. This was different from the Syracuse "Y Formation" where the center placed his back to the defense so that he could better see the backs. Because the center was facing away from the line of scrimmage, the Syracuse Y only existed for one year before the rules prohibited its use. Morrison's Y- Formation used both a balanced line and an unbalanced formation. *Figure 126* He offsets the backfield to one side or the other. It did not matter if the line was balanced or unbalanced. This was a power formation.

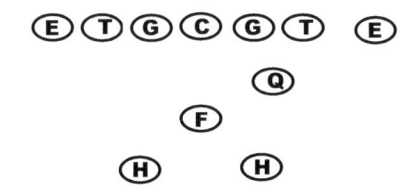

(E) (T) (G) (C) (G) (T)　(E)
　　　　　　　　　　(Q)
　　　　　　　(F)
　　　　　(H)　　(H)

Figure 126 Morrison's Y-Formation

Intentional Grounding Rule

1924 brought a change in the penalty for intentional grounding. The penalty increased from 10 to15 yards. This rule change would bring about a significant transformation in passing strategy.

Restrictions on the Shift

A second very significant rule change was enacted requiring that on all shift plays all players were required to come to a complete stop and remain stationary, "momentarily." Of course, this rule was inserted to combat Knute Rockne's Notre Dame shift. However, there were different interpretations as to what "momentarily" meant. In 1927, the rule became more explicit by demanding all players remain stationary for one full second. The Notre Dame shift stands with both the Minnesota shift of Dr. Harry Williams and the Heisman shift at Georgia Tech as the most widespread shifts in football. However, as stated previously, it seems that all shifts go back to the early 1900's and Amos Alonzo Stagg. In his *"Scrapbook"*, Stagg discusses those early shifts. "Although many Notre Dame supporters denied it, the new rule did have a significant impact on how shifts were used."

Notre Dame & the New Shift Rule

Harry Stuhldreher, who quarterbacked the renowned Four Horseman of 1924, defended the Notre Dame system saying, "The Notre Dame system is based upon three fundamental, their importance scaling down in the order named. First, in importance is speed; second, deception; and third, power. The Warner system, for example, rates, power first, deception second, and speed third.

"The Notre Dame system depends for its success upon fast breaking. By fast breaking we mean getting to the point of attack as quickly as possible a great number of interferers, as opposed to the Warner system of delayed attack – delayed because of its fakes, spins, and reverses, which are the keynote of the Warner attack and which take more time to develop and get under way.

"In proof of its power of adaptability to changing conditions, I would like to mention three of the many developments which have taken place in the Notre Dame system in the past five years. The first development I want to talk about is the incorporation – not the invention – of the spinner attack. This was brought about by football legislation which called for a one-second halt after a shift.

"Previous to this rule change, the Notre Dame weak side was just what it was called – namely, weak. It didn't have to be strengthened, however, under the old shift rules. We got along fairly well somehow, weak side and all. With the one-second stop, however, the opposing line had time to move with us, and even over-shift. It was imperative for us to make our weak side a real threat. The incorporation of the spinner took care of it. The incorporation of the spinner was done in accordance with the Notre Dame principle of fast breaking. Our opponents' spinners are delayed in their inception.

"Ironically enough, instead of crippling us, the passage of legislation enforcing a one-second stop in shifts really made it possible for us to strengthen our weak side; for without the one-second stop, we could not have used the spinner at all. Even with our fast breaking, our short side would still be our weak side.

"A second development within the Notre Dame attack is the increasing use of the lateral pass. The lateral pass fits into the Notre Dame system better than into any other system; one more because of our fast-breaking characteristics, which make a defensive man move out of position more quickly and, therefore, leaves them wide open against a lateral passing attack.

"A third development came about when opposing coaches came up with the idea that the best defense against the Notre Dame system is a fast-charging defense. When this idea became firmly fixed in our opponents' heads, it became easier and easier to suck them into traps. There, due to their off-balance position, they can be blocked one way or another with little difficulty. This opens up huge holes for our ball carriers."

"I have heard arguments against the Notre Dame system of individual blocking. I have heard it pointed out as a weakness. But if we couldn't develop men to do the job consistently, we would be the first to give them help. The Notre Dame system has been called the gambling system of play. It is a little fairer to say that it goes for the longer gain. We, therefore, believe in having linemen play line positions and letting the smaller trickier, speedier men play in the backfield.

"One of the reasons why those of us who have played under the Notre Dame system have such an affection for it (is that) it gives more boys and more varied types of boys the opportunity to play the game. It puts a premium on brains and smartness and coordination and physical cleverness, rather than on weight or beef or brawn. We ask only of a player that he possess speed, agility, a competitive spirit, and adaptability, and a well-knit, sound physique.

"Rockne knew that the average boy gets a bigger kick out of outsmarting an opponent than out of out bruising him or of beating an opponent with weapons emanating from his brain rather than with those from his thigh muscles. He knew that getting a kick out of this type of play, they would play it because they liked it, and play it harder and be willing to devote more time and pains to perfecting their parts in it.

"A bulwark of the strength of the Norte Dame system lies in the fact that all of the plays are run from one formation. The Warner system, for example, uses four separate formations from which certain definite plays originate. An opponent of the Warner system need only make himself familiar with these four formations and the well-known element of doubt, the chance for deception is considerably minimized.

"For example, when you see a Warner team go into its A-Formation, you can count on power plays and reverses, When it goes into its "B" or deeper formation, you can count on less power with more reverses and passes. The Norte Dame system, running all of its plays from one formation, provides no such tip-offs for its opponents.

"It does not seem reasonable to suppose that the Notre Dame system could have been so successful, so overwhelming, without being fundamentally sound in its conception. The elements which went into its making were speed, deception, precision in timing, and the perfection blocking. The man on the street and even some of Rockne's coaching opponents probably felt that he possessed a form of magic, a sort of football legerdemain, that he worked in a superhuman fashion his wonders to perform. But the wizardry, the magic, the supernatural element of his success was, in the main, sweat and hard work and toil and attention detail and then more sweat coupled with organization." [156]

Incomplete Pass Rule of 1926

1926 brought a new rule intended to rein in the passing game. It called for a 5-yard penalty for any incomplete pass after the first in any series of downs.

Passing from the Single Wing

There was a widespread belief that the Single Wing had some fundamental deficiencies as a passing formation. The unbalanced line presented pass protection problems. Also, some people felt the tight formation limited longer passing. However, using the Single Wing, Texas A&M made successful use of the run-pass option in 1927. In a letter to Allison Danzig in 1954 Joel Hunt, the A&M quarterback during that period stated, "our best long gainer was a single wing option run or pass to the strong side." [157] This is same play would help Dick Kazmaier of Princeton win the Heisman trophy more than twenty years later. Hunt went on in that same letter, "We had a passing offense that swept Southern Methodist, the heralded 'aerial circuit,' off the field."[158]

Man in Motion

It was also in 1927 that Stagg introduced the man in motion with the objective of using him as a pass receiver. Stagg had used the "man in motion" as early as 1898 as a decoy. He used him going away from the formation and as a trap blocker, motioning him back toward the center. It was not until 1927 that he began to use, what he called his "flyer" as a pass target for the passer.[159]

Deep Punt & Short Punt

The Deep Punt, sometimes called the Long Punt formation, was fundamentally a configuration used for punting but it did allow the fullback to receive a direct snap. He could then fake the punt and carry out a buck in the middle of the line. Alternatively, he could hand the ball to one of the up backs on an off-tackle or sweep play.

Numerous teams used the Short Punt Formation at this time, most notably Minnesota, Michigan, Yale, and Cornell. The formation is a versatile attack from a balanced formation. It was ideal for passing because the ends were loose, the backs were in a position to go to either side, and the passer was in a good position. The balanced line created good protection for the passer. At the same time, it was strong for bucking and lent itself well to lateral passing. The inherent weakness of the Short Punt formation was that none of the backs aligned outside the defensive tackle or end. This weakened any misdirection in the running game. When there was an attempt to position a back outside the defensive end the formation at once lost its balance.[160]
Figures 127, 128

Figure 127 Deep Punt formation

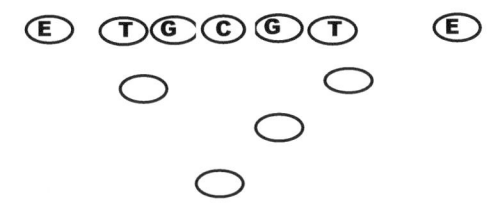

128 Short Punt formation

Some typical plays from the Short Punt formation follow. *Figure 129-131*[161]

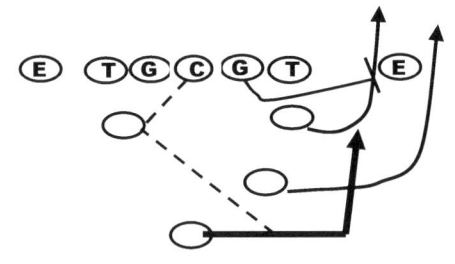

Figure 129 The Short Punt Off Tackle

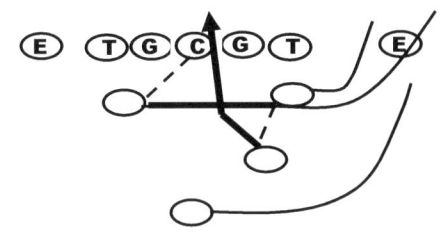

Figure 130 The Short Punt Cutback Play

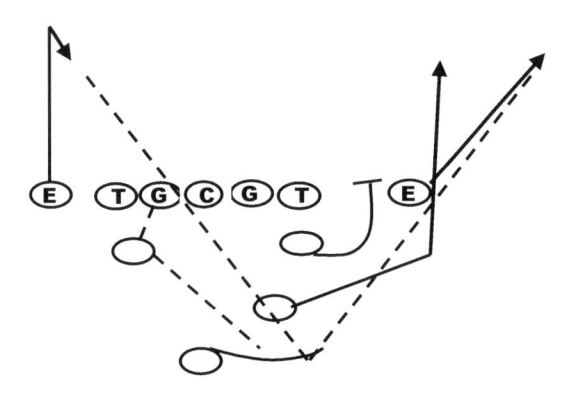

Figure 131 Short Punt Forward Pass   **Note** The "Button Hook Route by the left end.

Defending the Short Punt

The over shifted 6-2-3 defense was frequently used in an attempt to stop the short punt's bucks and the slants off tackles to the strength of the formation.

Figure 132 [162]

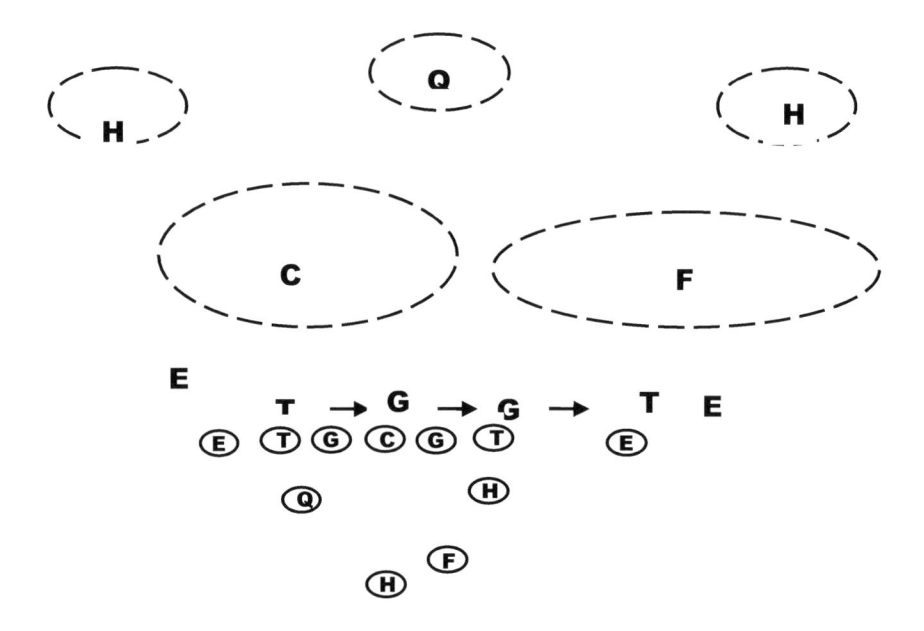

Figure 132 The Over shifted 6-2 used to defend the Short Punt's strong side bucks and off-tackle slants.

Five Man Line Versus Single Wing

The origins and limited use of the five-man line were discussed in a previous section of this text.

Although the five-man line was used by Percy Haughton at Harvard in 1914, he used it sparingly and only in particular situations. There is evidence that Ray Morrison of S.M.U. used the five-man line in the waning moments of games when they were protecting a lead in 1917.

In writing to Allison Danzig in 1951, Andy Kerr stated, "Against Notre Dame in the Rose Bowl game on January 1, 1925, Pop Warner played a type of five-man line with the Stanford team." [163] However, the five-man line was not a primary or every down defense even into the 1920s. That will change shortly. Doc Wilce's Ohio State team used it repeatedly in their upset of archrival, Chicago, in 1923.

Teams began to use the 5-3 versus the Single Wing. *See Figure 133* [164]

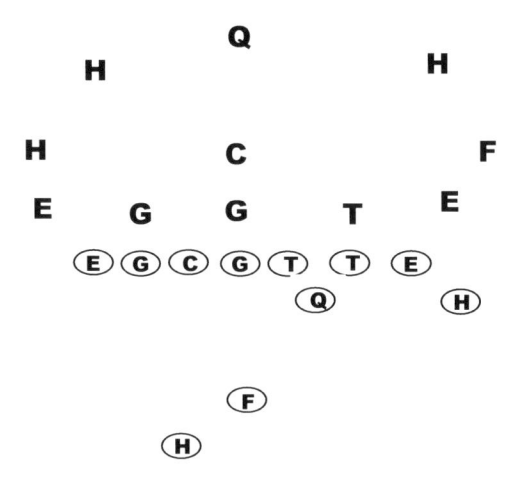

Figure 133 The 5-3-2-1 Defense versus the Single Wing

Double Wing Reappears

As the decade neared its end, the Double Wing formation made a significant reappearance. Powers such as Army, Holy Cross, Colgate, Pittsburgh, Yale, Harvard, Princeton, and Brown were all using it. *Figure 134*

There were numerous forms of the Double Wing. It was run from a balanced or unbalanced line. Obviously, the common element to all of these formations was the presence of two wingbacks. The two inside backs were aligned as either a tailback and fullback or a tailback and a blocking back. In one unusual formation, Dutch Meyer aligned the two inside backs at an equal depth, creating a twin tailback set. The Double Wing is an excellent passing formation, with a balanced and deceptive running attack. Some claim to see several weaknesses with the Double Wing formation. It is susceptible to crashing defensive ends. Mastering the timing of the deception plays is hard. Also, it is thought to be difficult to create an inside power running game.[165]

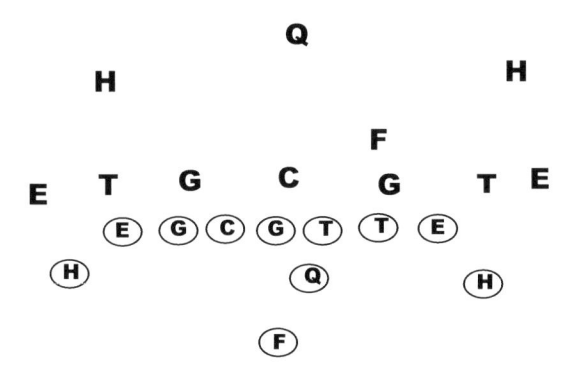

Figure 134 The revival of "Pop" Warner's Double Wing; Shown vs. an over shifted Seven Diamond.

[155] Daly, Charles D., *American Football*, (New York and London, Harper & Brothers Publishers, 1921), p. 37,40
[156] Danzig, *The History of American Football*, pp.64-65.
[157] Danzig *The History of American Football*, p. 45
[158] Danzig *The History of American Football*, p. 45
[159] Danzig, *Oh How They Played the Game*, p. 57
[160] Dana X. Bible, *Championship Football*, (New York, Prentice-Hall Inc., 1947) p.71, 111
[161] Rockne, Knute K., *Coaching The Way of the Winner*, (New York, The Devin-Adair Co., 1925) p.32-35
[162] Killinger, Glenn, W., *Football*, A.S.Barnes and Co., New York, 1939, p. 79
[163] Danzig, *The History of American Football*, p. 111
[164] Killinger, p. 76
[165] Bible, p 71

CHAPTER EIGHT

The Game Opens up

(1930 –1939)

Four-Spoke Secondary

History shows that the first use of a "four spoke secondary" was in 1930. This was a defense initially used against the spread formation. There were six men on the line of scrimmage, a single linebacker, and four secondary defenders. It allowed for both a good pass rush and four pass defenders. *Figure 135*

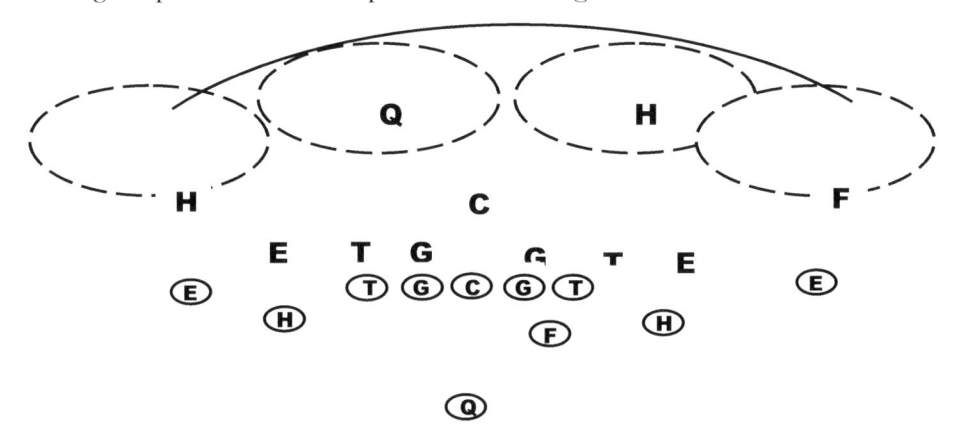

Figure 135 The 6-1-4 Defense Thought to be the first use of the "4 spoke secondary".

George Halas and the T-Formation

On offense, the "T" formation began its revival in 1930 when Ralph Jones used the "T" as the Head Coach of the Chicago Bears. Jones only coached the Bears for three seasons 1930-1932. Along with George Halas the team owner, and a consultant named Clark Shaughnessy, who was then the coach at the University of Chicago, they began to adjust Amos Alonzo Stagg's old "T". Stagg had used the "T" much like the other offenses at the turn of the century. He ran dives, bucks, and power plays. However, the Single Wing and Double Wing of "Pop" Warner displaced it. Halas believed that the Bears had become boring and predictable on offense at times, so he, Jones, and Shaughnessy devoted much time to transforming Stagg's old "T." At the time, football was mostly an up-the-middle power game, so Jones worked on opening things up. They created a "T" formation attack using two split ends at times. And using a halfback in motion. *Figure 136*

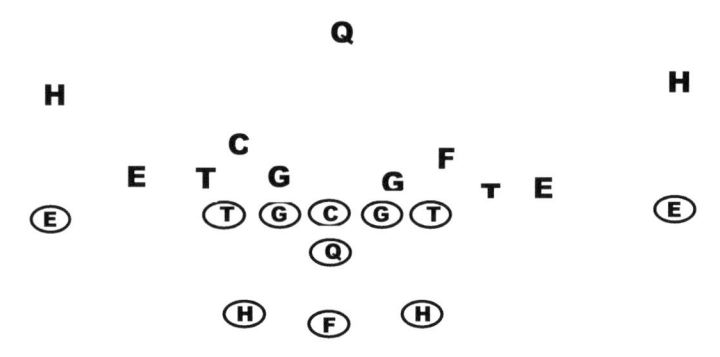

Figure 136 The T-formation with two split ends

The T-formation is a simple set-up that lines three backs in a row behind the quarterback. The QB takes the snap directly from the center. In today's game, the quarterback taking a direct snap from center is not unusual. However, back in the 1930s, it was a radical idea. The quarterback would then hand the ball off to one of his backs. The hand-to-hand snap from the center to the quarterback was quick and allowed the running backs to hit the holes at full speed. In the Single Wing, or Double Wing the tailback had to wait for the ball and then start running. Debatably, this small change has had the biggest influence on any innovation in the history of the game.

Clark Shaughnessy and Ralph Jones

Ralph Jones (c. 1880 - July 26, 1951) coached Wabash College for a short time. He previously had coached at the Lake Forest Academy but was working as an assistant at the University of Illinois when George Halas hired him. While at Lake Forest, he had experimented with simple alternatives on the basic "T" formation. With "Red" Grange, "Bronko" Nagurski, and the new "T" formation they turned the Chicago Bears into a winner. In addition to lining the quarterback directly under center, they increased the spacing of the offensive line and devised blocking schemes that would allow the running backs to run through the line and run to daylight. They designed plays that allowed the running back to fake a run and throw a jump pass. When Jones left the Bears in 1932, Halas teamed up with Clark Shaughnessy, who was still the head coach at the University of Chicago. Shaughnessy devised very complex formations and by 1935, the T became, even more, efficient.

Ralph Jones and Shaughnessy worked tirelessly to develop their T-formation. They began sending one back in motion toward the sideline before passing the ball to him. *Figure 137* Using a man in motion was not groundbreaking but was unique in that up until that time a motioning back nothing but a decoy. The motion spread opposing defenses out and allowed more room to run in the middle of the field. As stated earlier, the three men also created larger splits between the offensive linemen. This wider alignment forced the defensive line to open up accordingly. On a quick dive play, which became a fundamental part of the Bears offense, the linemen did not have to double-team at the point of attack. This was a significant difference from what was done in the Single Wing. Instead, with the back now hitting the hole so quickly, all the linemen had to do was achieve a "stalemate" with their opponents. He could keep them in place, and let the runner slip through the opening created by the wide splits.

Since most defenses attempted to be quick in responding to the first move of the quarterback, Jones and Shaughnessy produced a series of counters, or 'misdirection' plays to deceive them. The quarterback would spin away from the line and fake a dive before either handing off or pitching the ball to another back headed in a different direction. The fake handoff also came in handy for play-action passes. The Bears would fake the dive to a halfback before throwing a pass. Defensive coaches now not only had to worry about the multitude of running plays being run to both sides of the line, but they also had to worry about the pass on any given down. It was a drastic change from the ruthless power game of years past.

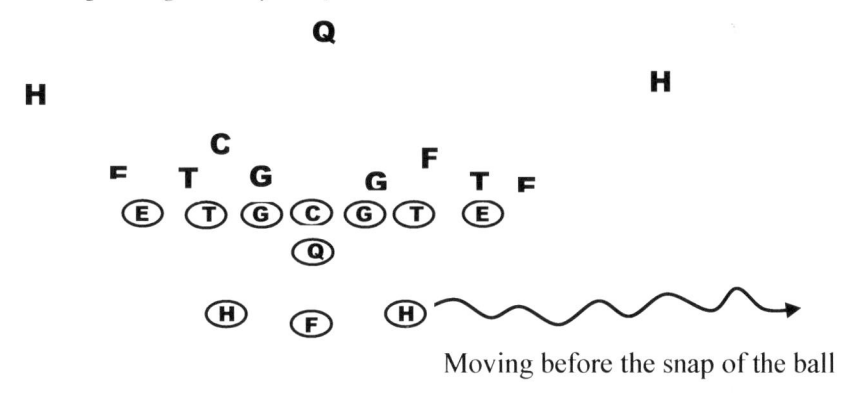

Moving before the snap of the ball

Figure 137 The Halfback in motion

It's Still the Single Wing

Although the "T" formation would soon dominate the game, the prevailing offense of the 1930s, and well into the 1940s, was the Single Wing. The typical Single Wing of this period operated out of an unbalanced line. Some teams would split the end to the short side. The primary objective of this offense is power and deception. The Single Wing provides, perhaps, the best power blocking or any offense in the game. The quarterback, fullback, and tailback can receive a direct pass from the center. Three cycles of plays can develop from these three different snaps. There is excellent deception by the quarterback and fullback handling the ball with fakes, spinners, fades, and laterals. Although it was not thought of as a passing offense at that time, there were excellent opportunities to execute some very fast passes. There are four quick receivers; the wing, the quarterback, the long side end, and the short side or split end. The pass protection is superb on the long side, but coaches had to be cautious about the short side rush. The off-tackle and tackle smashes to the strong side were devastating. Perimeter or outside runs to the long side could also be overwhelming to a defense. Additionally, it was a good quick kick formation. Offensive coaches found that running to the short side of the formation was problematic. Also, because of the short side rush, throwing longer passes were a problem. Below are some examples of plays of the Single Wing formation of this period. *Figures 138-143* [166]

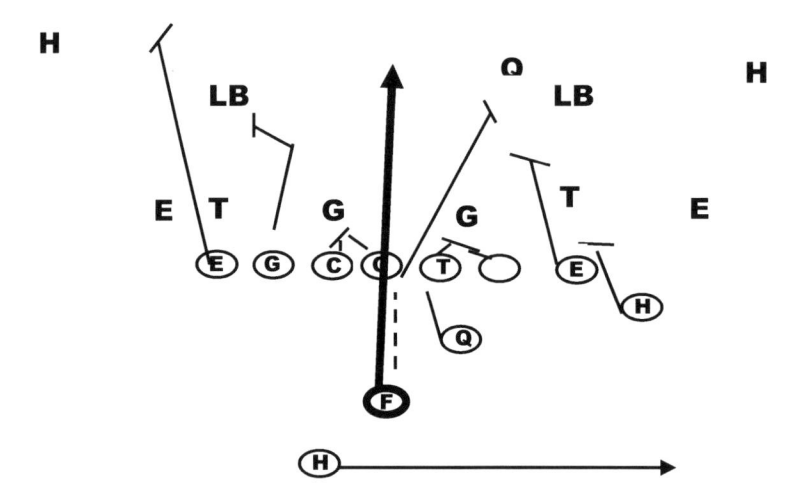

Figure 138 The Straight Buck

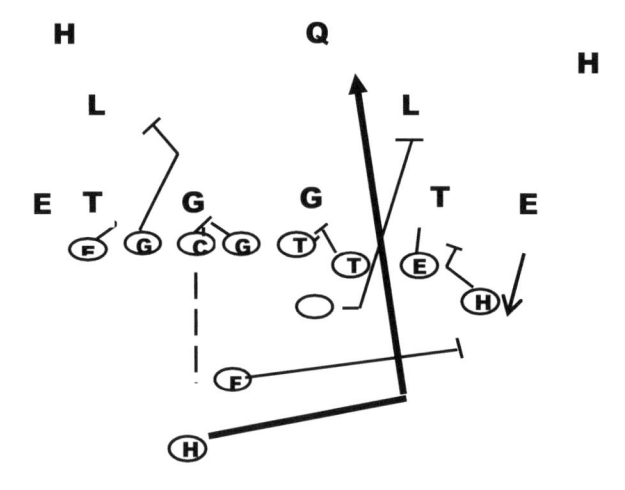

Figure 139 The Slant Off-Tackle

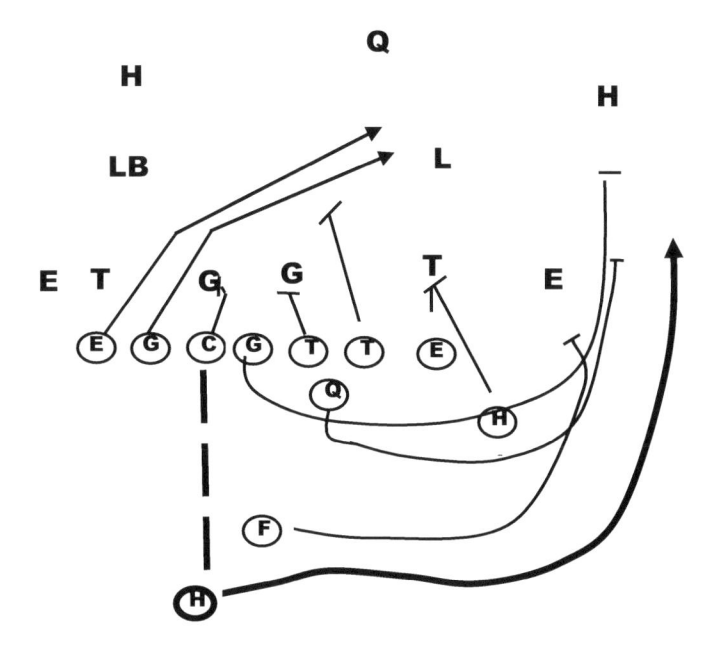

Figure 140 The Sweep

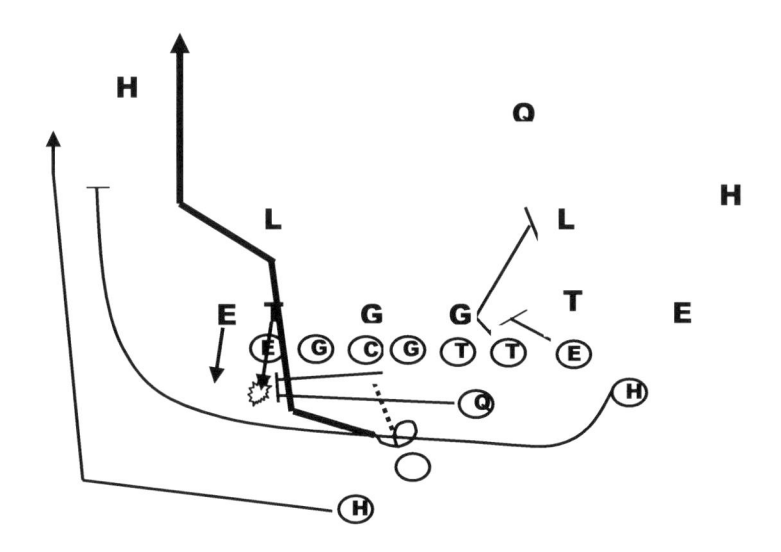

Figure 141 The Spinner

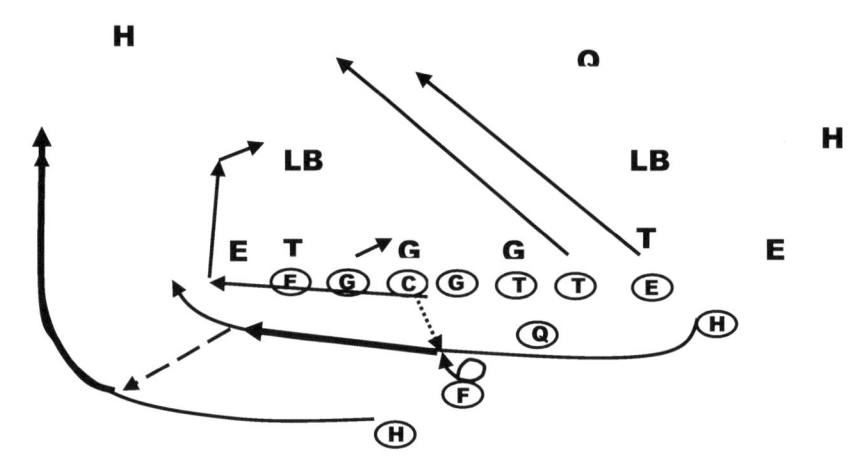

Figure 142 The Lateral Pass from the Spinner

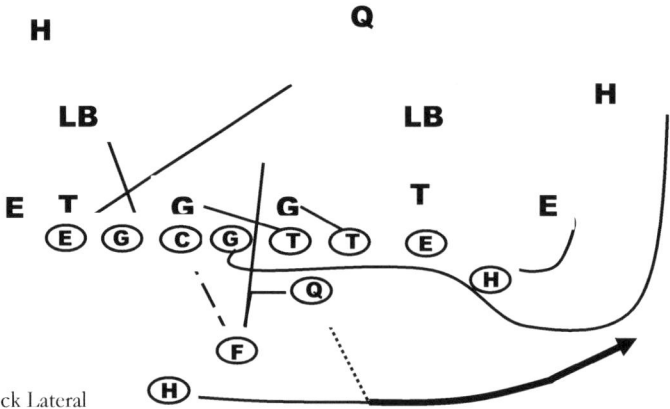

Figure 143 The Buck Lateral

"Fritz" Crisler

One of the predominant coaches during that time was Friz Crisler. He had some trouble at the start, winning only 10 of 17 games at Minnesota. He coached at Princeton University from 1932-1937 and won 35 games while losing only nine and tying two. It is thought that Crisler was one of the first to implement a new blocking principle. He abandoned attempting to drive the opponent straight back toward the goal line but rather had his blockers turn the defenders to the sideline creating a larger hole for the ball carrier to run through.

In 1938, Crisler left Princeton and took over the University of Michigan program. It was during this time while he was in the process of winning 71 games while losing only 17 and tying 3, that Crisler fathered two-platoon football, later he would also help kill it.

In a 1956 interview, Crisler discussed his late night conversations with F. Scott Fitzgerald the night before Princeton Games. The famous author was an avid Princeton fan and liked to make suggestions to Crisler. "He was a smart football fan. Sometimes he had a play or a new strategy he wanted me to use," said Crisler. "Some of the ideas Scott used to suggest to me over the phone were reasonable—and some were fantastic."

In the fantastic department, Crisler cited an example: Fitzgerald, he said, "came up with a scheme for a whole new offense; something that involved a two-platoon system." [167]

Crisler's explanation regarding the two-platoon system; "We arrived at the two-team system at Michigan not out of any great ingenuity but pure necessity," he points out. "Michigan was to meet Army in 1945. It was a veteran Army team, and Michigan had mostly freshmen. I was perfectly aware that our youngsters could not stand up against Army for sixty minutes and we would have to spell them off at intervals.

"We divided the line into two groups, one whose abilities were best suited to offense, the other best gifted in defense. Then we ran the offensive team in whenever we gained possession. When we lost possession which was frequently, the defensive line took over." [168]

Two-platoon football grew enormously, right from the start. However, it was costly for the schools and appalled disciples of pure old-time football. Crisler recognized the problem and moved to abolish it. He headed the football rules committee that eliminated unlimited substitution in early 1953.

Defending the Single Wing: Overshifted 6

To defend against the Single Wing, defenses continued to "Overshift" their 6-man line by sliding the defensive line toward the strength, or long side, of the offensive formation *Figure 144*.

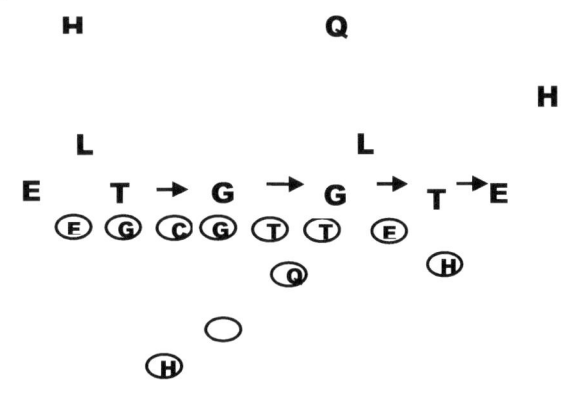

Figure 144 The Overshifted 6 Man Line Defense. It had also been used against the Short Punt.

Lou Little: The Columbia Defense

Lou Little at Columbia had a unique approach to stopping the Single Wing. Described by Arthur Sampson of the Boston Herald on December 26, 1933; "Unlike most teams, Columbia linemen are taught a low, fast, head and shoulder charge on defense. The linemen do not attempt to make tackles. The sole job is to break through into the opposing backfield and spill the interference. There is only one assignment for the guards, tackles, and ends. They do not use their hands to fight against the charge of the offensive e team. They charge on defense just the way all teams do on offense, driving head and shoulders into the opposing linemen with the attempt to work straight across the line of scrimmage."

As described in Danzig's *The History of American Football*: "The end play which Little teaches also is the type to bother the Cardinals (the article was written as Columbia was preparing to play Stanford in the Rose Bowl.) Columbia wingmen do not wait for the slow forming Warner interference to snowplow over them. They crash into the opposing backfield from a sprinter's start and, instead of trying to fight off the interference, they are taught to do the hitting themselves. By driving head and shoulders into the blockers who are headed their way, Columbia ends close up any opportunity to make a hole between tackle and end. They are responsible for plays inside their position only. If the end cleans out all interference on wide end runs, he has done his complete job in the Little system of defense. There always is a flanking backer-up who has the job of bringing down any runner trying to circle the flank." [169]

Lou Little is credited with implementing another significant defensive adjustment. He was the first to employ a true rotated or "squirmed" secondary to combat the strong side power of the single wing. He moved his halfback (H) on the strong side of the formation up and moved his free safety (Q) closer to the wingback side. *Figure 145* [170]

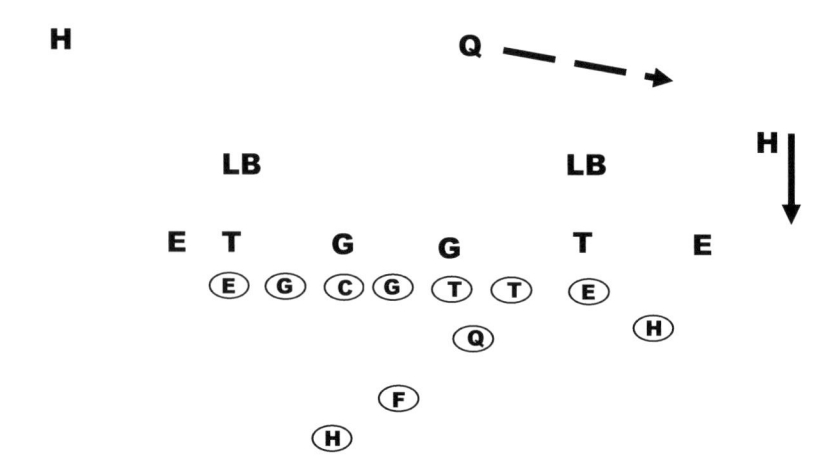

Figure 145 The rotated or "squirmed" secondary

More on The Notre Dame Box

What set the Notre Dame Box apart from other offenses was the unique backfield set behind a balanced line. They often shifted into the box from a "T" formation. In our section on shifting offenses, we have written at length about the Notre Dame system. The formation relied on deception, speed, disciplined blocking and passing. It has excellent power to the strong side of the formation along with a good perimeter attack to the strong side. The end runs were a big part of the system. Because of the balanced line, the formation also had a superb weakside attack inside the end. There were three "quick" receivers in the passing game and because of the balanced line and tight formation, exceptional pass protection. We showed several of the more common adjustments in the offensive formation in other sections of this text. The basic alignment of the backs allowed for outstanding deception in backfield play. Since almost all of the plays started very much alike, Rockne referred to them as his "sequence" of plays. He stated in his book "*Coaching, the Way of the Winner*" – "This sequence also means that they (the plays) depend on one upon the other and that their successful use lies in their being used in an intelligent and logical sequence. In other words, the use of one play may not gain much ground, but has the effect of making another play which looks much like it, very strong." [171]

Finally, the location of the deep back presented many opportunities for the quick kick.

The shortcomings of the Notre Dame system was the outside attack to the weak side of the formation, especially when there was a split end to that side. The use of shifting made it imperative that all eleven players be well disciplined, precise in their execution, and well practiced in the timing. Although Rockne seemed to be able to achieve that discipline and timing with regularity, others who tried to replicate the Notre Dame system had difficulty. Finally, with the regularity with which the two guards are pulling there is added pressure on the center in performing his assignments.

Following are several popular plays from the quarterback sequence of the Notre Dame Box. *Figures 146-148* [172]

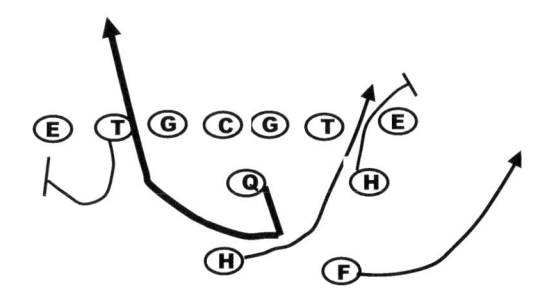

Figure 146 Quarterback fake to halfback, pivots and dives backside

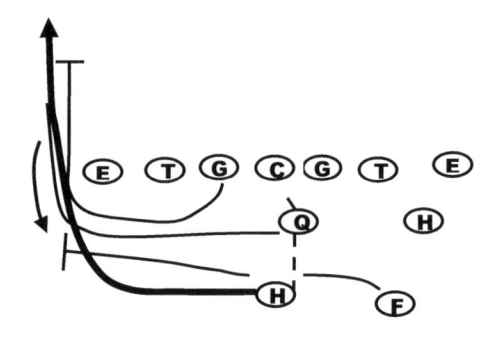

Figure 147 Weakside Sweep by Halfback

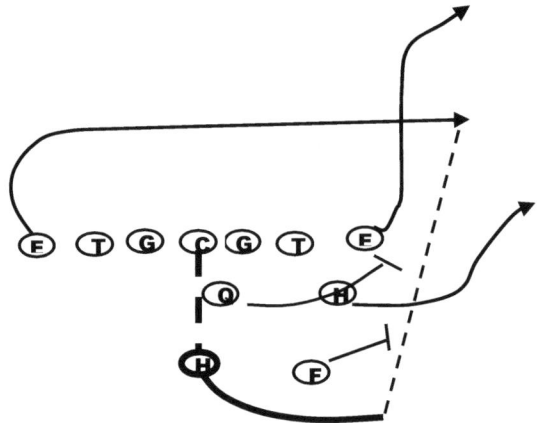

Figure 148 Flood Pass

Rockne stated his thoughts on the Notre Dame system and shifting in his book "*Coaching; the Way of the Winner*":

"Some of the older coaches who have been unsuccessful in stopping shift attacks want the shift legislated against. However, I think the rules today are perfectly clear and concise, and are for the best interests of the game. A shifting team is a beautiful thing to watch; it has color, and it appeals to the spectator. It has become an integral part of offensive football, and when fairly used, under good officiating, has no advantage over the set and go offense except that it is harder to stop.

"It is best to keep your shift formation just as simple as possible. It is possible, of course, to work up complex offensive shifts, but, as a rule, the coach using these spends so much time practicing the shift that his team is weak on tackling and blocking, and is beaten because of these weaknesses. And besides, in these days of intensive scouting, we cannot fool the defensive team like we should like to. We find that we can get better results by the perfection of execution with some deception, rather than by depending entirely on complex shifts.

"A team which uses just a single shift is not using the shift to its fullest efficiency. The arrangement, which we use, is to work plays without a shift; after one shift; after two shifts, and even after three shifts. However, the three changes are used more to kill time than anything else.

"It is also well, if you can, to develop a change of pace in your shifts. By this, I mean develop two shifts, which look alike, one slow, and one fast. By mixing up your shift attack in this manner, the defense is just as much in the dark as to when the ball is to be passed as they would be in the set formation when the offensive team is using the snap signal. The team using a single shift, with always the same cadence and rhythm, allows the defense to get used to the rhythm and in a short time, the defensive line will be getting the jump on the offensive line. This would be fatal. If, however, you keep changing the rhythm and keep using plays with no shift, one, and two shifts, then you have the defense back on their haunches, waiting, which is just where you want them." [173]

Dick Harlow and the Single Wing

In 1937, Dick Harlow at Harvard began to run Double Wing Plays from the Single Wing formation. This was significant because it created confusion for defensive coaches who were planning different defenses for each of those formations. Harlow put a great emphasis on spinners, reverses, double reverses, and fake reverses.

Running Shift

Carl Snavely, first at North Carolina and Later at Cornell had a great deal of success on offense using the "running shift". Snavely said that Alabama in 1934

" employed some maneuvers from the short punt formation that looked awfully good to me. Alabama was using the Notre Dame system and would shift from the original "T" Formation into the Notre Dame box or into the short punt.

"We could not do this in quite the same way from our single wing and with an unbalanced line. So I hit upon the idea of a running shift, on the initial movement of which our men moved almost exactly as they did on a reverse to the weak side. Two linemen pull out, one moving from the strong side to the weak side, the other dropping into the spot vacated by him. Thus, we have a balanced line from which we used a small number of reverses, mousetraps, and passes, employing the spinner idea and copied to a great extent, I confess, from the Alabama attack. "[174]

Triple Wing

While coaching at Brown, Tuss McLaughry was the first to use the "Triple Wing". Notice the use of the unbalanced line. *Figure 149* [175]

Figure 149 The Unbalanced Line Triple Wing used at Brown

The formation was used extensively by, and is very much associated with, "Dutch" Myers at Texas Christian University. Certainly, Myers was the biggest name in spread formation football at the time.

Used less frequently than the Single Wing, Double Wing, or Notre Dame System, the Triple Wing was still a significant development. We have shown the typical Myers Triple Wingback formation below *Figure 150*. They also used two split ends, creating a spread formation. *Figure 151* The objective of the formation was deception, speed, and passing. It contained a strong perimeter attack and naturally a strong passing attack. It was good for lateral passes and an excellent quick kicking formation. The shortcomings of the Triple Wing were severe. There was absolutely no power for line bucks. There was no short side attack. No ability to produce power at any spot on the line of scrimmage, and with only one back to receive the snap there was only one series from which to create plays.

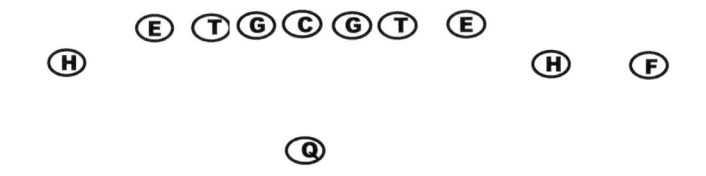

Figure 150 The Triple Wing Formation

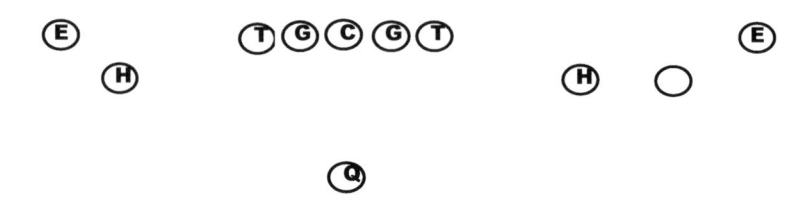

Figure 151 Aligning the Triple Wing with Two Split-ends, creating a Spread Formation: Today called an "empty" set

The Rediscovered Minnesota Shift

Bernie Bierman improved and further developed his Minnesota shift. Bierman believed in the need for a balanced attack between running, passing and kicking. However, he felt that the emphasis on each was dependent upon the defense his team faced in any given week.

"We have built up, let us say, what we consider a well-balanced attack. We can plunge, pass, kick, handle the ball well and fake. But a team can never have exactly the same strength in all of these departments at the same time. Now the defensive strength of our opponents as applied to these different abilities varies. As a result, it behooves us each game to emphasize the style of play with which our opponents of the day are least able to cope.

"Maybe we have taken great pride as the season progressed in our driving and running strength. Our line has outstanding offensive power and, in addition, we have a sturdy bucker and a good off-tackle attack. There comes a Saturday however when we meet a defense that loves to stop that kind of football and has the ability to do it. Perchance our passing and kicking games can't begin to compare with our running game, but, comparatively speaking, they would be our best bet against this particular opponent.

"We all have heard the expert who complained that a certain team 'played a dumb game' on a particular Saturday.

'I saw team A play team B,' he'll say, a couple of weeks ago and it tore B's line to pieces. The A men marched through for three touchdowns. The blooming fools played team C last week and wasted all afternoon throwing passes, running wide and trying trick stuff. Of course, the time they went into the line, they didn't do so well, but if they had kept at it, they would have gotten things going just like they did against.'
"The answer is that against C's defense, A's offense undoubtedly was of an entirely different shade than against B's. Football is not an exhibition. It is a contest which demands that the strength of one team be applied against that of another team in the most practical way possible." [176]

Two variations of Bierman's Minnesota shift are below. *See Figure 152*

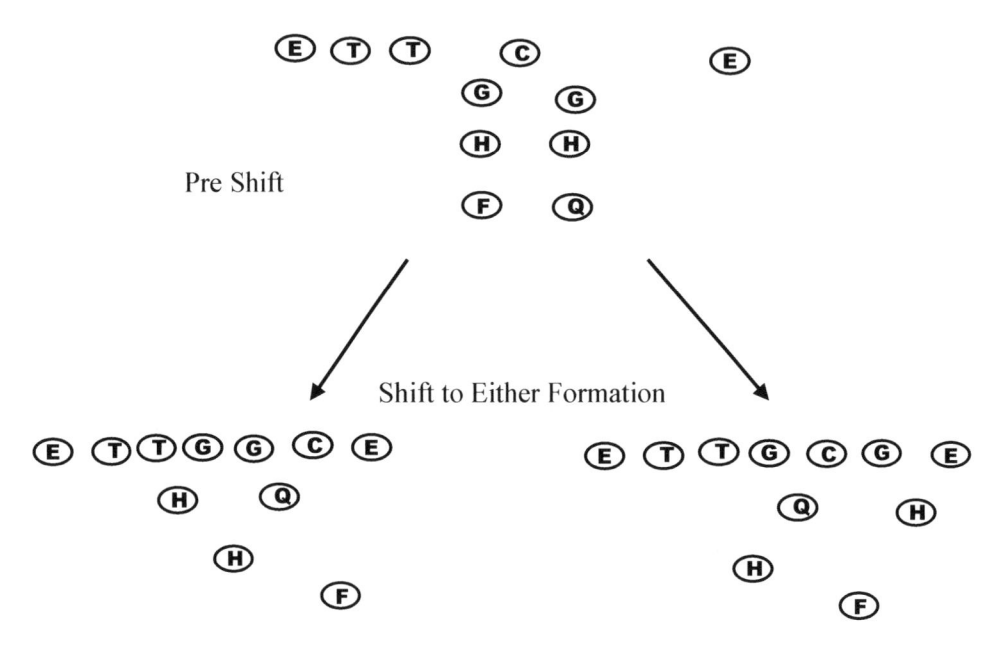

Figure 152 The Minnesota Shift in its later years.

The 5 Man Line Defenses

The origins and limited use of the five-man line were discussed in a previous section of this text.

Clyde Littlefield used the five-man line as his primary defense at Texas in 1930. When he defeated Ray Morrison's S.M.U. Team 25-6, it got the country's attention. By the middle of the decade, several collegiate teams throughout the country were using it. As the decade ended, the five-man line was a central element of college football.

In the November 22, 1937, issue of the Boston Herald sports writer, Arthur Sampson wrote, "The success that some of the teams had in using the five-man line defense started a wholesale use of this arrangement this fall. It also started a cry for some defensive legislation on the theory that so many defensive arrangements were hurting the offense." [177]

The 5-4-2 is thought to be have been introduced by the University of Illinois around this time. The 5-3-3 appeared everywhere during the final years of the decade.

The 5-3 proved to be good versus the pass. With the three linebackers, it was excellent against the buck and good against the lateral passes and deception of the "T" formation, especially when the linebackers used a zone defense. The combination of five linemen and three linebackers made the defense superb for stunting to rush the passer. However, if the linebackers played inside the end or if they played man-to-man against a man in motion, the defense was weak against the end run. On the other hand, if the linebackers stacked the defensive ends or played outside, the defense was weak against the inside plays. Below is a diagram showing the 5-3-3 adjustments against a man in motion from the "T" formation. The outside linebacker picks up the man in motion and carries him through his zone. If he goes deep, the linebacker passes him off to the halfback who plays him man-to-man. The safety then must pick up the end man-to-man and the opposite halfback will play the other end man-to-man. *Figure 153*

Figure 154 shows a standard pass rush stunt from the 5-3-3 defense.

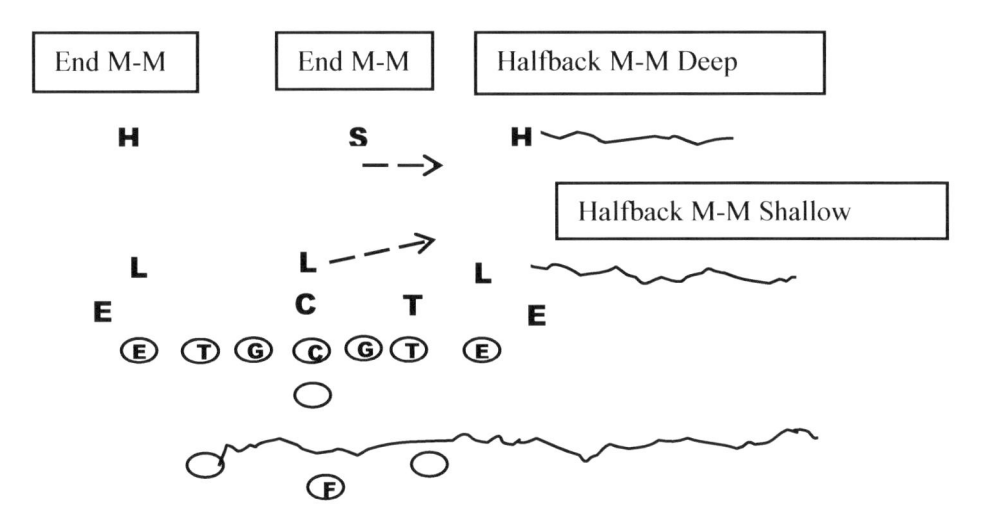

Figure 153 5-3-3 defensive adjustment versus the "T" Halfback motion

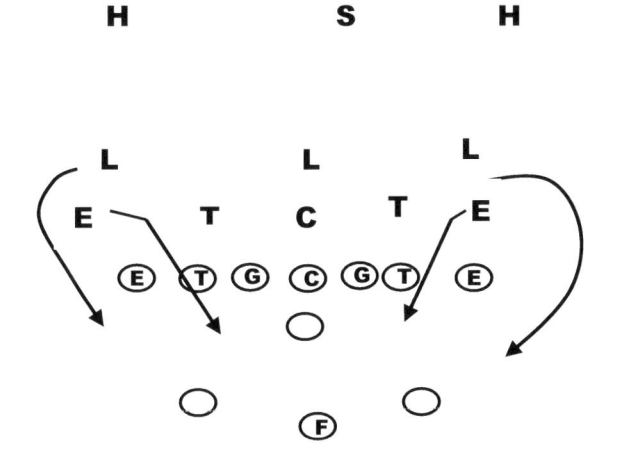

Figure 154 Pass stunt by the defensive ends and outside linebackers from the 5-3-3 defense

A fundamental 5-4-2 defense was then, and remains, an outstanding defense against the "T" formation. We have shown how this defense would adjust differently from the 5-3-3 against the same motion as above. *Figure 155*

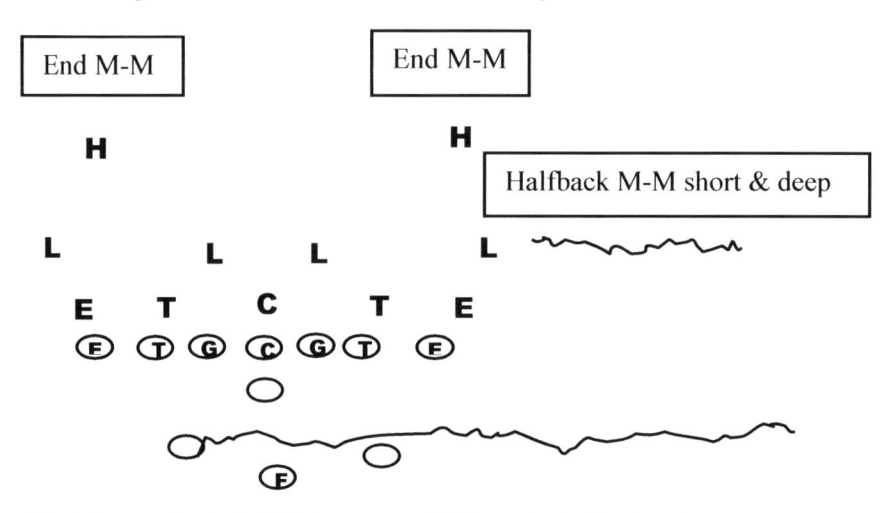

Figure 155 Adjustment by the 5-4-2 defense versus "T" formation halfback motion

Defensive Six Man Line Shifts

The standard defensive arrangements during the first part of the decade were some form of the Six-man line or the Seven-man line. As the decade wore on adjustments were made to these basic alignments to cope with the changing offenses. New ideas were developed that would change how the defense was played. As attacks became more sophisticated, defensive coaches realized that they could no longer line up in a standard defense and cope with the multitude of offensive possibilities.

Offensive coaches could no longer prepare their blockers for a particular defensive alignment. They could no longer spend their practice time preparing for a specific six-man line or seven-man line defense. Blockers now had to have the ability to adjust their blocking scheme from week to week and from team to team. It would even be necessary for them to change their blocking pattern in the midst of the game.

There are numerous defensive alignments characterized by having six players on the line of scrimmage. The Loose Six, which has the defensive tackle playing outside the offensive tackle and the linebacker inside, was a common defense against the Single Wing and Double Wing formations that employed a balanced line. The Overshifted Six and the Under shifted Six were used versus teams that used unbalanced lines, most notably the Single Wing.

As discussed earlier, the Overshifted 6 has the defensive line moved either a ½ man or full man to the strong side of the formation. The two linebackers are under-shifted. It is excellent against the running game, having the equivalent of a seven-man line on the strong side. The linebacker on that side is in a position to meet the charge of the fullback or to move with the blocking of the play. The weak side backer and defensive end on that side were in a ready position to stop reverses and end runs to that side. *Figure 156*

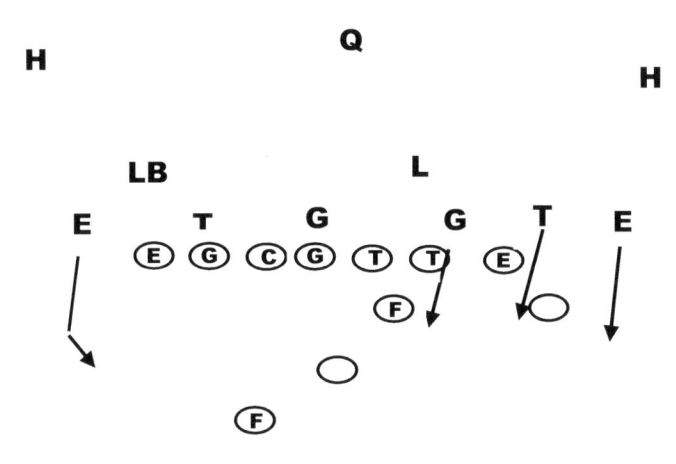

Figure 156 The Overshifted Six-Man Line. Used when the defense was expecting the offense to run to the strength of the formation.

The Under-Shifted Six-man line has the line moving to the short side of the formation and the linebackers sliding to the strong side of the formation. The common use of the Under-shifted line combated the offensive formation aligned to the short side or boundary side of the field. That left many opportunities for them to run to the weak side of their formation but to the wide side of the field. The flanking position of the defensive end to the short side of the formation prevented the offense from taking advantage of their alignment. The strong side linebacker played wide to defend both the off-tackle and outside run to the strength of the formation. On the pass, he would defend the strong side flat. The weak side linebacker moved inside where he could meet the power plunges of the fullback. From this alignment, he still had to defend the short side outside zone on the pass. This left a rather large void in the short middle of the pass defense. To remedy this weakness teams dropped the strong side defensive Guard into pass coverage in the broad area between the two linebackers. See *Figure 157*

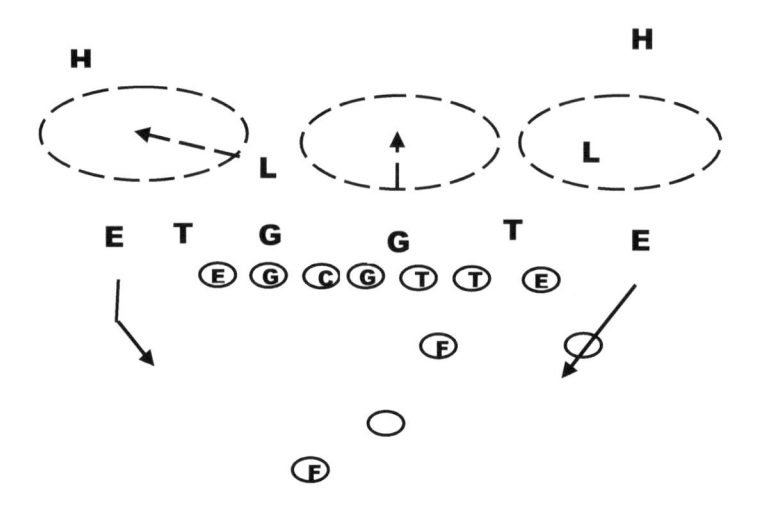

Figure 157 The under Shifted, Six man line, showing the middle zone of short pass defense created by dropping the strong defensive guard into the pass defense.

The Tight Six evolved from the Loose Six. It was often used when playing against the "Bears" "T" or what later became known as the "Tight" "T" formation. This balanced defensive alignment positioned the defensive tackles inside where they were in a better position to play the quick hitting dives of the "T" formation. It also placed the linebackers wider, which enabled them to play the short pass and the pass to a back coming out of the backfield. As motion by the halfbacks became a central aspect of the "T" formation, an added benefit, was the ability of the linebackers to quickly widen with the motioning back. *Figure 158*

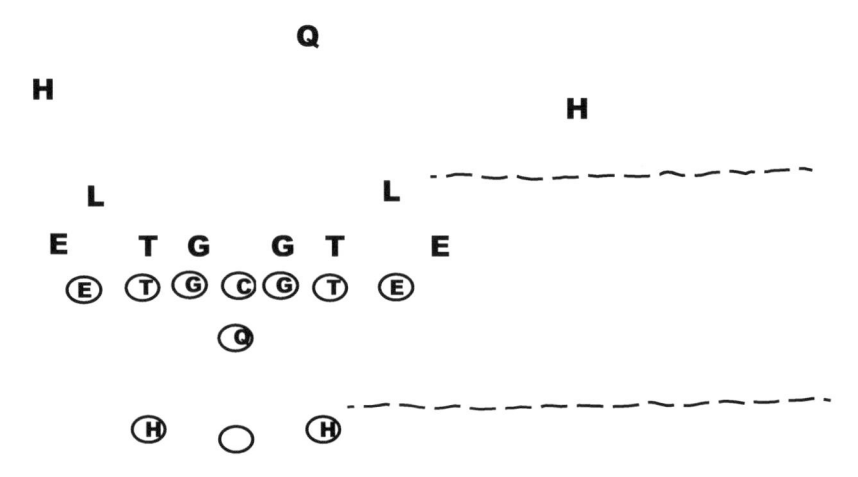

Figure 158 The Tight Six Defense versus the "Tight" T-formation. The dashed line indicates the reaction the linebacker had when a halfback went in motion.

It was around this time that the 6-3 defense made an appearance. The 6-3 placed nine men on or near the line of scrimmage and made it difficult for teams running the "Tight "T" to move the ball without the use of motion. *Figure 159* However, with only two halfbacks in the secondary there was definitely a problem in guarding against the "T"'s play action passes.

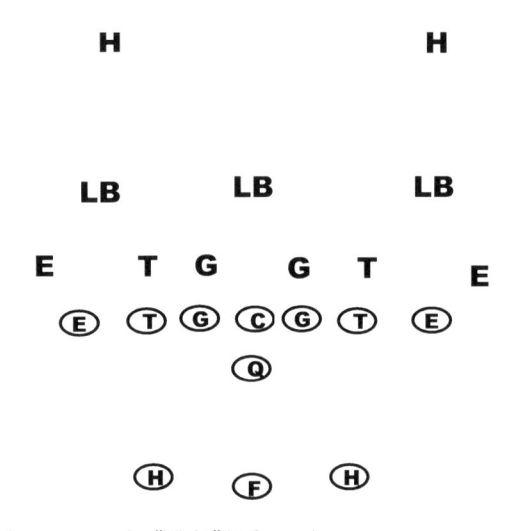

Figure 159 The 6-3 Defense versus the "Tight" T-formation

The 6-3-2 defense also proved to be very effective against the Double Wing formation. Dana Bible devised a defense in which the defensive ends crashed through the wingback and into the backfield while the defensive tackles delayed the offensive ends. This left seven defenders, the remaining four interior linemen, and the three linebackers, to defend against the inside run. *Figure 160* [178]

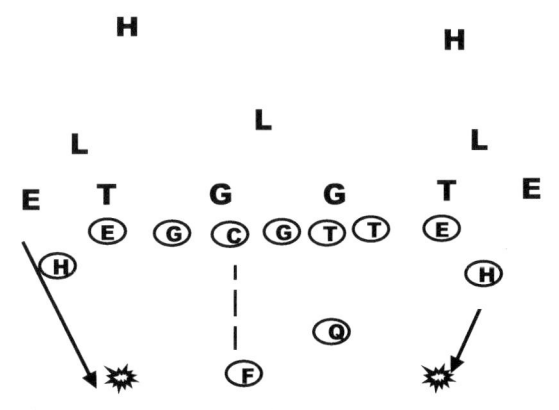

Figure 160 Bible's 6-3 Defense versus the Double Wing

In the middle part of the decade, some teams began to use a 6-1-4 defense against the spread formations. This defense allowed the teams who were using the basic six man line defenses to align against the spread without altering their fundamental philosophy of defense. They spread their defensive ends with the offensive formation and dropped them into pass coverage. By playing with a single linebacker, they were able to play with a four-man secondary defense, playing six men in the primary pass defense.

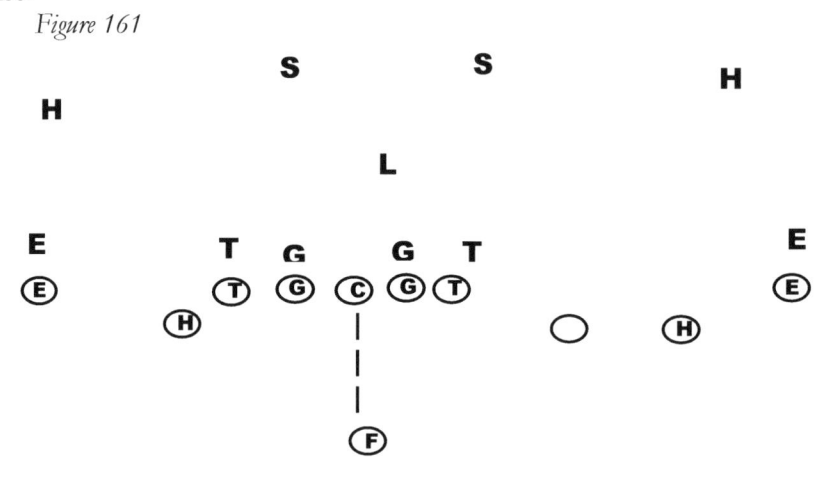

Figure 161

Figure 161 The 6-1 Defense versus the Spread formation

7 Man Line Defense

The 7-1-2-1 Defense proved to be very effective against Single Wing teams and Short Punt teams that stressed power running over passing. Because of the single linebacker in the middle, it was not a good defense in defending the "T" formation's quick openers. It had a difficult time breaking up the flat passes thrown by the "T". It could be capable of mounting a good pass rush against teams that operated from an unbalanced line. With the release of the short side end into a pass route, there were only two offensive linemen to block three rushing defenders. *Figure 162*

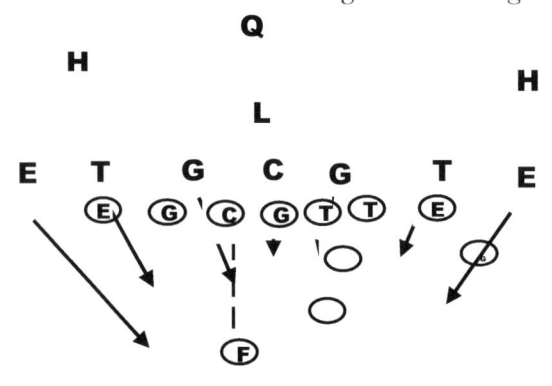

Figure 162 Effective pass rush of the 7-1-2 defense versus the unbalanced line

The 7-2-2 Defense

Against the "standing" "T" formation, the 7-2-2 was an excellent defense.

According to Don Faurot, the father of the "Split T" formation, "This defense is the best of the nine-man lines for the standing "T". Any seven-man spacing, with tight linebackers on each side, is an ideal rushing defense against any formation.

"The two defensive safeties must play man-to-man on the ends while the backers-up or ends pick up the halfbacks as they come out for passes. The defensive tackles and ends play wide to meet the outside plays. The defensive guards converge to stop the plays over the middle.

"This 7-2-2 defense has definite pass weaknesses over the center and in both flats. It is most practical against an opponent with a weak passing attack and strong rushing game. *Figure 163*

"When the flanker is sent out, a linebacker or an end must drop back to a halfback position. This adjustment converts the 7-2-2 defense into a 7-1-2- or an over shifted "six." [179]

He preferred to play his ends wide so that they were in a good position to widen with any halfback motion.

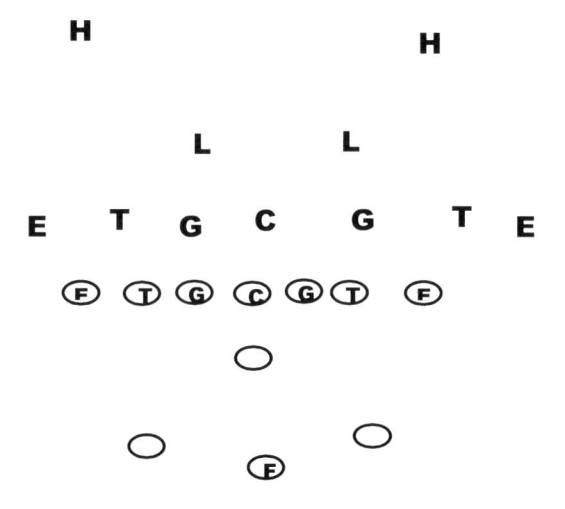

Figure 163 The 7-2-2 Defense versus the "Standing T" offense

The 8-2-1 Defense

This decade also brought the introduction of the 8-2-1 Defense; it proved to be exceptionally good versus the run and in rushing the passer. It was weak on the longer passes and had severe problems in adjusting to spread formations and semi-spreads.[180] The use of the 8-2-1, which would later become the 8-3 or "Gap 8" defense, would become nearly universal as a Goal-Line defense for years to come. *See Figure 164*

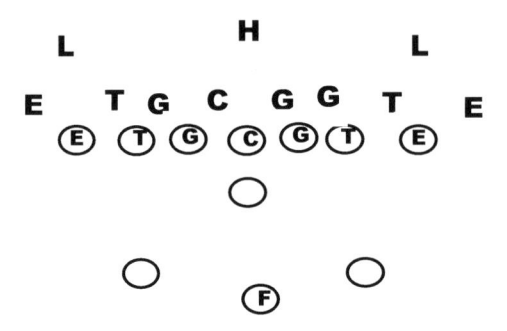

Figure 164 The 8-2-1 Defense. Later to become the 8-3 or "Gap 8 Defense

Attack Defense: Carl Snavely

In 1938, Carl Snavely took the unprecedented step of mounting a defensive attack using an abundance of defensive alignments. This served to create much confusion on the offensive side of the ball. Writing to Allison Danzig on June 22, 1951, Snavely said of his new approach,

"I believe that we were the first team to use a definite combination of defenses, including over shifted, under shifted, and standard 6, 5-5-1, and 7-1-2-1. We started using this at Cornell in 1938. Next, I believe we were the first team to use a jumping defense, jumping from one to another of these defenses after the offensive team had lined up and was waiting to start play.

"We first used this against Pennsylvania so as to make it difficult for the Pennsylvania quarterback to call his signals to advantage. The Penn quarterback called his signals after the team had come to its starting formation while he was looking over the defense. Our jumping defense was successful in counteracting their quarterbacking to the extent that they ceased calling the signals at the line of scrimmage and called them in the huddle." [181]

"Some definite attempt should be made on every play to get at least one of the defensive linemen well behind the opponents' line and on his feet. It is a better defense to throw the opponents for a loss whenever possible, even if the tactics used to accomplish this sometimes permit them to make an appreciable gain than to concentrate on stopping them for a short gain on each play. Nothing is more disconcerting to an offensive team than to find an opponent continually mixed up in its backfield. Even though the offense gains occasionally, a defensive lineman jumping through and tackling for a loss every few plays tends both to destroy confidence and frequently to cause bickering, faultfinding, and inefficiency in the ranks of the other team.

"Obviously, tactics that will result in getting well across the line standing up are more or less reckless. A man has to take a chance on being taken out of the play or getting through for the tackle. More conservative tactics might enable a man to stop the play at or near the line of scrimmage, but they seldom put him through for a clean tackle behind the line. Therefore, when a player gambles on getting through, the man next to him should employ more conservative tactics. The method of play may be interchanged between players as the game progresses, or sometimes one man may attempt to go through during the entire game while his teammate holds the fort. The important thing is that adjacent linemen should not employ reckless tactics at the same time." [182]

An interesting segment in Crisler and Wieman's Book *"Practical Football"* written in 1934 suggests that the philosophy of defenses attacking the offense rather than playing traditionally has been around for a while.

Dutch Meyer: Spread Formation Football

At TCU Dutch Meyer used a tailback spread with much success when he took over as head coach in 1934. Meyer, more than anyone else, is associated with the original spread formation. His book *"Spread Formation Football"*, [183] which was not published until 1952, details the spread formation as a systematic method of offensive football.

Meyer's record in 19 years as the Horned Frogs' coach was 109-79-13. He led TCU to a national championship in 1938 and Southwest Conference championships in 1938, 1944 and 1951.

The "Normal" Formation

From Meyer's "Normal Formation," some variations of the shovel pass became a key series of the spread formations. *Figures 165-167* [184] Note the conflicts created for the defenses. Defenses had to place players more suitable as run-stoppers off the line of scrimmage and have them defend against the pass. At the time, the rules did not allow for offensive and defensive "platooning" or "situational substitutions." Also, note the consistent use of both guards and tackles as trap blockers for the shovel pass.

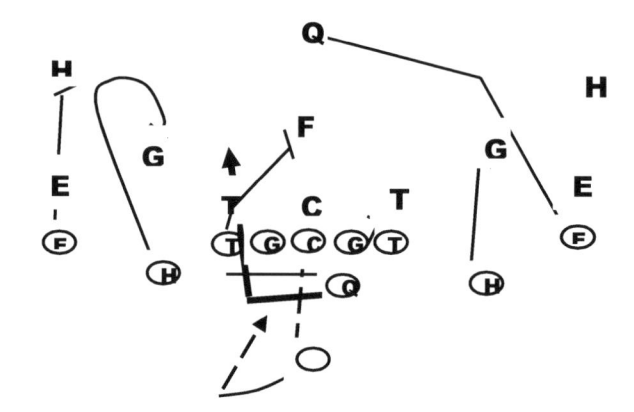

Figure 165 Shovel Pass to the Quarterback

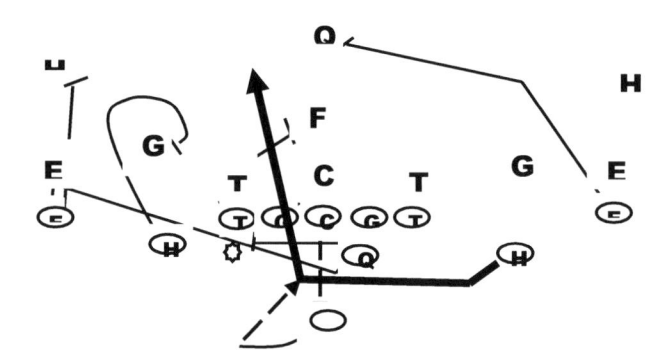

Figure 166 Shovel Pass to the Right Halfback. Note the Right Guard's trap block on the defensive tackle

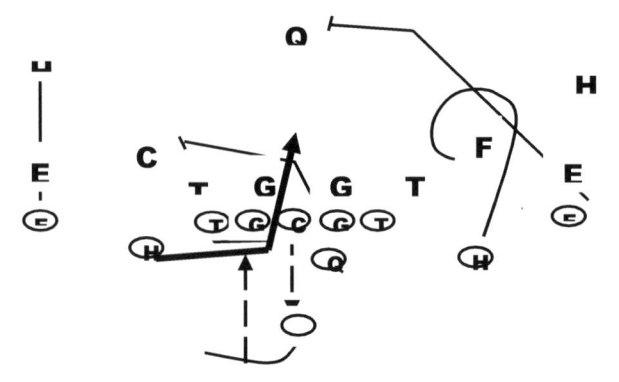

Figure 167 Shovel Pass to the Left Halfback with the tackle trapping the defensive guard

Below are two interesting pass patterns from Meyer's book. The first is "the Short" and the second is the "Spot" pass. We selected them because of the similarities between them and two popular routes found in present day offenses.

Figures 168, 169 [185]

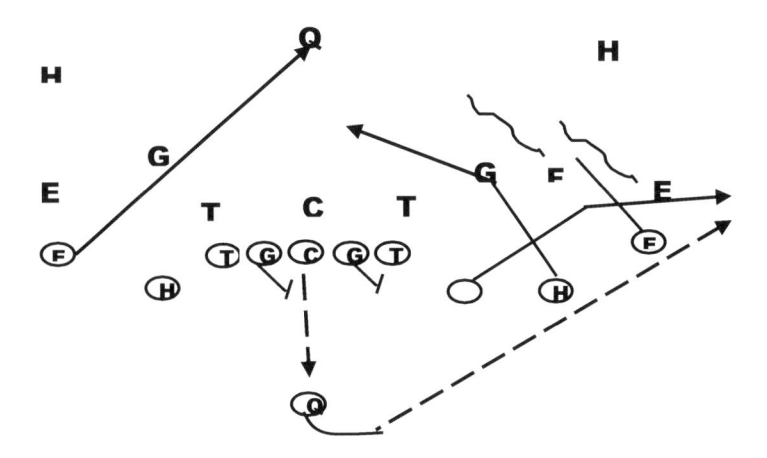

Figure 168 The "Short" Pass Very similar to modern day pass play used in short yardage and goal line by many teams today.

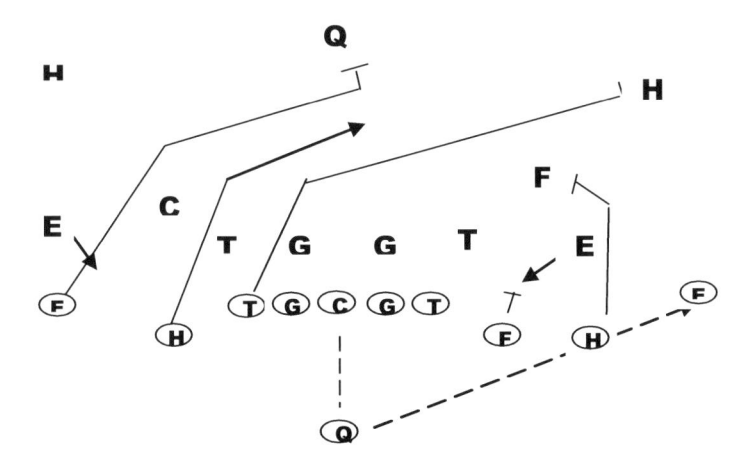

Figure 169 The "Spot" pass thrown to an uncovered or loosely covered end.

Frank Bridges: Baylor

Keeping with the wide-open game employed in the southwest, Frank Bridges at Baylor was not only innovative with the pass. He also had special plans for his kick returns. He made extensive use of the quick kick and utilized the tackle around play.

Below are three of the more highly used southwest spread formations. *Figures 170-172* Notice the similarities between these formations and the spread formations found today, especially the "empty set.". (*Figures 171 and 172*)

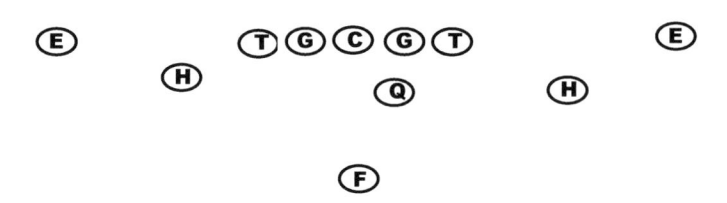

Figure 170 Spread formation used for both passing and running. Meyers called this his "Normal" formation. The position of the fullback allowed for a direct snap to him or snap to the quarterback, a fake buck by the fullback to provide deception in the running game.

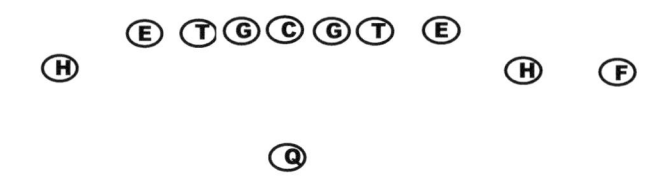

Figure 171 The Spread formation with two tight ends and triple wings. This was an attempt to force the defense to keep more defenders on the line of scrimmage.

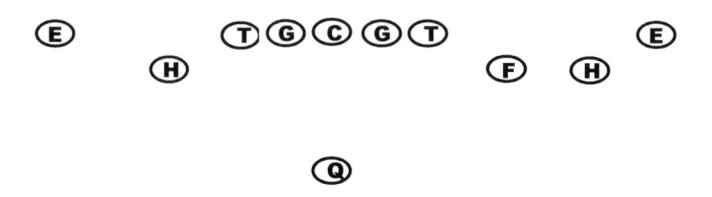

Figure 172 The most popular of the spread formations used in the 1920s and 30s. Meyers referred to this as his "Basic" formation

Defending the Spread formation

Below are two common defenses vs. the spread formations of the period as depicted in Killinger's book "*Football*" [186] *Figures 173, 174*

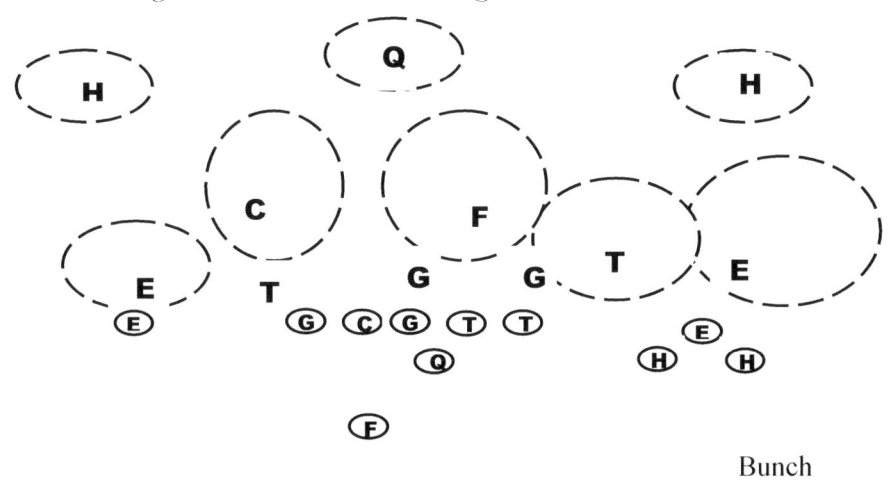

Bunch

Figure 173 Defense used against what is today called a "Bunch formation

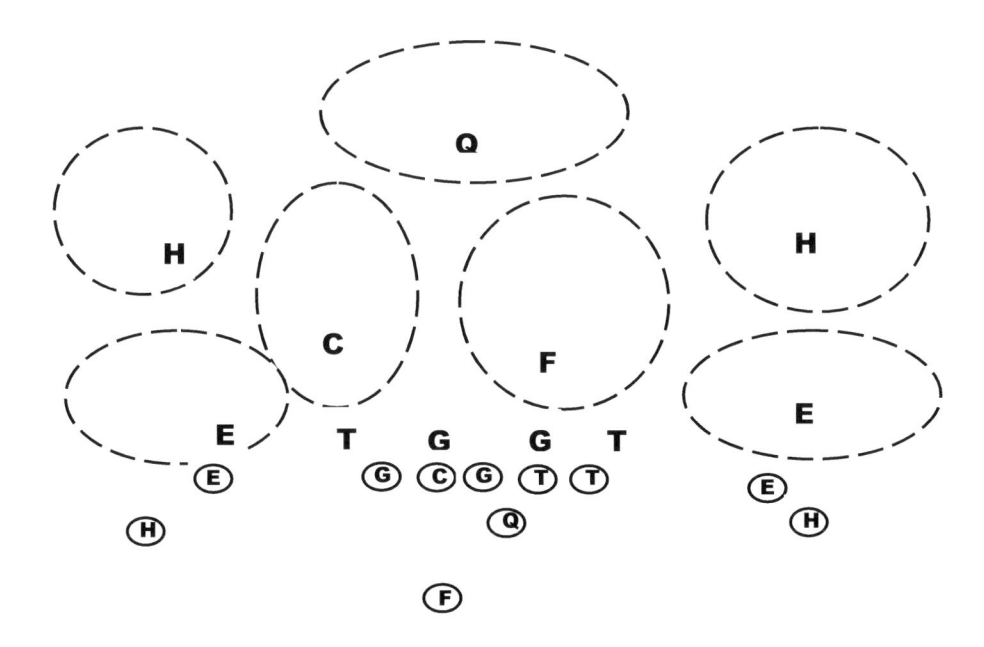

Figure 174 Killinger referred to this as a common defense versus the Spread

Ohio State versus the Spread
Ohio State's defensive answer to the spread formation was somewhat different
Figure 175 [187]

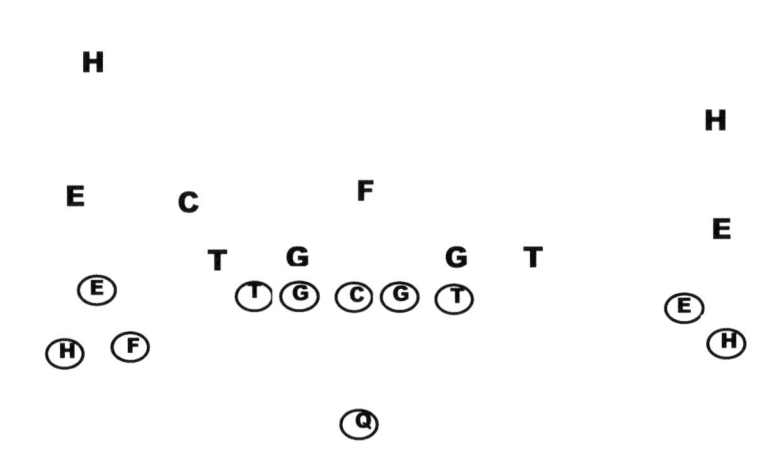

Figure 175 The Ohio State defense versus the Spread formations

"Standing T" Formation
Faurot used the term "Standing T" formation for any "T" formation that has both halfbacks and the fullback in the backfield. This is later called the "full house T" or "Straight T" formation. *Figure 176*

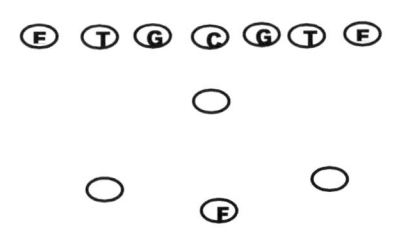

Figure 176 Straight T-Formation or Full House T

[166] Crisler, Herbert "Fritz", and Elton Wieman, *Practical Football*, (New York, Whittlesey House, 1934), p157-162

[167] Helliker, Kevin. *The Football Genius of F. Scott Fitzgerald*. The Wall St. Journal, Oct. 24, 2014. http://www.wsj.com/articles/the-football-genius-of-f-scott-fitzgerald-1414166403

[168] Pope, Edwin, *Football's Greatest Coaches*, (Atlanta, GA,Tupper & Love, Inc., 1955, p.59.

[169] Danzig, Allison, *The History of American Football*, p. 112.

[170] Little, Lou, Arthur Sampson. *Lou Little's Football*. (Leominster, MA.,Leominster Printing Co., 1934) P.151

[171] Rockne, Knute, *Coaching,*; the way of the Winner p. 28.

[172] Rockne, Knute, *Coaching; the way of the Winner*, p. 29-31

[173] Rockne, Knute, *Coaching; the way of the Winner*, p. 96-97

[174] Danzig, Allison, *History of American Football*, p. 69

[175] Danzig *The History of American Football*, p. 56

[176] Bierman, B.W."Bernie", *Winning Football Strategy, Psychology nd Technique*. (New York and London,McGraw-Hill Book Co., Inc.,, 1937). P. 216.

[177] Danzig, Allison, *History of American Football*, p. 112.

[178] Bible, Dana, *Championship Football*. (New York, NY, Prentice-Hall, Inc.,1947). p. 161.

[179] Faurot, Don. *Football Secrets of the "Split T" Formation*. New York, NY, Prentice-Hall, Inc.,1950). P. 243-244.

[180] DaGrossa, *Functional Football*, p. 236

[181] Danzig, Allison, *History of American Football.*, p. 112.

[182] Crisler, Wieman, *Practical Football*, p. 188-189.

[183] Meyer, L.R. "Dutch", *Spread Formation Football*, (New York, NY, Prentice-Hall, Inc., 1952)

[184] Meyers, *Spread Formation Football*, p. 168-173

[185] Meyers, *Spread Formation Football*, p. 175,176

[186] Killinger, Glenn, W., *Football*. (New York, A.S.Barnes and Co, 1939), p. 81

[187] Wilce, J.W., *Football*, p. 169

CHAPTER NINE

Innovations Abound

(1940 –1949)

The decade of the 1940s brought multiple changes in the approach to both offensive football and defensive football. The variations in the different offensive systems, especially the "T" formation, seem boundless. Also, for every small adjustment made by the offensive coaches, the defensive coaches respond with a corresponding rejoinder. The following two quotes, one from Fielding "Hurry Up" Yost of Michigan and the other from Curley Grieve, a reporter for the San Francisco Examiner provide insight into how little even knowledgeable football people were of what was to come. Said Yost, "There are no longer any distinctive systems in football. They've become standardized. Nobody sees a balanced line anymore except at Notre Dame, and even some Rockne-trained coaches are getting away from it. There is only one formation that's any good and it's the Single Wing."—Michigan Athletic Director and former Coach Fielding H. (Hurry Up) Yost on the eve of the 1940 college football season.[188]   And Grieve's comment; "That hocus-pocus which is called the T-Formation made 90,000 spectator converts and seemed definitely to signal the arrival of a new era in college football. The day of the tug-of-war is out, Clark Shaughnessy and his Stanford Indians have definitely killed it."—Curley Grieve, writing in the San Francisco Examiner after the Rose Bowl game of Jan. 1, 1941 [189]

T-Formation

The modern "T-Formation" came into its own in 1940. Although George Halas and the Chicago Bears had used it for nearly a decade, few other teams seemed interest in adopting it. It was not until Clark Shaughnessy became the head coach at Stanford for the 1940 season that people took notice of the new "T-Formation". Shaughnessy had left the University of Chicago after the 1939 season. His final team at Chicago had scored just 37 points while having 308 scored against in just eight games. After the 1939 season, the University of Chicago dropped football. Shaughnessy had the option of staying on as a tenured professor at Chicago with no team to coach or move on. Shaughnessy chose to move to Stanford. Although he had provided George Halas with much of the offense that the Bears were using from 1935 on, he had not used the "T" at Chicago. However when he took the job at Stanford, much to the chagrin of the Stanford faithful, he installed the "T". Stanford, which had won one game in 1939, was undefeated in 1940 and Shaughnessy's "T-Formation" became the mania of the football world.

The country was taken by surprise with the Shaughnessy "T" with its quick hitting dives and disarming deception. An entire age of coaches and players had grown up without seeing the "T." Previously Amos Alonzo Stagg at the University of Chicago had used the "T" before the turn of the century. Under Stagg, power was the central feature of the formation. The "Pop" Warner double wing, the Notre Dame box, and the power oriented Single Wing, soon displaced it. No one had ever seen a "T" that placed such an emphasis on wide-open play. The new "T" would change the game dramatically. By the end of the decade, according to a survey by Football Digest, 250 of the top 350 college teams were using it. [190]

Conventional defenses were having a tough time stopping the new "T-Formation. Until now defensive football teams stacked the line of scrimmage with six, seven, and sometimes even nine-man defensive lines to stop the run-heavy offenses. Now with the Bears "T", coaches needed to devise ways to prevent the straight ahead run but also provide defenders who could pursue the ball all over the field and cover the pass. By the mid-1940s, it became apparent that linebackers were being forced to cover fast halfbacks who were motioning out of the backfield. When that occurred, there was a lack of support on the second level inside.

Paul Brown's T-formation

Near the of the decade, Paul Brown and a balanced Cleveland offense featuring a power running game accompanied by an exacting passing attack was scoring at will on the five and six-man defensive fronts that were dominating the league. It was only a matter of time before the Philadelphia Eagles with Greasy Neale's new Eagle defense and Brown's Cleveland offense would meet.

Eagle Defense

Greasy Neale, the coach of the Philadelphia Eagles, came up with the idea of the "Eagle Defense". He adjusted the old 5-4-2 defense that was first introduced at the college level in the late 1930s. This provided for two fast outside linebackers to defend against the motion back or flanker and two deep defensive backs covering the two fast ends. He further adjusted the defense by placing the two defensive tackles on or just outside the offensive guards making it harder to double team any defensive lineman. It also made it more difficult to pull a guard and to trap. Moving the tackles in also allowed the two inside linebackers to play wider, protecting them from direct blocks by the guards. It also placed them in a better position to defend against any pass receiver swinging out of the backfield.

The problem of stopping the prolific ""T" offenses was solved. On the other hand, was it?

See *Figure 177*

```
              S                           S

     L       L           L              L  ~~~~~~~
        E       T G T         E
        Ⓔ  Ⓣ  Ⓖ Ⓒ Ⓖ Ⓣ  Ⓔ
                   Ⓠ
              ~~~~~~~~~~~~~~~~~~~~~~~~~~~
             Ⓗ    Ⓕ    Ⓗ
```

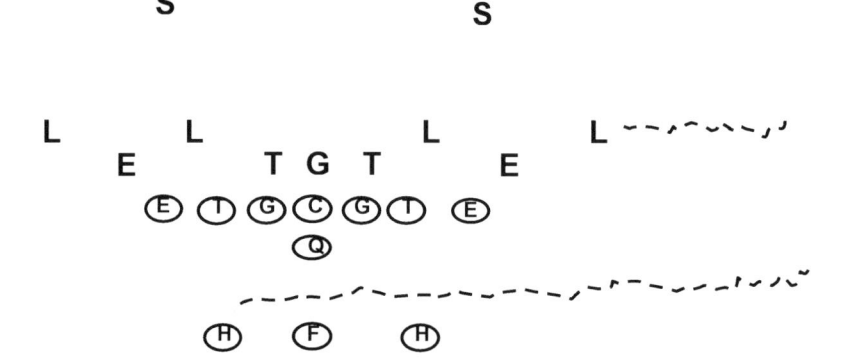

Figure 177 The Original Eagle Defense versus a man-in-motion

Split T: Don Faurot

In 1940, Don Faurot, then the head coach at the University of Missouri experimented with adjusting the "Tight "T"" formation. He originated a new idea in line spacing and introduced an entirely new theory of backfield action. His new style of offense became known as the "Split "T"", or "Sliding" "T" offense. It was an immediate success. Because of the Second World War, his pioneering ideas did not spread as quickly as they might have otherwise. During the war, Faurot was stationed at the Navy Pre-Flight Training Program in Iowa. Two of his aides were Jim Tatum, who would become the head coach at Oklahoma and Bud Wilkinson who would follow Tatum as the coach at Oklahoma. The three studied and discussed the "Split "T"" endlessly during that time. Following the war, the principles of the "Split "T"" spread rapidly, most notably at Oklahoma and Maryland. In the ensuing years, there were many variations of the "T" formation created by countless coaches. They revolutionized the game.

Over the years, there have been some misconceptions regarding the "Split "T"" offense. Probably the greatest of those is that the distinguishing characteristic of the offense is the split of the offensive line. Although the line splits are critical to the success of the offense, arguably the most unique aspect of the offense is the fact that the quarterback's maneuvering is on the line of scrimmage rather than several yards in the backfield.

The basic premise of the offense was its ability to attack over a wide area very quickly. In attacking quickly over a wide area, the "Split "T"" formation created a tremendous problem for the defense. The effective pursuit of the ball carrier by the defensive line was reduced because the rapidly hitting plays were past the line of scrimmage before any defender, not near the point of attack, had an opportunity to react and pursue.

The primary series in the offense consisted of the quarterback sneak, the handoff, off-tackle to the fullback, an option play by the quarterback to the offside halfback, a counter play to the fullback, and a running pass off the fake of the option. Each of these plays would be run to each side of the line of scrimmage. *Figures 178-183*

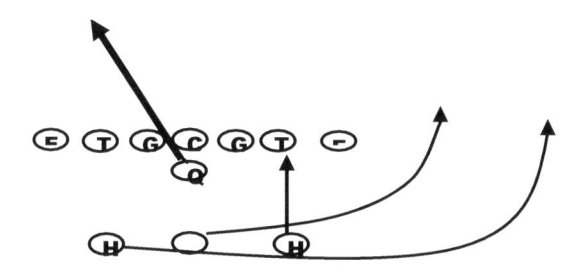

Figure 178 The Quarterback Sneak

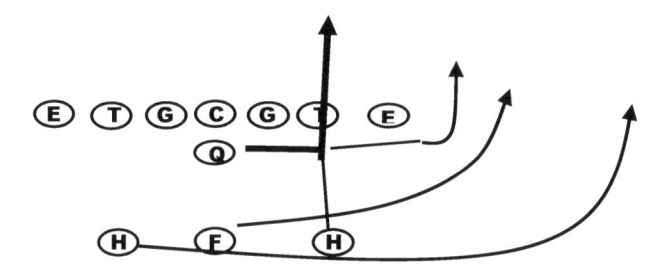

Figure 179 The Halfback Handoff

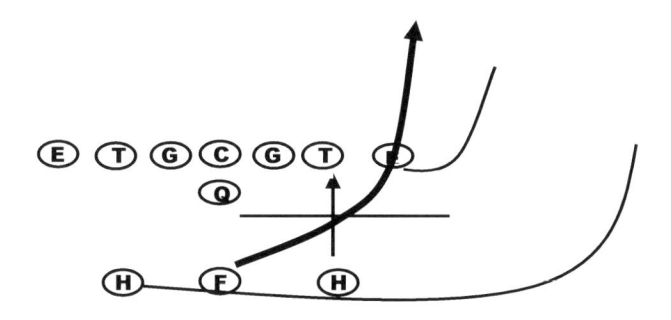

Figure 180 The Off-Tackle to the Fullback

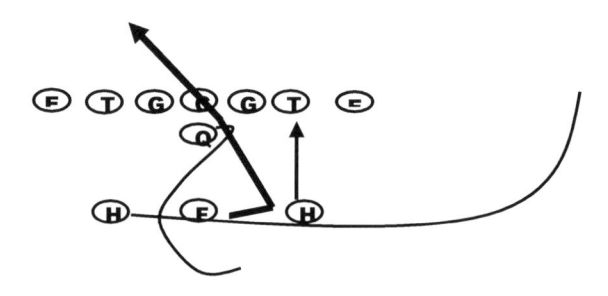

Figure 181 Counter Play to the Fullback

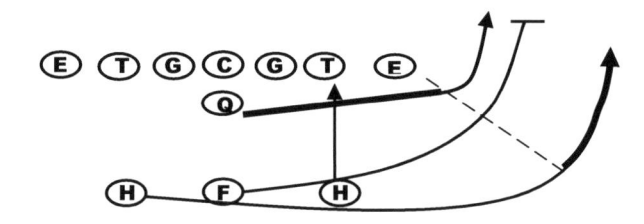

Figure 182 Option to the Offside Halfback

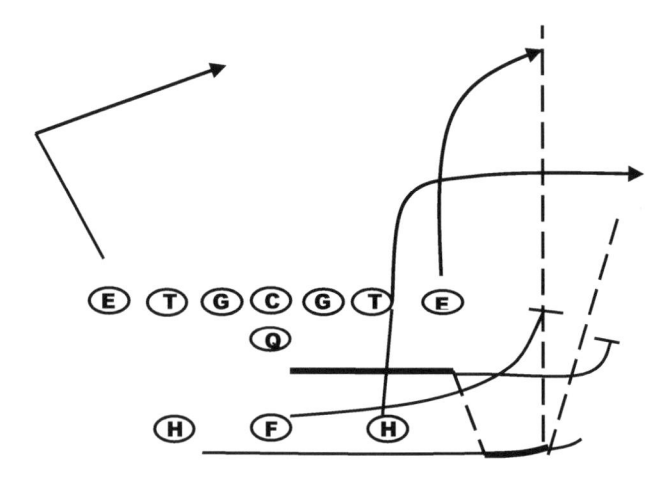

Figure 183 The Running Pass

153

The fact that the "Split "T"" could hit quickly over a broad area had a significant bearing on the type of blocking that was used. Faurot's original "Split "T"" had very few double team, cross-blocks, or traps. Because of the large splits in the line, he would forgo those blocks in favor of the one-on-one containing block. Offensive linemen were not asked to drive a defender laterally to open the hole. The defense was already spread due to the splits in the offensive line. In addition, the faking in the backfield helped the line in carrying out their assignments.

Said Faurot of his offense; "The "Split "T"" has been very successful against the basic five, six, or seven-man lines. "The splits in the line open the defensive holes wider, thus affording better blocking angles for the offensive linemen. It also permits the one-on-one blocking that is necessary to get some other interference men ahead of the play. The blocks need not be sustained as long, nor must the defensive man be moved as far, since he is more or less screened out of the play with a high block. If the defense refused to open up when the offense splits its formation, outside blocking angles are easily gained, and wide plays have increased chances of success.

"A considerable number of our opponents have brought up nine men to within one yard of the line of scrimmage in an effort to stop the running game of the "Split "T."" Simple arithmetic shows that this weakens their pass defense. In the short time available to coaches preparing for a game, improvised or new defenses have not generally been sufficiently perfected.

"Although the slanting and looping lines have been fairly effective in stopping the "Split "T"" plays, the linebackers are generally used as linemen, again weakening the defense just over the line against quick or hook passes. This unorthodox slanting defense is a guessing game and the guessers are apt to come up with the wrong answer." [191]

Faurot was aware of how Shaughnessy used motion in the use of his "T" formation. He realized he needed to have other formations than his "Standing "T." However, he had doubts about the effectiveness of using motion in his "Split "T"". He believed that the easiest defense for his team to work against was a stationary defense. When a halfback goes into motion, the defense adjusts to that change caused by his movement. He felt that this provided the offensive line only seconds to "readjust" their blocking assignments. He believed that the most important ingredient in the success of his "Split "T"" was the ability of his offensive line to determine exactly who they would block and how they would carry out their blocking tasks. Therefore, he reasoned, any change made in his offense had to be made from a set position. He decided on using a "flanker" offense for a number of reasons. First, he thought it would widen a tight defense so that it would be easier to run the offensive plays. With a flanker outside, the defensive end would usually play wider. Secondly, it caused adjustments in the opponent's pass defense. The halfback to the side of the flanker had to widen with the flanker. To maintain the stability of the defense, the safety then had to rotate toward the flanker taking him out of the middle of the defense. It made it difficult for him to offer any help to the linebacker in defending against the pass. He states the reasoning for creating the flanker formation briefly in his book.

"When an opponent tries to defend against our running plays from the standing "T" by placing nine men near the line, we generally resort to a flanker offense. These defenses – the 5-4-2, the 6-3-2, and the 7-2-2- are strong against any running game, whether the offensive is the "Split "T", the "Bears "T", the Single Wing, or the Notre Dame System. Known as "box defenses" because they feature a double safety, these alignments are well equipped to hamper a rushing attack. Since one player must widen to cover the flanker, use of a flanker will take an opponent out of the defense position that he wishes to play. Usually, the linebacker moves back to the halfback position under these circumstances.

"With the flanker out approximately ten yards from the offensive end, it is essential that the three deep defensive secondary players fan out across the field to ensure a sound pass defense. Then, only eight men are left at close range to defend against the running game." [192]

He used four flanker formations. *Figures 184-187*

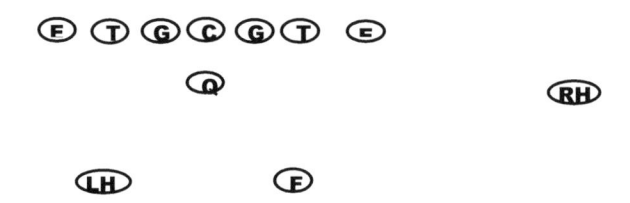

Figure 184 Flanker #1 (Right). Right Halfback flanked with the Fullback taking over his position. The formation was also aligned to the left.

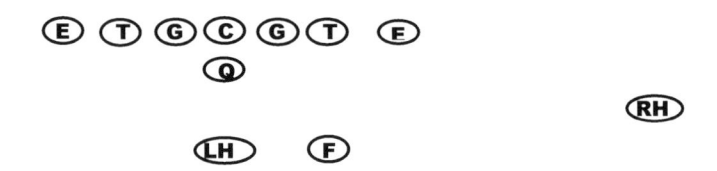

Figure 185 Flanker #2 (Right). Right Halfback flanked with the Fullback taking over his position and the Left Halfback aligning directly behind the Quarterback. The formation also aligned with the Left Halfback flanked Left, Fullback taking over his position, and the Right Halfback aligning directly behind the Quarterback.

```
        E  T  G  C  G  T  E
                 Q                           LH
              F    RH
```

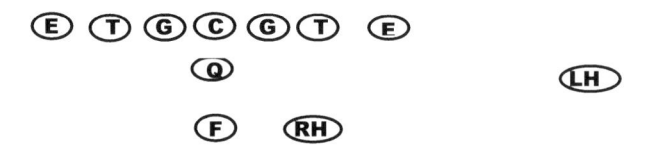

Figure 186 Flanker #3 (The Left Halfback flanked to the Right with the Fullback directly behind the Quarterback and the Right Halfback in his normal position. The formation can also be aligned to the left with the Right Halfback flanking to the left.

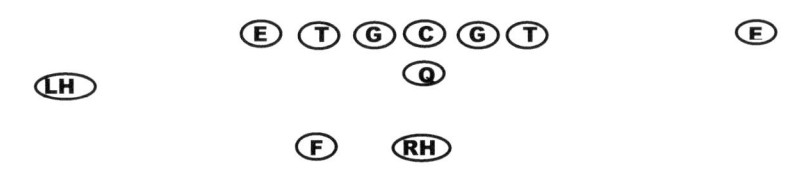

```
               E  T  G  C  G  T              E
     LH              Q
                  F    RH
```

Figure 187 Spread Formation (Right). Right End spreads and the Left Half flanks left. The Fullback and Right Halfback remain in their normal T positions. This formation also aligned left with the Left End split and the Right Halfback flanked.

Split-T Veer Blocking

An interesting note regarding Don Faurot's blocking for the "Split T" is how it differs from the current blocking schemes used today. This varies considerably from today's Veer blocking. Faurot used the term veer blocking" to describe a blocking system he used with his split-T offense. By 1949, he had established what he called his "veer blocking" where the offensive linemen would shield the defender allowing him to charge in the direction he chooses.

> He describes the veer block; "We use veer blocking on the straight handoff over the guards. …"Our guards or tackles must practice taking this defensive player in the direction in which he charges and helping him on his way. The backs hit a trifle more slowly on veer blocking and wait for the hole to open up. …
>
> "The point to remember in veer blocking is that the ball carrier must avoid running through what appears to be a defensive hole. When the line is slanting, the defensive players will fill up this opening. The real opening will be directly over the position occupied by the defensive player before the ball is snapped. The offensive blockers on either side of the veer blocking guard or tackle must protect the course taken by the halfback."[193] *See Figure 188*

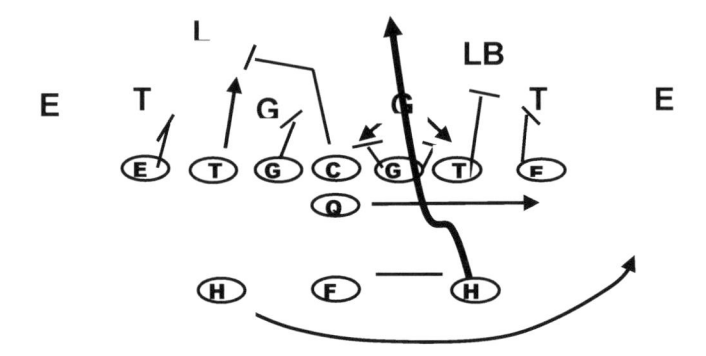

Figure 188 Veer Technique of blocking and ball carrying. If the defensive guard slants in, the offensive guard will block him in. If the defender slants out, the offensive guard will block him out.

Notre Dame T

In 1941, Flank Leahy, the newly appointed head coach at Notre Dame traveled to Chicago to study the Bears "T" formation. The previous season Leahy had been the coach at Boston College. He had only recently accepted the position at Notre Dame. Leahy and his line coach Moose Krause watched as the Bears, with their "T" formation, defeated the NY Giants. Following the game, Leahy, Krause, Halas, and one of the Bears players, Bob Snyder, had a lengthy discussion about the "T" formation and about the possibility of installing it at Notre Dame.

The following spring Leahy contacted Snyder and invited him and his wife to visit him at his summer home and the two would talk about the "T" formation. Leahy and Snyder talked football from 1:00 pm to 4:00 pm. When it was apparent that the conversation was going to continue for a while longer, Snyder sent his wife back to the hotel. The next day Snyder's wife returned to their home in Toledo Ohio while Leahy and Snyder continued to talk. Snyder returned home three days later. The two agreed that Bob Snyder would return to South Bend, Indiana to help install the offense. The Notre Dame "T" was born. Notre Dame went on an unprecedented run from 1942-1953 when they would have six unbeaten seasons and four national championships.[194]

Leahy created a "T" formation that was very similar to the "Bears T" but carried many of the same principles of Don Faurot's Missouri "Split T". Just like the "Split T" the Notre Dame "T" widens the defense and hits over a broad front with a variety of quick hitters, and off-tackle slants. For the most part, he kept the quarterback close to the line of scrimmage. He retained the complexity of the "Bears T" along with a broad assortment of blocking combinations. Unlike Faurot's offense where the blocking was called by the quarterback, Leahy's blocking schemes were called by his tackles, or guards, depending upon the defensive alignment.

157

"At Notre Dame, even the basic quick-opener, known as "43" or "the bread & butter play," has a maze of variations. When the Notre Dame quarterback has called the play number ("43" signifies that the "No. 4" back is to ram through the "No. 3" hole) and the team has swung out of the huddle, Leahy's tackles have about two seconds to size up the position of the defensive team.

"Then both tackles call signals for blocking assignments on the play. It sounds confusing, but to good T-men, it isn't; on a play to the right side of the line, the players listen only to the right tackle and let the left tackle chatter his deception signals unheeded. If the right tackle sees the "3 hole" is clogged, he may cry "Up two," and play "43" becomes "45." If the defense shifts heavily to the "play" side, he may shout, "Cancel," whereupon the quarterback calls "Opposite," and the play hammers at the other side of the line. Obviously, Notre Dame Tackles need to be quick-witted as well as big." [195]

Many claim only a taskmaster such as Leahy could achieve the success of the Notre Dame "T." Time Magazine said of Leahy, "His great weakness as a coach lies in his aloofness. He is a superb organizer, a wonderful tactician, has a talent for inspiring Great Spirit in his players, who respect him but don't love him." [196]

Split T Option: Oklahoma

At Oklahoma, Jim Tatum, and later Bud Wilkinson would begin to experiment with changing the emphasis of their "Split "T" offense. Faurot, Tatum, and Wilkinson knew the simple concept of option Football was to force the defender, who was to be optioned, to make a choice and for the quarterback to ensure it was the wrong one. Oklahoma was to run a "Split "T" very much like Don Faurot's, however, they tended to run more option plays and more play action passes in their offense. The emphasis was on the option. Wilkinson felt that if there was a delayed commitment by the defense, regarding the area the offense was attacking, the offense had a distinct advantage. The quarterback option provided the offense with that delayed commitment, as did the play action pass. Oklahoma would dominate college football for the next decade.

Unlike many of the Single Wing, Double Wing, Short Punt, and most other "T" teams, Oklahoma chose to run a single "series" in their offense. The play selection consisted of the following: the handoffs, the jump pass, the quarterback option play, the running pass, the fullback counter. There was also the quarterback sneak, the fullback counter pass, and the reverse.

On the topic of presenting the defense a tremendous variety of offensive formations, Wilkinson believed, "We do not use men-in-motion, or as many flanker variations as do the standard T-formation teams. We have only one reason for this, but we believe the thinking behind it is important.

"As we have attempted to bring out earlier in the text, our attack is based on our ability to hit quickly through any spot along the line of scrimmage. We, therefore, like to look over the defense before we snap the ball. We expect our quarterback to come up to the line, look over the defense, and then change his pay if the one he has called in the huddle is not good against the defensive alignment being used. Men-in-motion cause the defense to go in motion too as they adjust their positions. Any offensive player who moves before the ball is snapped will create some movement on the part of the defensive team. Because we do not want the defense to be in motion, but rather to remain set, we use flankers in preference to men-in-motion for our formation adjustments.

"Our fullback is used most often as our flanking back. At times, we have used the halfbacks, but we feel that the fullback is the best man to use with our style of attack. *Figures 189*

"...we can run every play in our offense without using the fullback except the fullback counter and the fullback counter pass.

"Therefore, because we do not like to change or add offensive plays in order to get flanker variations, we use our fullback as our flanker. He is the only man who can be dropped out of the formation without changing many of our plays.

"Flankers always force the defense to adjust its alignment. We believe that by using flankers properly, we can actually change the defensive alignment in many instances. This is particularly true when the defense is using a box-type secondary." [197]

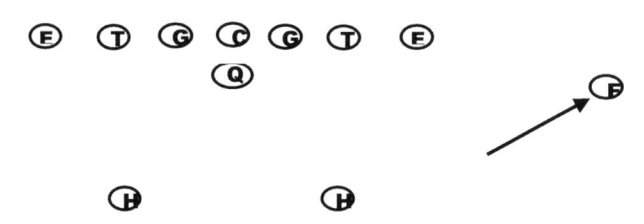

Figure 189 Oklahoma's Flanker formation with the Fullback flanked

Defensive Adjustments

Because of the extraordinary changes in offensive football at the beginning of the decade, defenses made some exciting changes of their own. Defensive coaches stayed up late devising ways to stop the new offenses of quick-hitting plays, men in motion, and flankers.

At the end of the 1940s, defensive linemen were largely interchangeable. There were no coaching strategies for the sizes of defensive tackles, defensive ends, or nose guards. The roles of defensive linemen were not as detailed and precise as they are today.

Shifting & Changing Defense

In the 1941 Football Guide, Bob Hall and John DaGrosa wrote; "shifting and changing defenses were more widely used (in 1940) than ever before. ...While five and six-man lines were the popular alignments, it was the additional developments in the use of subterfuging, sliding and looping lines that constituted the major achievements in defensive play. Varied defensive alignments were observed: for example, five-man line distribution against weakness and six-man line distribution against strength, and vice-versa. Both the offense and defense 'played the percentage', according to the position on the field, the score, and the down and distance to go. The defensive signal-caller had to consider each change in the tactical situation and call his play accordingly." [198]

However, in the 1942 Football Guide Hall and DaGrosa wrote; "Most of the shifting and changing defenses noted throughout the country were basically unsound and were used solely for their surprise value. The defense gambled with unorthodox alignments and in many cases succeeded in upsetting the offensive blocking assignments. However, such defensive strategy is risky and can be fully exploited by a well-equipped attack. " [199]

Although many people like to think of linemen falling back into zone pass defense as a recent development, the scheme was used as early as 1947. In his book *"Championship Football,"* Dana Bible shows a guard dropping into a zone from a 6-2 defense versus the Single Wing. [200] As noted earlier, Zuppke was dropping his defensive guards into pass coverage as far back as 1910.

Screwballistics:

Harvard was the team most associated with the unorthodox defenses. Their coach, Dick Harlow said of his system, "We are going to come up with the ultimate in screwballistics." [201] Harvard used as many as 28 different defensive maneuvers during the season. At the call of a signal, they went into a five-, a six-, or a seven-man line. They over-shifted to the strong side and they over-shifted to the weak side. They charged straight ahead or they looped. Guards became tackles, tackles became ends and ends dropped back off the line. Backers-up moved up to become guards.

Hall and DaGrosa wrote, "The enemy blocking assignments were screwed up. Enemy ball carriers, heading for a big hole, found themselves knocked down by masked marvels coming seemingly from nowhere at blind angles until they slammed their headgear down in disgust, and their own downfield blockers swore in disgust at the futility of mopping up ahead of a runner who never got past the line." [202]

In 1941, Arthur Sampson wrote in the Boston Herald; "The tricks Dick Harlow has taught those sturdy forwards of his are enough to drive a field general insane. It is next to impossible to operate an attack against such a baffling set of defenses. About all a quarterback can do is select his plays at random and trust he will have the good fortune to call something that will, by luck, hit the vulnerable spot in the defense Harvard happens to be using at the moment. It does no good to look at the Harvard defense as it is arranged. It doesn't help any to change signals after the team has left the huddle. The only individuals in the stadium who know what the Harvard linemen are going to do when the ball is snapped are the seven members of the Crimson forward wall and backer-up George Heiden continued.

"The Harvard coaches sitting on the bench don't know exactly which one of the several schemes their pupils are going to try on any given play."[203]

Defending the Split T

Some specific defensive adjustments were made in an attempt to control the "Split 'T'".

The 5-3-3 was enhanced in the following way. The three interior defensive linemen were asked not to look for the ball carrier but rather penetrate to a particular spot to stop the quick thrusts. The defensive ends were instructed to slant hard and go after the quarterback. They were to ignore the possibility of the quarterback pitching a lateral pass to the halfback coming around. It was felt that much of the strength of the "T" perimeter runs was in creating indecision on the part of the defensive end. The three linebackers played conservatively because it was thought that any ball carrier would be slightly slowed or delayed by the five defensive linemen who were penetrating to spots. *Figure 190*

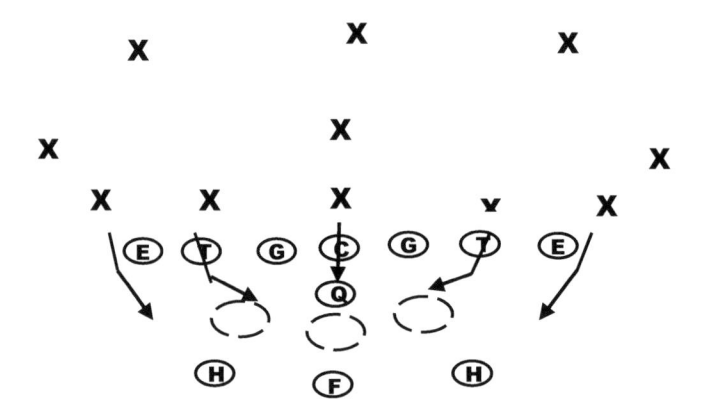

Figure 190 Angle Charge 5 Man Line. Three interior defenders charged to spots. Defensive ends angle charged and attacked the quarterback

A second defensive modification to stop the "T" was a 4-4-1-2 Rover alignment. The two guards pinched the middle. The two inside linebackers crashed the gaps with abandon. The two outside linemen (the ends) hit the offensive ends and held their area. The middle linebacker acted as a "rover" if there is no motion. If either of the halfbacks went in motion or became a flanker, the middleman would widen with him. *Figure 191* [204] The change-up for this defense was to have the defenders playing over the offensive guards to slant out and the two inside linebackers to crash inside.

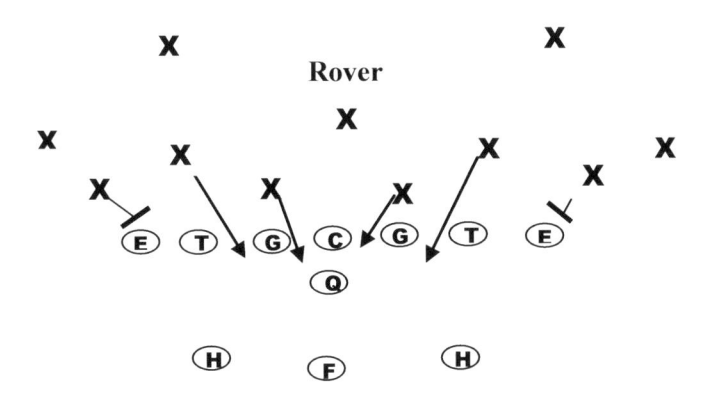

Figure 191 The 4-4-1 (rover) defense versus the "Split T."

When the ball was near the inbounds mark, the defensive coaches playing the 4-4 defense created an adjustment to defend the wide side of the field *Figure 192*

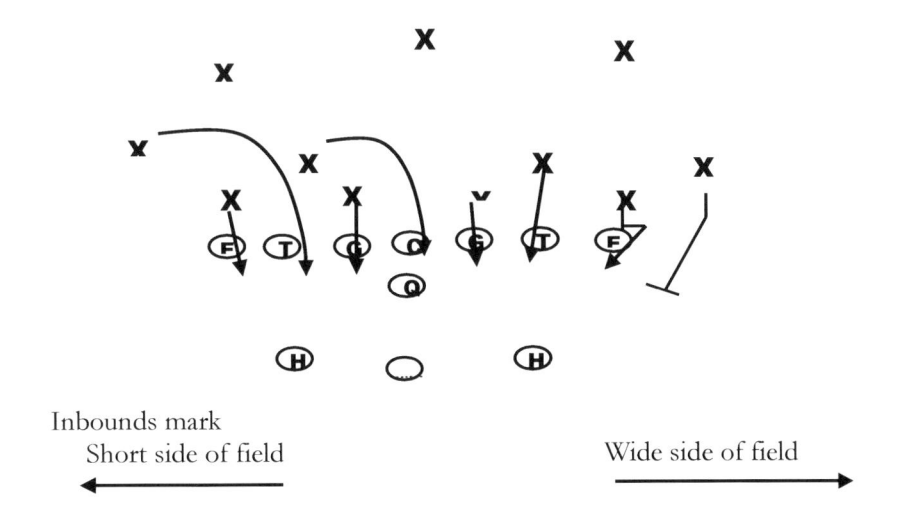

Inbounds mark
Short side of field ← → Wide side of field

Figure 192 Using the 4-4 Defense when the ball is near the inbounds mark

Some defensive coaches who were playing the 5-3-3 Defense over-shifted their defensive line one way and under shifted the linebackers the other making their defense look, much like a wide tackle six defense one way and a 4-4 defense on the other side.
Figure 193

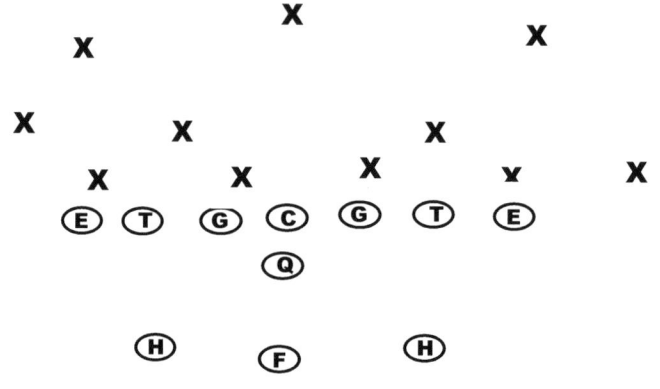

Figure 193 The Overshifted 5-3 Defense against the "Split T."

Coaches who were wed to the 6-Man line used the following over-shift.

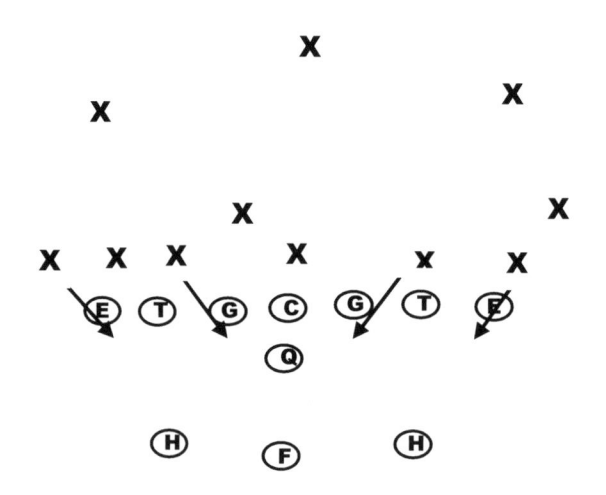

Figure 194

Figure 194 The Over-shifted 6 Man Line versus the "Split-T." (shifted to defensive right)

Defensive Adjustments to the Split-T Line Splits

Those who played a standard defense were forced to cope with the variable line splits of the "Split "T"". This was especially true for the teams who were playing the 5-man line.

Bobby Dodd describes the instructions given to his defenders playing the 5-3-2-1 defense. "The most common adjustment necessary is for the linebacker and the tackle. The linebacker should keep his relative position to the tackle (still playing the end) if he can reach him with his first step. If the end is taking a split greater than this, the linebacker should loosen up and go straight back two or three yards. Tackle should maintain his initial position. If the tackle takes a maximum split, the defensive tackle will be in about a nose-on position and will still have the responsibility of not being hooked. This defense cannot be played if the tackle tries to keep the outside shoulder position with a tackle split. The guards will have more territory than they can possibly cover." [205]

Princeton Single Wing Adapts

While the T-formation began to flourish, there were still many teams that clung to the Single Wing. Charlie Caldwell at Princeton adjusted his Single Wing during the '40s and '50s and had the Tigers ranked nationally in both 1950 and 1951. Caldwell's Single-Wing, complete with some of the greatest spinner and buck-lateral plays ever devised, played havoc with opponents.

Herman Hickman of Yale stated in a Sports Illustrated article in 1957 that he believed Caldwell overwhelmed teams with   ..." over 30 variations of offensive alignments, including double flankers to the strong side, the fullback set as a flanker to the short side, the tailback set as a flanker, any of the backs in motion to either side, split ends on either or both sides with any combination of the above. Yet all the time the offense seemed to function with the utmost efficiency." [206]

Caldwell's book on the Single Wing, "*Modern Single Wing Football*" and Ken Keuffel's *Winning Single Wing Football* are considered the two essential books on the formation. Dick Coleman took over at Princeton in 1957 and continued to use the Single Wing successfully until 1968.

Michigan State's Multiple Offense

No discussion of football in the decade of the 40s would be complete without addressing the Michigan State Multiple Offense of Clarence "Biggie" Munn. Munn took over at Michigan State in 1947. The Michigan State Offense evolved to its multiple status for the following reasons; 1. Munn's experiences as an assistant coach at Minnesota under Bernie Bierman, Ozzie Solem at Syracuse, and Fritz Crisler at Michigan, 2. The various offensive maneuvers, techniques, and formations were added together to get the maximum use of the personnel at hand, and 3. These aggressive methods were used as counter-movements because teams had successfully halted the existing formation by placing their defensive alignments so that it stopped the strongest parts of the offense.[207]

Munn began his coaching career at Albright College (PA). He ran the unbalanced Single Wing that he brought with him from his experience with Bierman at Minnesota. This version of the Single Wing emphasized the buck lateral series with the ball being directly snapped to the fullback who fakes or gives it to the quarterback. By the time he took his second head-coaching job, at Syracuse, he had added the unbalanced Single Wing with the spinner series by the fullback. It was the series used so successfully by Crisler at Princeton and later at Michigan. To this, he added an unbalanced line "T" formation from which he ran dives and pitchouts and shifted back to his Single Wing. *Figure 195* He always ran from an unbalanced line so that there would be no changes in his blocking assignments. Another element he added to his offensive arsenal was the use of a Single Wing with the Wingback deep. *Figure 196*

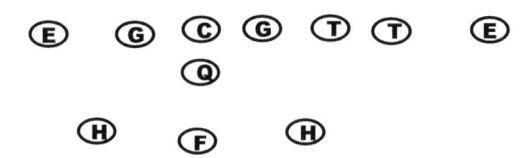

Figure 195 The Unbalanced T-formation

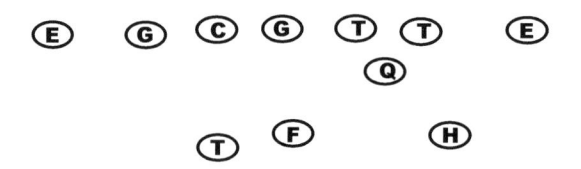

Figure 196 Single Wing with the Wingback Deep

As the 1947 season progressed, Michigan State found that their opponents were lining up in a 6-man line and under-shifting if they remained in a "T" formation. This was done to stop the short side running plays, which were so strong. Alternatively, they over-shifted if they lined up in a Single Wing, to stop the long side plays.
See Figures 197, 198

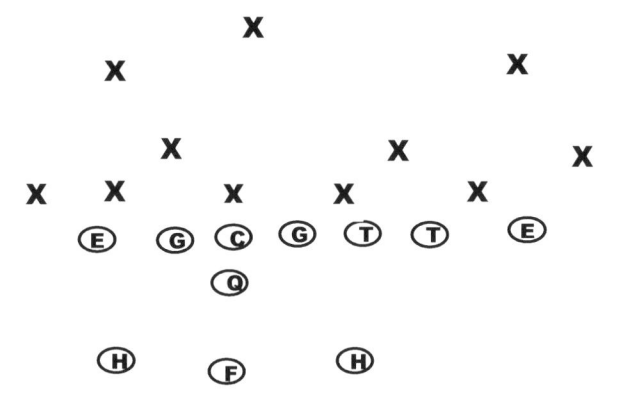

Figure 197 The Under shifted 5 Man Line versus the Unbalanced T-formation

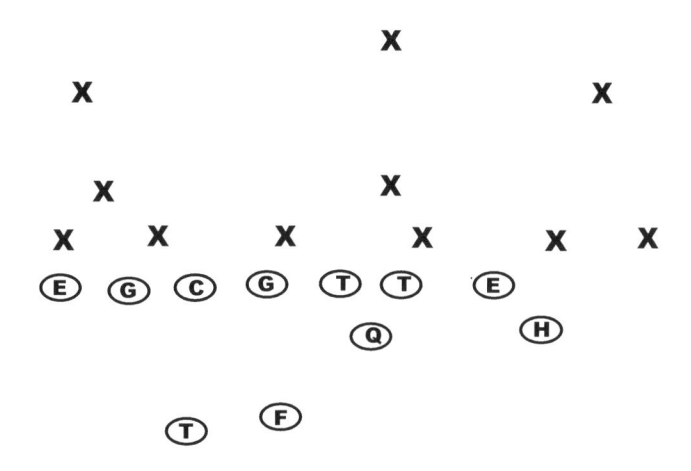

Figure 198 The Overshifted 6 Man Line versus the Single Wing

Munn's solution, in 1948, to the over-shift by the defense to the "T" and under-shift by the defense to the Single Wing, was to create a "Winged T" formation. He could snap the ball through the quarterback's legs directly to his fullback and run the buck lateral or spinner plays. He could also shift from his "T" or "Winged T" back to the Single Wing. *Figure 199*

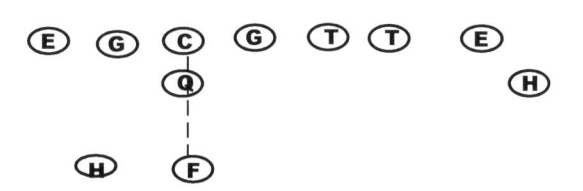

Figure 199 Wing-T Direct to the Fullback from which either the "spinner" series or "buck lateral" series could be run

T Double Wing: Eventually the Michigan State Multiple Offense would add a "T" Double Wing formation. Some teams are still using this formation today. *Figure 200*

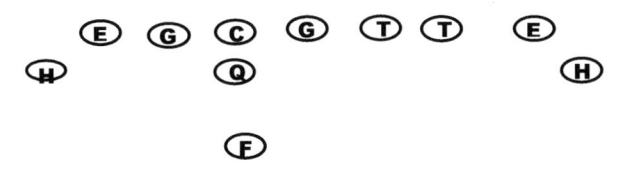

```
        E   G   C   G   T   T       E
    H               Q                   H
                        F
```

Figure 200 The "T" Double Wing Formation

Munn also began to run an unbalanced T-formation with the short-side halfback up. *Figure 201* Both formations were run from an unbalanced line. The intent being that each would allow Michigan State to throw the ball more.

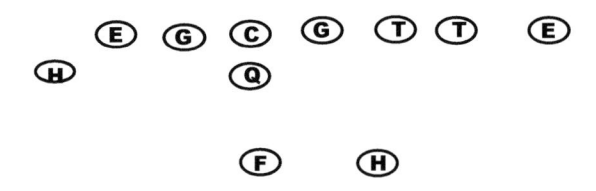

```
        E   G   C   G   T   T       E
    H               Q
                        F   H
```

Figure 201 Unbalanced T-formation with the short-side halfback up. Shown with the left halfback up

Syracuse Y Formation

Another short-lived innovation is worth mentioning. Ozzie (Ossie) Solem, coaching at Syracuse, introduced the Y- Formation. He reversed his center, turning his back to the line of scrimmage. From this position, he could snap the ball directly out to a wide back and get a quick sweep play. After just one season, the reverse position of the center during the snap was outlawed in 1942.

Free Substitution

A significant rule change came about in 1940. It allowed free substitution. This ushered in the two-platoon system allowing teams to spend more preparation and practice time on each facet of the game. Offenses now spent more time adding to the sophistication and variety of their systems. On the other hand, defenses now had more time to prepare individual adjustments for the opponent's offense. The result of this new rule would be a plethora of innovative ideas on both offense and defense. Football would be changed forever.

Earlier, Knute Rockne had used a two-team system at Notre Dame. It was Rockne's practice to send in his "shock troops" to soften up the opposition and then revert to his first group to overrun the opponent. However, Rockne's "shock troops" played both offense and defense. The new rule allowed for unlimited substitution.

As mentioned earlier, Michigan, under Fritz Crisler, was the first to take advantage of the free substitution rule, but not until 1945 when they were playing Army. By substituting by platoons, they were able to put different players on the field for offense and defense. The new system had Michigan tied with, what was thought to be, a far superior Army team in the third quarter. Although Army went on to win the game Crisler was so satisfied with his new idea that he was to keep using it in subsequent games. The Army coach, Colonel Earl Blaik was so impressed with the platoon system that he began using it himself. Army, being the national power at the time, brought visibility to the new system and it quickly spread.

Revised Substitution Rule

The unlimited substitution rule ended in 1953 and reverted to the same regulations that existed before 1941. However, by 1955 the substitution rules were revised once again, allowing for a player who started a quarter to be replaced and still allowed to return once in that quarter. Later, there was revision again, allowing for free substitution.

Birth of the I Formation

Ted Nugent devised the I-formation in 1949, while at Virginia Military Institute. Although many think Notre Dame was the first to use the "I," they came upon it when a when a Notre Dame assistant coach, Bernie Crimmins, visited VMI. The I- formation will play a significant role in offensive football beginning in the1950s.
Figure 202

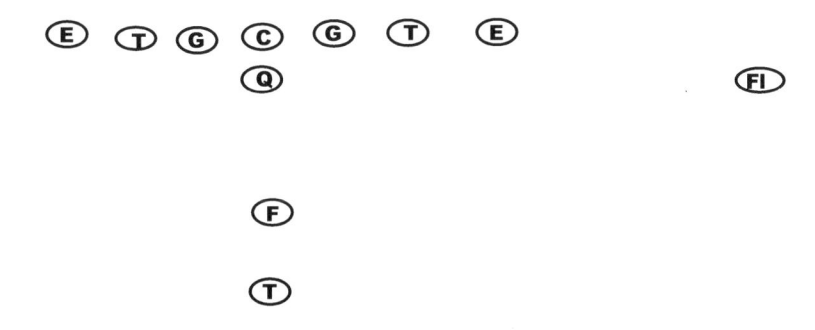

Figure 202 Ted Nugent's I formation

[188] Fimrite, Ron, *A Melding of Men All Suited to a T*, Sept. 5,1977. http://sportsillustrated.cnn.com/vault/article/magazine/MAG1092785/index.htm#ixzz11Vwg6TIU,
[189] Fimrite, Ron, *A Melding of Men All Suited to a T*, Sept. 5,1977. http://sportsillustrated.cnn.com/vault/article/magazine/MAG1092785/index.htm#ixzz11Vwg6TIU
[190] Fimrite, Ron, *A Melding of Men All Suited to a T*, Sept. 5,1977. http://sportsillustrated.cnn.com/vault/article/magazine/MAG1092785/index.htm#ixzz11Vwg6TIU
[191] Faurot, Don, *FOOTBALL Secrets of the "SplitT" Formation*. (New York, NY, Prentice-Hall, Inc.,1950). P. 8.
[192] Faurot, Don, *FOOTBALL Secrets of the "Split T" Formation*, p. 128.
[193] Faurot, Don, *FOOTBALL Secrets of the "Split T" Formation*, p. 162-63
[194] http://www.profootballresearchers.org/Coffin_Corner/22-01-839.pdf, Oct. 19, 2010.
[195] Time Magazine, Monday Sept. 19, 1949, Sport: *T Secrets*
[196] Time Magazine, Monday Nov 8, 1948, Sport: *Those Irish*
[197] Wilkinson, Charles (Bud). *Oklahoma Split T Football*, Prentice-Hall Inc. New York, NY, 1952. P. 224-226.
[198] Hall, Bob, John DaGrosa, *1941 Football Guide,* 1941. Hist. 112
[199] Hall, Bob, John DaGrosa, *1942 Football Guide*, 1942. Hist. 113
[200] Bible, DanaX., *Championship Football*, Prentice-Hall, New York, NY, 1947, p.156
[201] Cornell-Dartmouth program, 1942.
[202] Danzig, Allison, History of American Football, p. 113
[203] Sampson, Arthur, Boston Herald, October 27, 1941.
[204] England, Forrest, W., *Coaching The T-formation*, (Jonesboro, AR, Arkansas State College Press, 1948), p. 108
[205] Dodd, Robert, "Bobby", *Bobby Dodd on Football*, Prentice-Hall, Inc., New York, NY, 1954. P.220
[206] Hickman, Herman, "*Caldwell of Princeton*" Sports Illustrated, November 11, 1957
[207] Munn, Clarence,"Biggie", *Michigan State Multiple Offense*, (New York, NY, Prentice-Hall,Inc. 1953).P. 9

CHAPTER TEN

A Growth in Defensive Tactics

(1950 -1959)

With the growth of the offensive passing attacks, the game's best defensive minds knew they had to adjust and adapt quickly. They looked at their current systems, made a few changes and, among other adjustments; the 4-3 was born.

Defensive theories in football were advancing, but not yet to the level of offensive theory. I am saying this because the focus of defensive line play was more physical in nature. The objective was to defeat the man in front of you, hunt down the ball carrier and tackle. Major adjustments were rare. Probably the biggest changes were in defending a man in motion. There really were no defined sizes of defensive tackles or defensive ends. Also, the assignments for defenders were not nearly as detailed and precise as they are today.

During this time, there were several far-reaching developments in the game. Firstly, there was a growth in the emphasis on defense and with teams varying their defenses both before and after the snap. Secondly, there developed a delayed commitment on the part of the offense, after the snap, until the defense had definitely committed itself. Thirdly, there was an escalating academic or cerebral approach to the study of defense.

After World War II, numerous men brought new methods and attitude to coaching defense. Coaches such as Clark Shaughnessy at Stanford, Bernie Bierman at Minnesota, Fritz Crisler at Princeton and later at Michigan, Wallace Wade at Duke, Earl "Red Blaik at Army, Lou Little at Columbia, Bobby Dodd at Georgia Tech, Bear Bryant at Kentucky, Texas A&M, and Alabama, Forest Evashevski at Iowa, "Woody" Hayes at Ohio State, Eddie Erdelatz of Navy, "Bud" Wilkinson at Oklahoma, Colonel Robert Neyland at Tennessee, and a host of others brought a new, analytical approach to the college game.

From the above men, as well as others who we may have failed to mention or remain nameless, came the tenets of defense that still survive today. During this time, defensive coaches recognized several fundamental principles that are still relevant today.

Development of Defensive Alignments

What did defensive coaches realize?

For defenders aligned on the line of scrimmage, there are generally three possible alignments, nose-up (face-to-face), on the outside (or inside) shoulder, or align in a gap. For defensive ends, there is, of course, no gap alignment but they may align outside (wider than a shoulder alignment) or wide. *Figure 203*

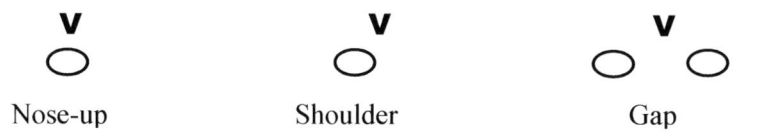

```
      V              V                V
      O              O              O   O
   Nose-up        Shoulder           Gap
```

Figure 203 Possible Defensive line alignments

Each of the potential alignment positions provides the defense with certain advantages and disadvantages. What did they conclude?

Nose-Up Alignment: When aligned in a nose-up position it was difficult for the offensive lineman to release and block a linebacker. The nose-up position facilitated a cross-charge with another defensive lineman and looping. Key reading (reading and reacting to the actions of the offensive blocker) was easier from a nose-up position. Generally speaking, defenses that aligned in nose-up positions allowed the linebackers to stack defensive lineman without having the immediate threat of a double team block. The nose-up position was best for "read and contain" defenses. On the other hand, the nose-up alignment allowed for the potential block by three different offenders on the nose-up defender. There was also the threat of a double team lead-post block either side. The defender was faced with the possibility of some different "false read" problems. The nose-up position made rushing the passer harder for the defender. As a rule, the defender had to have greater size and be stronger to play the nose-up position. If the offensive line took wide splits, the widening forced the nose-up defender to either shift his alignment to a shoulder or gap alignment or play a single gap. Lastly, the nose-up alignment facilitated the offense if they attempted to "wedge" block.

Shoulder Alignment: In a shoulder position, there was less chance of a defender being "hooked" in (or out) by an offensive blocker. A defender in a shoulder alignment was better able to pursue a play away from his position. It was easier to defeat an attempted double team block from a shoulder position. The shoulder alignment does allow a large area or "bubble" between defensive linemen, especially if the adjacent lineman is in a nose-up position. The shoulder alignment allows for an easier release by the offensive blocker onto the linebacker. It required more linebackers to cover the vacant areas. Finally, the shoulder alignment leaves the defender vulnerable to a successful one-on-one block in the direction of the offset.

Gap Alignment: Coaches realized that in the gap alignment there were only two potential immediate blockers. It would decrease the threat of a double team block, creating sizeable lateral movement. It allowed for better penetration by the defensive line. The gap alignment created problems when teams attempted to down block behind pulling linemen. By positioning in a hole, the defense effectively could resist the spreading of the defensive front using wide split lines. Defenders aligned in gaps did not read keys and, therefore, were not susceptible to false keys. It assisted in the success of stacked defenses. The gap alignment was a vital necessity in goal-line situations. The shortcomings of the gap arrangements were that they created good blocking angles for one-on-one blocks. They also were more prone to the trap block since the gap defenders rushed hard. Defenders aligned in gaps had more difficulty in pursuit. Gap defenders made it less difficult for the down blocks necessary for sweeps to be successful. Teams that wanted to "pivot" block on pass plays found fewer problems with gap defenders. Versus a split line, gap defenders could not hold up two adjacent offensive linemen from attacking a linebacker, as they might be able from a shoulder or nose-up alignment.

Alignment and the Neutral Zone

It was also determined that the distance from the neutral zone or ball was as important as the lateral positioning. When shooting a gap, a lineman should align as close to the ball as possible. Reading an offensive lineman's movement, however, required more distance "off" the ball.

Linebacker Alignment

At the second level, linebacker alignment was very similar to that of the line. They would position themselves in a nose-up, shoulder, or gap alignment with their depth depending on several different factors. Below are some examples of the various arrangements. *Figure 204*

Nose Alignment

Shoulder Alignment

Linebacker Stacked on

Gap Alignment

Linebackers Gap Stacked

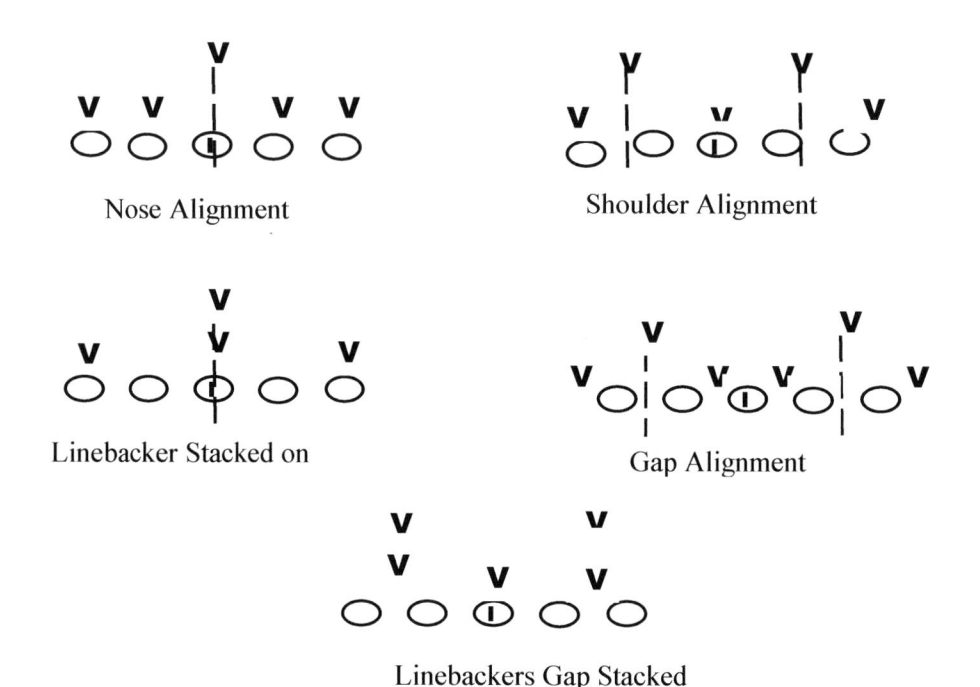

Figure 204 Examples of various Linebacker alignments

Just as with defensive linemen, there were advantages and disadvantages to the different arrangements for linebackers. They were comparable to that of the defensive line. However, the variations in blocking combinations that were available for use by the offense against the linebackers were more numerous. Below are some blocking combinations that linebackers had to be prepared for at that time. *Figure 205*

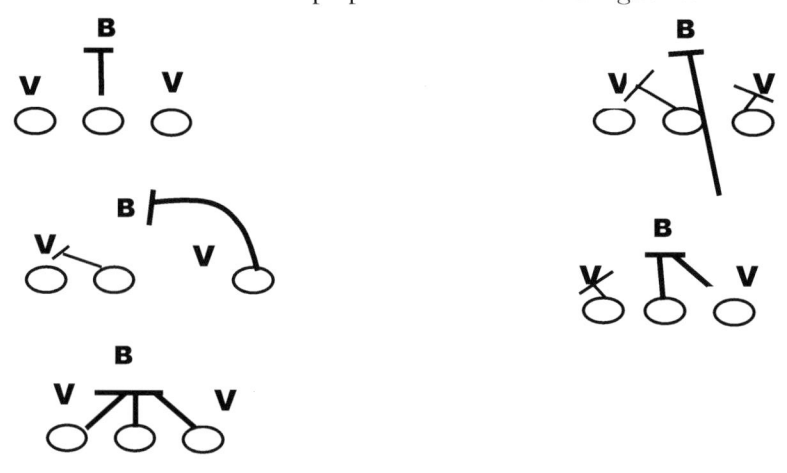

Figure 205 Examples of typical blocking combinations used on Linebackers during the 1950s

Secondary Adjustments

Coaches began to improve their matching of pass defense or secondary with the defensive front (defensive linemen and linebackers). They identified pass defenses as being either zone, man-to-man or a combination of the two. They further defined the secondary play as being a "five spoke defense" or a "four spoke defense". The five-spoke defense was associated with an eight-man front (4-4, 5-3, 6-2, 7-1) and the four-spoke defense was associated with the seven-man front (5-2, 6-1, 4-3, etc.). In the Five Spoke defense, there are three deep pass defenders and the defensive ends or linebackers are involved in the perimeter defense in both stopping the outside run and defending the short pass in the flat. The ends/linebackers adjusted to motion and flanker sets and the three deep defenders mostly remained in place. *Figures 206, 207*

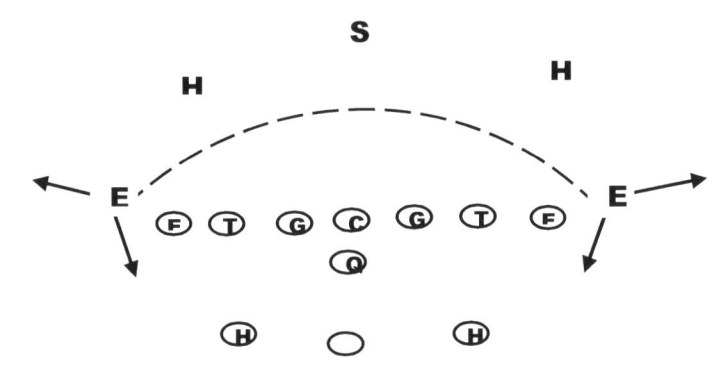

Figure 206 The Five-Spoke Defense

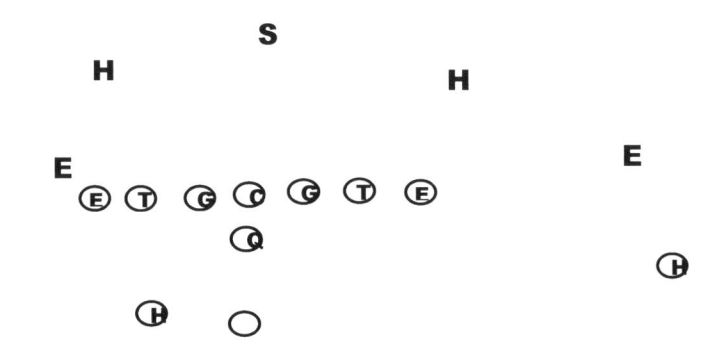

Figure 207 Adjusting to the Flanker using the Five Spoke Defense

In the Four-Spoke defense, there are four deep pass defenders. *Figure 208* The four secondary defenders adjusted to a flanker by rotating in the direction of the flanker. *Figure-209* Although in some defenses the defensive ends were a part of the perimeter defense, it was not a necessity.

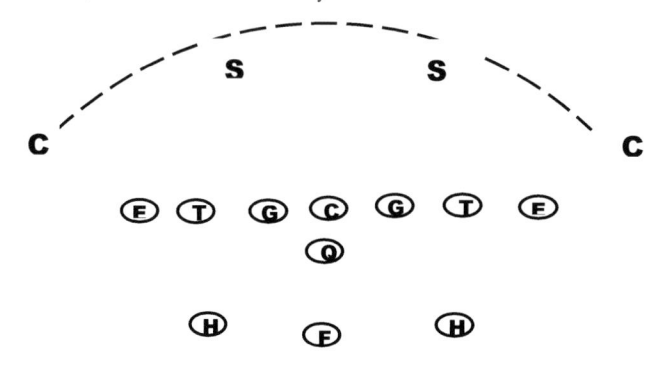

Figure 208 The Four-Spoke Defense

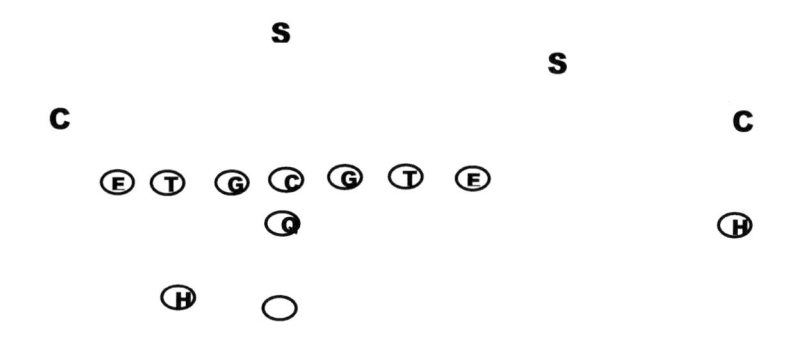

Figure 209 Adjusting to the Flanker using the Four-Spoke Defense

The Alabama Defensive Numbering System

One of the most significant innovations during this period was by Paul "Bear" Bryant of Alabama. He is credited with devising a numbering system for the many possible alignments of the defensive front. Bryant himself gives much credit for the new system to O.A. "Bum" Phillips while he was a Texas high school coach. Although some coaches have made minor changes in the system, it is still widely used today.

In his book *"Building a Championship Football Team,"* the "Bear" describes his innovation in the following way, "After coaching for a number of years, and always trying to find something that would make football easier to understand for the average player, I came upon a system of defensive numbering that has proven very valuable to me since then. In the past, I have used many different defenses. I always employed the technique of giving each defense a name. Most of the time the name had little in common with the defense, and this confused, rather than helped, the players. After discussing the possibility of the numbering system with my own and other college and high school coaches, while at Texas A & M in 1956, I finally came across a feasible plan for numbering defensive alignments. I must give credit to O.A. "Bum" Phillips, a Texas high school coach, for helping work out the solution as he experimented with the numbering system with his high school football team. In the numbering of our defense now, we give each offensive man a number, as well as the gaps between the offensive linemen. Figure 1 is an example of our defensive number system.

"Accompanying each number is a particular 'technique,' which will be explained shortly. If a defensive player lines up in a 2 position, he will play what we call a '2 technique'; a 3 position plays a '3 technique,' etc. Therefore, from end to end of the offensive line we can line-up our defensive men and each position has a particular technique." [208]

Figure 210

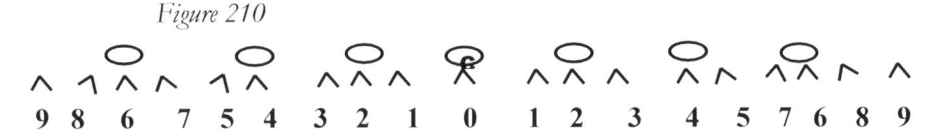

9 8 6 7 5 4 3 2 1 0 1 2 3 4 5 7 6 8 9

Figure 210 Alabama Numbering System

Colonel Robert Neyland

Colonel Robert Neyland, at Tennessee, is the man who many consider the most influential coach in advancing new principles and theories of defense. Sports Illustrated named Neyland as the one of the best defensive coordinators in its "Best of the 20th Century" edition.[209] He served as Tennessee's Head Coach on three different occasions, leaving during World War II for service in the Army where he achieved the rank of brigadier general.

A great advocate of both the seven-man line and 6-man line, he was painstaking in his attention to detail. On the Goal Line - he was the first to tighten up his 7-1 to a 7-4. His "Wide Tackle 6-2" became a timeless defense. Versions of it are still in use today. His Over-shifted 6-2 was the precursor of today's 5-2 defense and the 3-4. Also, when looked at carefully, you can see that by taking Neyland's Wide Tackle 6-2 and moving one linebacker down into a "nose" position over the center and stacking the other linebacker over him you have a defense the highly resembles the old 7-Diamond defense.

Wide Tackle 6 Defense

The defense favored by General Neyland at Tennessee and his many disciples was the "Wide Tackle 6" defense. Although Neyland did not write books, nor did he write many articles on his defense, there are a few outside sources for information on the defense and how it was played. The Guards play nose-up on the offensive guard, what Bryant called a "2 technique." They were to hit the offensive guard and pursue the ball. On the pass, they handled the middle screen, the draw and rushing the passer. The defensive tackles aligned on the inside shoulder of the offensive ends, what Bryant called a "7 technique." They handled the off-tackle play to their side and they were the trail man on plays away from them. The defensive ends played wide outside the offensive ends, an "8 technique". They handled contain. On plays away from them, they were to pursue, taking a deep angle. On drop back pass, they covered their flat area. The linebackers lined up on the inside eye of the offensive tackle. They were to attack aggressively any blocker who approached them. If there was flow away(offensive attack moving away from them), they were to check for the counter play before pursuing the ball. The defensive secondary played a standard 3 deep coverage. *Figure 211*

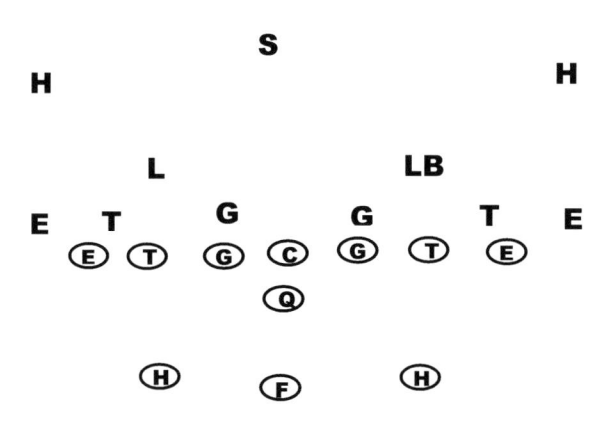

Figure 211 The "Wide Tackle 6" Defense preferred by Neyland

Three well-liked stunts from this defense taken from "Bear" Bryant's book are below.[210] *Figures 212-214*

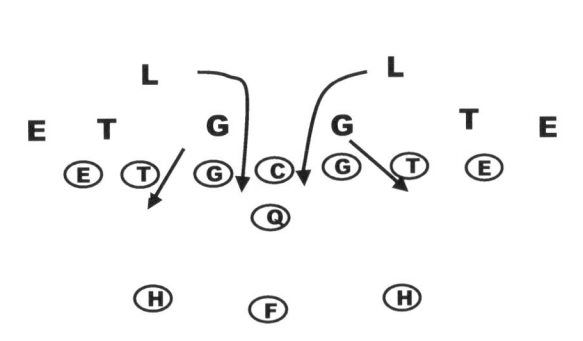

Figure 212 The Guards loop to the outside over the offensive tackles and the Linebackers fill inside the Offensive Guards

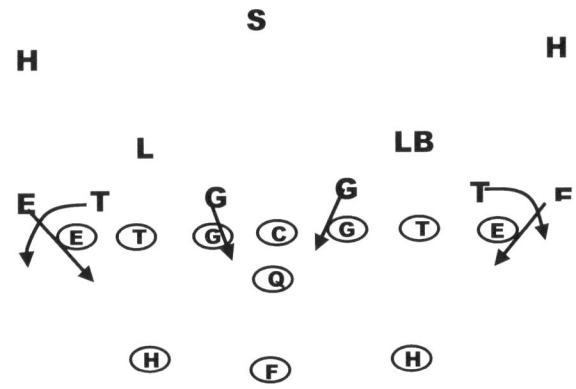

Figure 213 The "X" Stunt. Ends slant in and Tackles loop outside. The Guards slant in or what Neyland called a "Pinch."

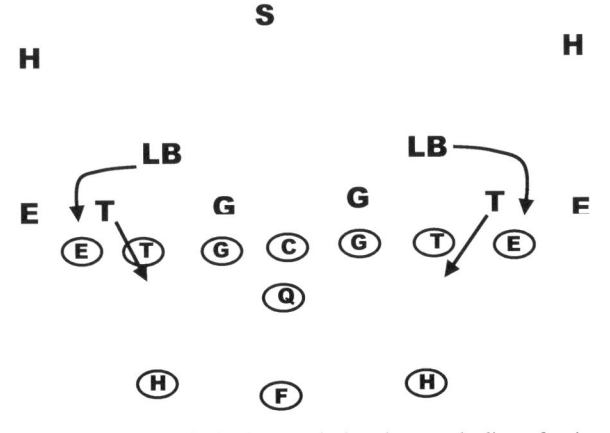

Figure 214 The Tackles pinching and the Linebackers replacing them at the line of scrimmage positioned on the inside shoulders of the offensive Ends

5-2-4 Defense

As the decade wore on, the primary defense of choice was becoming the 5-2-4 that "Bud" Wilkinson and his inventive assistant Gomer Jones used at Oklahoma. In the preface of his (and Gomer Jones) book, *"Modern Defensive Football"*, he states a fundamental principle that will serve to guide him in the advancement of his defensive schemes.

> "The rules of the game are reasonably well balanced between the offense and defense. However, the rules do give a slight advantage to the offense. If the offensive team is well coached and well conditioned and if its personnel are physically equal to that of the defensive team, the offense should be able to move the ball with reasonable consistency. Therefore, we do not know of, nor believe there is, any defense, which will completely stop the opponent. In this sense of 'stopping the opponent', we mean holding them to absolutely no gain for several successive plays.
>
> "We feel it is realistic to assume that the offensive team will move the ball reasonably well. Thus, the mission of the defense becomes one of 'slowing up' the opponents, of keeping them from making the long gain or the easy touchdown, and of battling them to gain possession of the ball before they can score." [211]

The 5-2-4 defense that Wilkinson called his Defense 72 came about precisely to stop the "Split "T"" formation. It quickly became the primary defense against the "T" formation. High school teams and some colleges, employ it today using the same primary assignments as Wilkinson taught his teams. The ends lined up almost in front of the offensive end. They charged hard, straight into the offensive end, being sure that the end is not able to "hook" him (block him in). If the offensive end attempts to block him out, he "fights the pressure" and holds his ground. If the offensive end tries to release downfield, hold him up as long as possible. They taught the two defensive tackles to line up almost head up on the offensive tackle and charge straight into him being sure that the offensive player could not block them in. Today most 5-2 teams line their tackles on the outside shoulder of the offensive tackle (5 technique). The Nose Guard lined up directly on the offensive center about 2-2 1/2 feet off the line of scrimmage. He was taught to vary his charge by, at times, charging hard into the center and at other occasions charge with less force. The idea was to control the center and not allow him to cut-off the Nose Guard's pursuit either way. The linebackers lined up about 1 ½ yards off the line of scrimmage on the outside shoulder of the offensive guard and reacted to the movement of the offensive guard. Their pass zones were the "hook" zones. The Corner men lined up 3 yards behind the line of scrimmage and 4-5 yards outside the Offensive end. If the ball started moving toward the Corner, he was to give ground laterally and maintain outside position on the ball. If the ball moved away or the quarterback dropped back, he was to drop back and play pass until he was positive the play was a run. The two Safeties were to line up 8-9 yards deep on the inside shoulder of the offensive end. They were to key the offensive guards and come up quickly if the key indicated a running play and to play pass defense when they were sure the play was not a running play.   *Figure 215*

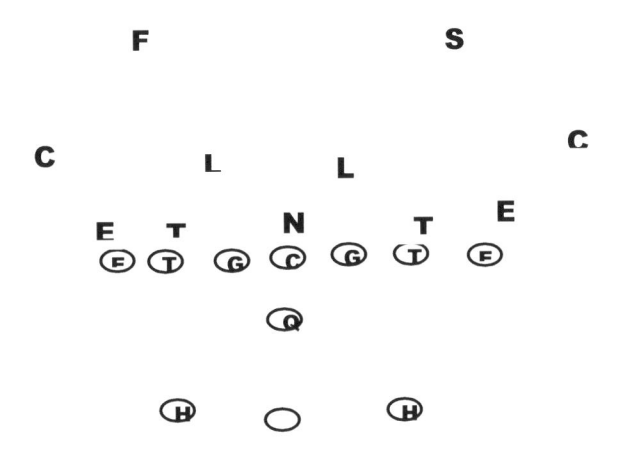

Figure 215 Wilkinson's primary "Defense 72" (5-2-4)

Wilkinson and Jones considered this defense to be a "4 spoke secondary" defense with the two Corners and the two Safeties each being one of the spokes. The defense's adjustments to the split-ends and/or flankers of the "T" formation were a relatively easy process made by the Corners. There were virtually no changes necessary by the interior seven defenders and only minor "tweaks by the Safeties *Figure 216*

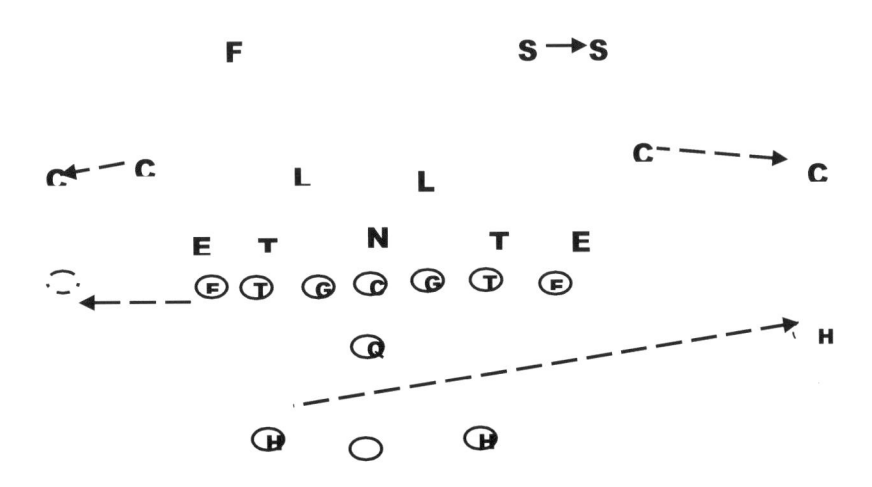

Figure 216 The 5-2-4 defensive adjustments to a Split end and Flanker

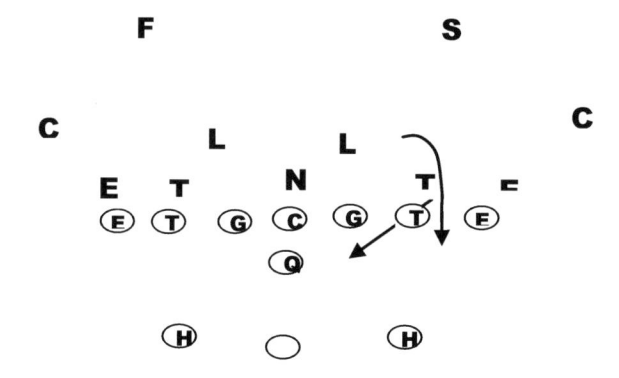

Four of Wilkinson's early stunts are below. *Figures 217-220*

Figure 217 Tackle & Linebacker "Cross Charge."

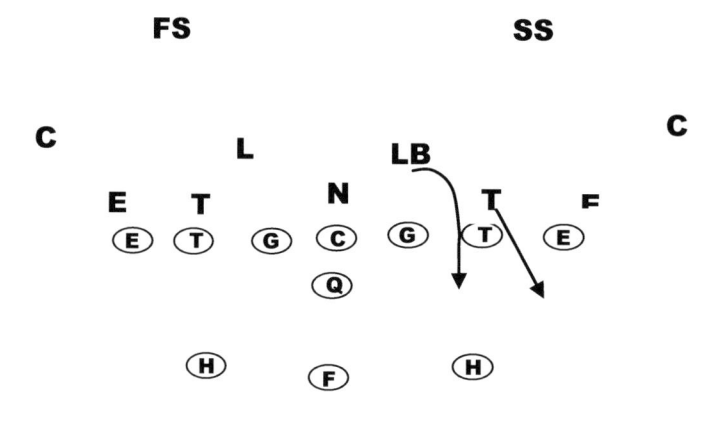

Figure 218 Tackle & Linebacker "Shoot the Gaps."

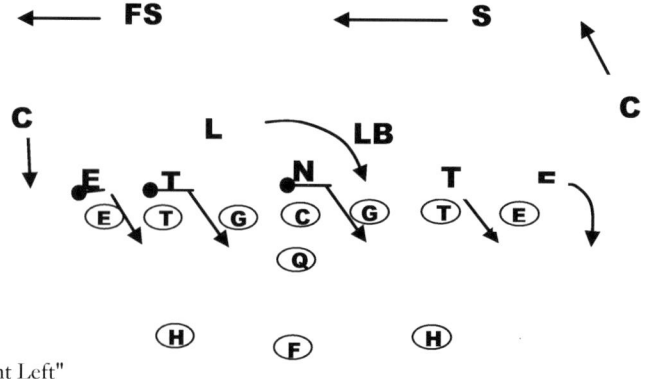

Figure 219 "Slant Left"

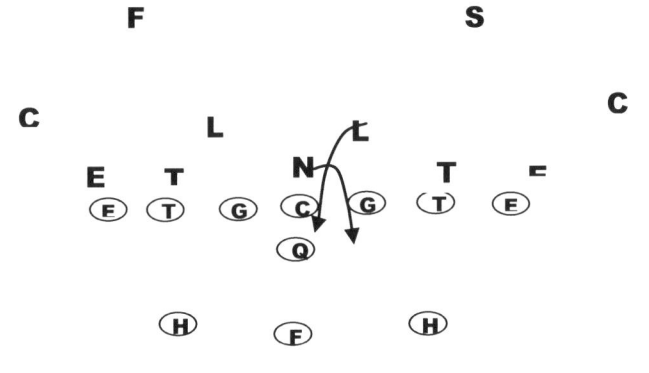

Figure 220 Nose Guard & Linebacker "Cross Charge."

6-1-4 Defense

Another defense that became widespread during this period was the 6-1. Some believe that the 6-1 was actually one of Dick Harlow's 28 different defenses at Harvard in 1942.[212] *Figure 221*

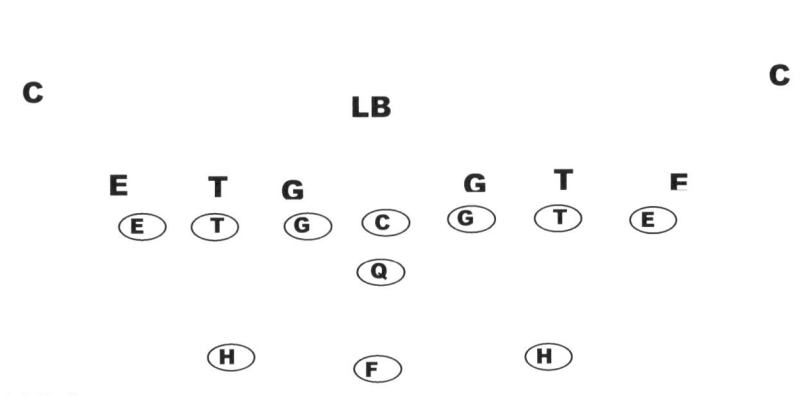

Figure 221 The 6-1 Defense

Growth of the I- Formation

We have previously mentioned that there are some who claim, in 1951, Notre Dame, under Frank Leahy, was the first to use the I- formation. However, Tom Nugent who coached at Florida State and previously at VMI is said to have come up with the idea in 1949. He began using the formation at Virginia Military Institute in 1950 as a substitute for his Single-Wing and another choice to the T-formation. In fact, Leahy himself gives Nugent credit for the first use of the formation. Another early advocate of the "I" formation was Don Coryell. Although he became famous for his Air Coryell offense in later years, he was also a pioneer of the "I". He helped lead the way with this innovative new attack. He used it as a high school coach in Hawaii, at

Wenatchee Valley College in 1955, and at Whittier College in 1957-1959.

The quarterback now actually crouched behind the center with his hands underneath. Before this, the quarterback stood behind the center and looked under his legs for the short snap.

Red Smith, the famous sportswriter for the New York Herald Tribune, describes the new look this way "The "I" is a tandem with all four backs in a single file directly behind the ball. The quarterback in the normal "T" formation position crouched under center. Ordinarily, the order behind him is a fullback, right half and left half.

"The quarterback gets the ball from center, spins, and either hands-off or fakes to playmates who rush past him to the right and left. Fake runs always precede passes" He quotes Frank Leahy, the Notre Dame coach at the time, as saying "Our lads who play defense in scrimmage tell me they find it difficult to guess where those backs mean to go when they all start from the same place, so to speak." [213]

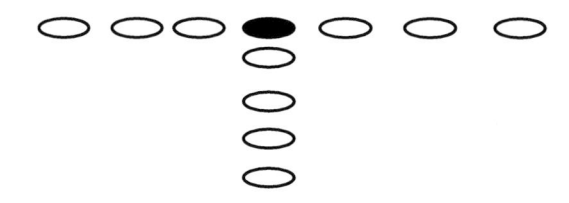

Figure 222

Figure 222 The Straight "I" formation. Later to be known as the Maryland I

The disciples of the new offense felt that the "I" had advantages over both the Single Wing and the "T" formation. They cited the ability to utilize one or two good backs to attack all the holes on either side of the center. The best blocking back became the fullback and he could use those blocking skills leading the way on both the right and the left side of the center. They felt the "I" provided enhanced backfield patterns for both the belly play and the option with the tailback lining up directly behind the quarterback. There was an increased speed at hitting the hole with a lead blocker on the inside plays. The "I" made it harder for defenses to read keys to find the ball carrier. Finally, the new offense made it easier to free an offensive back for use as a flanker without reducing the effectiveness of the attack. Some of the basic "I" plays from that era are below.

See Figures 223-227

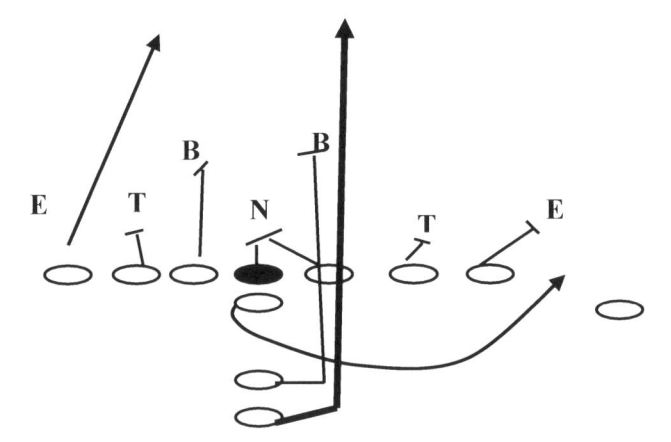

Figure 223 The Inside Power Isolation play

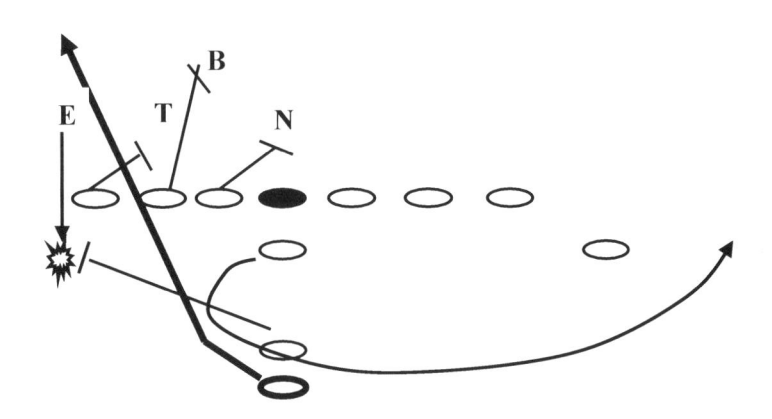

Figure 224 The Power Off-Tackle play

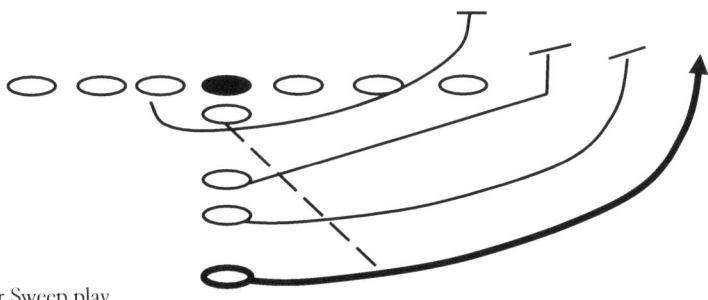

Figure 225 The Power Sweep play

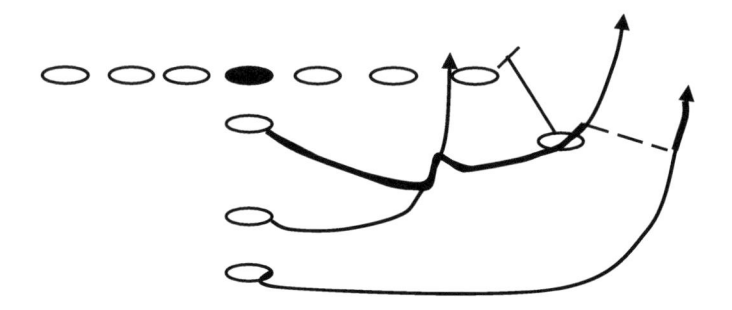

Figure 226 The Quarterback/Tailback Belly Option

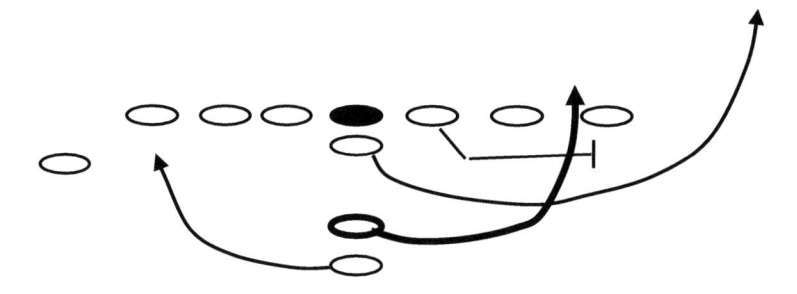

Figure 227 The "Upback" (Fullback) Off-Tackle play

As the decade ended, the I- formation developed some different looks. Although the "Maryland I" and the "Wing I" were the primary formations, many of the same basic plays were run from other formations. *Figures 228-233*

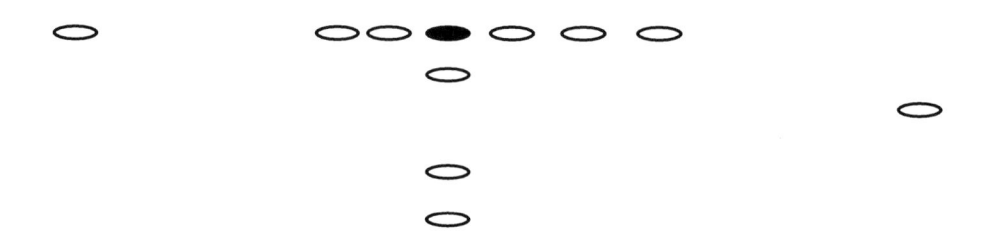

Figure 228 The "Spread I" Later called the "Pro I."

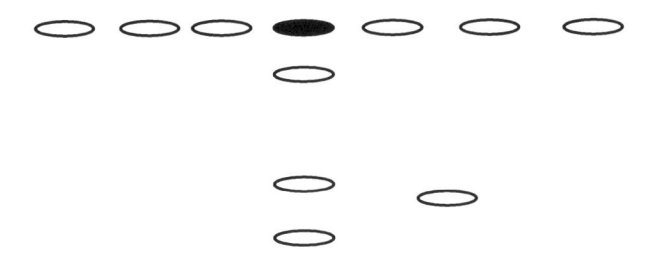

Figure 229 The "Power I" or "Triangle I."

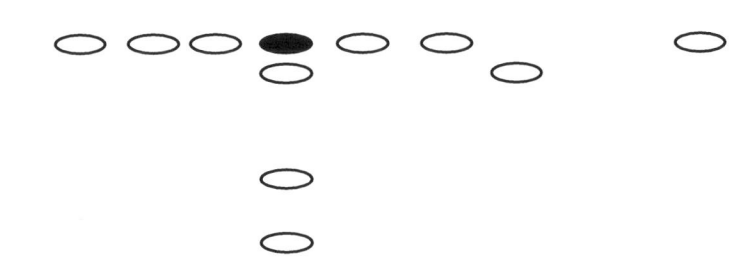

Figure 230 The "Slot I."

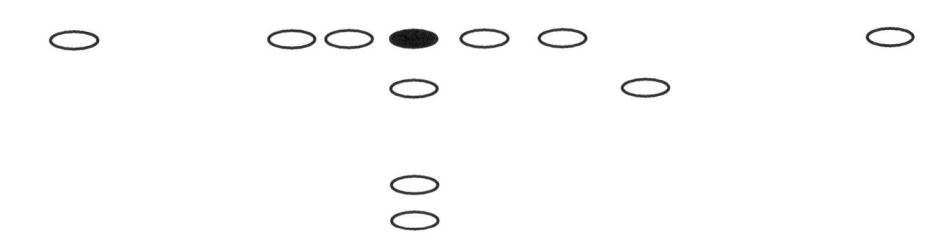

Figure 231 The "Double Split I."

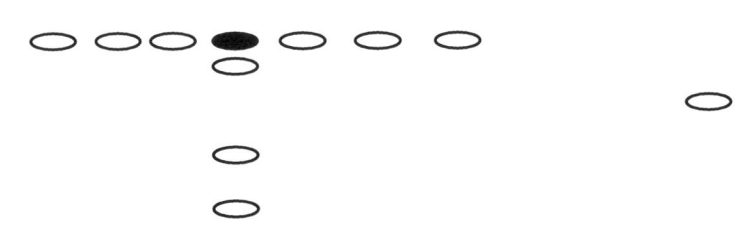

Figure 232 The "Flanker I."

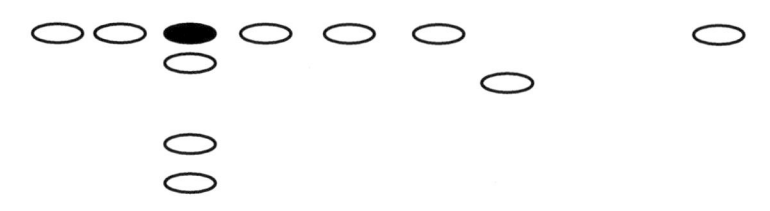

Figure 233 The "Unbalanced I."

Evolving T-Formation

Those teams that chose to play the "T" formation continued to evolve that offense during the 1950s. Many of the same configurations shown above in the ""I" formation were also used with the "T" formation. The "Spread T, the "Slot-T", the "Flanker T", the "Double Split T", the "Unbalanced T" all became familiar formations.

Professional football teams began to make news by allowing the halfback to become a flanker while keeping the fullback in the backfield but in the position of the halfback. This adjustment allowed teams to place the quicker, more agile halfback out at the flanker and place the bigger and more powerful fullback in a position to dive straight ahead and lead block for the remaining halfback. *Figure 234*

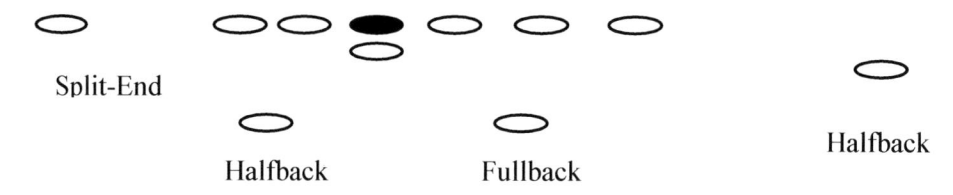

Split-End
Halfback   Fullback   Halfback

Figure 234 The "Split Back T" formation

In 1953, teams began using more spread formations. The slotback was used to combat the 6-1 umbrella defense. This loosened up the 6-1 and gave offenses greater passing areas.

By 1956, coaches found, with the waning of the 6-1 and the increased use of the 4-3, that the offense had to present a stronger blocking picture for the running game. This resulted in more teams playing with the offside end continually spread and the end on the flanker side closed (or tight) for greater running strength.

Need for Change

In 1954, the football purists tried to restore the old style of football, by forcing the same players to play offense and defense, but by 1965, unlimited substitution returned. The return of platoon football was here to stay.

In spite of the success in reforming the rules, criticism of commercial abuses of football and other sports lingered, and the complaints of commercialism in major college sports were reminiscent of the criticisms in the early 1900s. Although the NCAA was, in the 1940s, given broader investigative and enforcement powers, there were still significant problems. Professors and coaches did not love one another, and some college presidents faced pressures—and quandaries. Although violence plays a role in the uproar at this time, there are other greater concerns. Illegal payments to athletes, violations of academic standards, and drug abuse among players trouble the major programs.

David Nelson: The Wing-T

David Nelson, best known as the coach at the University of Delaware, developed the Wing-T offense. We should also note that in 1962 Nelson became Secretary-Editor of the NCAA Football Rules Committee. He held that position for 29 years. Nelson had played at the University of Michigan under Fritz Crisler where he got his Single Wing experience. He combined the Single Wing with the "T" formation to arrive at the Wing-T. Nelson was head football coach at The University of Maine from 1949 to 1950. While at Maine, Nelson, along with his assistant coaches Mike Lude and Harold Westerman began to develop the Wing-T-formation. The Wing-T, which is still in use extensively today, was not just a formation but also a complete system of plays.

When he became the Head Coach at Delaware in 1951, Nelson continued, along with his assistant Mike Lude, who he brought with him from Maine, to develop the Wing-T. Tubby Raymond, Nelson's eventual successor, joined the Delaware staff the fourth year of the Wing-T offense and became the Head Coach in 1966. Delaware was selected as the top small college in the East in 1959, 1962, and the 1963 team finished as the top small college team in the nation, according to the United Press International poll. When Nelson finally retired from coaching, after the 1965 season, he had an impressive 105-48-6 record. By combining the Single Wing and the trap series Earl "Red" Blaik used at Army, utilizing the buck sweep, and adding a QB bootleg the Wing-T developed into a complete system. The Wing-T sweep came directly from the Single Wing. They adjusted the blocking so that they could run the sweep away from the wingback to the split end side. In 1955, they added the counter.

Many other teams adopted Nelson's Wing-T formation. Forest Evashevski, coaching the Iowa Hawkeyes, won the Rose Bowl in 1957 and 1959 using the Wing-T-formation. Paul Dietzel won the national championship at LSU in 1958 using the Wing-T. Arkansas coached by Frank Broyles had much success. Also, Ara Parseghian won the national championship at Notre Dame in 1973. This elite list would be incomplete without mentioning Eddie Robinson of Grambling State, who had tremendous success using the Wing-T.

The two primary alignments for the original Delaware Wing-T were the "Wing" and the "Slot." They can be seen in *Figure 235*

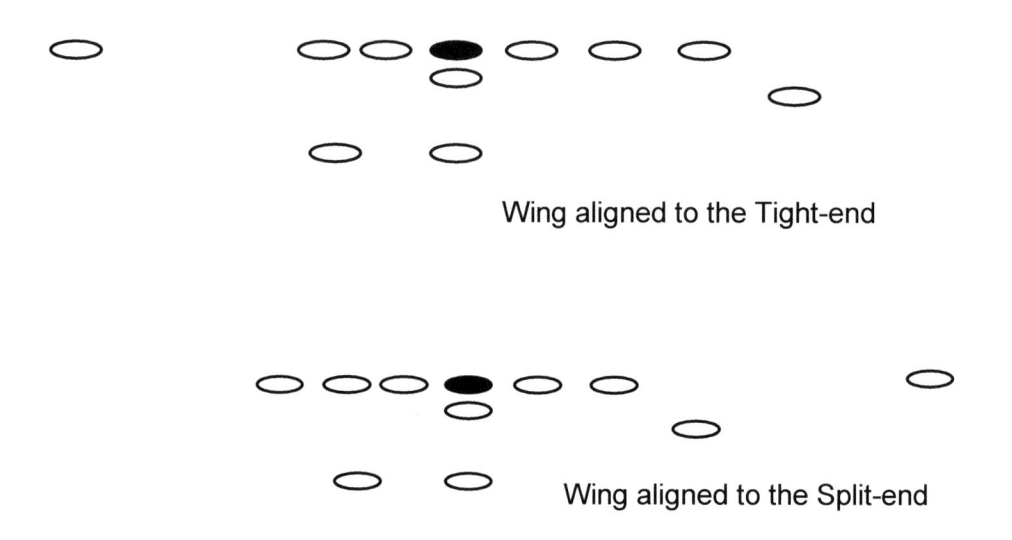

Wing aligned to the Tight-end

Wing aligned to the Split-end

Figure 235 Two Basic Wing-T formations

When "Tubby" Raymond took over for Nelson in 1966, he continued to evolve the Wing-T. He used more open formations with spread receivers. Raymond introduced the Delaware Waggle in 1968 which was a play having the quarterback faking the sweep in one direction and keeping the ball in the opposite direction with a run/pass option. The play was enhanced by having both guards pulling opposite the fake sweep and blocking for the quarterback. The Waggle is still a mainstay of many of today's offenses. *Figure 236*

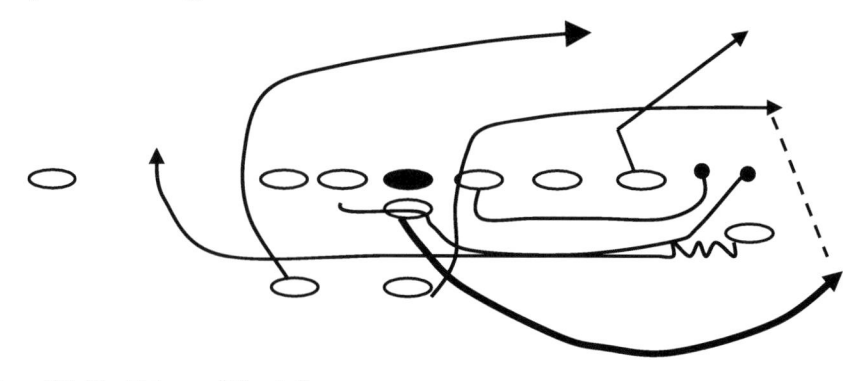

Figure 236 The Delaware "Waggle."

Raymond also experimented with opening the formation and using only one back in the backfield. *Figure 237*

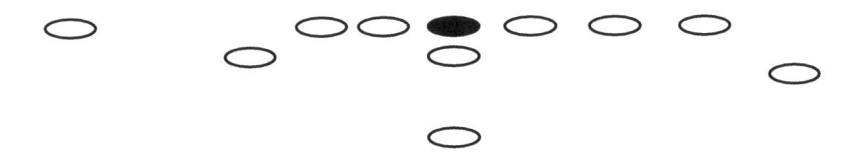

Figure 237 The Delaware One Back Formation

Paul Brown's Double Split T

The Coach of the Cleveland Browns, Paul Brown split both of his ends to put pressure on the defensive secondary.

Brown had his offensive linemen take wide splits, creating an immense "bubble" between the defensive tackle aligned over the guard and the defensive end, aligned wide because of the split-end. He attacked the secondary with the pass, both deep and shallow, with his split ends. He then had the halfback to the side he was going to run the ball, sprint wide as if he was running a sweep around end. This left a gaping hole for the fullback to dive through the defense. He had discovered the vulnerability of the Eagle defense.

Brown had found the way to defeat the Neale's Eagle defense. He spread the field, pressured the edges (flanks) with speed, threw short timing passes, and attacked the middle with the run. When the two powerhouses met in 1950, Brown destroyed Neale's Eagle defense 35-10. *Figure 238, 239*

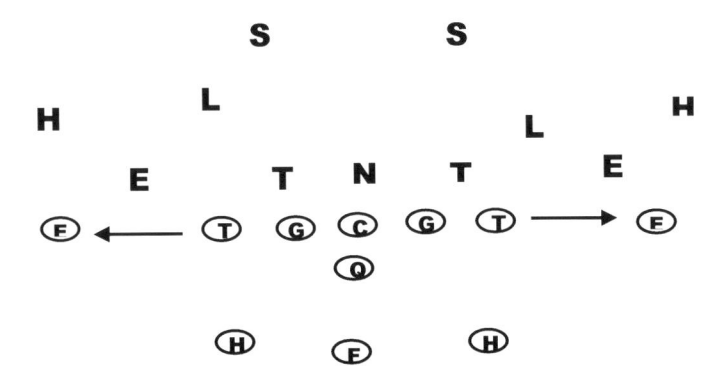

Figure 238 Paul Brown's "Double Split T." that allowed his offense to score 35 points on the "Eagle."

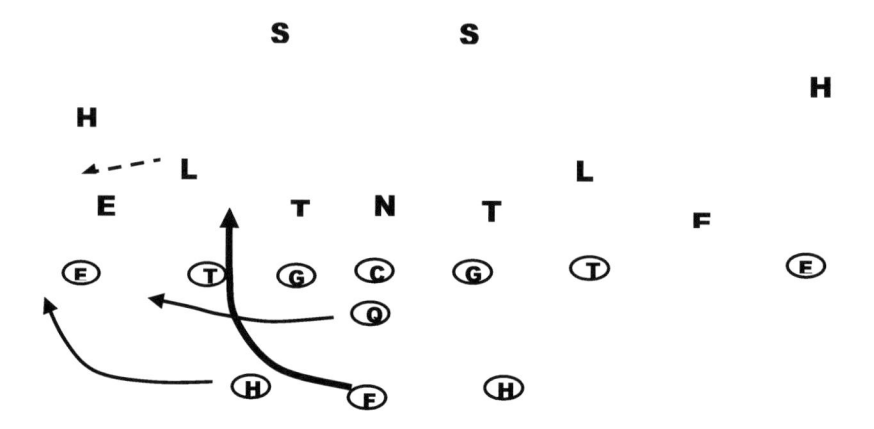

Figure 239 Paul Brown's Fullback dive versus Neale's "Eagle" Defense

Forerunners of the 4-3

Two significant developments contributed to the creation of the 4-3 defense.

We have discussed Greasy Neale and his Eagle defense. Neale began to drop the Nose guard off the line of scrimmage into a linebacker position. His Eagle defense made regular use of a seven-man front and four defensive backs. *Figure 240*

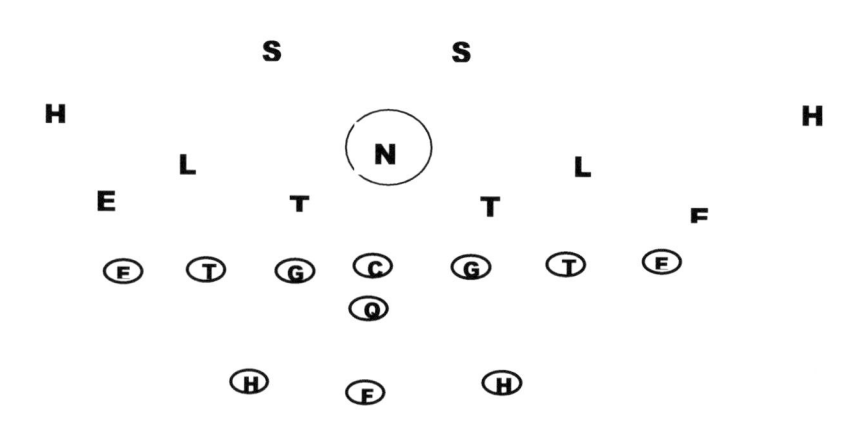

Figure 240 Figure 36 The Eagle Defense with the Nose Dropped Off

191

The Umbrella Defense

The New York Giants Coach Steve Owen found a way to strengthen his defense versus the run while still pressuring the short passing that Brown preferred for his timing routes. Owen's system, eventually known as the "Umbrella" defense, was another significant structural change in moving closer to the 4-3. The defense originally was a modified 6-1 with six defensive linemen, one linebacker, and four pass defenders. *Figure 241*

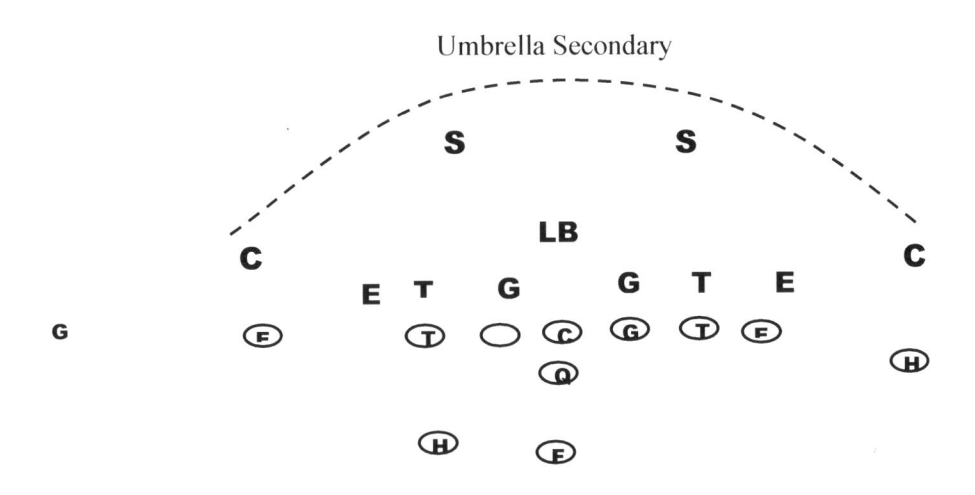

Figure 241 Owen's original 6-1 umbrella defense

Birth of the 4-3 Defense

Like Neale, Owen had previously used the 5-3-3 defense and he liked the versatility of having three linebackers. Effectively he took the two defensive guards out and replaced them with linebackers. Owen moved his tackles down over the offensive guards and his ends to a position outside the tackles. He replaced the guards with two linebackers, which he placed outside his tackles. Thus he, along with his gifted defensive back, Tom Landry, created the 4-3 umbrella defense. This new scheme had all the advantages of the 6-1 versus the run with the added versatility of three linebackers who could rush the passer or drop into pass coverage. Tom Landry became the Giants Defensive Coordinator in 1956, making some noteworthy adjustments to the defense. Landry developed some of the first innovations in the process, many of which still shape 4-3 fronts five decades later. Under Landry, the four defensive linemen were only responsible for one gap. It became a "keying" defense, with each of the lineman having a specific assignment that depended on what the offensive lineman in front of them did. A primary responsibility of the defensive linemen was to keep offensive blockers from getting to the middle linebacker allowing him to pursue quickly to the ball. [214]

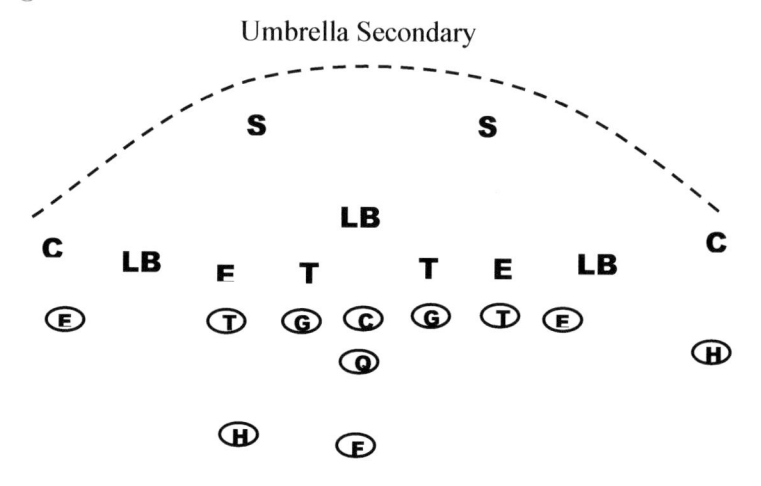

Figure 242

Figure 242 The evolved 4-3 Umbrella Defense.

As the decade ended, and many more teams began to use Owen's new defense, some teams lined their traditional 6-1 ends up as linebackers. The 4-3 defense was born.

Remember, in Philadelphia, Neale dropped his middle guard off the line and changed his Eagle Defense into a variation of the 4-3. Some college teams picked up this alignment and the defense became known as the "College 4-3."

The Lonesome End

In his last year of coaching in 1958, Army's Earl Blaik won 8 and tied 1 without a loss. That team used the "Lonesome End" formation, in which one end split very wide, near the sideline, and never entered the Army huddle. The quarterback relayed the plays through hand signals. If the opponent's interest in him diminished, or they left him unguarded, Blaik would have him sprint down the sideline for a long touchdown pass. Unfortunately, for many defenses, the long throw to the "Lonesome End" occurred much too often. In two games that year, Army scored 71 points. Teams seemed to have difficulty deciding whether they should concentrate on the "Lonesome End" or the rest of the Army offense. Eventually, the rules outlawed the "Lonesome end". *See Figure 243*

End stayed near the sideline. He never entered the huddle.

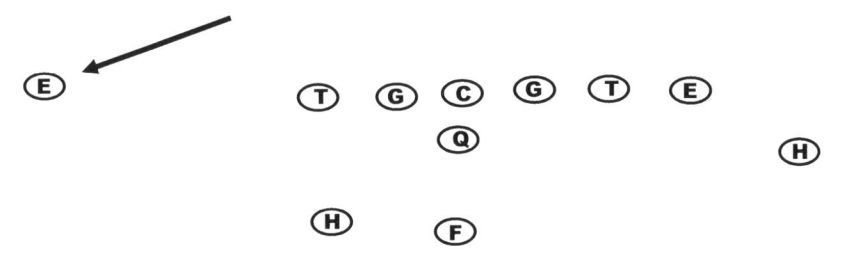

```
  (E)              (T) (G) (C) (G) (T) (E)
                           (Q)              (H)
                       (H)     (F)
```

Figure 243 Army's "Lonesome End."

Two Point Conversion
In 1958, the NCAA ruled that college teams now would have the option of going for a two-point conversion after scoring a touchdown.

Modifying the 4-3
By 1959, Allie Sherman of the New York Giants as well as some other defensive coaches tweaked the basic 4-3 defense somewhat and began to play defensive linemen in the "gaps". The intent was to destroy the stronger blocking combinations created by the Tight End and add defensive strength to the strong side of the attack. Vince Lombardi would create the offense to combat the "gap" defense.

---

[208] Bryant, Paul, jW. "Bear", *Building a Championship Football Team*,(Englewood Cliffs, NJ, Prentice-Hall Inc., 1960), p. 28-29
[209] http://sportsillustrated.cnn.com/*centurys_best*/news/1999/10/06/cfb_allcentury_team/
[210] Bryant, *Building a Championship Football Team*, p. 55
[211] Jones, Gomer, Wilkinson, "Bud". *Modern Defensive Football*, (Englewood Cliffs, NJ, Prentice-Hall, Inc., 1957), P. xi-xii
[212] Danzig, *A History of American Football*, p. 113.
[213] Danzig, *A History of American Football*, p. 58
[214] Lombardi, Vince, *Vince Lombardi on Football*, (New York Grapahic Society Ltd., Greenwich, CT, 1973),

CHAPTER ELEVEN

Development of the Contemporary Game

(1960 –1969)

"Red" Hickey's Shotgun

In 1960, "Red" Hickey, the coach of the San Francisco 49ers, devised a new system that he called the "Shotgun." Actually, there had been many variations of the formation since the 1930s, often as part of the Double Wing and Single Wing Formations.

At times, he brought one of the wide receivers back into the backfield and lined him behind the weak side guard.

Hickey felt that the "shotgun" provided his team with a couple of distinct advantages. One of the benefits of the shotgun formation was that the passer had more time to set up in the pocket, which gave him a second, or two to locate open receivers. Another advantage was that standing further back from the line before the snap gave the quarterback a better "look" at the defensive alignment. Although the 49ers did run the ball from the "shotgun", everyone considered it a passing formation. Hickey ran the offense with much success until defenses learned that, through blitzing, you could stop the new "shotgun." Under Tom Landry, the Dallas Cowboys revitalized the formation in the 70s. Moreover, today it is seen at every level of football. *Figure 244*

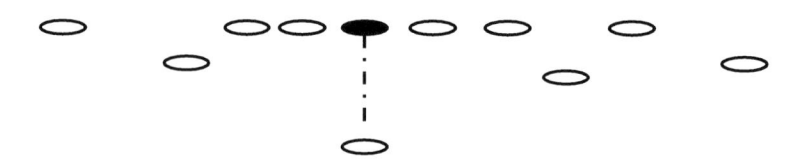

Figure 244 Shotgun formation of "Red" Hickey

Growth of the "I" Formation

At the college level, the decade opened with some changes in the I- formation. John McKay became the Head Coach at the University of Southern California. During his first two seasons, he had limited success. In 1960-61, he was 8-11-1. Before the 1962 season, McKay implemented some changes in his "I" formation. Before this time, the "I" had been used predominately from a three-back set. McKay opened up the formation and used a Pro set and a Slot set. There were times he removed his Tight End and played with two Split Ends. He increased the splits in his offensive line and an entirely new form of the "I" was created. His USC Trojans were 11-0, won the Rose Bowl and selected as the National Champions. Using their new adaptation of the "I", they repeated as National Champions in 1967 and again in 1972 and 1974.

The Trojans' favorite play was a simple sweep that came to be called "student body right," although it was just as effective when run to the left. It was, in fact, a simple sweep. Because it seemed the entire team was running toward the sideline and the student section of the stadium the name "Student Body Right" caught on.

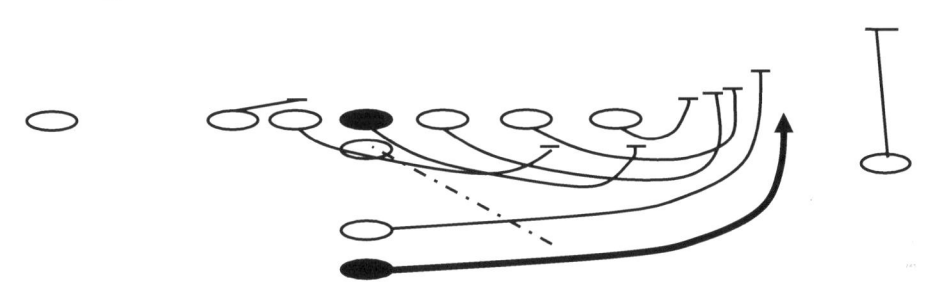

Figure-245

Figure 245 USC's "Student Body Right" play

Two Platoon Football Returns

It was in 1964 that Two-platoon football returned to the college game. It would prove to be, perhaps, the single most change in the game effecting positional technique and complexity of execution on both offense and defense.

Bill Yeoman: The Veer Option

The option, used for decades and, at the time very widely utilized by the Split "T" teams, went through a new transformation with the creation of a new option.

Considered "equalizers" on the playing field, option offenses allowed less athletic teams to compete with larger and faster defenses. Option offenses traditionally relied heavily upon running plays, though modern option offenses now incorporate a large quantity of passing plays. Because it was a run-based offense, option offenses were very efficient at maintaining ball control, giving the opposition less time to score, and allowing their own defense to rest. However, this also meant that when the option team was losing near the end of the game and needed to score quickly, they were at a disadvantage. The option schemes relied on timing, deception, and split-second decision-making under pressure, which, in turn, required flawless execution and discipline.

Bill Yeoman developed the new option in 1965 while he was the head coach at the University of Houston. Even today, some refer to it as the Houston Veer. Additionally, it is also called the "split-back" Veer because, in the original "veer" formation, the two running backs were split, with one behind each guard. In its basic form, there is normally one tight end.

Yeoman created his Veer to attack the 5-2 defense that was in fashion back then. *Figure 246* depicts the "true triple option" or "Inside Veer" play to a tight end side.

The line would take large splits to widen the defensive tackles. The back on the play-side would dive, and the far back would sprint to play-side as an option pitchman.

Yeoman would double-team the nose man using the Center and play-side Guard. The play-side offensive tackle would release inside to block the inside linebacker just as he would on the Split T-trap play.

The design was for the quarterback to extend the ball into the dive back's pocket (waist) while "reading" the reaction of the unblocked defensive tackle. If the defensive tackle did not step down to grab the dive back, the quarterback had, what they called a "give" read. He handed the ball to the dive man (Option "1" in the diagram). If defenses could not stop this play, they would see a good quantity of plays to that dive back for the rest of the game. However, if the tackle did close down to stop the dive, that accounted for him without anyone having to block him. The quarterback pulled the ball from the dive back's waist and kept it. He then continued down the line to his next "read", on the defensive end. The large split of the Tight End served to widen the defensive end. The defensive end was left unblocked, just as the defensive tackle had been. The Tight end would go outside the defensive end. As he released from the line of scrimmage, he would widen. This would later to be referred to as an "arc" block. The Tight End would look to block whoever had the responsibility for tackling the halfback or "pitchman". This would be the "SS" (the Strong Safety) in *Figure 246*. Should the quarterback pitch the ball, the wide receiver on the play-side would block the cornerback (C). The quarterback would option the defensive end. If the defensive end attempted to tackle him, he would pitch the ball to the running back (option "3"). If the defensive end widened, to cover the halfback, the quarterback would turn up into the area created between the defensive tackle that was crashing down to tackle the dive back and the defensive end widening to tackle the pitchman (option "2").

The line play of a veer team was very aggressive. They were low in their stance with their weight forward. Some veer coaches have advocated four-point stances.

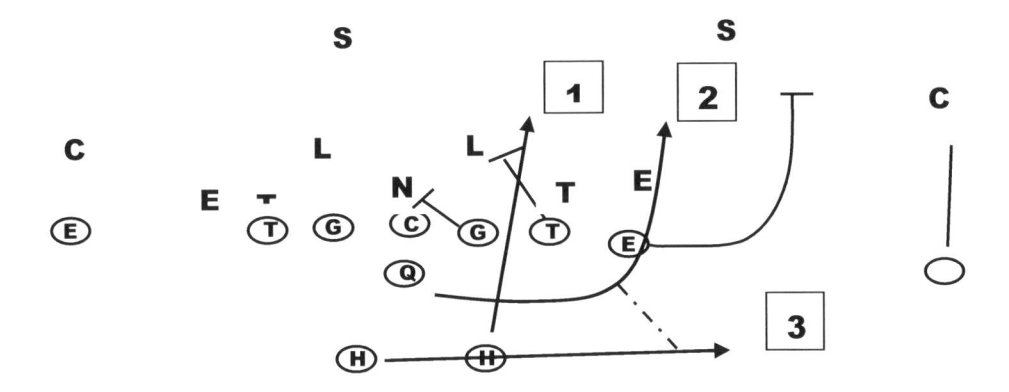

Figure 246 The Veer Option

The play above is shown in its very basic form. As defenses adjusted to survive the threat of the triple option, veer teams had to devise all sorts of blocking schemes to deal with them.

It is a "series" offense. A defense stacked to stop one particular play finds itself vulnerable to another play that starts out looking the same as the first. Other plays that are usually included in complete veer attack are the Dive, Outside Veer, Lead option, Counter Dive, Counter Option, and the Tight End dump pass.

The Wishbone

The Wishbone Triple Option traces its roots to West Texas High school football. History has it that in the summer of 1968, Emory Bellard became the father of wishbone triple option football. The wishbone's roots, according to Barry Switzer, date back to the 1950s. In his book *"Bootlegger's Boy"*, Switzer credits the foundation of the Wishbone to Charles "Spud" Cason, who was the coach at William Monnig Junior High School of Fort Worth, Texas. Cason first modified the classic T-formation by moving his fullback up to get him to the line of scrimmage quicker.[215] Switzer claims Bellard learned about Cason's tactics while coaching at Breckenridge High School in Texas.

In 1967, The University of Texas hired Bellard to coach the linebackers. That following spring, Texas head coach Darryl Royal moved him from coaching linebackers to the offense. Bellard always liked option football. Moreover, he wanted the advantages three-back formations gave an offense. He had started toying with the Wishbone concept while coaching at Ingleside and Breckenridge High Schools. Ballard liked the idea behind the Houston Veer but felt that a three back setup would provide a lead blocker for the pitch back.[216] The principle of Ballard's Wishbone Triple Option was the same as Yeoman's Houston Veer. Royal, who was always a fan of the option offense, listened to Ballard's idea and took a chance on the new offense. That year Texas tied their first game, lost their second, and then won thirty straight games and two National Championships using the wishbone. *Figure 247*

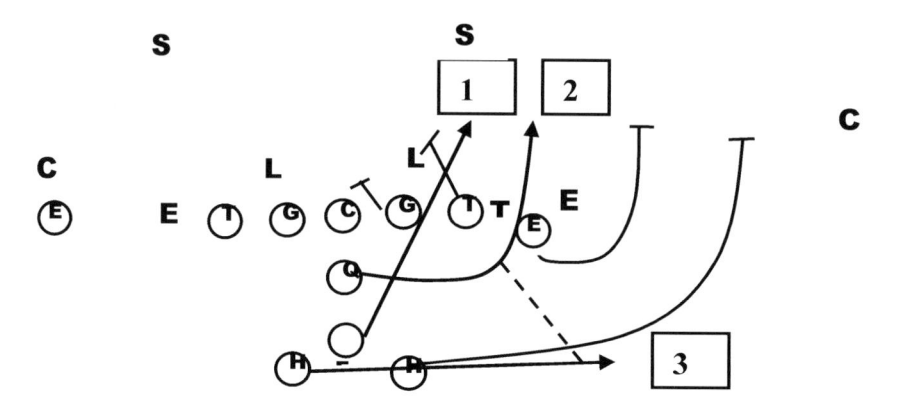

Figure 247 Wishbone Option

    Homer Smith and Pepper Rogers stated in their book *"Installing Football's Wishbone T Attack"*: "There is no Wishbone offense without the triple option play. It is the single most important part in the machinery and it must be understood for what it is not as much as for what it is." [217]

    The Wishbone became extremely popular at both the college level and high school level. Oklahoma under Chuck Fairbanks, UCLA under Pepper Rogers, and Alabama coached by Paul "Bear" Bryant all adopted the formation. Both Alabama and Oklahoma won National Championships using the Wishbone. During the decade, Alabama using the wishbone won three National Championships under head coach Paul "Bear" Bryant. Bryant is considered one of the greatest head coaches in college football history. He compiled a 323-85-17 record in his 25 years at Alabama. Along the way, he won six National Championships.

    Coach Bellard went on to coach at Mississippi State, where he introduced the "Wing-Bone", moving one of the halfbacks up to a wing formation and frequently sending him in motion. This was also called the "Broken Bone."

    As we will see later, the wishbone concept is still alive and still run effectively. It is in the form of a Stack-I, and a sort of Power-I formation called the I-bone. Navy, Air Force, and Georgia Tech still run it, but mostly from a spread formation and mostly with motioning wingbacks. These schools have created a new generation of triple option football. More on this in a later chapter

    The triple-option from the wishbone would be hurt at the high school level when the high school rules prohibited blocking below the waist. At the college level, it has been damaged by several factors, including the increased popularity of the passing game, and by the pro offense influence.

Backbone Defense to Stop Wishbone

Phil Jack Dawson, a high school coach from Westbrook Maine, devised a defense that was very successful in stopping the Wishbone attack. Frustrated with the difficulty of facing the Wishbone teams he was playing each year he created a different defense for the Wishbone that he named the "Backbone Defense".[218] *Figure 248* Note how the middle linebacker (M) and the two Inverts (I) mirror the alignment of the three Wishbone backs. Ara Parseghian and his staff at the University of Notre Dame were working on a similar approach to defending the Wishbone around the same time.[219] Parseghian and Dawson had many conversations regarding the structure of the defense. Notre Dame used the defense successfully in the 1971 Cotton Bowl with Texas and again in the 1974 Sugar Bowl against Alabama.

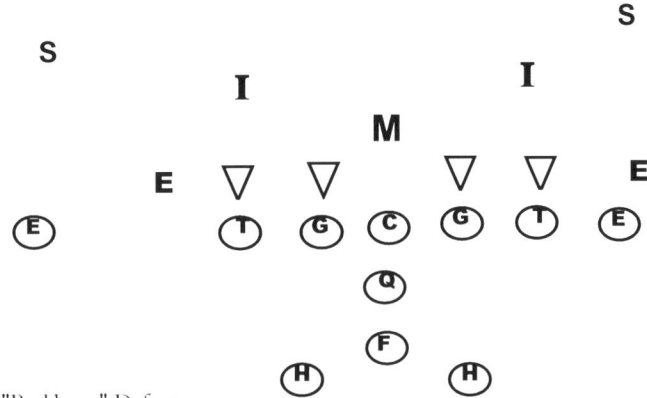

Figure 248 The "Backbone" Defense

Vince Lombardi

No discussion of football during the 1960s would be complete without a discussion of Vince Lombardi. The following statement by Lombardi sums up his thoughts on the game.

> "Every football team eventually arrives at a lead play. It becomes the team's bread and butter play, the top-priority play, the play that the team knows it must make go. It is the play opponents know they must stop. Continued success with the play, of course, makes for a number one play, because from that success stems your confidence, and behind that is the basic truth that it expresses the coach as a coach and players as a team and they feel complete satisfaction when they execute it and it's completely right."[220]

For Vince Lombardi and the Green Bay Packers that play became the "Lombardi Sweep". From his time in college at Fordham Lombardi had been impressed with the Single Wing and its power blocking. He combined the guard pulling technique of the Single Wing with the T-formation he had learned under Earl "Red"

Blaik at Army. He actually began using the play as an assistant coach with the NY Giants in the late 1950s, but it was not until he became the head coach at Green Bay that the play became legendary. *Figure 249*

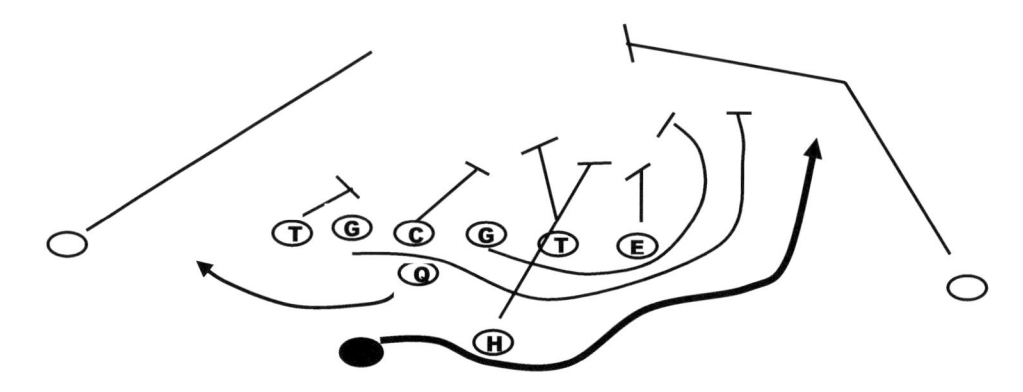

Figure 249 The Green Bay Sweep

Lombardi's "do-dad" or area block" may be the precursor to the present day "Zone Block".

States Lombardi, "The guard and the center do-dad or "area block" the defensive tackle and the middle linebacker. Do-dad blocking is used against stunting lines or lines that stack one defensive man behind the other. In the case where the defensive tackle has an inside charge and the middle linebacker is keying fullback and has the outside responsibility, the middle linebacker will, with the snap of the ball, move immediately to the hole, making it impossible for the offensive center to cut him down because of the middle linebacker's key on the fullback. In this case, we will use do-dad blocking.

"The center is the lead blocker – the apex. He will lead step, the same technique as the down block, for the crotch of the defensive tackle. The offensive guard, using the same technique as he does in the drive block, will aim for a point which is outside the hip of the defensive tackle. If the defensive tackle has an inside charge, the tackle immediately releases the defensive tackle, picking up the middle linebacker who would be moving with the key of the fullback toward the hole. The center, since the tackle is moving into him, would pick him off.

"If the defensive tackle has an outside charge that means that the middle linebacker would first have a responsibility to the inside. Remember, however, that the middle linebacker still has the key of the fullback. But the fact that he has inside responsibility would hold him long enough so that the center, coming off the down block on the

defensive tackle, could recover and pick off the middle linebacker." [221]
Figure 250

Defensive Tackle Slants in   Defensive Tackle Stays

Figure 250 "Do-dad" Blocking

Run to Daylight

Lombardi initiated the phrase, "Run to Daylight." In Lombardi's "Run to Daylight" design, the back ran for an area where the blocking was focused, and then he would sprint to where he saw "daylight." Instead of hitting a pre-designated spot, he had the freedom to run to any open area. The Packers' off-tackle slant, for example, might have the fullback hit the guard hole or the tackle hole depending where the open area was. This is an essential element of the zone-blocking scheme of today.

The Evolving 4-3 Defense

It was during this period that defensive coaches discovered that it was difficult to play the 4-3 defense with the two tackles in a "head-up" position. From the head-up position, both tackles were responsible for two gaps. Coaches began to align the tackles with one on the inside shoulder of an offensive guard (a 1 technique) and one aligned on the outside shoulder of the other guard (a 3 technique.) This created a situation where each tackle was now responsible for one gap. *Figure 251*

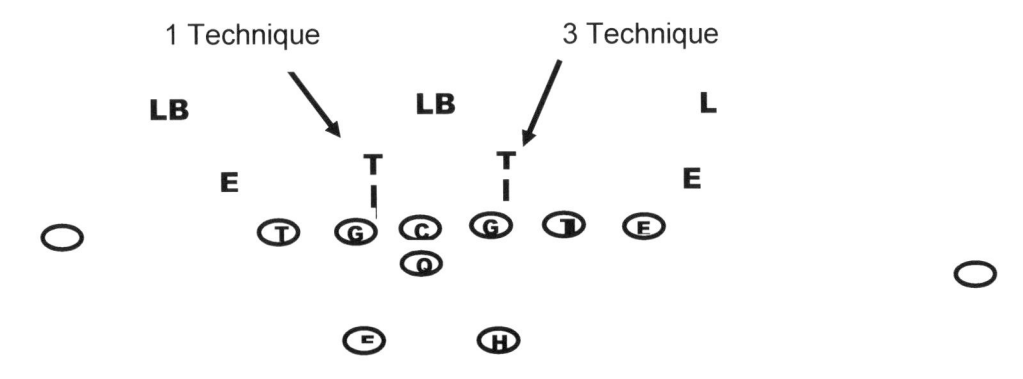

Figure 251 The 4-3 showing a "one" technique tackle and a "Three" technique tackle

Hank Stram's Odd Front

Tom Landry and the defensive coaches in the NFL were not the only ones tinkering with the basic 4-3 defense. In the AFL, coaches were experimenting with creating mismatches of larger defenders aligned over smaller offensive blockers and quicker defenders aligned over larger, slower blockers. They began to make the defense harder to block by suddenly shifting the defenders just before the snap of the ball.

Hank Stram, the innovative coach of the Kansas City Chiefs, made a dramatic change that would influence defenses for decades. Stram moved one of his defensive tackles from the typical 4-3 even front to a position directly over the center. He shifted his middle linebacker to a position over the guard to that side. He now had something that looked like an "odd" front (meaning a defender is aligned over the offensive center). *Figure 252*

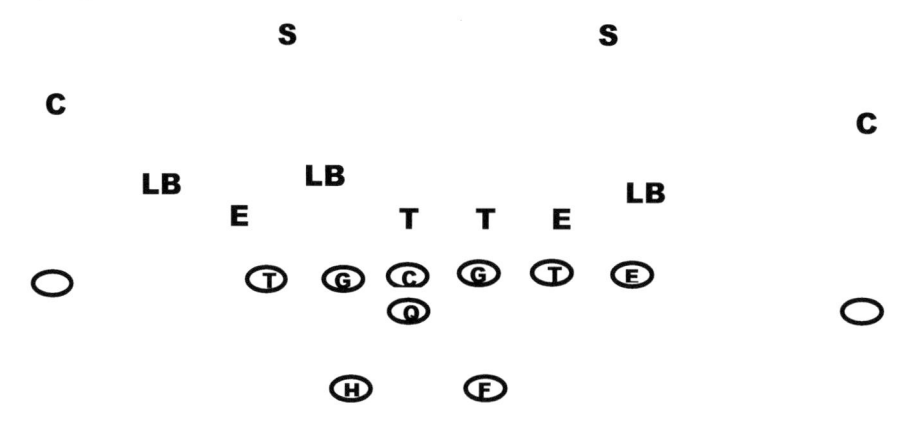

Figure 252 Hank Stram's 4-3 Odd front

4-3 Over Front

Defensive coaches are continually searching for ways to make their defensive linemen more effective. As mentioned previously, one of the difficulties for the 4-3 tackles playing head up on the offensive guards is that they become responsible for 2 gaps, the center-guard gap, and the guard-tackle gap. By sliding the defensive tackles to an offset position, the defenders are now responsible for only one gap. This freed them to be more aggressive in their play and harder to double team.

When coaches took the 4-3 alignment and shifted the defensive line either weak or strong and the linebackers in the opposite direction, the 4-3 "Over" and 4-3 "Under" defenses were formed. These adjustments allowed the defense to shift more linemen to the suspected point of attack. The alignment created a 3-technique tackle (the defender aligned on the outside shoulder of the offensive guard) and a 1-technique defender (the defender aligned on the shoulder of the center or inside shoulder of the guard.) The alignment presents four down lineman and three linebackers in the front seven, just as in a basic 4-3.

Figure 253 shows the 4-3 "Over" defense. Notice one defensive end lines up on the inside shoulder of the tight end. The other defensive end lines up on the outside shoulder of the weakside tackle. One defensive tackle lines up on the outside shoulder of the offensive guard to the tight end side. One defensive tackle lines up in the weakside gap between the center and the guard. On the strongside, the linebacker lines up head up on the offensive tackle. Another linebacker lines up on the outside shoulder of the weakside guard. The third linebacker lines up in a position outside the weakside defensive end.[222] In moving to the Over 4-3, the defensive strength has shifted to the strong side of the offensive formation. The "Over" defense was popularized by Hank Stram of the Kansas Chiefs.

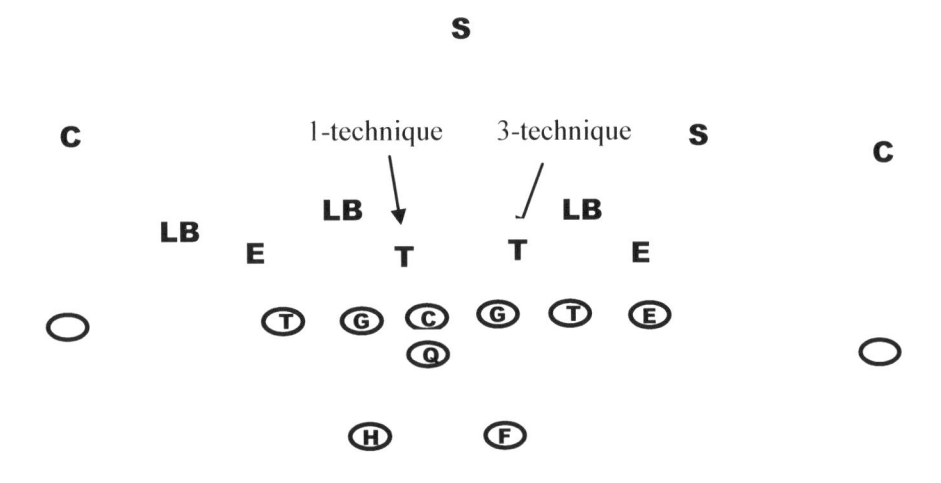

Figure 253 The 4-3 "Over" defensive front

4-3 Under Front

When defensive coaches want the strength of the defense to move to the weak side of the formation, they have the 4-3 under front. *Figure 254* It is a simple task to get from the Over front to the Under defense. One end aligns on the outside shoulder of the offensive tackle to the tight end side. The other defensive end is outside the offensive tackle to the weak side. One tackle aligned in the strongside gap between the center and strongside guard. The other tackle is on the outside shoulder of the offensive guard on the weak side. The linebacker on the strongside will position himself on the line of scrimmage on the outside shoulder of the tight end. Another linebacker will be off the line of scrimmage on the outside shoulder of the strongside guard. The third linebacker will align off the ball head up on the weakside offensive tackle.[223] The "under shifted" front makes it tough for the offensive line to double team the 3-technique, or, in this case, under tackle. Additionally, this protects the weakside linebacker from the offensive blockers and he is in an excellent spot to make a significant number of plays. The Monte Kiffin and Tony Dungy philosophy was to turn back the ball carrier in the direction of the weakside linebacker. Coaches talk of "spilling" the runner to the weakside linebacker. We have the creation of a new concept in run support.[224]

In the future, the "under" will be adapted to the Tampa-2 defense popularized by Dungy and Kiffin

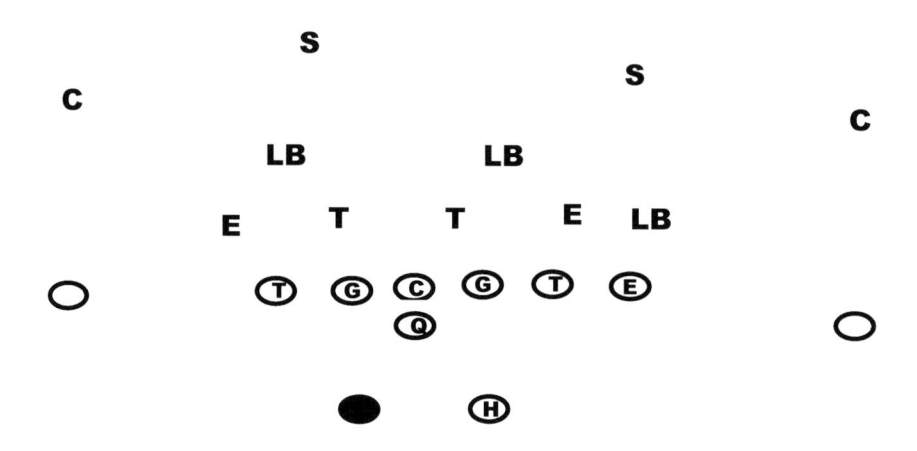

Figure 254 The 4-3 "Under" defensive front

The Flex Defense

Coach Tom Landry, who many actually credit with refining the 4-3 defense when he was a player-coach with the New York Giants, became the Head Coach of the Dallas Cowboys in 1960. He continued his innovative ways by creating an adjustment in the 4-3 defense to combat Lombardi's "Run to daylight" concept. Landry devised a defense to create problems for the "do-dad" blocking. He altered some of the defensive alignments in the 4-3. They called it the "Flex Defense." The Flex defense abandoned the fast-pursuing linebacker preferred by most 4-3 defenses. Because the "Flex" altered its alignment to counter what the offense might do, the defense created unique problems for the offense. There were three variants of the Flex Defenses — strong, weak, and "tackle" — where one or two defenders were off the line of scrimmage. The idea with the flexed linemen was to improve pursuit angles to stop the Green Bay Sweep. Each player had a particular responsibility to "key" or read the actions of the offensive players in the area. The defense created unique problems for offenses.[225]   *See Figures 255, 256*

205

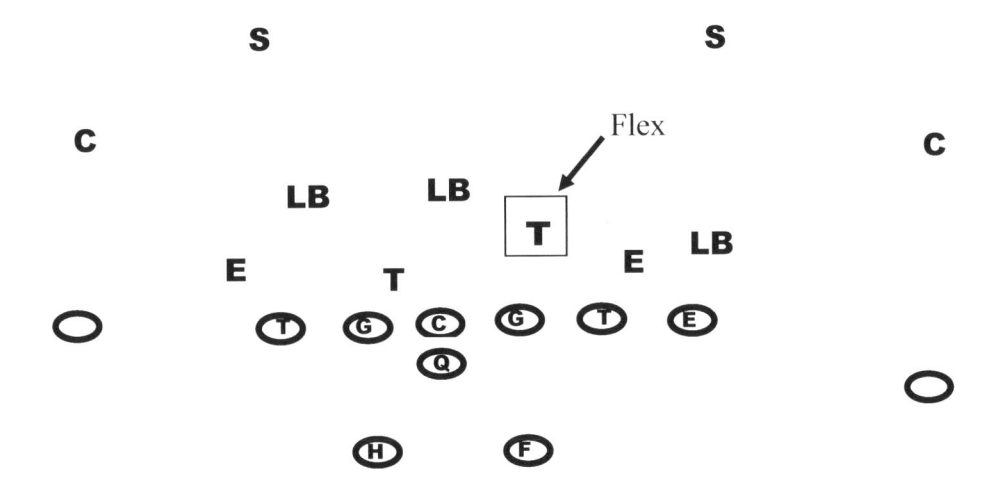

Figure 255 Dallas "Flex" Defense: One Tackle flexed

As can be seen in *Figure 255*, the "Down 3" aligned in standard alignments for typical 4-3 players of their positions. The defensive ends stayed in an outside shade the offensive tackle. To the split end side, the defensive tackle went to an inside shade of the offensive guard. The fascinating change is the "Flex" player, who could really do many things for them. Some years he was a linebacker and other years he was a true defensive lineman who just played out of a two-point stance.[226]

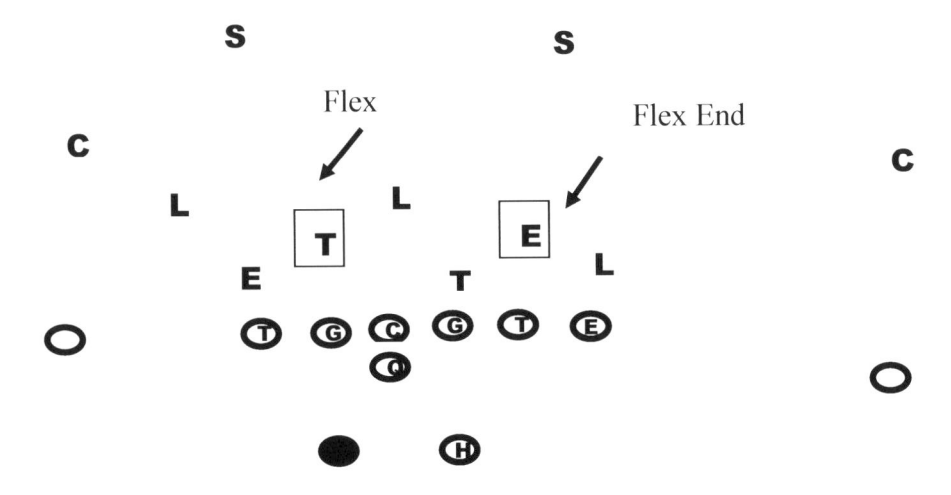

Figure 256 Dallas "Flex" Defense: Tackle & End flexed

The Dallas Shift

Landry was not only inventive on defense. He revived the man-in-motion and the shotgun formation. However, one of Landry's biggest offensive contributions was the use of "pre-shifting". He had his offense shift from one formation to the other before the snap of the ball. Such shifting certainly was not new. Coach Amos Alonzo Stagg used it around the turn of the 20th century. Landry had the offensive line run up to the line of scrimmage, get into pre-stance and in unison, all stand back up as the offensive backs shifted. They would then resume their original position. What seemed like a small thing played havoc with defenses. The idea was to break the keys the defense used to determine what the offense might do. The "up and down" movement made it more difficult for the defense to see where the backs were shifting (over the tall offensive linemen) and thus cut down on recognition time. [227]

The Run & Shoot

Many claim Glenn "Tiger" Ellison, a high school coach in Ohio, created the precursor of the "spread" offense. It started with an attack that he called the "Lonesome Polecat" but quickly evolved into his new offense, the Run and Shoot, which referred to run first and shoot second. The fundamental principle of the Run and Shoot was to line up in a four or five-wide receiver formation and then adjust the play call, according to the defense. In the right hands, this is vicious since any defense you can think of has a hole somewhere. The receivers and QB have to be on the same page so they both know what route to run. If the defense lines up with five or six defensive backs, the offense can then gain an advantage by running the ball.

Said Ellison of his new idea; "From the opening whistle to the final gun, the Run-and-Shoot offense went for the home run – it tried to score on every play, except for an occasional punt (1.2 punts per game). We refused to punt when the ball rested in front of the 50-yard line. We considered the entire playing field offensive territory. We were willing to pass anywhere on the field on any down.

"We made every pass look like a run and every run look like a pass. Offenses that pass from a pocket split their attack into two phases – their running game and their passing game. The setting up of the quarterback in the pocket screams "Pass" to every defender on the field. Even though pocket-passing teams often fake the ball to a runner before setting up in the pocket, still the fake wards off detection for only a moment, after which all defenders spring into anti-aircraft action. The Run-and-Shoot offense did not split its attack – it was just one game, running and passing performed anywhere anytime with no distinguishing clue to signal run or pass." [228] *See Figure 257*

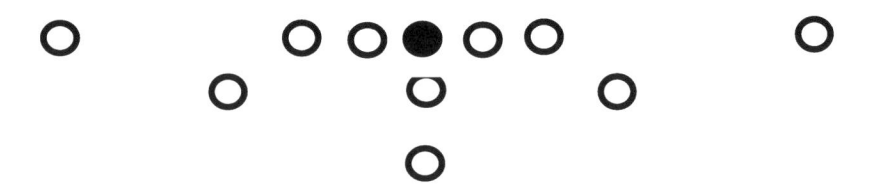

Figure 257 Ellison's Run and Shoot Formation

    Darrel "Mouse" Davis helped make the Run & Shoot offense famous with his own Run & Shoot offense at Portland State University where he coached from 1975-1980. Davis embraced the theories of Middletown (Ohio) High School coach Glenn "Tiger" Ellison. Davis utilized the offense throughout his long coaching career. His experience included coaching at the high school level in Oregon, at the college level, and professionally in the NFL, CFL, USFL, WLAF, and Arena League. During his time at Portland State, Davis's Run-and-Shoot teams owned a 42–24 record over 6 seasons. His teams averaged 38 points and nearly 500 yards of offense per game. PSU led the nation in scoring three times.[229] Mouse Davis later was the offensive coordinator for Wayne Fontes with the Detroit Lions. John Jenkins, who worked with Davis, became the offensive coordinator for Jack Pardee at the University of Houston. He followed Pardee to the Houston Oilers in 1990 where they continued to spread the field and placed an ever-increasing emphasis on the passing attack. June Jones at Hawaii used his version of the Run & Shoot with great success in 1999 and later with the Atlanta Falcons. We will discuss more on the Run and Shoot later.

    There are two prominent disciples of the passing game that must be considered at this point. Don Coryell and Sid Gillman. Although both Coryell and Gilman coached into the 1980s and continued their innovative work with the passing offense, both coaches began their work with the passing attack in the 1960s.

Don Coryell

    In the late 1950s and early 1960s, Don Coryell was a pioneer in the use of the I- formation. He was an assistant under John McKay when McKay was making history with his "I" formation. However, the largest part of his work with the pass offense came after that time.

    Originally, his offense was known as the West Coast Offense. However, an article about San Francisco Head Coach Bill Walsh in Sports Illustrated in the early 80s incorrectly called Walsh's offense "the West Coast offense," This mislabeling stuck. Subsequently, Coryell's offensive scheme has been referred to as "Air Coryell". He continued to refine his passing system while coaching the San Diego Chargers from 1978-1986. Several of the more successful advocates of Coryell's system are Norv Turner, Mike Martz, Cam Cameron, Al Saunders, and Joe Gibbs.

The "Coryell Offense", was at times, referred to as a "Vertical Offense". Moreover, the "Vertical Offense" is probably a more descriptive term for the offensive philosophy Coryell espoused. He promoted a mixture of deep and mid range pass plays, along with power running.[230] The offense relied on getting all five receivers out into patterns that stretched the field and had the Quarterback throwing to a spot on time where the receiver could catch the ball and turn up the field. Pass protection was critical to Coryell's success because at least two of the five receivers would run a deep in, a skinny post, a comeback, speed out, or shallow cross. All are routes that take time to complete.

Overall, the goal of the Coryell offense was to have at least two downfield, fast wide receivers who could adjust to the deep pass very well. This was combined with a solid pocket quarterback with a strong arm. Coryell used three key weapons.

The first was a strong inside running game. The second weapon was the ability to strike deep with two or more receivers on any play. And the third was, to not only use those two attacks in collaboration with each other but, to include an abundance of mid-range passing to the Tight Ends, Wide Receivers, or Backs.

The Coryell offense had the ability to both "eat the clock" with the ground game and to strike deep and fast without warning. Critics argue that the Coryell offense was ill-suited for coming from behind, as the deep passing attack could be predictable and, therefore, easy to defend. However, structured around a power running game with tall Wide Receivers with breakaway speed make this contention hard to support. This offense does not only emphasize deep passing, but it is also good in short yardage and red zone situations. When evenly matched, the Coryell offense could produce big drives and big scoring efficiency. If teams sat back to cover the deep field, offenses were able to run the ball on them. If the defense tightened down to stop the run, the offense could go deep. When defenses confronted him by using three deep defenders, with an eight-man defense up front, the quarterback picked apart the defense with 10-20-yard passes

Joe Gibbs, who won 3 Super Bowls with the Washington Redskins, was an ardent supporter of the Coryell offense. The Redskins featured a ferocious running game. Gibbs often kept the Tight End in as an extra blocker to pass protect. The Redskins offense combined Coryell's passing game with a strong, powerful running game. Gibbs was one of the first to use the three Tight End offense that we will discuss later. He made extensive use of the counter trey play. Gibbs was also one of the first to make frequent use of the bunched receiver concept.

Generally, the Coryell offenses concentrated on stretching defenses vertically with deep passing. This was in contrast to the short passes that will be a mainstay in the Bill Walsh West Coast offense. Some were critical of the Coryell offense because it depended on a higher risk passing game. Another criticism was the offense's inability to stretch defenses in the red zone. While Coryell, himself, schemed and selected personnel to defeat short yardage and red zone situations, some Coryell offense supporters did not consider those needs and suffered in those areas. Coryell's offensive innovations are on display every week in the wide-open passing game of today

Sid Gillman

The other significant name that stands out when discussing the modern passing game is Sid Gillman. Gillman's San Diego Charger teams were some of the most offensively explosive in football thanks, in large part, to his wide-open passing game, that today is the standard of both college and pro football. The great success of his assistants Al Davis at Oakland, Chuck Noll of Pittsburgh, Jack Faulkner of Denver validates the impact Gilman has had on the passing game. Actually, Gillman was the first NFL coach to use a vertical passing game, even before Coryell.

Gillman is credited with inventing the concept of "timing," and calibrating quarterback drops with receiver routes. Unlike many innovative coaches who are caught up in their own generation, Gillman continued to be in the forefront of the game largely up until his death: he coached many great NFL teams in his later years.

Before Gillman became the Head Coach of the Los Angeles Rams in 1955, the NFL used a run game with short, quick passes to the backs or receivers. When the American Football League started in 1960, Gillman became the Head Coach of the Los Angeles Chargers. The Chargers moved to San Diego in 1961. He led the team to 5 Western Division titles, the league championship in 1963, and an 82-47-6 record in the first six years of the league.[231]

One of the major tenets of Gillman's passing game was that the timing of the delivery of the pass was essential. He believed that it was the single most important aspect of successful passing. He analyzed each route and established a timing concept between the quarterback and receiver for each respective pass route. He was, most likely, the first to attempt to have the quarterback deliver the ball before the receiver even made his break or final move. He believed that if you wait until the receiver is well into his last move, you are too late.[232]

Gillman was one of the first coaches to advocate attacking defenses with the pass first to set up the run, which was the opposite of what conventional wisdom promoted. He felt coaches should use all five receivers to attack the defense both vertically and horizontally.[233]

Between Gillman's affinity for detail and Paul Brown's meticulous approach to coaching the Cleveland Browns, there developed a new approach to football. Brown is credited with instituting detailed game planning, the use of film study, drawing up plays, and the modern convention of Xs and Os and diagrams. Although inventive in many ways, Gillman was particularly thorough in the planning of his passing game.

Bump and Run Coverage

Defensive coaches, in an attempt to compete with the teams that were beginning to pass the ball with so much success with timing routes, found a way to slow down receivers. In the upstart American Football League, professional teams were throwing the ball all over the field.

The Oakland Raiders and defensive back Willie Brown came up with a defensive technique that resembled the tight man-to-man defense played in basketball. Brown had learned this technique from Jack Faulkner when he was playing with the Kansas City Chiefs. However, he never used it in any games. The unique technique intrigued Al Davis, the coach of the Raiders. In 1967, the only restriction on a defensive back was there could be no contact when the ball was in the air. Brown started covering receivers at the line of scrimmage. He had little fear of getting beat deep. He would align on the shoulder of the receiver and immediately strike him when he first moved. This served to prevent or delay the release of the receiver and to disrupt the timing of the precise pass routes used by the passing advocates of the Coryell and Gillman systems. Brown would continue to bump him as he attempted to run his pass route. As the Raiders continued to press the shocked and confused receivers on the line of scrimmage, they prevented them from getting into their routes. The bump and run became the most talked about innovation of the year. Raiders' opponents completed only 41% of their passes. The lowest pass completion percentage in the AFL. When other teams copied the technique, it became nearly impossible for receivers to escape quickly into their routes.

As with any new defensive maneuver, the offense developed measures to combat the "bump and run coverage". Offensive coaches began to teach their pass receivers aggressive moves to fight the bump and run. They used escape techniques, some of them very similar to those used by defensive linemen, to shed offensive blocks. Coaches also found that keeping the wide receiver off the line of scrimmage provided them with an extra couple of yards to prepare for or avoid the defensive back. Offensive innovators began to use motion by a wide receiver to prevent the defender from getting a proper alignment and bump on the receiver. However, most importantly there were rule changes. In the NFL, 1974 brought restrictions on the amount of contact defenders could make with a receiver. The contact rule was strengthened in 1977. Defenders could make contact with a receiver only once. In 1978, in the NFL, defenders were no longer able to maintain contact with a wide receiver beyond 5 yards from the line of scrimmage. Not so coincidently, that same year brought a revised rule in pass protection that allowed offensive linemen to extend their arms. They now were also allowed to use open hands to protect the passer. The passing game once again flourished.

Even with the restriction, the bump and run/press coverage is still widespread today. The techniques of executing the coverage have changed, but the general concept remains.

[215] Switzer, Barry, Shrake, Bud, *Bootlegger's Boy*, (New York, NY, William Monroe, 1990), p. 72
[216] "Emory Bellard, *Creator of Wishbone Dies*", ESPM.com. Feb. 10,2011.
[217] Smith, Homer, Rogers, Pepper, *Installing Football's Wishbone T Attack* (West Nyack, NY, Parker Publishing Co., 1973), p.1
[218] Dawson, Phil Jack, "*Defeating the Triple-Option With the Backbone Defense*", Parker Publishing Co., West Nyack, NY, 1974
[219] Dawson, Phil Jack, "Defeating *the Triple-Option With the Backbone Defense*", Parker Publishing Co., West Nyack, NY, 1974, p. 38
[220] Lombardi, Vince, Vince *Lombardi On Football*", Vol. 1, New York Graphic Society Ltd. And Wallynn, Inc.,New York, NY,1973, p. 19
[221] Lombardi, Vince, Vince Lombardi on Football. Vol I, (Greenwich, CT.,New York Graphic Society Ltd. Inc. 1973). P. 92-93
[222] Arnsparger, Bill, *Coaching Defensive Football*, (Boca Raton, Boston, London, New York, Washington, DC, St. Lucie Press, 1999), p.64,65
[223] Arnsparer, p. 66, 67
[224] http://subscribers.footballguys.com/2009/09bramel_idpguide.php
[225] http://en.wikipedia.org/wiki/*Tom_Landry*
[226] http://competeinallthings.blogspot.com/2010/01/*4-3-flex-defense-basics-as-i-know-them*.html
[227] http://ezinearticles.com/?*That-Strange-Up-And-Down-Thing-The-Cowboys-Once-Did*&id=798594
[228] Ellison, Glen. *Run-and Shoot Football*. (West Nyack, NY. Parker Publishing Co., Inc. , 1965. P. 29-30
[229] Schlabach, Mark (July 20, 2009). *"Spread concepts around for decades"*. ESPN.com. Retrieved 2009.07.21
[230] Shannhan, Tom. 2008. "*Don Coryell Belongs in the Hall of Fame*", July 1 (accessed October 4, 2008) ?
[231] http://inmyheartblog.wordpress.com/2008/01/02/*remembering-sid-gillman-innovative-football-coach-jan-3-2003/*
[232] http://smartfootball.blogspot.com/2009/04/*sid-gillman-father-of-modern-passing*.html
[233] http:// *Sid Gillman, "Father of the Modern Passing Game," notes on passing offense*, Saturday, April 04, 2009. smartfootball.blogspot.com/2009/04/sid-gillman-father-of-modern-passing.htm

CHAPTER TWELVE

The Option Dominates

(1970–1979)

Option Football truly exploded during the 1970's and into the 1980's. From 1969 to 1990, option teams would win or share 11 National Championships. Usually thought of as running formations, they do not necessarily scorn the pass. However, as Ohio State's Woody Hayes once said, "When you pass, three things can happen and two of them are bad." [234]

The Oklahoma Wishbone

Following the 1966 season, Barry Switzer became an assistant coach at the University of Oklahoma under new head coach and his good friend, Jim Mackenzie. After Mackenzie had died of a heart attack in the spring of 1967, Switzer continued as an assistant under Oklahoma's new head coach Chuck Fairbanks.

As Oklahoma's Offensive Coordinator, Switzer quickly made a name for himself with the wishbone offense. He built Oklahoma into, what would become one of the most productive rushing offenses in college football history. Under Switzer's wishbone, Oklahoma set an NCAA rushing record of 472 yards per game in 1971.

When Fairbanks became the coach of the New England Patriots following the 1972 season, Switzer became the head coach at Oklahoma. He led Oklahoma to an undefeated season that year and the next. Oklahoma was selected as the National Champions in 1974, 1975 and 1985. From 1973 to 1980, Switzer's team won or shared the Big Eight Conference championship every season. The triple option continued its evolution when Emory Bellard now at Mississippi State, "broke the bone" with the formation shown below. Tony DeMeo, who coached at Iona College and Mercyhurst College, had a significant influence on the "broken bone" advocates. DeMeo, who many consider the chief of triple option football, most recently, coached at the University of Charleston. DeMeo would gain fame with his Triple Gun Option offense. Nebraska began to run the "triple" from a Power "I" set. The I-Option Offense offered a typical I balanced attack. At its heart, the offense relied on a devastating combination of the option, power running, and play-action passing. All are easily run from the I- formation and its variations. The concept of a balanced offensive attack combined with the big play potential of the option enticed vast numbers of college teams and high school teams to include some components of the Nebraska I. *Figures 258, 259*

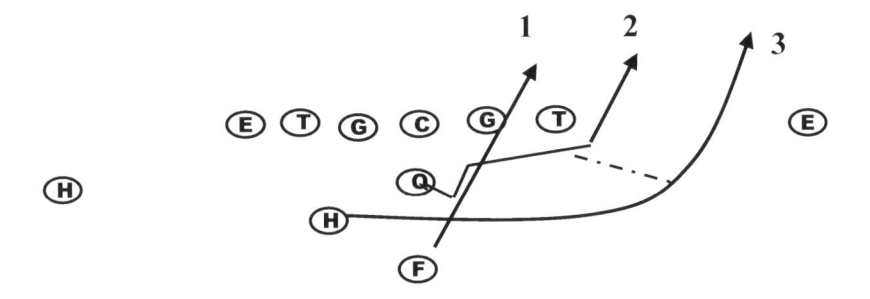

Figure 258 "Broken Bone" option

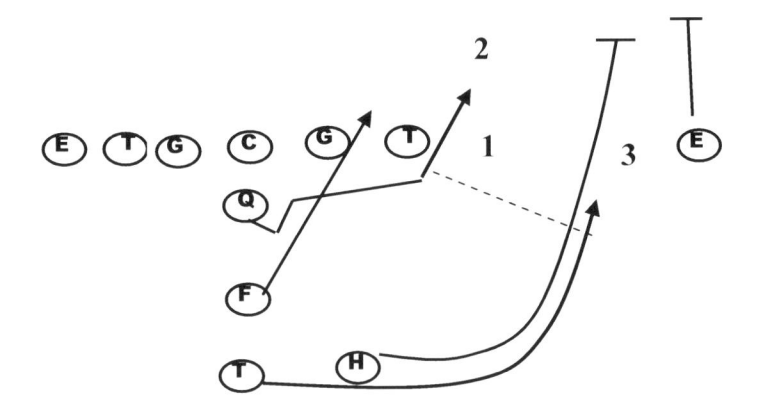

Figure 259 Power I Triple option

Advances in the "I" Formation

The "I" Formation continued its growth in the 1970s with several formational adjustments. Coaches began to offset their fullback to both the tight end side and the split-end side. *Figures 260, 261*

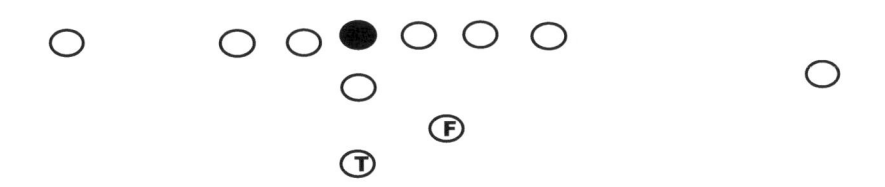

Figure 260 "Offset" I Strong

Figure 261 "Offset I Weak

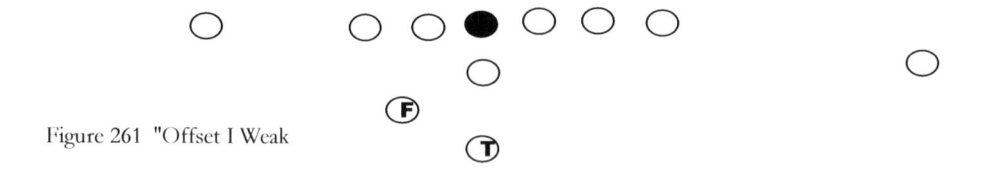

The "I" continued to grow, with offenses that did much shifting and motioning. The I coaches began moving backs around. They motioned men into the backfield and motioned men across the formation.

Flexible T

The "Wing-T" continued to flourish and Ben Martin at the Air Force Academy kept the "T" thriving with his "Flexible T Offense". His "Flexible T" created an integrated system for the pass and run that revolved around an unbalanced line and the movement of the halfbacks to generate a variety of formations. Three of his more traditional formations are shown in *Figures 262-264*.[235]

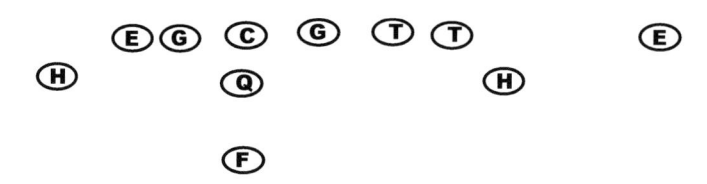

Figure 262 Ben Martin's Double Wing Right

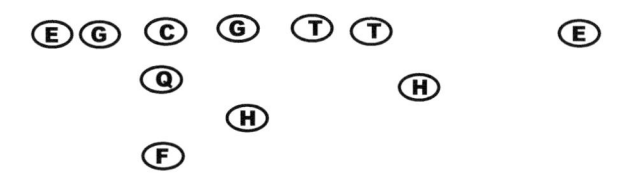

Figure 263 "Peel" Right

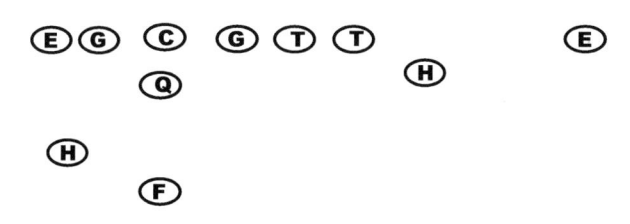

Figure 264 Slot" Right (unbalanced line)

Eddie Teague at the Citadel ran a very similar offense that he called the "Unbalanced Line Open End T Offense."

By this time, the Single Wing had all but disappeared. It will rise again, however.

The NCAA Creates "Divisions."

In 1973, the NCAA organized the colleges into divisions based on attendance and scholarships offered. The three divisions were aptly named Division I, Division II, and Division III with Division I competing at the highest level and Division III the lowest level. In 1978, Division I split into two groups, Division I-A, the highest level, and Division I-AA. In 2006, Division I-A was renamed the Football Bowl Subdivision (FBS) and I-AA was renamed the Football Championship Subdivision (FCS).

Stunt 4-3

In the early 1970s, the NFL's standout defensive units were identified with nicknames. There was the Doomsday Defense (Cowboys), Steel Curtain (Steelers), Fearsome Foursome (Rams), and the Purple People Eaters (Vikings). Defensive strategy underwent some changes at both the professional level and the collegiate level.

In 1972, Pittsburgh Steelers head coach, Chuck Noll, hired Bud Carson to coach his defensive backs and hired George Perles as defensive line coach. In 1973, Carson became the Steelers Defensive Coordinator. Carson and Perles worked closely in developing the "Steel Curtain" defense that dominated professional offenses in the 70s.

At the core of the Steelers defense was a concept they called the "Stunt 4-3." Although Pittsburgh was renowned for its run defense, statistically their pass defense was stronger. Also, Carson was a strong advocate of the two-deep zone defense. He would have his cornerbacks "jam" the wide receivers and had the outside linebacker on the side of the tight end, reroute him to the inside and not allow him into the flat zone. Some say the first use of the Stunt 4-3 was in the 1974 playoff game vs. the Buffalo Bills. However, Woody Widenhofer, who was a linebacker coach with the Steelers that year, claims the first use was in the Championship game vs. The Oakland Raiders.

Consistent with Widenhofer's claim, rumor has it that Perles devised the "Stunt 4-3" on a napkin before the 1974 AFC championship game with the Oakland Raiders. So many new ideas are credited with having been first drawn on napkins, it seems that without napkins football coaches would be unable to make any progress. The defense yielded Oakland just 27 total rushing yards. That was the first of four Super Bowl titles the Steelers would win. The basic concept of the Stunt 4-3 was to place the strong-side tackle in the A gap and angle him across the center's head. The weak tackle played a 3 technique on the outside shoulder of the weakside guard. They executed a series of "stunts" from these positions on almost every play. *Figures 265-268*

The Atlanta Falcons led the NFL in defense in 1977 allowing a paltry 9.2 points per game using a defense very similar to the Stunt 4-3.[236]

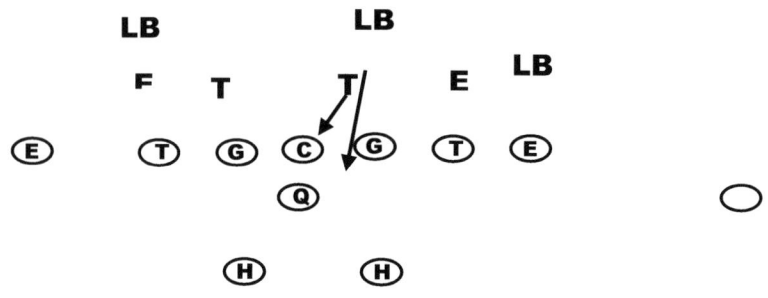

Figure 265 "A" gap Stunt

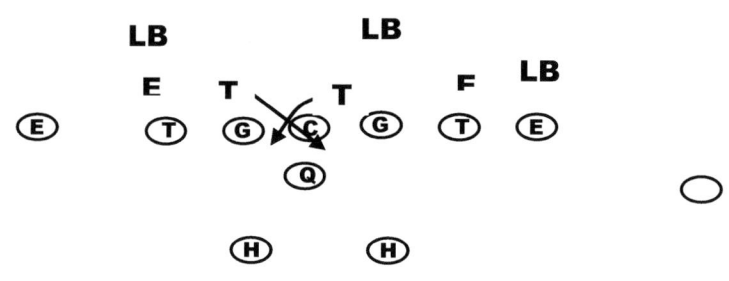

Figure 266 Tackle Twist Stunt

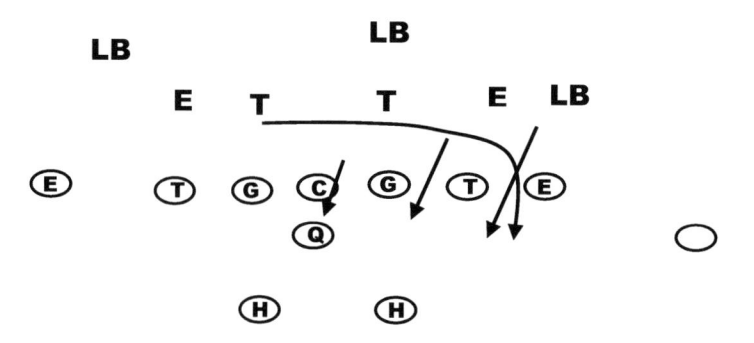

Figure 267 Tackle Loop Stunt

217

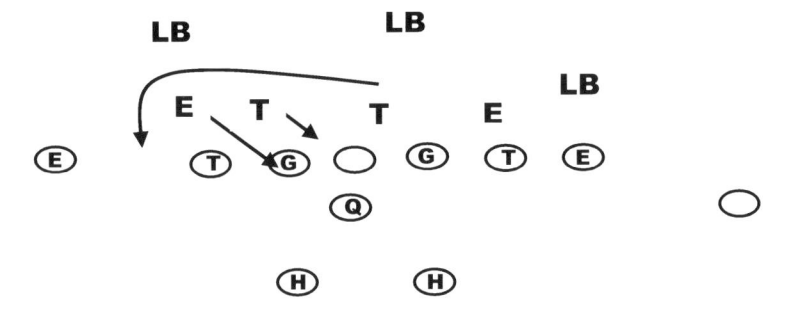

Figure 268 Nose Loop Stunt

3-4 Defense

Perhaps as much as any other aspect of the modern game, the origin of the 3-4 defense is uncertain.

There are those who say the 3-4 originated at the collegiate level, at the University of Oklahoma in the 1940s under Jim Tatum. Others say it was created at Oklahoma but by Chuck Fairbanks, much later. "Bill Arnsparger is the guy," former Browns Head Coach Sam Rutigliano said. "He's the guy who invented it. He's the architect of the 3-4." [237] Some credit Fairbanks with the "regular" use of the defense in 1974 during his tenure as coach of the New England Patriots. Others say Bum Phillips as coach of the Houston Oilers used it that same year. People who follow the Kansas City Chiefs put in a claim that Hank Stram used the defense to win a championship in the early 70s but did not stick with the scheme. Joe Collier claims to have used that same defense with the Buffalo Bills in 1964. "We initially used it in 1964, but we used it quite a bit against San Diego in 1965 in the AFL Championship Game," Collier said. [238]

All of these men can lay claim to having created the 3-4, but none can do it solely. Like so many other things in football history, the 3-4's first use is uncertain and often hard to follow and define.

The 3-4 defensive formation is as its name suggests. There are three down linemen with four linebackers behind them. Two cornerbacks cover the outside receivers. A strong and free safety completes the defensive backfield. The idea of playing with only 3 down defenders is not new. Hank Stram was known to hide linebackers directly behind his three down lineman in a "stack" formation. Don Shula and Bill Arnsparger used a three-man line primarily to get eight men back in coverage. Arnsparger called his defense the "53" after the jersey number of their fourth linebacker, Bob Matheson. [239]

In the 3-4 set-up, the front seven players are crucial to the defense. The front three defensive linemen are comprised of two defensive ends and nose guard. The 3-4 defense requires a nose guard who can consistently jam up the middle.

The linebackers in the 3-4 are different from linebackers found in the other common defenses of the day, the 4-3 and 5-2. Generally, one of the linebackers will line up on the Tight End with the other outside linebacker lining up to the open-end side. In its purest form the Nose and both Ends line head-up on their offensive counterpart. Each of the three has a two-gap responsibility. This was Arnsparger scheme. *Figure 269* Other systems found the Nose shaded to one side and/or the Ends in a shoulder alignment with single gap responsibilities.

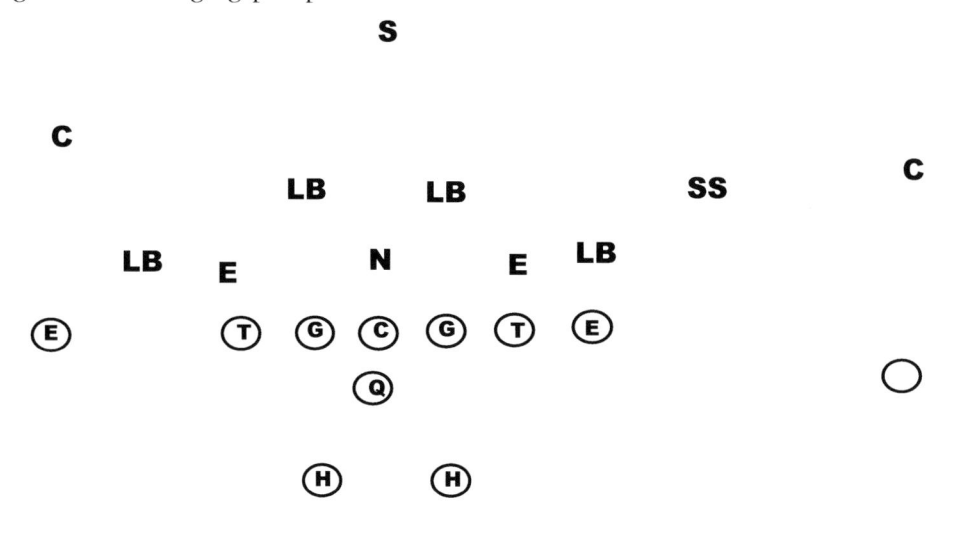

Figure 269 Arnsparger's Original 3-4 Defense

    The main advantage of the 3-4 defense is the alignment of the linebackers. Based 5 yards back from the play; the linebackers can read the flow of the action and give pursuit. The defensive linemen engage the blockers and clog the running lanes leaving the linebackers free to make the play.
    The 3-4 defense also can confuse offenses as at different times a different linebacker can line up on the line of scrimmage to rush the passer. A great number of blitz packages are also available to defensive coordinators as blitzes can come from many different locations.
    Pass rushers can come from all different directions. There are many stunts and blitzes with linebackers and safeties moving on and off the line of scrimmage. On occasion, a bundle of defenders will come and other times none will come. It can be head spinning to an unprepared offense.
    The 3-4 defense is not without its weaknesses. The 3-4 defense really is a personnel based defense. By that, we mean that if a team does not have the linebackers who have the speed and size needed nor the defensive linemen who can stymie the blockers, the 3-4 is very vulnerable.

The 3-4 defense is also susceptible to the inside rush. With just a nose guard to close the middle, the inside rushing game prevails with many offensive teams who play against the 3-4.

Due to the responsibilities put on the linemen and the linebackers, there are claims that the 3-4 defense is best run at the professional level. It has been said that unless a college or high school team has seven players who can play defensive line or play linebacker, the 3-4 is not really an alternative.[240]

Bum Phillips and the One-gap 3-4

Chuck Fairbanks and Hank Bullough created a 3-4 scheme with the New England Patriots that was more of an attacking system. Bum Phillips took it one-step further and developed his own version of the 3-4. How and why did Phillips develop this exceptional defense? "Coaching is pretty simple really. If you don't got something, find something you do got. Really we didn't have but one [defensive lineman] - [Hall of Famer] Elvin [Bethea] - until we got Curley [Culp] in the middle of that season. Then we had two. What we did have was four real good linebackers so all I done was find a way to get our best players on the field."[241]

Phillips brought the "Under" concept to the 3-4. Unlike the pure 2-gap 3-4, there's no clear "bubble" in a 1-gap front. The strong side end will slide down into the guard-tackle gap. The Nose will slant to the weak side center-guard gap and the weak side end will align in a 5 technique (outside shoulder of the offensive tackle) or he may be head up. *Figure 270*

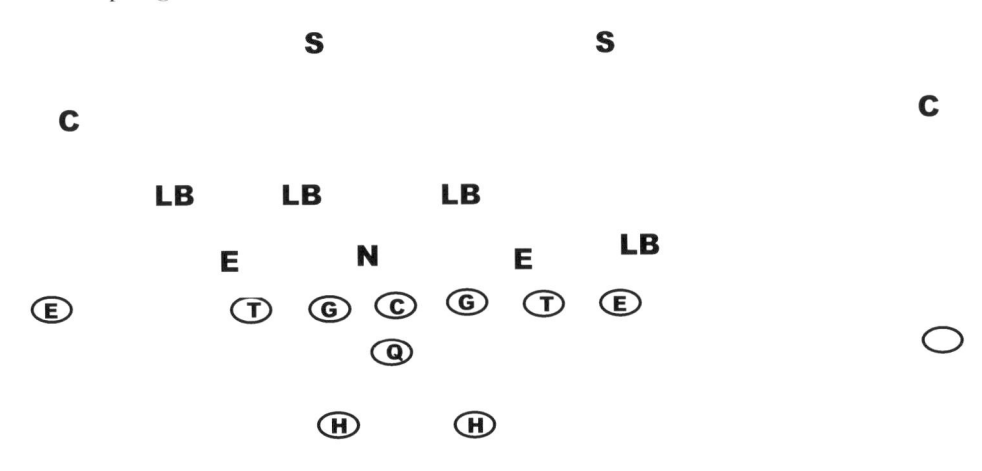

Figure 270 Bum Phillips 1-Gap 3-4 (Under 3-4)

Just like the Fairbanks-Bullough 3-4 scheme that was being used in New England at the same time, Phillips was looking to suppress the run and create mismatches in the pass rush. Though Phillips based his scheme on the same concepts that the New England coaches did, he preferred his attacking style. He used some one-gap techniques in his front seven, stunting and slanting his lineman. The attacking manner of play with 1-Gap defenders continues today because it allows the defense to disguise who the pass rushers will be.

At the collegiate level, the mid-seventies brought several new defensive developments, which would influence the game profoundly.

5-2 Defense

While the 5-2 defenses were still highly used by a high percentage of teams, offenses were beginning to catch up with it. They had found the weaknesses and were exploiting them. However, some adjustments helped the 5-2 defense to continue to present problems for offenses.

Gap Control Defense

It was also during this decade that the theory of "Gap Control" in defensive systems became more prevalent. In his book, *Coaching the Gap-Control Rover Defense* Tom Olivadotti states, Gap control itself is not a new concept, but it would be brought to a new level of sophistication.

> "Controlling a gap does not mean the lack of reading by defenders. On the contrary, it is based on reading. The basic theory is that the defensive down men are generally responsible for a gap before the snap of the ball while the linebackers are responsible for a gap or an area depending on the movement of their key.
>
> "The defensive linemen read once they feel the pressure of the blocker. It might be said that on some occasions they are sacrificed. However, this is not true. Their pursuit is enhanced and they become most proficient in fighting pressure of the offensive blockers
>
> "Once we have controlled every gap along the line of scrimmage to the side of the ball, we can close to the ball. Theoretically, the ball carrier should have nowhere to go.
>
> "Our defense is not a standard penetrating defense, yet it is not a pure reading defense either. We want to control the line of scrimmage, reading on the move and pursuing to the ball. To get penetration, we will stunt and/or move our defensive linemen to a gap. These are 'called moves.'."[242]

The 5-2 Monster Defense

Improved scouting systems brought about the need to use "unbalanced" defenses such as the one, originally, called the Arkansas Monster, and later just the monster defense.[243] Until this time, most defensive teams using the 5-2 defense lined up with two cornerbacks and two safeties. The monster defense aligned one of the two safeties closer to the line of scrimmage. This placed him in a position to better play the run. The monster defenses allowed teams to outnumber the offensive players to either the strong side of the offensive formation or the wide side of the field. This put the defense in a position where they outnumbered and overpowered the offense in the area they wanted to run. *Figure 271*

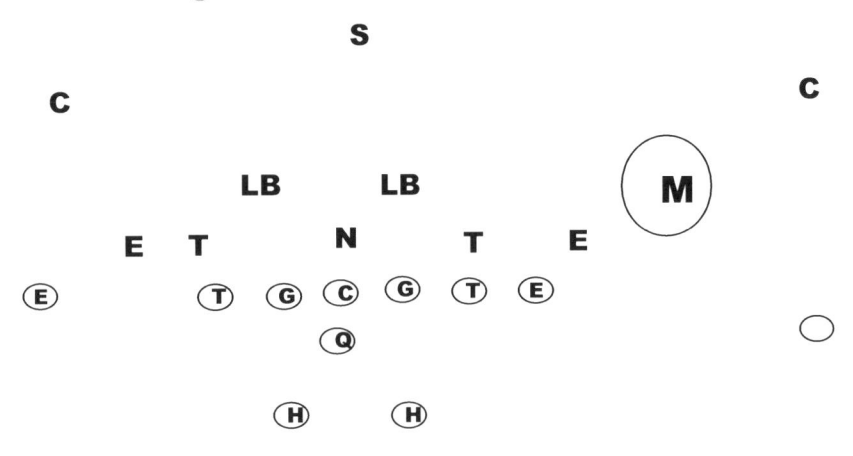

Figure 271 The 5-2 Monster Defense

Michigan Angle Defense

Seeing what the monster defenses were doing, the response of offensive coaches was to begin to run to the weak side of their formation and run into the short side of the field. We will see in the following paragraphs how defensive coaches aligned to the strength of the formation and invited the offensive to run weakside. They then slanted their line back to the weak side again creating a numbers advantage for themselves.

When Bo Schembechler, the Head Coach at Miami of Ohio, became Michigan's Head Coach, he brought with him a defense that people would later call the "Michigan Angle."[244] It was a different kind of defense. Operating from a five-man line with two inside linebackers and a Strong Safety that would become the "Monster", the Safety was said to be "inverted" and aligned close to the line of scrimmage. The linebackers keyed the ball and had no counter responsibility as in a regular 5-2. Against this defense, it was difficult to run the "I" isolation play as well as the trap.

See Figure 272, 273

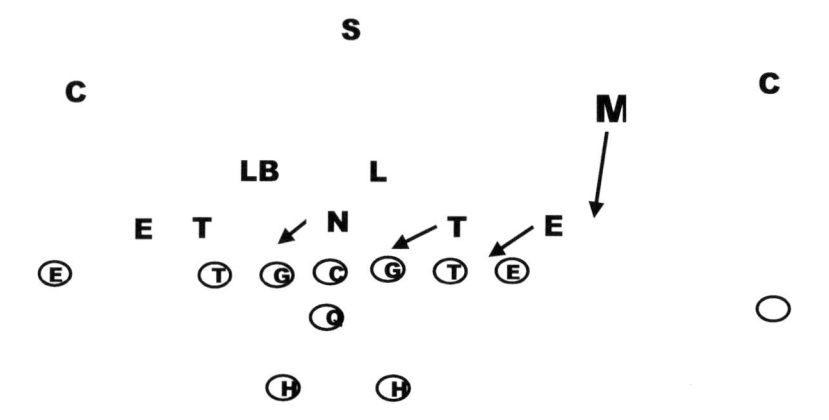

Figure 272 The initial alignment of the Michigan Angle defense with arrows showing the potential movement of defenders on the snap of the ball.

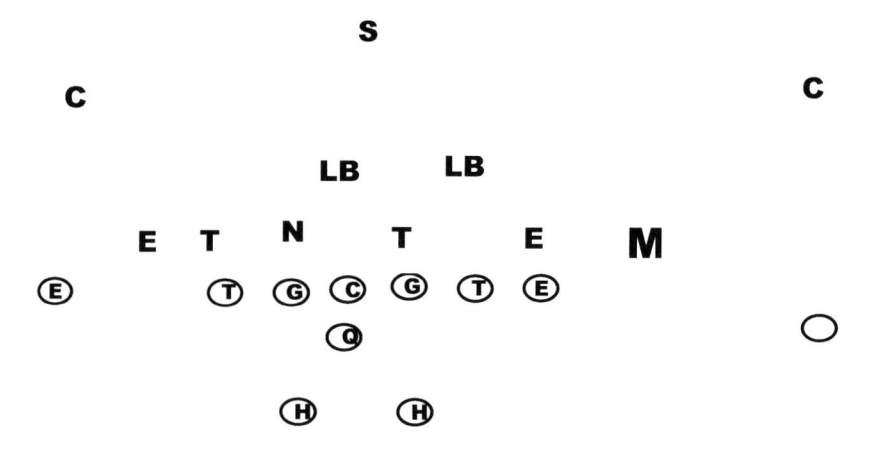

Figure 273 The "Michigan Angle" Defense - The final position of defenders after the angle movement.

Double Invert Defense

In an attempt to bring secondary players closer to the line of scrimmage to play contain on the run, some 5-2 teams began to play what they called the "Double Invert" defense. The corners would play softer, very similar to their play in a 3 deep secondary. The two safeties would both "invert" and align closer to the line of scrimmage than was customary in the 4 deep secondary. The initial deep-outside position of the cornerbacks and their freedom from immediate run responsibility encouraged sound pass defense, so the Invert certainly measured up in that respect. The invert's ability to hide behind the defensive end and to take the wide sweep with an inside-out tackling angle made him a difficult target for pulling guards and fullbacks leading the play. [245]

The invert away from the action would rotate back to the middle 1/3 of the field and become, essentially, a free safety. *Figure 274*

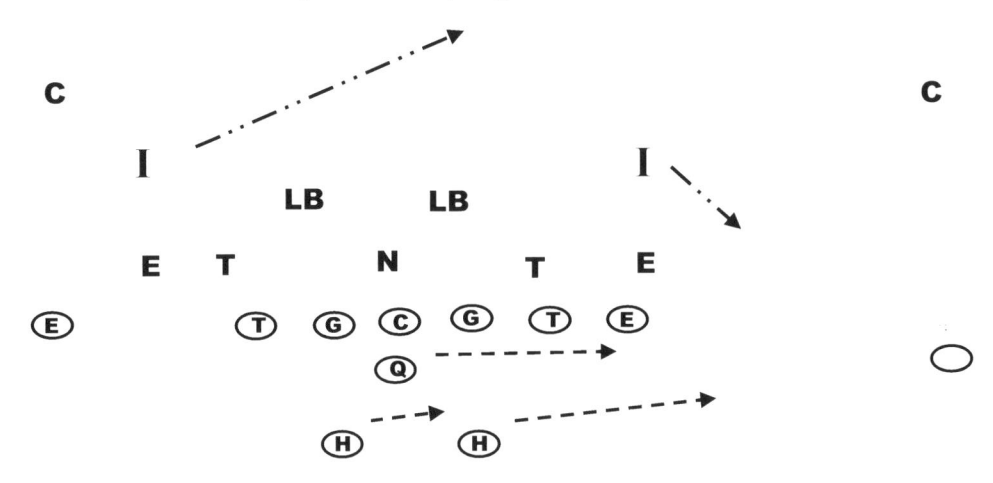

Figure 274 Reaction of the Inverts to backfield action

      Ralph Kirchenheiter, in his book *Coaching Football's Invert Defense*, makes the following comment. "Far more than a mere variation in alignment of the defensive backs, the Invert Defense is flexible enough to contend with all offensive sets from all positions on the field.

      "The Double Invert was a logical successor to the Monster defenses. "The Monster-type defenses established a strong side by placement of the "monster" than slanting the line away from him, essentially neutralizing the manpower advantage initially created. The Invert Defense, on the other hand, presents a balanced appearance, but on the snap of the ball, the line is slanting to gain an advantage to one side or the other. The inverts, reacting to a key, can react toward the slant, thus creating an overpowering manpower advantage, or opposite the slant of the line, again establishing a balanced front." [246]

Jerry Claiborne: The Split-6 Defense

      At the University of Maryland, they were using the "Split-6 Defense" that was created by Warren Geise, the defensive coordinator at that time, under Head Coach Jerry Claiborne. Geise later became Head Coach at South Carolina. [247] *See Figure 275*

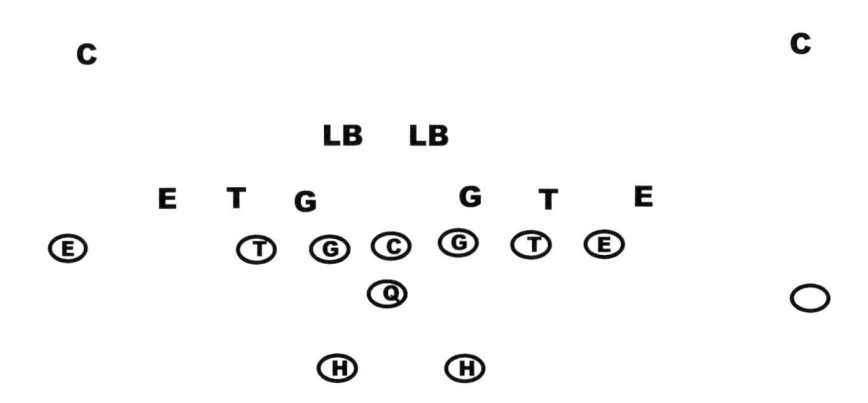

Figure 275 The Maryland Split-6 Defense

4-4 Defense

It was not long before coaches began using the Split-Six principles but replacing the defensive ends with outside linebackers, creating a 4-4 defense.

Joe Paterno, at Penn State, was one of the first to switch to the Split-Four defense. At Notre Dame, Ara Parseghian used the 4-4, and at Georgia, Vince Dooley instituted the 4-4. However, many say the creator of the 4-4 defense was John Ray, who was the Defensive Coordinator at Notre Dame in the mid-1960s.

In basic terms, the 4-4 defense is set up with four linemen, four linebackers and three players in the secondary

The 4–4 defense relies on speed and intelligence rather than relying too heavily on size and strength as many other defenses do. Flexibility is a key as every player can have a variety of roles from one play to the next. It is an attacking defense that has available to it multiple blitz packages that can be easily concealed and modified. The principal priority of the 4–4 defense is prohibiting the run. With eight men on or near the line of scrimmage on every play, 4-4 teams have shown that it is tough to run on this defense. Also, with eight men so close to the line of scrimmage, it is hard for the offense to identify when or from where the blitz pressure will be coming. One final noteworthy plus of the 4–4 defense is that it can quickly adjust to the many formation changes offenses can make.

Some say that the potential to give up the big play is a major disadvantage to the 4-4. Others cite the fact that the Cornerbacks are "on an island" and may have difficulty covering the deep pass. *Figure 276* shows the basic 4-4 defense and *Figures 277, 278* show two of the frequently used adjustments.

225

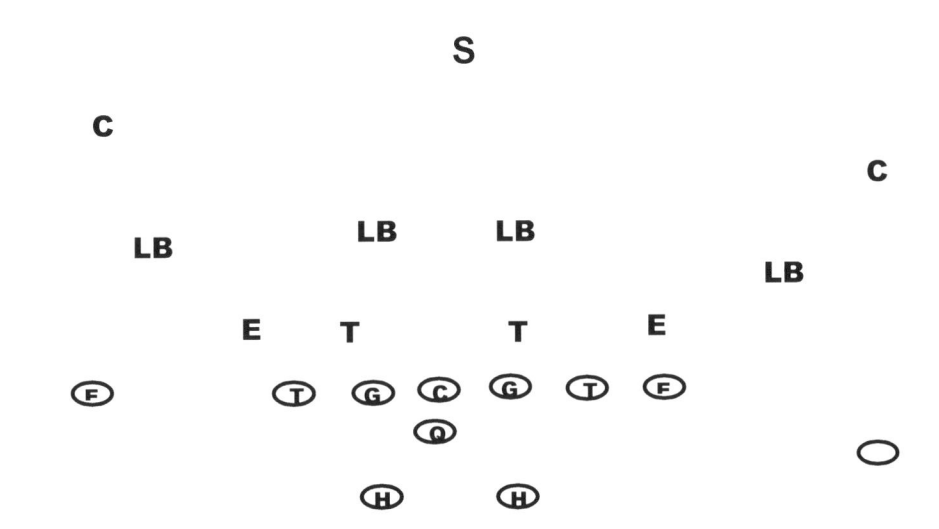

Figure 276 The Basic Split-4 Alignment

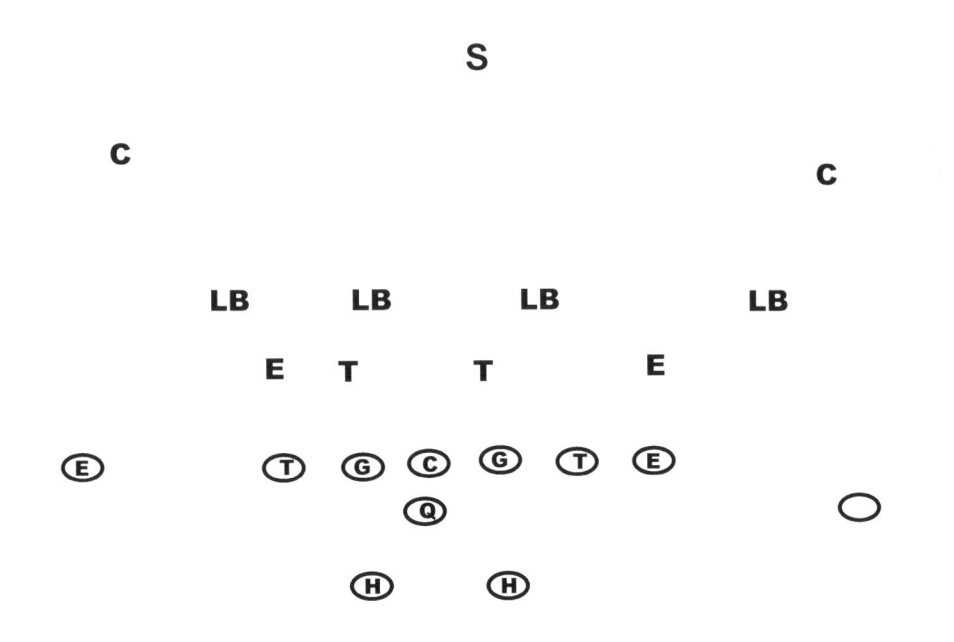

Figure 277 Common "Offset" Adjustment in 4-4 Defense

226

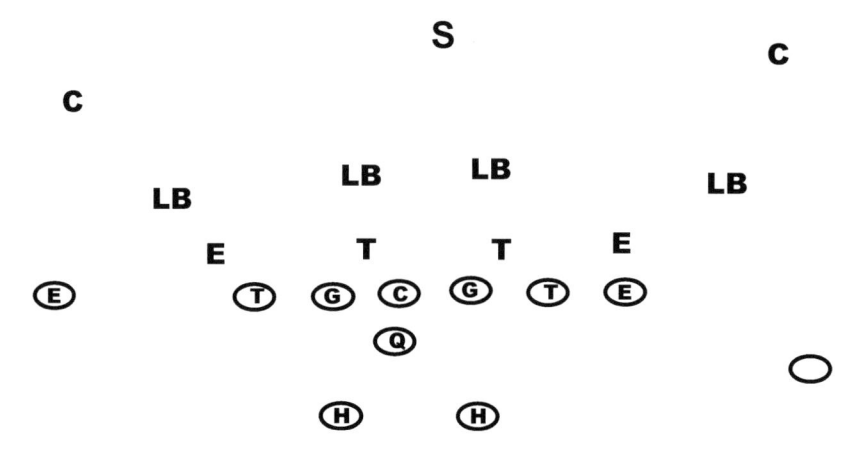

Figure 278 4-4 Stack Defense

Expansion of the Coryell & Gillman Passing Concepts

During the 1970s, there was also a proliferation of teams who showed a willingness to use the pass as an integral part of their offense. The success of coaches Sid Gillman, Don Coryell, and Paul Brown persuaded others to incorporate the pass into their offense. New passing records were set on an annual basis.

The growth in the number of coaches using The Don Coryell and Sid Gilliam concepts grew rapidly. The use of vertical passing, forcing the defense to defend the whole field, demanding detail, timing in route running and using four and five receivers in the pass routes became commonplace. There was a wealth of passing, with wide-open offenses using the pass first to set up the run philosophy. Gillman emphasized physical conditioning. Throwing the ball as much as they did, his teams had to be in excellent physical condition. It should be noted, Gillman was also one of the first coaches to have his players follow a weight lifting routine.

The success and glamor of the American Football League with its aerial circuses attracted many to the possibilities of the passing offense. Defenses were slow to adjust.

Birth of the One Back Spread Offense

Offenses had been lining up with one back in the backfield for decades, but many give credit to Jack Neumeier, Head Coach at Granada Hills High School in California, for the introduction of the modern day one back offense. Neumeier wanted to spread the field with his receivers to create more space in the passing lanes and at the same time generate bigger holes for his running backs. He used option routes similar to those Glenn Ellison used with his Run & Shoot. Jack Elway wanted a high school where his son, John Elway, could exhibit his passing talents. The older Elway, who was coaching college football, was intrigued with Neumeier's offense and John Elway enrolled at Granada. Jack Elway began to use the offense while coaching at Cal State Northridge. In 1979, Elway took his "One Back" offense to San Jose State where he and offensive coordinator Dennis Erickson continued to fine-tune the attack. Elway later took the offense to Stanford while Erickson went on to use the "one back" as the Head Coach at Idaho, Wyoming, Washington State and Miami. Both coaches stressed an offense of three wide receivers, one tight end, and one running back. The early running game was kept simple, using the inside and outside zone, the Power-O and the Counter Trey popularized by the Washington Redskins. The passing game emphasized the short three step drop passes using the option routes of Glen Ellison. Below are a few of the more common "one back" formations from that time.

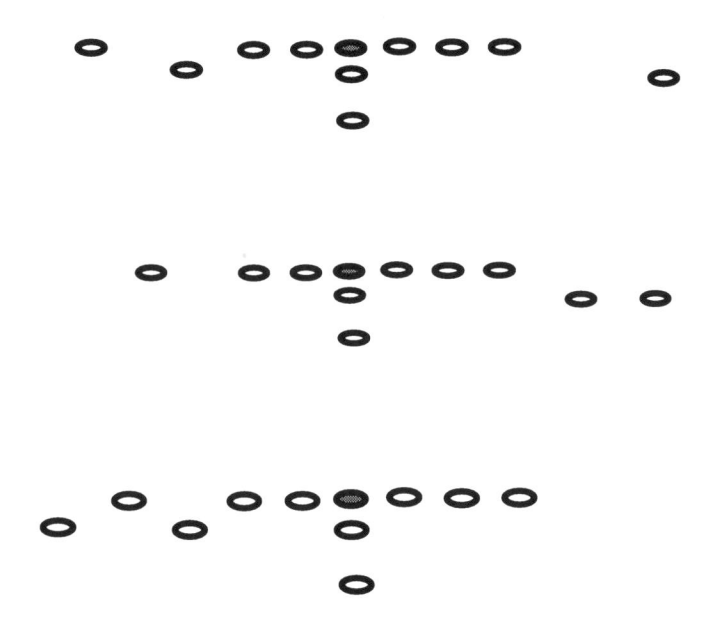

Figure 279

Figure 279   Three Common One Back Formations

We will see later, almost all today's spread teams have embraced the philosophy of the "One back" offense. Virtually all those who use the "one back" offense count the safeties. They identify how many defenders are in the "box" (an area generally existing from offensive tackle to offensive tackle) to make a run/pass decision. They will use formations to get the match up in personnel that they want and then run pass patterns that allow the receivers various options in running their individual routes.

The "Nickel" Defense

The "Nickel Defense" was created to reduce the effectiveness of the new passing offenses. The "Nickel Defense" was called so because it brought a fifth defensive back to the field. The defense, with its five defensive backs, usually had four down linemen and two linebackers, but there were those who elected to play with only three down linemen and three linebackers.

Some people familiar with the coaching of Clark Shaughnessy give him credit for coming up with the term "Nickel". They say Shaughnessy was devising and naming defenses with any number of defensive backs in the 1950s. However, many believe the Nickel defense actually originated as an innovation of Philadelphia Eagles defensive coach Jerry Williams in the 1960s as a means to defend against celebrated Tight End Mike Ditka of the Chicago Bears. The Eagles, however, did not use their five defensive back defense extensively. These same people would give George Allen, then an assistant coach with the Chicago Bears, credit for the name "Nickel". Allen is widely thought to have developed the format that used five defensive backs as a natural extension of his many coverage systems. Allen was an assistant under George Halas and worked with Clark Shaughnessy on the defensive staff. Moreover, he had many opportunities to witness how Philadelphia tried to defend Ditka.

The Miami Dolphins, under Head Coach Don Shula and Defensive Coordinator Bill Arnsparger, popularized the Nickel in the 1970s. With the proliferation of passing and multiple formations in the NFL, Arnsparger was searching for a defense he could implement with a limited number of defensive linemen. *Figure 280*

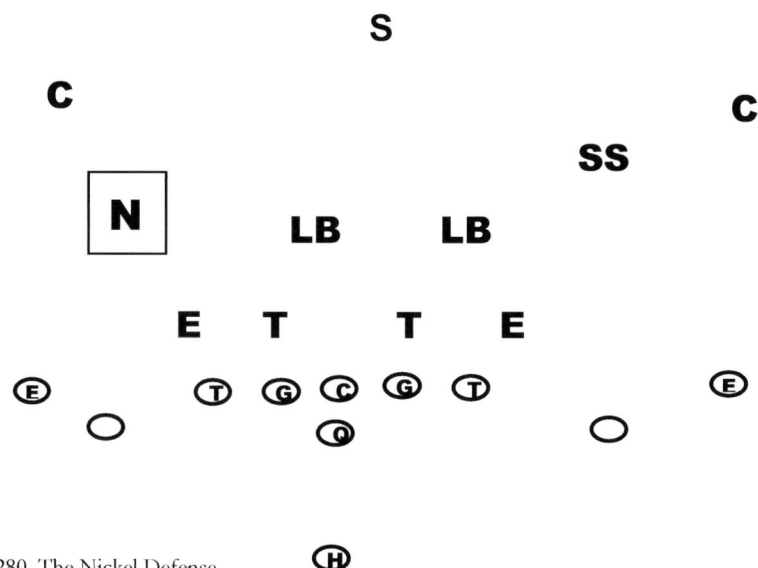

Figure 280 The Nickel Defense

Trap Option

Wichita State University developed a new option series in 1978. They named it the "Trap Option but it has since been called the Freeze Option and the Midline Option by high school and college coaches over the years. *Figure 281*

Wichita State called it the 40-60 Series. Syracuse University under Paul Pasqualoni successfully ran the Freeze Option for some years.

As the 40-60 Series developed through the spring of '78, it became apparent that it could be an equalizer for a team that needed every advantage it could muster to be competitive.

This new concept took the place of the older trap option where the QB opens up left (for trap option right), fakes the FB trap and then reverse on around for the option. In the 60 series, the play looks exactly like freeze option left (if the option is going to the right). The QB steps off the midline and fakes to the FB right up the gut, but then he turns back to the LOS and options the end. In the Syracuse instructional tapes, George DeLeone calls this their Counter Freeze Option.

The "Freeze Option alters the reactions of the linebackers when it forces them to "freeze" as they try to decide if the fullback or the quarterback has the ball. It forces the defensive tackle to step down to stop the fullback run. It limits the number and kinds of blitzes and stunts a defense might use. It limits the over shifted secondary coverages that some defensive coordinators like to use. [248]

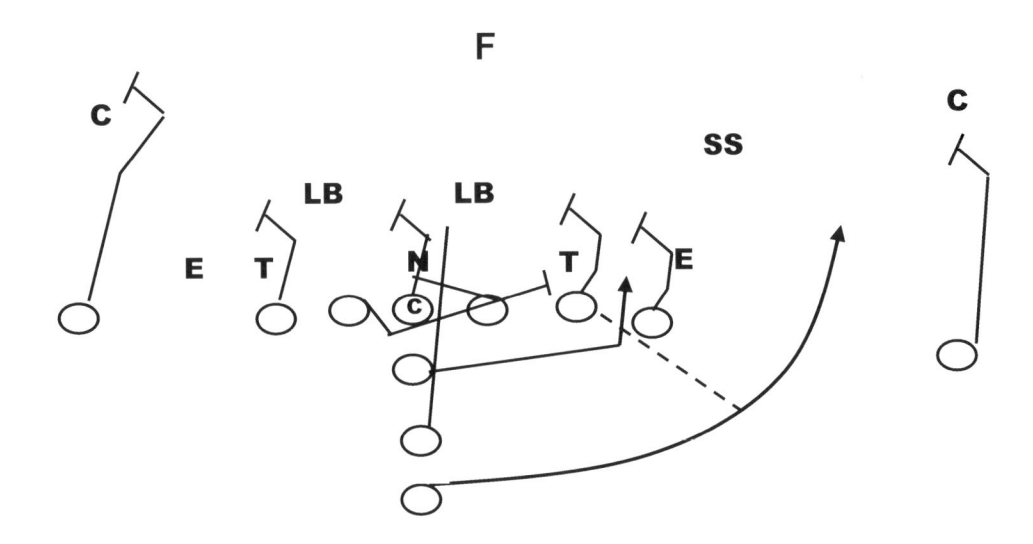

Figure 281 The Trap Option

234 http://en.wikipedia.org/wiki/Barry_Switzer
http://www.compusportsmedia.com/main/articles.asp?StoryID=214
235 Martin, Ben. Flexible T Offense.(Englewood Cliffs, NJ, Prentice Hall, 1961). p. 33-34
236 http://www.coldhardfootballfacts.com/Articles/11_2234_The_greatest_pass_defenses.html
237 http://www.brownsgab.com/2009/06/26/history-of-the-3-4-defense/
238 http://www.brownsgab.com/2009/06/26/history-of-the-3-4-defense/
239 Arnsparger, Bill, Coaching Defensive Football, (Boca Raton, Fl., St. Lucie Press,1999), p. 68-69
240 http://www.suite101.com/content/the-basics-of-the-34-defense-in-football-a13577
241 http://www.milehighreport.com/2013/4/8/4194504/mhr-university-the-3-4-defense
242 Olivadotti, Tom. Coaching the Gap-Control Rover Defense. (West Nyack, NY, Parker Publishing Co.,1975).P. 25-26.
243 http://www.suite101.com/content/the-basics-of-the-34-defense-in-football-a13577, retrieved 4/23/2012
http://smartfootball.com/defense/overload-blitzes-and-angle-stunts-against-one-back-formation.
244 Richards, Gregory B. and Melissa Larson, Big-10 Football, (Wingdale, NY, Crescent Books, 1987), page 95
245 Kirchenheiter, Ralph, Coaching Football's Invert Defense. West Nyack, NY,Parker Publishing Co.,1974), P. 21
246 Kirchenheiter , p. 20
247 http://www.dumcoach.com/classic/viewthread.php?tid=5973
248 http://www.compusportsmedia.com/main/articles.asp?StoryID=163

CHAPTER THIRTEEN

Changes in the Passing Game

(1980 - 1989)

Air Coryell

In 1980, the exciting offensive system of the San Diego Chargers, known as "Air Coryell," underwent some significant changes that would permanently change the look of offensive football. The Chargers had acquired an impressive tight end by the name of Kellen Winslow in the 1970 draft. He was such an impressive athlete that, when the 1979 season had completed, Coryell knew he had to get Winslow more involved in their offense.

During the 1979 season, the Chargers primary use of their tight ends was to bring in plays. They served as run blockers next to the offensive tackles. However, for the most part, outside linebackers could still "outmuscle" the tight ends in defending the running game. In the passing attack, they occasionally ran some short-to-intermediate pass routes; drags, hooks, flat routes. That was it. They were all big people, essentially 'tackles' who could catch the football. During the off-season, Don Coryell and his staff considered better ways to take advantage of Winslow's extensive skills. Joe Gibbs, the Chargers offensive coordinator at the time, felt that there were needed changes regarding the conventional restrictions of the position. When Winslow lined up in the traditional tight end position, the linebackers made it difficult for him to release and get off the line of scrimmage. It was decided that the thing to do was, to take him off the line of scrimmage. They could then move him around in the formation making it hard for the defense to identify where he would end up. Coryell had lined up wide receivers at the tight-end position in the past. The intent was to get a faster, more agile receiver on a bigger and slower defender; to get the receiver open down the middle of the field. However, Coryell had never placed an emphasis on the maneuver nor did he use it frequently. Some examples of how Coryell and Gibbs wanted to align Winslow are shown in See *Figures 282-284.*

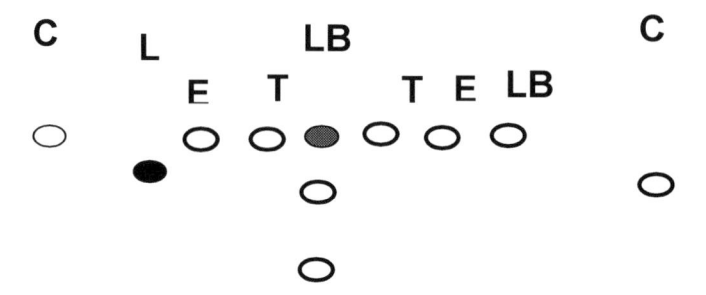

Figure 282 Winslow's alignment is shown as a dark oval

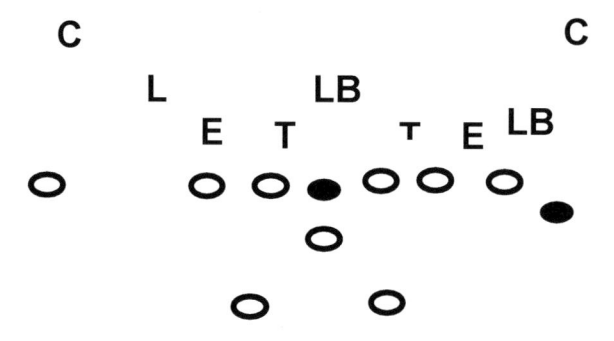

Figure 283 Winslow's alignment is shown as a dark oval

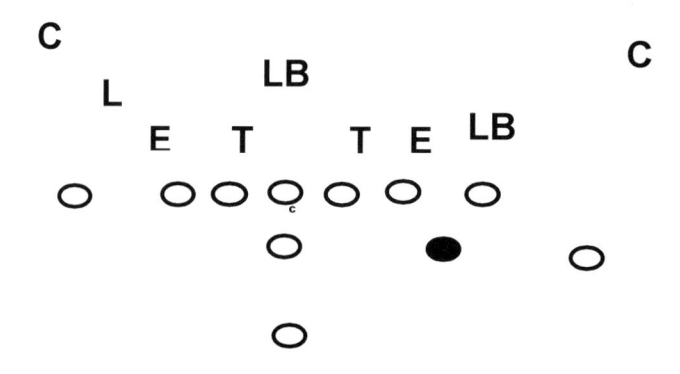

Figure 284 Winslow's alignment is displayed as a dark oval

Wanting to keep Winslow involved in their experiment, the coaches met with him during the off-season to show him their ideas. They would indicate a formation that they wanted to end up in and then tell Winslow he could begin anywhere he wanted as long as he ended up in the formation that was indicated. This helped significantly during the season as defensive coordinators had a difficult time charting the relationship between Winslow's initial alignment, his alignment at the snap, and the play being run. Coryell and Gibbs planned pass routes for Winslow that were typically reserved for wide receivers. The innovations proved to be highly successful

Joe Collier, the Denver defensive coordinator who had to face the Chargers twice a year made this statement. "During the early years of Air Coryell," he said, "the strong safety wasn't much more than a glorified linebacker; basically, a run defender who could cover an average tight end. You put a guy like Winslow out in the slot and he's going up against coverage that's a lot slower than he is. It's not the matchup on defense we liked. So we'd try to give that strong safety some help, like bringing a linebacker out to help him or bringing the other safety over to help. Of course, this weakened us in other areas. It forced us to do things we didn't want to do." [249]

For the first time, a tight end led the NFL in receiving for two consecutive years. Kellen Winslow led the league in receiving in both 1981 and 1982.

Zone Blocking

As was indicated earlier, the origin of the zone block can be traced back to the 1960s with Vince Lombardi's "Do-Dad" block. In his book, *Lombardi on Football* he describes his "Do-Dad block. Along with that description, there are several diagrams showing the "Do-Dad" block. The zone schemes being used today appear quite similar.

Some claim the modern zone-blocking scheme was the invention of Jim McNally, who coached with the Cincinnati Bengals during the 1980s. There is no doubt that the Bengals were one of the first and one of the finest zone blocking teams during that period.

However, McNally himself has this to say about zone blocking and the Inside and Outside Zone plays; "There were teams who were doing zone blocking already; that's what Cleveland was doing with running back Kevin Mack," McNally says. "We were one of the first teams to combine the inside zone and the outside zone. We made the defenses go away from being a reading defense to more of penetrating in the gaps. Because big holes would open up in that 3-4. Everybody (on the defensive line) would be a little wrong, maybe reading one guy who went too far, and the back would make the cut." [250]

Discussing zone blocking Sam Wyche, who was coaching the Bengals during this time had this to say about the zone. "Before then, the concept had been to push the defense off the ball," Wyche says. "The zone scheme takes the defensive guy where he wants to go, but you take him there faster. You don't engulf him and the back is coming from a deeper starting point downhill, he sees the crack and hits it." [251]

Howard Mudd, who coached with a large number of NFL teams, must be given credit for being a major contributor to the growth and sophistication of the zone block, especially during his time with the Indianapolis Colts.

Perhaps the coach most often identified with the zone scheme is Alex Gibbs, who coached at several colleges before joining the Denver Broncos in the NFL in 1984. He also had coached with the Oakland Raiders, San Diego Chargers, Indianapolis Colts, Kansas City Chiefs, Broncos again, Atlanta Falcons, Houston Texans, and Seattle Seahawks. That is a lot of coaching stops. At every stop during his coaching career, he produced teams that excelled at zone blocking and running the inside and outside zone plays. Below, *Figure 285* a typical zone-blocking scheme.

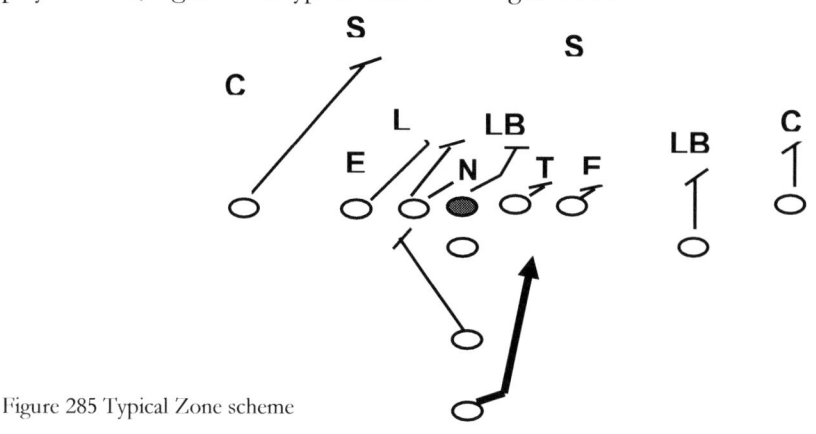

Figure 285 Typical Zone scheme

BYU Offense

Coach Lavell Edwards stated in several interviews, that the BYU offense actually got its start in the mid 1960's while he was the offensive Coordinator at Brigham Young University. When Edwards became the Head Coach at BYU, out of necessity, he and assistants Dewey Warren, Doug Scovil, and Norm Chow created a scheme that was pass oriented and unique in its simplicity. With Warren, the BYU offense turned every running play into a passing play and overpowered defenses with four, and sometimes five receivers, being deployed on every down. Although Warren left BYU after only two seasons, BYU continued to use his attack, with further refinements, for many years. During four seasons as BYU's offensive coordinator (1976-77 and 1979-80), Doug Scovil continued to refine the offense. With Scovil aboard, BYU won the NCAA passing title all four years. Under Edward's leadership, Norm Chow continued BYU's prolific passing offense through the 80s and 90s. Norm Chow created an offense that they thought would allow them to compete with schools with better athletes. Edwards is quick to give credit to Dewey Warren and Doug Scovil, as well as other assistants on his staff for bringing concepts from the professional game in the development of the offense. The BYU pass offense depended on timing. From the design of the quarterback drops to the route depths, to the protection schemes, everything depended on a timed sequence. If the defensive rush and coverage prevented execution of the rhythm or timing, then they converted to designated route adjustments

They sent receivers deep to stretch the field vertically and used their two running backs in the flats to extend the field horizontally. They incorporated timing routes just as Bill Walsh would do with the West Coast offense. The offense was an attempt at ball control that depended primarily on the pass. They also made frequent use of "option" routes with receivers altering their routes depending on how the defense played them. If the defender was on the outside shoulder of the receiver, he would break to the inside. If the defender was on the inside shoulder, the receiver would break to the outside, etc.

Both Edwards and Walsh made use of "hot routes" to combat defensive pressure. Every pass pattern had a receiver assigned a short route so that if an unblocked blitzing defender attacked the quarterback, he could throw quickly to that short receiver. Edwards explains the principle in - LaVell Edwards, *"The Football Coaching Bible."*

Figure 286 shows a BYU pass pattern from the 1980s called 65 Flood or Y-Sail. It was the beginning of the "Air Raid" offense to be discussed later. It is shown because both the routes and quarterback "reads" are typical of their offense.

"Preplay (prior to the ball being snapped): Read cover 2- "Where are the corners? Cushion... if yes, then cover 2."

"During play :(quarterback progression) 5 step drop

"Before he does anything, he "peeks" at the Z (#1, fade underneath him) to see if some massive breakdown in coverage occurred for the big play.

"He then goes to the Y (#2 Tight End, Sail---> [Sail is a corner route, with an over-middle-under policy, or go where the guy/s covering you aren't])

"Your safety valve is your fullback, which has been a primary route this year.

"Also, your running back is also able to go across the middle as a safety valve for the safety valve, but it is unlikely that he will be able to escape the pileup.

"Coverage Pending: If it is cover 2, the QB has to read the Strong Safety

"You can use your Z (#1, fade underneath him) as either a safety valve or tunnel vision lockdown guy because it will be one on one, no matter what. Also, the Y receiver can be a tunnel vision candidate because he will be up 1 on 1 with the SS, or wide open." [252]

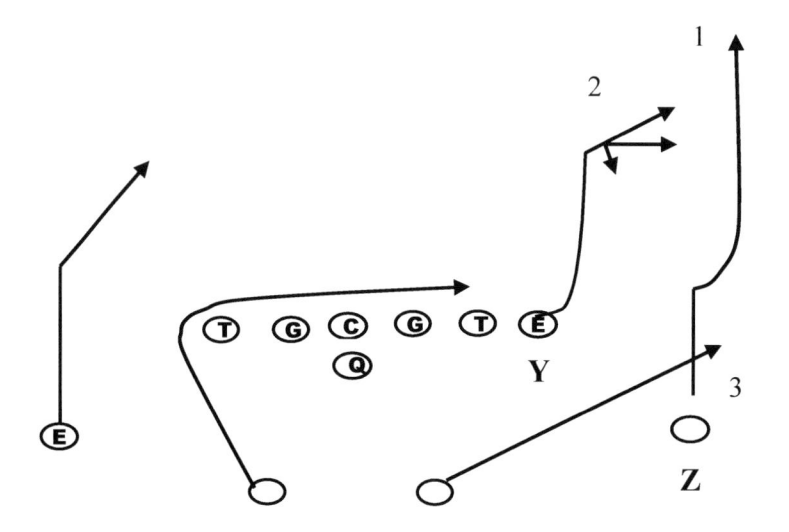

Figure 286 65 Flood or Y-Sail

According to Chow, one reason for the success of this version of the offense was in its simplicity. He has said the offense had around 12 basic pass plays and 5 basic run plays. The plays were run from several different formations, with only some plays tagged for extra flexibility. The players knew the offense by the second day of practice.
Two other favorites of BYU's 12 basic pass plays are shown below.
Figures 287, 288

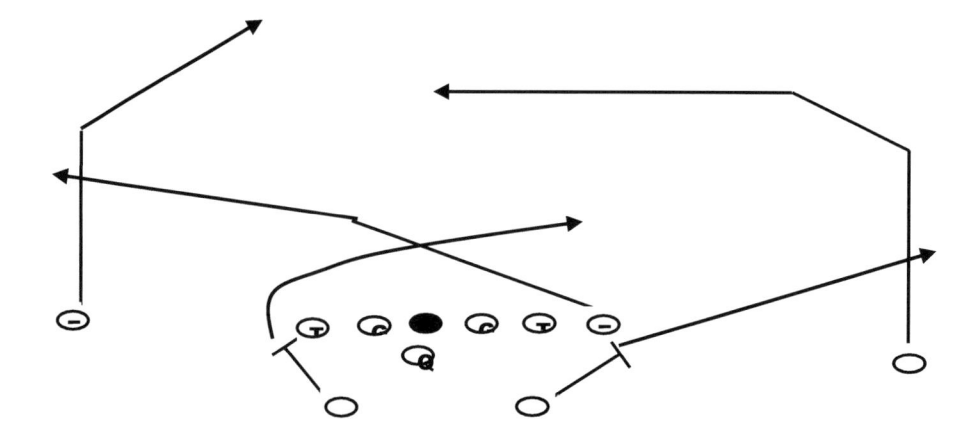

Figure 287 60 Y H Option

Figure 288 68 Smash

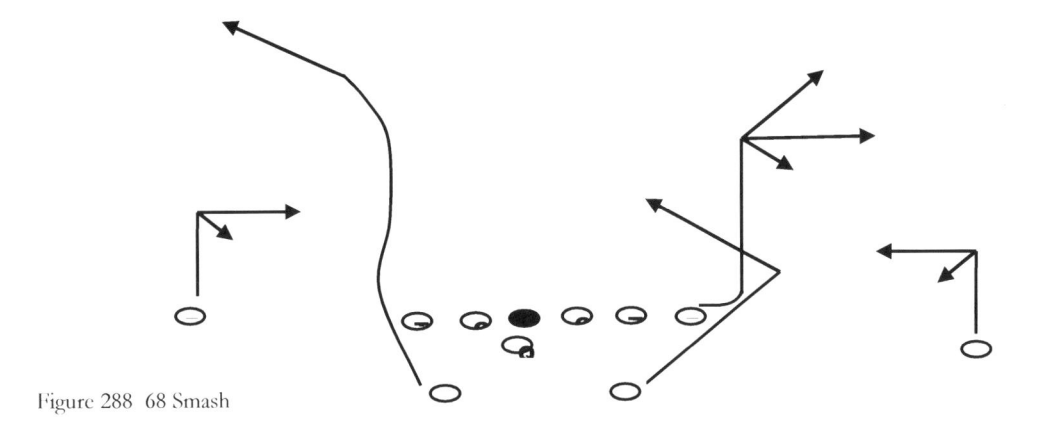

Joe Gibbs: H-Back

When Joe Gibbs left the Chargers and became head coach of the Washington Redskins, he further refined the use of the extra tight end. Gibbs used the single back formation with the extra tight end, which he called an "H" back. In Gibbs' formations, the traditional Tight End was, almost exclusively, a blocker, while the "H" back was primarily a receiver.

Gibbs started out using the same formations he had used during his tenure as the Offensive Coordinator in San Diego. Added to these formations was a "two tight-end" set. *Figure 289*

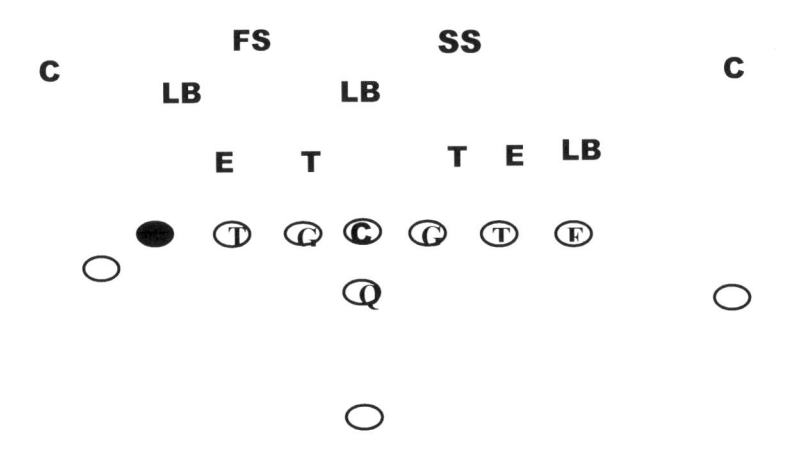

Figure 289 Gibbs Two Tight End Formation   Note the use of a Wingback (a potential 3rd Tight End)

238

The creation of the two tight end, two flanker formation was a countermeasure against 3-4 and 4-3 defenses in general but more specifically to counter the outside linebackers who aligned to the open end of the formation. In a typical, one tight-end formation the defense has seven gaps to defend. When you line up with two tight ends, the defense now has eight gaps to support. *Figure 290*

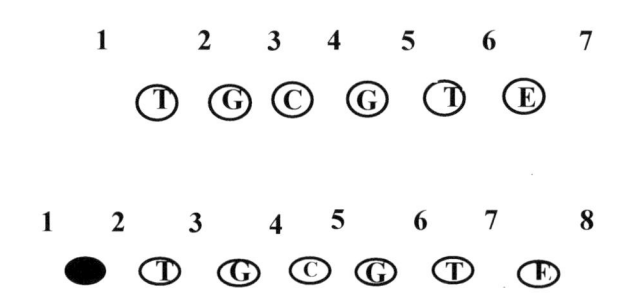

```
      1     2  3  4  5   6    7
      T     G  C  G  T   E

      1   2   3    4  5   6    7    8
      ●   T   G    C  G   T    E
```

Figure 290   7 gaps versus 8 gaps

The extra Tight End proved as Gibbs suspected, to be in a better position than a fullback to stop the outside linebacker when he blitzed. It also forced the linebacker to align wider, thus lengthening the distance between him and the quarterback. This alignment presents problems for defenses because they have to show their hand much earlier.

The two-tight end set allows teams to load up blockers at the line of scrimmage. Gibbs discovered a second advantage. It allowed him to disguise the directions of the play and still get maximum blocking at the point of attack. The presence of the second tight end extends the offensive line, allows them to pull either tackle or to use the tight end to block inside on delays or draws.

Taking it a step further, Gibbs used his second Tight End as an all-purpose blocker. He would usually line up one step behind the line of scrimmage. Gibbs sent him in motion across the formation to change the offensive strength. He motioned him into the backfield to act as a fullback. He placed him in a position to be a pass protector, and then slipped him into the pass pattern.[253]

The term H-back meant, "Motion TE." The Redskins would typically use one running back, one tight end, two wide receivers, and this H-back as their base offensive personnel grouping. The "regular" tight end would be a bigger, more blocking-focused player. The H-back would be a somewhat more maneuverable type, but still a blocking-focused person. The Counter Trey Play, made famous by Gibbs's Redskins, quite often had the H-back motioning to the strong side of the formation, where the regular Tight

End was aligned. This had the effect of making it look like they were overloading that side to run there. The Tight End and the H-back would seal that side while the tackle and guard pulled leading the counter play.

Gibbs felt that offenses needed the versatility that the new position provided. The multi-tight end sets allowed the Redskins to gather as many as four eligible receivers near the line of scrimmage. The extra tight ends gave him plenty of options in the passing game. However, as we know, two-tight end sets can also be very efficient when running the ball.

West Coast Offense

Almost everyone acknowledges that Bill Walsh, of the San Francisco 49ers, was the creator of, what is referred to as, the West Coast Offense. However, there is some dispute over the origin of the West Coast concepts. As was mentioned earlier much of the West Coast Offense can be traced back to Sid Gillman of the 60s-era San Diego Chargers. Some say the West Coast schemes extend all the way back to Francis Schmidt, who was the coach at Ohio State in the 1930s. Others have put Don Coryell of the '70s Chargers in the West Coast tradition. Walsh himself, in an article in The Sporting News, January 1999, says that he actually began using the West Coast concepts as an assistant coach with the Cincinnati Bengals.

Surprisingly, left unmentioned, in the West Coast conversation by most experts, are the Vikings of the 1970s. Coached by Bud Grant and offensive coordinator Jerry Burns, Fran Tarkenton directed an offense consisting of a short, ball-control passing game. Tarkenton has stated that, he believes, the Vikings ran an offense that was the forerunner of Walsh's West Coast offense.

It was not unusual to find offensive teams using ball control. Traditionally, those teams were founded on a strong running game. Walsh's West Coast offense was unique in that, although it was based on the ball control aspect of the game, he did it with quick, well-timed, passes. This short pass strategy had the added advantages of compensating for blocking breaking down and it had lots of yardage being picked up by the wide receivers after the catch. Walsh became Head Coach of the San Francisco 49ers in 1979. His approach to using short passes to control the ball met with a great deal of success. Ball control teams attempt to use the running game to draw the linebackers and safeties up to the line of scrimmage so that a long vertical pass can be thrown downfield. The West Coast Offense does, almost, the opposite. He attempted to throw short passes stretching the field horizontally to loosen the defense so that he could run the ball. There is little else unique about the West Coast Offense. In fact, many of the West Coast concepts are from BYU's offense of LaVell Edwards and Norm Chow. Walsh hired Mike Holmgren as his quarterback coach with the 49ers. Holmgren coached at BYU from 1982-1985. Walsh also used some of the Run and Shoot theory in his scheme.

The West Coast offense quickly grew to utilize a variety of formations and motions designed to confuse defenders. The initial Walsh concept uses a standard pro-set offense; two backs in split alignment, two wide receivers, and a tight end. The offense makes use of both three and five step drops by the quarterback, with the ball thrown on or before the receiver's break. The idea was to rely on the three- and five-step drops by the quarterback to compensate for most blocking breakdowns. Walsh wanted to throw the ball quickly and on the break. Just as in the Lavell Edwards/Norm Chow offense, it also relies heavily on flooding a defense with more receivers than they can cope with. The quarterback often moves around more than in a conventional offense with designed rollouts and bootlegs tied in with the patterns run by the receivers. [254] *Figure 291*

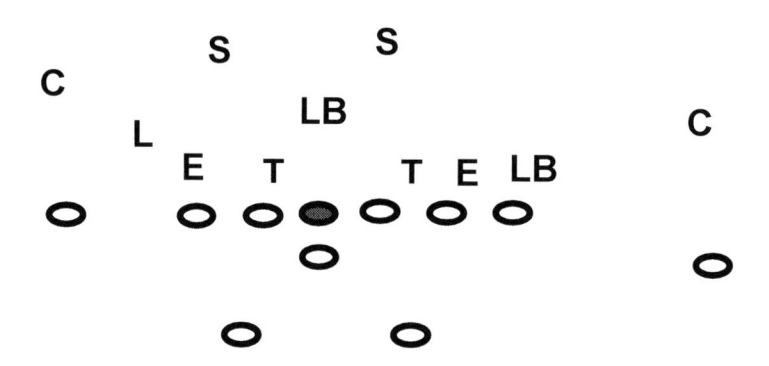

Figure 291 Basic West Coast Alignment

Triangle Passing Concept

The use of Triangles in the passing game is an extension of Sid Gillman's passing scheme. When Sid Gillman created the modern passing system, it focused on three "pass concepts". Those concepts are still the foundation of pass offenses. The three concepts are stretching the defense vertically (example smash concept or flood concept). Secondly, stretching the defense horizontally (example: all curl concept). Finally, attacking individual defenders of a man-to-man defense (example: mesh concept). In the 1980s, both BYU and Bill Walsh's 49ers developed variations of the Gillman concepts. Walsh combined all three concepts into one "triangle" read for the quarterback.

When first introduced the vertical and horizontal concepts had seemed unstoppable. If the three-man flood route, being a vertical stretch, attacked a cover 2 defense it was impossible to defend. There were two defenders (corner and safety) to play three receivers. If the All Curl route, being a horizontal stretch, was run against a cover 3 defense there were just too many voids in the under coverage to defend all the curls. As long as the offense could identify the coverage there was not much a defense could do. However, defensive coaches are not stupid and not without their own "geniuses". They began to change up coverages and disguise coverages so that the offense did not know which pass route(s) to run because they did not know what coverage the defense would be using. With all the movement of defenders, it became difficult for quarterbacks to identify the pass defense even after the play began.

The Triangle concept could be used to answer the defensive disguises. Below is an excellent example of the versatility of the triangle concept used in today's game. Many teams call this route "Snag", but it is so common some call it simply "Triangle."

The triangle has one receiver in the deep third on a corner route. The corner route is excellent versus man to man. One receiver goes into the flat. In this example, it is the running back. A third receiver runs the short hook, sometimes called a "sit" or "snag" route.

If the cornerback stays in the flat, the corner route will be open. If the cornerback drops with the corner route, the quarterback will have a high/low read on the Strong Safety (SS). If the SS goes to the flat route, the quarterback throws to the short hook receiver. If the SS sinks under the short hook route, the quarterback will throw to the flat receiver. *Figure 292*

Another traditional triangle route is the "Stick Route" shown below. *Figure 293*
It has very similar reads but with different pass routes.

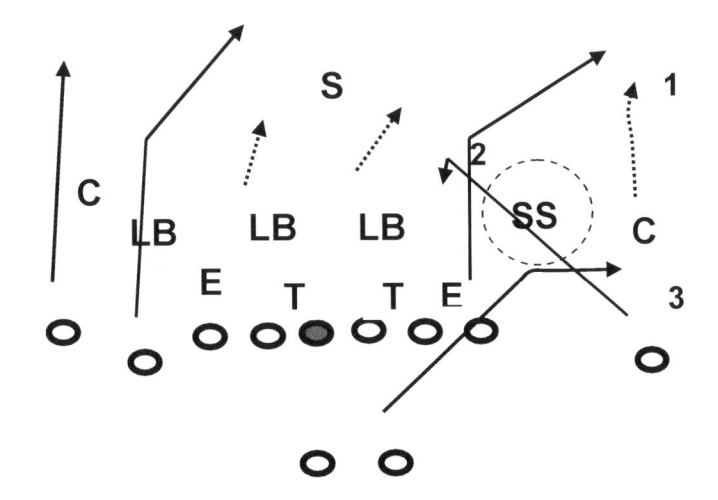

Figure 292 The "Snag" Route

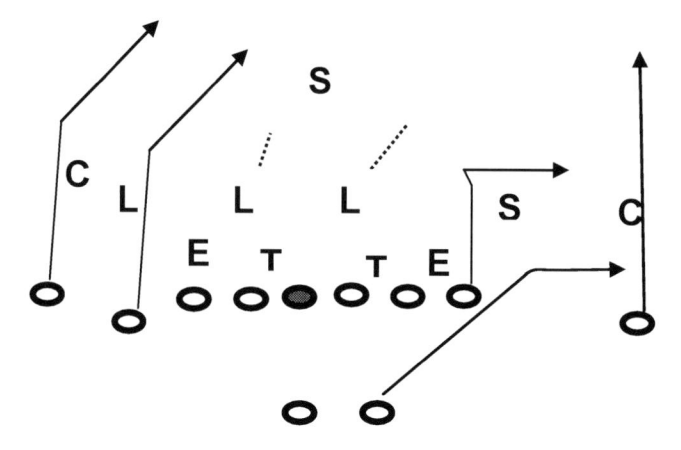

Figure 293 The "Stick" Route

In recent years, in an attempt to combat the triangle reads, defenses have begun to roll the defensive the secondary in the direction of the triangle side. This places an additional defender on the side of the triangle read and allows the defense to cover all three receivers. Since the extra defender comes from the backside, the natural response of the offense has been to create a backside combination route to combat the loss of one backside defender.

In the 40 years since Sid Gillman, defenses have become more multiple and better at disguising how they will play. The Triangle concept has given offensive coaches an opportunity keep up with the defense.

Jimmy Johnson: Miami 4-3

Jimmy Johnson popularized the Miami 4-3 Defense at the University of Miami in the mid-1980s. He had actually begun experimenting with the concept while head coach at Oklahoma State University. In his first head-coaching job, at Oklahoma State, Johnson knew he could not recruit successfully against the big schools. Therefore, he focused on recruiting student/athletes who were fast and had natural talent. Johnson felt that football talent was nice, but he made speed and athleticism his priority in recruiting.

He simplified the 4-3 scheme. There was no reading and reacting, no sitting in a specific area and attempting to control a gap. Instead, he coached his players to attack and penetrate the line of scrimmage. He used simple zone coverages in the secondary. The original intent of the defense was to stop the Wishbone Option offense of Coach Barry Switzer, who was overpowering teams at the University of Oklahoma. He later brought the Miami 4-3 defense with him to the Dallas Cowboys when he became head coach there. It might be a bit of an exaggeration to say that Jimmy Johnson was the most significant influence on the move, by many teams, back to the 4-3 front in the 1990s. However, the attacking style of defense brought about by Jimmy Johnson's Miami front continues to affect the game today.

The idea behind the defense was to have the front four align in something resembling an over front (9 and 3 technique strong side and 1 and 5 technique weak). From there the idea is to penetrate and wreak havoc in the backfield. He did not want his front four reading and reacting but attacking with the snap of the ball. He said that it was the linebackers and safeties jobs to do the reading and reacting. The defense also emphasized speed, especially on the outside. Johnson took outside linebackers and made them into defensive ends. He took safeties and made them into outside linebackers. He turned would be defensive ends into penetrating defensive tackles. His linebackers always had exceptional speed. Although the philosophy of the defense was the major difference from earlier 4-3 fronts, there were also a couple of minor schematic differences. Johnson had his strong side linebacker align off the line while his quick defensive ends lined up a little wider than the traditional 4-3. The alignment itself was not groundbreaking. It is a minor variation of the 4-3 Over. More accurately, the attitude and defensive team speed are what drives the system's success.

Johnson wanted his defensive line to explode into their gaps on the snap of the ball. He had them crowd the neutral zone as much as possible. The linemen were to make the offense react to them while they "read on the run", deciding what they would do next. The wide alignment of the ends allowed them to get up field quickly. This allowed the ends to both get a good pass rush and to disrupt a running play in the backfield. If they were not successful, they often forced the play back to the middle linebacker or "spilled" the play outside to the pursuit, where an outside linebacker was there to make the tackle. The smaller, quicker linebackers were protected by two solid, but still quick, defensive tackles that were disruptive enough to keep the linebackers "clean", to stop the run, and create negative plays. The perimeter rush by the line and tight coverage by the Cover-2 secondary provided excellent fortification against the pass. *Figure 294*

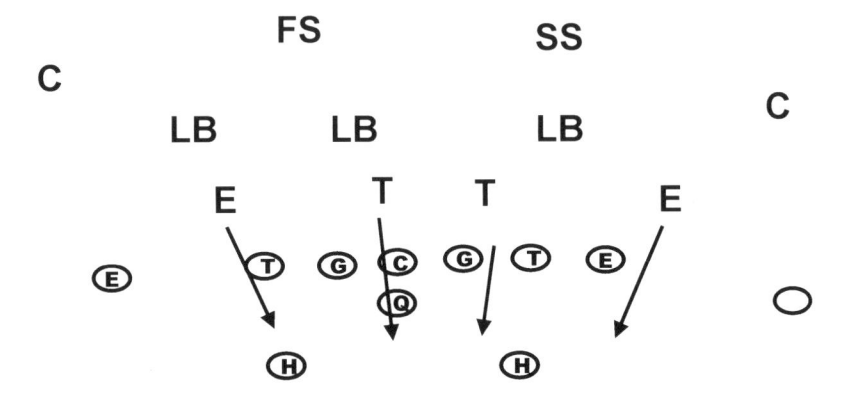

Figure 294 The Miami 4-3

In its zenith, it was a dominating scheme but it relied heavily on having a great front four because they rarely blitzed. If that front 4 did not do its job and get into the backfield, they were vulnerable to both the pass and run. If it did its job, the offense was helpless. However, the success of the undersized defensive players succeeding in a 4-3 front is still in evidence today and is directly traceable to the success of Jimmy Johnson and the 'Miami' 4-3.

Buddy Ryan: The 46 Defense

"Everything begins as an idea," Doug Plank (defensive back for the Chicago Bears) said. "The 46 was an idea, and with that little notion, Buddy changed football. There is no doubt. He changed the way the game was played." [255]

The 46 defense was an innovative concept with a unique defensive front. Mike Ditka was the Head Coach of the Chicago Bears, but the defense was the imagination of the highly creative Buddy Ryan, then defensive coordinator, that produced it. Ryan named the defense after the great Doug Plank, whose jersey number was 46. Ryan had a difficult time remembering names and he often called his players by their jersey number. It is one of only two defenses that we are aware of that is named after a player and not the actual defensive lineup.

Bill Walsh, the Hall of Fame Coach of the 49ers said that the 46 defense was the single most important innovation on the defensive side of the ball in the last 25 years.   46 Defense - *Figure 295*

This defense is based on pressure. The idea is to crush the run and force mistakes by the QB.

Homer Smith, perhaps the most analytical mind in modern day football, concluded that the 46 was a formidable defense. "Through football history, defensive coaches have tried to position their players so that blocking is more difficult than shedding blockers. Offensive coaches have always caught up with them and kept the ball moving to new yardage records. Now, however, if only in the NFL, this defense shut down offenses that had comparable talent and plenty of time to practice. Most offensive coaches can defeat defenses as long as they have the chalk, but his defense seems to hold its own on the chalkboard without a defensive coach in the room." [256]

The system starts with, what is in essence, a 4-3, but it employs a nose tackle, 3-technique tackle, and two Ends. The three interior defenders clog the middle of the formation lining up on the head of the center and the two guards. The weakside end acts as a "Rush End", lining up about three yards off the offensive tackle, his primary purpose, as the name implies, is to rush the quarterback.

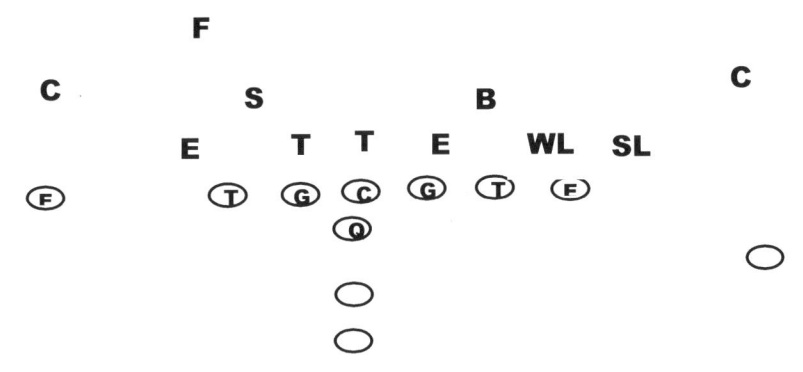

Figure 295 The 46 Defense

There are stories of offensive running backs, true or not, when faced with the 46, pleading with the quarterback to audible out of the run play.

In his book, *Coaching Football's 46 Defense*, Rex Ryan, Buddy's son, had this to say about the 46; "Without question the most dominating defensive scheme in the history of the National Football League, the 46 Defense applies pressure to every offensive flank and debilitates every phase of the hand-off running game. Unlike the popular 4-3 slide front and other 'pass-conscious' 7-man front schemes, the 46 is a fundamental defensive structure of the attacking 8-man front family. A 'stop-the-run-first' defense, the 46 presents a formidable defense for run-based offenses at all levels of play.

"The 46 defense is closely related to the dominant defensive scheme of professional football in the 1940s and early-to-mid-1950s. During this period, run-based attacks were the predominant systems of choice in offensive football. The solid run-stopping double eagle scheme credited to Earle "Greasy" Neale of the Philadelphia Eagles was a popular front structure of defensive football during this time frame in modern football history. In the post-World War II era, the double eagle front was a dominant force in professional football." [257]

The 46 was one of the most feared defenses ever, but like all defenses, this one had a shortcoming, and its shortcoming has been a major problem. The pressure created by the 46 left the flats unprotected. The cornerbacks were provided little help from the safeties. Also, with the coming of the short, quick West Coast offenses, the 46 fell out of use except in specialty situations.[258] This is not to say that Buddy Ryan was "a one-hit wonder," Buddy Ryan was influential in forming the Jet defense that helped Joe Namath pull off the upset in Super Bowl III. Moreover, he later had a significant role in the development of the Purple People Eater defense in Minnesota. Buddy Ryan was an impressive defensive genius. His 46 can still be found confusing offenses on fall afternoons.

More on the Wishbone

The Wishbone's popularity reached its peak in the 1970s. The wishbone was employed at all levels of high school and college football. Detractors said its demise was attributable to its run-heavy schemes and weak passing potential. However, in the 1980s, although it remained popular at the high school level, it was used less at major college programs. In his book, *Bootleggers Boy*, Barry Switzer commented that the wishbone was not dead but all of the coaches who knew how to coach the wishbone were dead. [259] However, the triple option concepts of the Wishbone are being used throughout the game today. Moreover, the triple option offense continues to flourish.

Wing T Changes

Two forms of the Wing-T had developed. In the Delaware type of Wing-T, the offense uses, in principle, two running backs along with the quarterback to move the ball. It also has more flexibility in its offense to pass the ball than the other type. The other type of attack, named after the first school to use it the state of Michigan, is the Bay City Wing-T. It uses three running backs and the quarterback to move the ball. In both forms, the fundamental aspect of the offense is the linemen. A vast majority of the plays are run by trapping or pulling one or more of the linemen; this includes the pass as well as the run plays. [260]

The traditional "Wing-T" offense began to employ many of the concepts of the wishbone offense. It often used three running back formations, especially in the Bay City version of the attack. As stated earlier, the Wing-T helped change the game of football in the 1950s and 1960s. The quarterback was used, fundamentally, as a means of getting the ball to one of the three running backs. As the triple-option became established, the Wing-T quickly incorporated the veer into its arsenal. However, it still made use of a large amount of misdirection running plays as the basis of its offense. The traps, the halfback crosses, fakes, sweeps, counters, and pulling linemen that characterize the Wing-T are now often accompanied by option runs; most markedly the veer triple option. The Veer is well suited to the Wing-T offense, especially the Delaware version.

The Delaware version of the Wing-T, with its use of two running backs, continued to gain significant support in the early 1980s. Today, both high schools and small college teams continue to utilize the Wing-T.

Flexbone

A new variation of the option offense called the "Flexbone Option" came to prominence in the 1980s and 1990s. The name is attributed to Air Force Head Coach Fisher DeBerry when he explained his team's need for greater variation in its wishbone attack, "We need to be more flexible in the Bone." As a result, the term "Flexbone" was born. [261] Running the triple option from a spread formation using two slotbacks or wingbacks was the idea of Ken Hatfield the Air Force Head Coach before DeBerry. One primary difference between the Flexbone and Wishbone is that the Flexbone replaces the halfbacks that align in the backfield of a wishbone with one or two "wingbacks" or "slot backs." They will align off the outside shoulder of the tackle or end. These players are typically very quick and must be adept at running, blocking (mainly cut blocking) as well as receiving. Due to the positioning of the "wingbacks", they assist the passing game as they serve to stretch the defensive alignment horizontally before the snap.

Paul Johnson, who began to run the offense in the mid-80s at Georgia Southern, chose to call it the "Spread Option Offense." Johnson thought his offense related more to spread formations such as the Run and Shoot. He uses the triple-option as a foundation of his offense instead of the vigorous passing game of the Run and Shoot. While at Georgia Southern, Paul Johnson won six Division I-AA National Championships. Johnson has brought the offense to Georgia Tech, in Division I, where he has achieved considerable success.

Oddly enough, as traditional wishbone coaches sought to make their offenses more dynamic, they began to imitate the alignments of this "spread offense". Most coaches use the term Flexbone. The name has since stuck, most likely to prevent confusion with other spread offenses. *Figure 296*

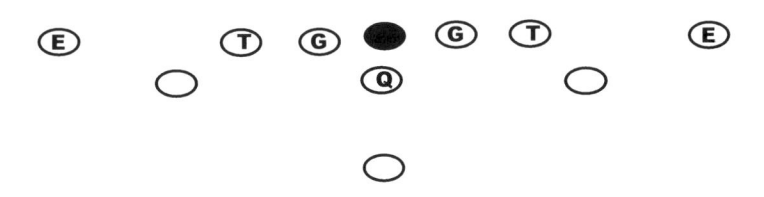

Figure 296 Flexbone

Nebraska I-Offense

The I Option offense, also known as the "Nebraska I-offense," derived its name from the extensive use of the I formation with the traditional straight-line alignment of quarterback, fullback and running back. Though balanced attacks from the I formation have been around for years, the "I-Option" gained recognition when Tom Osborne, at the University of Nebraska, brought it to the forefront. Using this offense, Osborne had outstanding success from the time of its introduction in 1980 until his retirement. Nebraska combined a strong running game with the option and play-action pass to create a dominant offense.

Homer Smith, the successful coach, and a leading expert in analyzing football strategies and tactics, provides an outstanding summation of Osborne's offense, "Tom Osborne understood what made option plays (and other run plays) work and what had stopped them. So, he ran them — he ran almost all of them — but only when they would work. He checked to them versus vulnerable defenses. His smash mouth runs, run-action passes, and QB runs kept defenses from mirroring properly against his options. The result was staggering totals of rushing yards. No matter how successful the options, etc. had been in their individual heydays, they were never better than when Coach Osborne "played a medley of tunes." [262]

No Huddle

Many believe that it was during his first season with the Cincinnati Bengals, in 1984, that Sam Wyche used the no-huddle offense. The Bengals were having problems with their 3rd down offense.

In a November 2008 interview with the Roanoke Times, Wyche posed the question, "We're going to go back here and [huddle] for 20 seconds and let them get all of their best rushers and best cover people in?" He then answered his own question, "And [then] we're going to line-up and do exactly what they thought we'd do—throw the ball." He felt that made no sense. The results of Wyche's thinking created the modern no huddle offense.

Actually, Wyche himself contradicts the common belief about the beginnings of the no-huddle. In a telephone interview with the Columbus Dispatch in 2013, while discussing the 1983 season, Wyche, at the time the University of Indiana's Head Coach, explained the origin of the No Huddle. He stated, "We played in the Big Ten against Ohio State and Michigan, and Iowa was good with Hayden Fry." "When I walked onto the field, I knew we didn't have the personnel to match up. We had to come up with a way to wear them down to our level.

"I thought if we can wear them out, out condition them, that'll close the gap. That's when the idea (of the no-huddle) really started." [263]

We realize that not huddling before each play goes back to the beginnings of offensive strategy. Additionally, the Dallas Cowboys under Tom Landry used the no-huddle infrequently from their shotgun in the 1960s.

In 1986, people were saying that the no huddle was creating as much havoc for Wyche's Bengals offense as it was for opposing defenses. Wyche defended the strategy to the Pittsburgh Post-Gazette, "We actually know what we're doing," Wyche said at the time. "Sometimes we use it to keep personnel off the field, sometimes to change the tempo of the game, and sometimes to force defenses out of a certain coverage." [264]

Because the Bengals used the no-huddle less than half of their offensive snaps, it was slow to catch on. It was not until 1988 when the Bengals were ripping defenses apart on their way to the Super Bowl that people began to notice. In the week leading up to the AFC Championship game between the Bengals and the Buffalo Bills, the Bills Head Coach Marv Levy questioned the fairness of the Bengals no huddle offense. "When you break the huddle - and I know he's not huddling so maybe it's hazy - they are not to come out with 12-13 players on the field," he is quoted in the Toledo Blade. There was talk that a Bills defender would feign an injury between every play. The day before the game the NFL declared that the Bengals offense was not in violation of the rules. However, just two hours before the game they reversed themselves and ruled that the Bengals could not have more than 11 men on the field at any one time. The Bengals won the game anyway 21-10. [265]

By 1990, Marv Levy, and the Buffalo Bills were running the no- huddle with Hall of Fame quarterback Jim Kelly. They referred to their version as the "K-Gun".

It is interesting to note that Chan Gailey, then at Troy State University, made a presentation to the American Football Coaches Association in 1985 his topic was "No Huddle Option Offense." [266] This implies that Troy State was also utilizing the "no-huddle" during the 1984 season.

The Dime Package

As offenses began to use more wide receivers, more defensive backs were needed. The dime defense grew from the need to cover more and faster wide receivers. In the Dime, the defense removes a linebacker and substitutes him with a fourth cornerback. This began as a defense used in obvious passing situations to one that is, with more frequency used on every down play. *Figure 297*

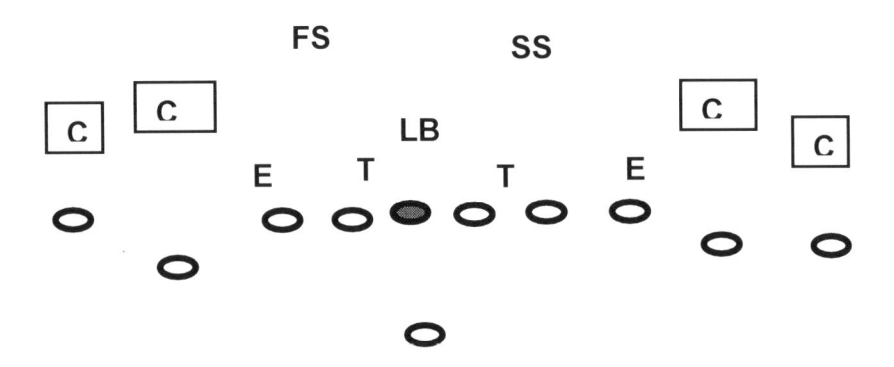

Figure 297 Typical Dime Alignment

Zone Blitz

Although technically the "Zone Blitz" found its origin in the 1980s, it did not become universally popular until the early 1990s. Because of that, we will discuss the zone blitz in the next chapter.

---

[249] http://thinkexist.com/*quotes/joe_collier/*
[250] Hobson, Geoff. *'88 Legacy Lives On in Playbooks*, Bengals.com, Nov. 23, 2013. http://www.bengals.com/news/article-1/88-legacy-lives-on-in-playbooks/e0794850-4b11-4a43-9fe6-85a525279238

[251] Hobson, Geoff. *'88 Legacy Lives On in Playbooks*, Bengals.com, Nov. 23, 2013. http://www.bengals.com/news/article-1/88-legacy-lives-on-in-playbooks/e0794850-4b11-4a43-9fe6-85a525279238
[252] *Norm Chows Airraid-Offense*, http://www.bruinsnation.com/2009/10/25/1100115/norm-chows-airraid-offense#comments
[253] http://www.footballoutsiders.com/strategy-minicamps/2006/*too-deep-zone-running-multiple-tight-ends*
[254] http://football.about.com/od/*offensivestrategy*/a/West-Coast.htm
[255] *Legacy of the 46 Defense* http://www.nytimes.com/2009/09/06/sports/football/06plank.html?_r=1&pagewanted=2
[256] Smith, Homer. *Understanding the 46 Defense and Ideas On How to Attack It*, American Football Coaches Association Summer Manual, 1986, p. 23-26
[257] Ryan, Rex & Jeff Walker. *Coaching Football's 46 Defense*. Coaches Choice, Monterey, CA. 1999. P. 9-10
258 *The 46 Defense*, http://www.windycitygridiron.com/2009/3/12/794822/the-46-defense
[259] Switzer, Barry. *Bootlegers Boy*, William Morrow & Co., Inc., 1990
[260] *Wing_T_Offense* http://en.wikipedia.org/wiki/Offensi...
[261] *Flexbone Offense*, The Resource For Flexbone Offense Football Coaches, http://flexboneoffense.blogspot.com/
[262] *Homer Smith on Tom Osborne's Nebraska Offense* http://smartfootball.blogspot.com/2009/04/homer-smith-on-tom-osbornes-nebraska.html
[263] Jones, Todd, *Sam Wyche Invented No Huddle Offense at Indiana in '83*. Columbus Dispatch, Thursday, Sept. 12, 2013. http://buckeyextra.dispatch.com/content/stories/2013/09/12/sam-wyche-invented-no-huddle-offense-at-indiana-in-83.html
[264] How the Cincinnati Bengals Changed NFL History: *The No-Huddle Offense Turns 25* By John Breech_, Correspondent Jun 17, 2009
http://bleacherreport.com/articles/201148-how-the-cincinnati-bengals-changed-nfl-history-the-no-huddle-offense
[265] Breech http://bleacherreport.com/articles/201148-how-the-cincinnati-bengals-changed-nfl-history-the-no-huddle-offense
[266] Gailey, Chan, *No Huddle Option Offense*, Proceedings Manual, American Football Coaches Association Convention, 1985, p. 21-22.

CHAPTER FOURTEEN

Adjustments

(1990 - 1999)

The Zone Blitz

There are, at least, four different accounts of exactly when the Zone Blitz was created. Some credit Dick LeBeau, who supposedly devised the scheme on a napkin while riding home from a game in 1988. The napkin bit is suspect. He was looking for unique ways to pressure and confuse the quarterback. Others claim the Philadelphia Stars of the USFL first used it in 1987. Their claim is that Jim Mora, Dom Capers, and Vic Fangio perfected an idea that was first put forth by John Rosenberg, who was also on the Stars staff at that time. Still others claim Joe Paterno at Penn State first used the zone blitz in the 1986 National Championship game against Miami.

Whatever the actual origin, the zone blitz came into its own as a defensive strategy of LeBeau and Capers, who were both assistant coaches for the Pittsburgh Steelers at the time. They refined the strategy and formed it into an every down defense in the early and mid-1990s. They remain good friends and have a genuine respect for each other's contribution to the zone blitz. "Very unique guy when you look at what he's done and what that defense has done," Capers said of LeBeau. "They've been the standard bearer really of the defense. If you look at him over the last 18, 19 years and probably put their collective stats together, I don't think anybody can compare with him." Added LeBeau: "He's been a success everywhere he's been. I'm one of his biggest fans."[267]

LeBeau, himself, credits much of the inspiration to conversations he had with Bill Arnsparger. Arnsparger's thinking on the blitz was unless you get to the quarterback, an all-out blitz leaves too many voids in the defensive coverage. The rewards of a big defensive play versus the risks of giving up a big play were not good. It was after this conversation that LeBeau was motivated to work on finding an effective but safe way to pressure the quarterback. LeBeau implemented his new scheme under head coach Bill Cower of the Pittsburgh Steelers.[268]

What is the rationale of the Zone blitz scheme? Confuse the offense by disguising the pass rush. Try to make a four-man pass rush function like an all-out blitz. Play zone coverage behind the blitz so that a mistake in the secondary does not result in a big play. Disguise the zone coverage so that a quarterback's usual sight adjustment leads him right into an unexpectedly covered route.

Before this new concept, defensive coordinators felt that blitzing a linebacker or safety would leave a wide-open zone in the secondary. Thus, the only possible coverage they could use behind a blitz was man-to-man. This way, all receivers are defended. However, this also puts enormous pressure on the cornerbacks and safeties to chase receivers all over the field.

The basic concept - the swapping of an expected pass rusher for an unexpected one - is relatively straightforward. However, the type of exchange and number of players involved in the rotation can become very complex. *Figure 298*

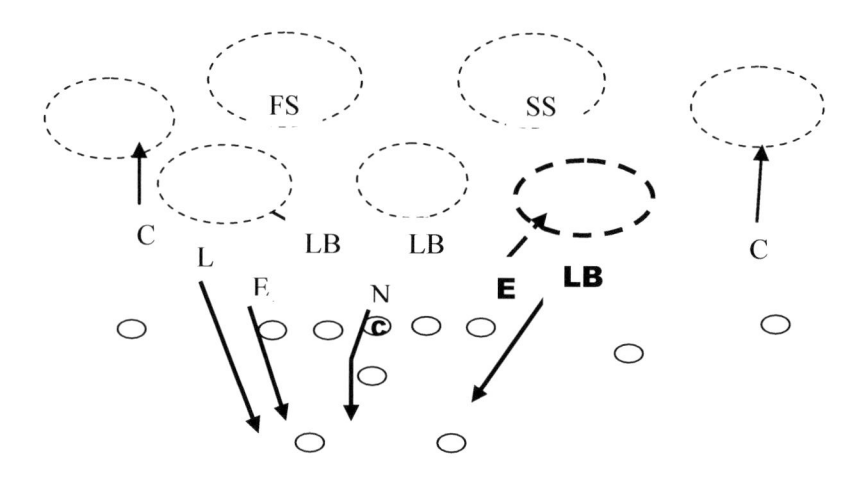

Figure 298 Simple Zone Blitz - with a defensive end and linebacker exchange

A more complex zone blitz might have two exchanges. Here is a more complicated example. In *Figure 299*, the defense shows seven men threatening the line of scrimmage at the snap. When you examine the rush, there are only five players rushing the passer (including the Strong Safety (SS)), leaving a three under zone and three deep zone coverage look.

253

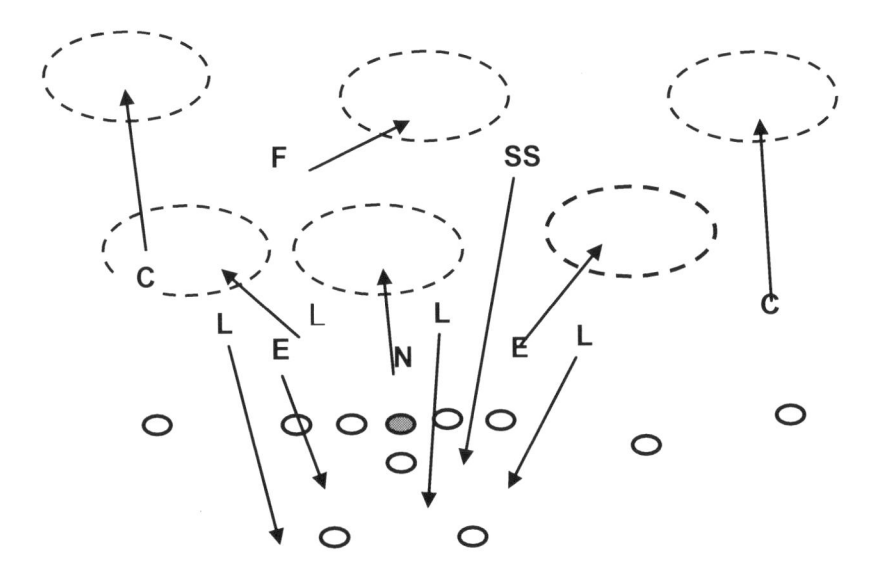

Figure 299 Zone Blitz with the Nose and End dropping

The Zone blitz can be run from a 4-3 front as well as the 3-4. However, both Dom Capers and Dick LeBeau prefer the 3-4 as a base for their Zone blitz schemes. They believe there are a wider variety of potential attack points.

Like any other defensive scheme, the zone blitz is beatable. A practiced offensive line and running back with good vision can spot the exchanges and adjust their blocking. If the favorable draw or screen pass is called, it can be extremely successful. The defensive line is suspect versus the play action pass because it forces a short pause before the lineman makes the exchange and drops into coverage. Finally, like any other blitz, if enough players stay in to protect the passer it is hard to overpower the blocking scheme.

"Tampa-2" Defense

The origin The "Tampa-2" Defense goes all the way back to the Pittsburgh Steelers of 1975 when Tony Dungy, the coach most famous for the "Tampa-2", played for Pittsburgh. It is actually Steelers Head Coach Chuck Knoll and defensive coordinator, Bud Carson, who Dungy credits with creating the defense. Carson is the one who initiated the idea of moving the middle linebacker into deeper pass coverage. His Cover 2 (two safeties in the secondary) system became very productive for the Steelers in the 1970s and 1980s. Dungy maintains he changed the defense very little since that 1975 season when he first learned the defense. Lovie Smith, most recently, coach of the Tampa Bay Buccaneers, claims to have played the system in high school in the mid-1970s. Also, similar principles were used by the Minnesota Vikings defense in the mid-to-late 1980s.

Bill Walsh's West Coast offense during the early 1990s was renowned for getting receivers down the middle of the field, behind the linebackers, for big gains. When Dungy became head coach of the Tampa Bay Buccaneers, he and defensive coordinator Monte Kiffin refined the old Steelers scheme to combat the West Coast tactic. The defense became the central element in Tampa's dominate defense in the late 1990s.

In the traditional cover two defenses, the corners have the flats, the outside linebackers have their respective curl zones and the middle linebacker has the hook area. The strong safety and free safety each has the deep 1/2 field. *Figure 300*

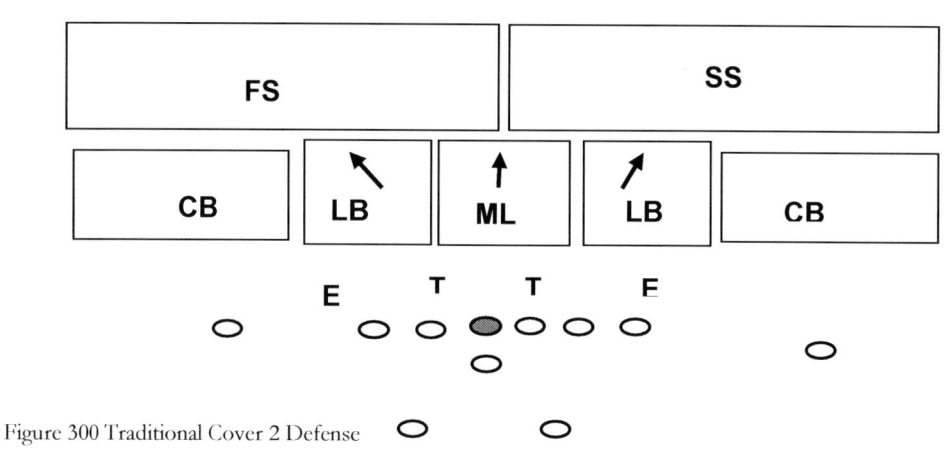

Figure 300 Traditional Cover 2 Defense

In the "Tampa-2", the middle linebacker's coverage area is much deeper (about 11-13 yards deep). He will drop almost as deep as the two safeties; making the "Tampa-2" resemble something close to a 3 deep secondary. In the simplest form, there will now be four under zones with the corners having the flats and the outside linebackers having the curl areas. *Figure 301*

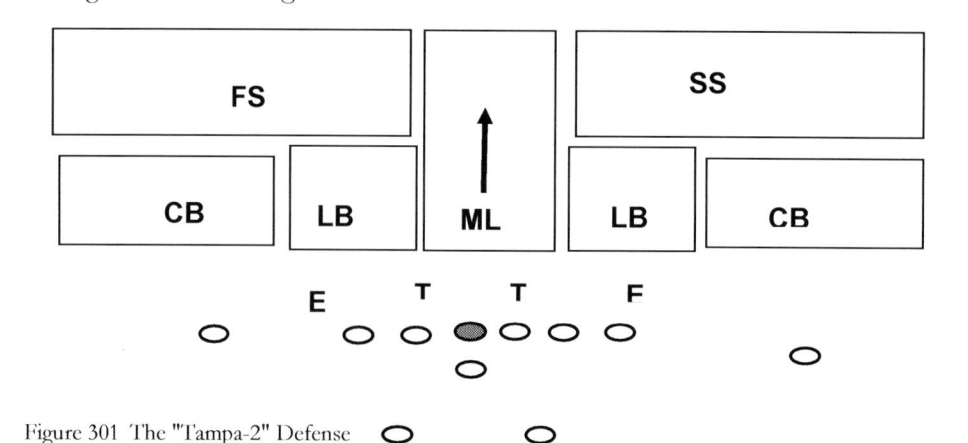

Figure 301 The "Tampa-2" Defense

One of the defensive tackles is usually lined up in a 3-Technique while the other may be a 0, 1, or 3 technique. In the beginning, both defensive tackles were only responsible for 1-Gap. However, it was soon discovered that offenses were beating the defense with the interior run. Defenses changed the scheme to have one tackle be a speed rusher (the 3-technique) and the other tackle plays more of a nose tackle technique. The remaining gaps are filled by the outside linebackers and occasionally by the middle linebacker. The Defensive Ends are in a 5-technique, playing on the outside shoulder of the offensive tackle or wider. From this position, they will rush hard off the perimeter. While the 3-technique is often an outstanding pass-rusher in the "Tampa-2", they sometimes fall short in their run-stopping capabilities.

While the "Tampa-2" was originally created to stop the West Coast offense, it is a misconception that it does not react well to the run. It does. It is a bend, but don't break defense. It is designed to allow the offense to complete underneath passes. Essentially everything is funneled underneath the middle linebacker and behind the outside linebackers thus creating a tiny window for the quarterback's throw.

The critical player in the defense, of course, is the middle linebacker. In the "Tampa-2", he does not immediately drop into pass coverage. He is not a defensive back. His first couple of steps is towards the line of scrimmage. This gives him the ability to react to the run quickly. If he reads pass, he takes his pass drop. This keeps him in the middle of the field, but takes away the possibility of crossing routes getting behind him. Where the Mike (middle linebacker) lines up in approximation to the line of scrimmage is situational. On a 3rd and 1, he will "crowd" the line of scrimmage. While the middle linebacker does have to have speed, he is not running with the quickest receivers on the field. His responsibility is to cover crossing routes or routes up the middle. These are usually tight ends or slot backs, although these receivers have demonstrated much more speed in recent years. The defense attempts to keep the offense off balance with a multitude of coverages, blitzes, stunts, zone blitzes, etc.

A second critical factor in the defense is the Cornerbacks. They must get a real "jam" on the wide receivers and disrupt their patterns. If the cornerback fails at this, the safeties have difficulty covering half the field. The safeties have to be able to see the entire field and know who is becoming their responsibility.

Options in the 1990s:

As was mentioned earlier, coaches have been successful running the triple option out of an I- formation. They called it the I-veer, or I-back veer.[269] This option was used with great success at Colorado under Bill McCarty and Nebraska under Coach Tom Osborne.

At the dawn of the 21st century, the "traditional" option offenses had all but evaporated from the college ranks, except for the service academies. Both the Veer and variations of the Wishbone can still be found at the high school level. So, if the offense was so successful, why did it disappear from the field of play? By most accounts, the decline of option football is related to the rise of professional football and television sports coverage. In the 1970's, rule changes instituted in the NFL favored the passing game and the high-paced and often spectacular nature of passing offenses were attractive to casual fans.

Today, most—if not all—Division I college players enter a college programs with at least a glimmer of hope of making it to the NFL. So, in the 1990s, recruiting high school players—particularly that player with outstanding athletic ability—to a school that ran a system, which may not have showcased their talents, is not an easy task. Teams at the college level had to adopt a more pro-like offensive scheme to attract the top talent. Unfortunately, for those teams that could not attract top talent—like the service academies and tier-two schools—winning a conference title (and sometimes-just winning) became a distant memory.

3-3-5 defense

In preparing for the opening game on Sept. 2, 1991, versus the University of Southern California, the Memphis Tigers defensive coordinator Joe Lee Dunn felt his defense was outmanned. He knew he could not line up in his usual 4-3 defense and compete with them, especially on the line of scrimmage. Dunn removed one of his down linemen and replaced him with a fifth defensive back. Memphis came away with a 21-10 upset. With a few shifts in alignment the 3-3-5 defense was born - a defense still in vogue around college football today. The defense plays with three defensive linemen and five defensive backs. The fact that the linebackers are often stacked over the linemen protects them from potential blockers. *Figure 302*. This defense has also been called the 33 Stack and the Spread Defense.

Dunn moved to the University of Mississippi, to Arkansas, and finally to Mississippi State where he perfected his 3-3-5 defense. Dunn did not hesitate to blitz anybody and everybody. It was not unusual, at the time, to see Dunn's defense blitz every player, at least, once in each game.

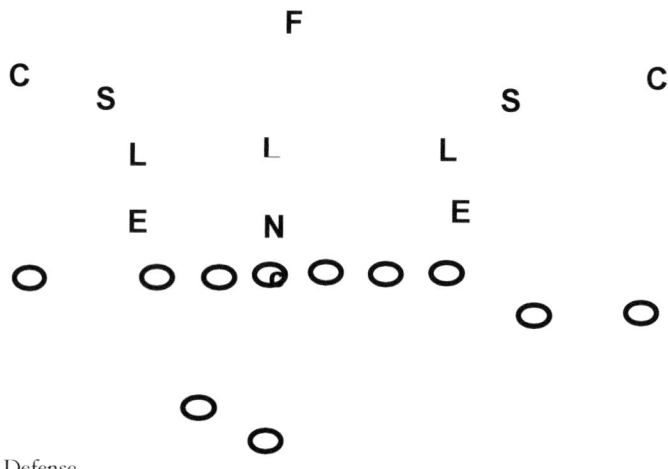

Figure 302   3-3-5 Defense

The 3-3-5 alignment allowed Mississippi State to Zone Blitz without dropping any defensive linemen. *Figure 303*

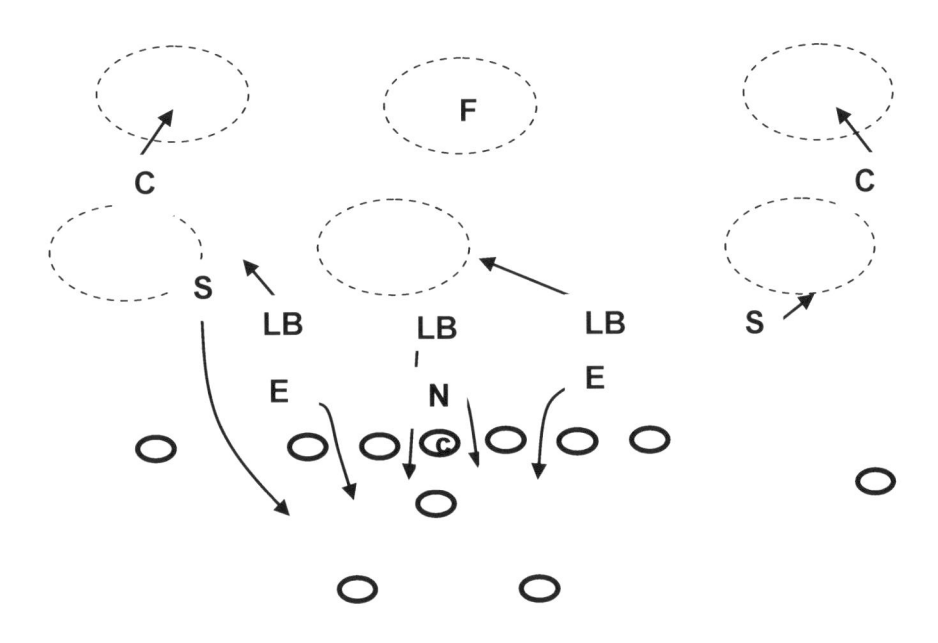

Figure 303 3-3-5 Zone Blitz

      Charley Strong, as Defensive Coordinator, brought Dunn's concepts to the University of South Carolina where he had much success with it. Strong mixed the 3-3-5 with both the 4-3 and 3-4 defenses to create an extremely multiple defense to combat the spread attack. Strong went on to become the Head Coach of Louisville and then Texas. Most teams today employ some variations with their 3-3-5 defense.
      It is not unreasonable to suggest that the 3-3-5 defense was the precursor of the "hybrid" defenses that are so popular in today's game

Game Preparation

      The scouting and analyzing of opponent offenses and defenses has been around since the beginning of the 20th century. In the late 1950s, its use became more universally recognized and specialized. In fact in 1962 Steve Belichick, an assistant coach at Navy, wrote a book on Scouting Methods.[270] He went into detail about how to organize the scouting procedures, what to look for, and how to best use scouting to take advantage of an opponent. He also stressed the need for "self-scouting" or scouting your own team. It is hard to determine how much your opponent knows about you if you do not know about yourself. With the advances in technology, in the late 1980s and the 1990s, there was a greater emphasis on detail and specialization.

In analyzing defenses, offensive coaches saw that when defenses played with a single safety, it did not matter if the offense had 1, 2, or 3 backs in the backfield. The defense would always be able to put one more defender on or near the line of scrimmage than the offense could block. *Figure 304.* On the other hand, when the defense aligned with two safeties, the offense will always have one blocker for each defender on or near the line of scrimmage. *Figure 305.* Offenses controlled their play calls by "reading" the safeties and determining the number of defenders on or near the line of scrimmage. They called this counting the defenders "in the box." Versus a single safety, the offense knew they did not have a sufficient number of blockers to run the ball. They went to the line of scrimmage and called a pass play. Versus two safeties, they knew their numbers matched the defenders "in the box" and they could run the ball. This created a whole new approach to offense.

It did not take long before defensive coaches began to disguise their defenses, moving defenders in and out of "the box" and stunting defenders. The number of defenders "in the box" was no longer apparent. Offensive coaches could no longer instruct their quarterback to merely read the safeties and count the defenders "in the box." This principle of play calling is still good; it just takes more preparation on the part of the quarterback to determine the actual alignment and intent of the defenders.

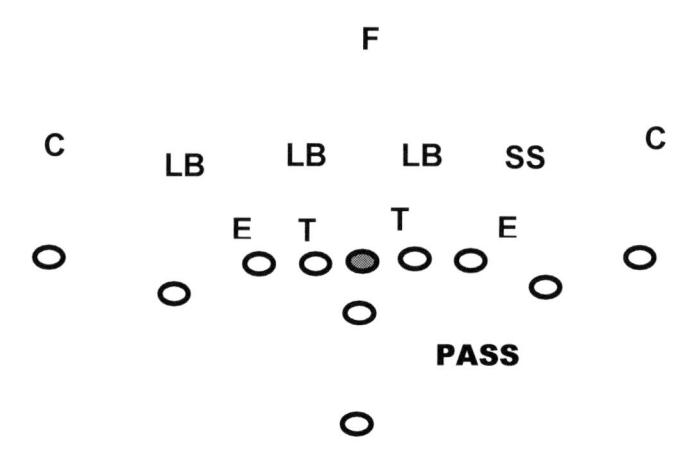

Figure 304 Single Safety -- Pass

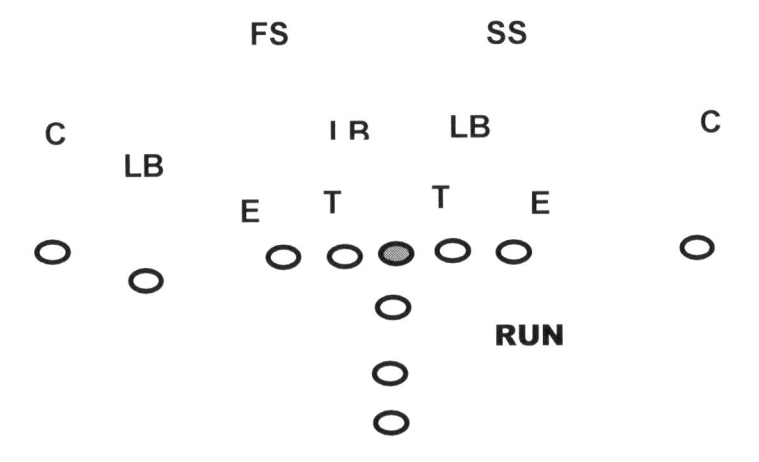

Figure 305 Two Safeties - Run

Although many coaches were using scouting methods that were detailed and precise, Bill Belichick, the son of Steve Belichick, played a significant role in changing game preparations. First with the Cleveland Browns and most recently with the New England Patriots the younger Belichick, greatly influenced by his father's philosophy of scouting, organized his defense on a weekly basis; each week's preparation being specific to that week's opponent. Operating out of both a 3-4 defense and a 4-3 defense, he created a pioneering hybrid defense. He was influenced by some great coaches. With Fritz Shurmur, he experienced the extensive use of both the Eagle concept and the nickel concept. From Maxie Baughan, he experienced George Allen's 4-3 with its many pre-snap movements. At Denver, he was with Joe Collier, who because of a significant number of injuries to his defense, created the Bronco's famous "Orange Crush" defense. This was one of the first truly multiple front defenses. He also worked with Bill Parcells running the 3-4 defense with the New York Giants and the New England Patriots. What all of these coaches had in common was a belief that to be multiple a defense had to have players who were adaptable and able to perform a variety of different functions for the defense.

Bill Belichick has brought the concept of individual game preparation to a new level. He is quoted as saying, "Every week is its own challenge. Every game brings its own set of circumstances, adjustments, play style, and matchups. We focus on what we want to do for that week, not what we did two weeks before or ten weeks before." [271] Belichick's hybrid defense is a labyrinth meant to puzzle and confound offenses.

Birth of Spread Option

Although the single back set with its "H"-back continued to be popular and have much success, the newest innovation in offensive football was the "Spread Formation" from a shotgun. This was very similar to the old single wing or "Red" Hickey's 49ers shotgun in the 1960s. *Figure 306* depicts a typical shotgun spread formation.

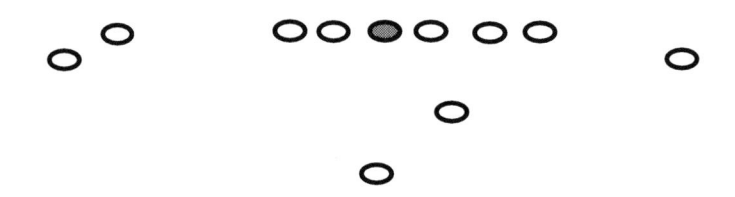

Figure 306 Typical Shotgun Spread Formation

Emerging during the late 1990s and 2000s, the spread is typically run from any variation of the shotgun formation such as the example above. The "spread" provides teams that have speed and athletic players to take advantage of holes in the defense created by the wide distribution of players. Many different systems are run from the spread. Although these offenses began in the 1990s, they grew and flourished in the twenty-first century and will be discussed in the next chapter.

Fun and Gun: Steve Spurrier

Steve Spurrier had played quarterback at Florida. He then went on to play in the NFL He later became "Head Ball Coach" at the University of Florida. The "Fun and Gun Offense" helped end the run first philosophy that, with few exceptions, was the paradigm for most offenses of the day. Steve Spurrier created one of the most exciting offenses of the modern era. The Fun and Gun was the predecessor of the spread offenses that were to follow.

Although they played with a Tight End, they often lined up with four wide receivers, no tight end, and only one running back. Spurrier liked to throw the ball down the field; especially fade routes and corner routes.

One pattern that Spurrier made popular was something he called Ralph (the compliment route was Lonnie). The #1 receiver to the outside had a rule that had him run a curl versus a 3 deep defense and to run a corner versus a two-deep defense. In combination with a flat route by the number 2 receiver, there was pressure on both the safety and corner. The curl versus a 3 deep defense exerted pressure on the linebacker. *See Figure 307A, 307B*

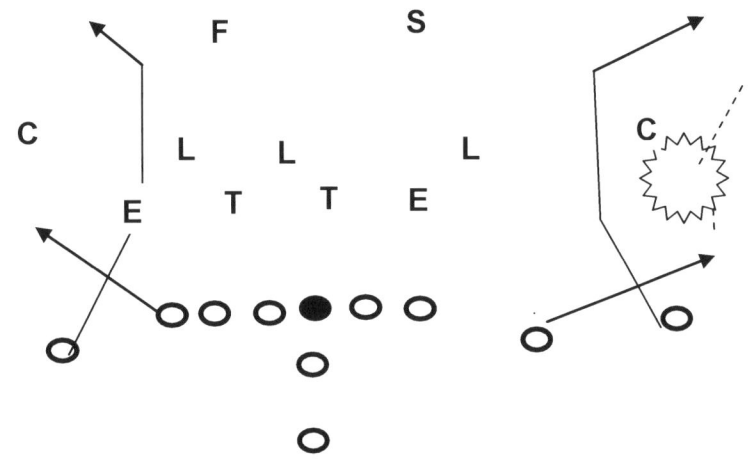

Figure 307A Ralph versus Cover 2

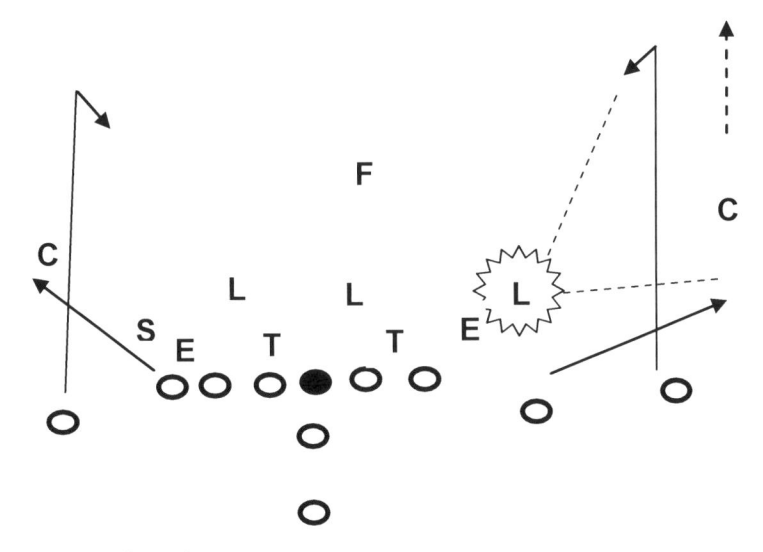

Figure 307B Ralph versus Cover 3

    Another route from Spurrier's playbook that became widespread was, what he called, his "Mills" route. This was a simple Curl/Flat route as above, with the added element of a post route over the top (deep in the secondary) of the front side Curl/Flat. When teams began to have the safety quickly "jump" the Curl/Flat, the quarterback had the "home run" post over the top, behind the defense.[272] *See Figure 308.*

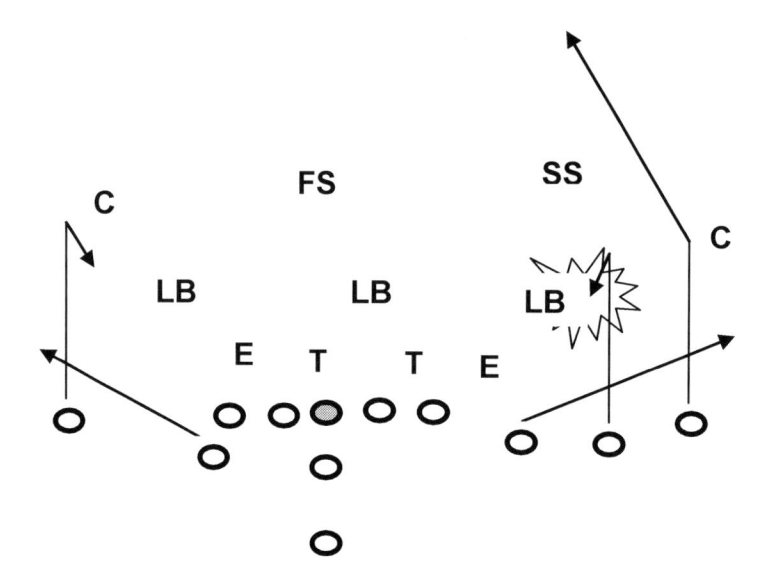

Figure 308 Spurrier's "Mills" route

Robber Coverage

Although defenses have attempted to disguise their intent since the beginning of the 20th century, more recently there has been an increased objective to use secondary defenders to act as "Robbers" or "Floaters." Just as there are two terms to describe what follows, the terms mean different things to different coaches. A Robber coverage may intend to take away a favorite run or specific ball carrier or the Robber may attempt to take away a particular receiver or pass route. In practice, there are innumerable forms of robber coverages; we will give only two simple examples of the execution.

What is frequently called "Cover 2 Robber" allows the defense to play with two defenders with each to handle half the field on deep passes. In the case of the example below, the two deep defenders are the cornerbacks (C). You can see there are four underneath zones (areas) that are defended by WS, SS, and the two linebackers (LB). If the free safety (FS) gets a run read, he will fly up to become the 9th defender in the front. On pass plays, he is free to stay with a deep pass route or to "jump" or "rob" shorter passes. *See Figure 309*

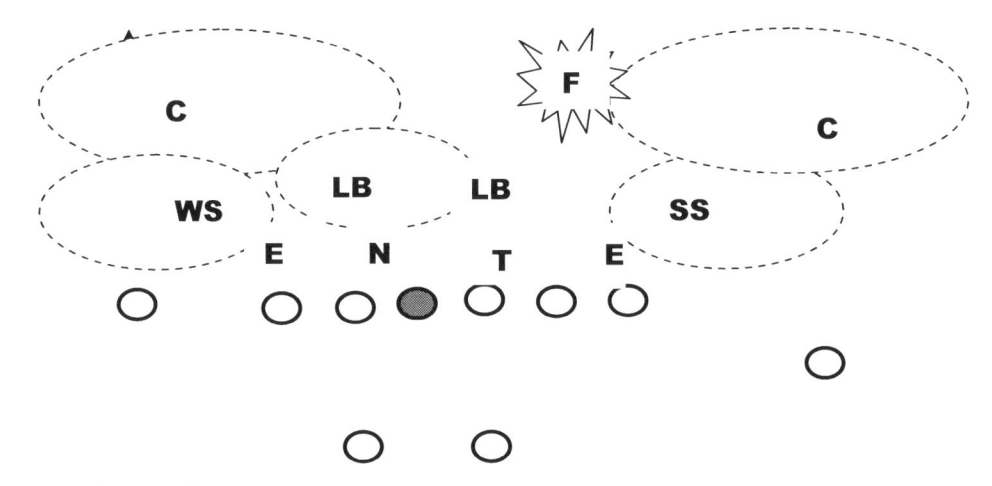

Figure 309   Cover 2 Robber

The diagram below, *Figure 310*, shows a typical man-to-man pass defense with a free safety and a "robber". This defense is often called a "Cover 1 Robber." The corners (C) will play the number one receiver (widest receiver) on their side, man to man. The S will play the tight end man to man. The W will play the running back on his side man to man. The strong side LB will play the running back on his side man to man. The weak side LB becomes the "robber" with the same responsibilities as above.

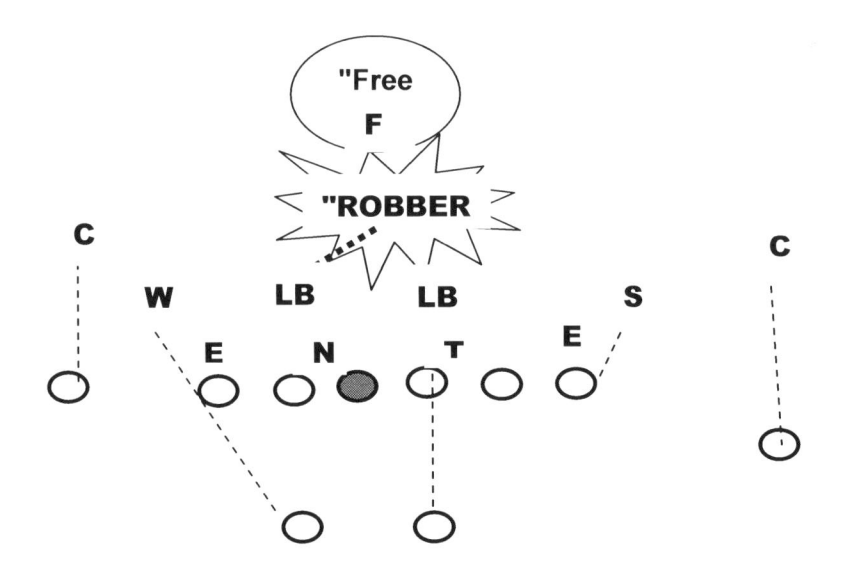

Figure 310   Cover 1 Robber

Wildcat

Creative coaches developed the Wildcat offense. In its basic form, it was a shifting of skill players. The quarterback is replaced with a running back who is a skilled runner and an able passer. Sometimes the quarterback is removed from the game and sometimes he will lineup as a wide receiver. Keeping the quarterback in the game creates an additional problem for the defense in that there is no prior indication that the Wildcat will be used. There is no tip-off to the defense that will allow them to substitute getting matching players on the field. *Figure 311*

When the Wildcat does remove the quarterback, a player who specializes in running the Wildcat may replace him or, as is sometimes done, he may be substituted by an additional wide receiver. Wildcat Teams may also place both tackles on the same side to create an unbalanced line. The Wildcat is much like the single wing and the double wing. Because of the direct snap to the running back, the Wildcat produces an 11 on 11 status for the defense. When a team uses a T-snap, the quarterback often is not involved in the play once he hands the ball to a running back; the defense now has 11 men to pursue 10.

The Wildcat is more of a strategy rather than an offensive philosophy. It can be used in combination with any offensive scheme.

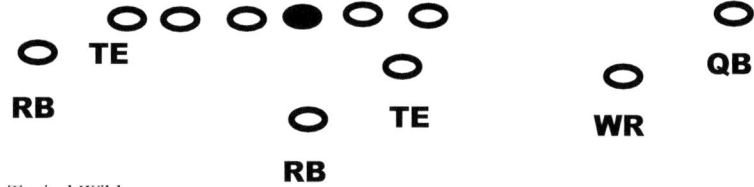

Figure 311 Typical Wildcat

The first use of the Wildcat is a much-disputed subject. Football purists will claim that this formation can be traced all the way back to "Pop" Warner, who, among other innovations, was the creator of the double wing and single wing.

"'This thing that they call 'the wildcat' is nothing more than what they call a direct snap," North Beach (Wash.) High School head coach Hugh Wyatt said. "So it's really not that original." In the late 1990s, La Center (Wash.) High School, then coached by Hugh Wyatt, used a formation that had two running backs line up in a shotgun formation Either back was able to take a direct snap. Wyatt's offenses ran a Wildcat-like system for more than 50 percent of their plays some years. "It was original for us because it meant that we could adapt some of what we did to single-wing principles," Wyatt said. "But I'm sure other people have been doing things similar to that. The main thing that I take credit for, and I could win this in the court of law, was giving it the name — 'The Wildcat' — that's all." [273]

In 1997, Coach Wyatt published an article about his new formation calling it "The Wildcat."

Andy Tally at Villanova ran a similar offense in the late 1990s. Talley has even laid claim to having invented the whole concept. "We used to direct snap the ball to Brian (Westbrook) and we called it the Wildcat ... because we couldn't think of a much better name for it," Talley said. "And I'd not seen anybody run that formation prior to us running it in college football." [274]

Another story contends that Coach Bill Snyder, a modern innovator with an impressive mind, is the father of the Wildcat coaching the Kansas State Wildcats. In 1998 Snyder's offensive coordinator, Ron Hudson while discussing the Wildcat one back offense asked, "Why can't the remaining back be the fullback, and let Michael Bishop be like the tailback." Hudson went on to say, "And that's how it evolved where now we started running the same plays out of one back with Michael out as the tailback with the remaining back as the lead blocker." [275] Snyder turned Bishop, his talented quarterback, into a direct snap Wildcat tailback.

A type of wildcat formation also made an appearance in 1998, when Brian Billick, the NFL's Minnesota Vikings' offensive coordinator began utilizing some similar formations.

There are still other sources who claim Billy Ford and Ryan Wilson invented the formation they called the "Dual" formation.[276]

Numerous teams began running the Wildcat in the new century. A second generation of the Wildcat was thought to be born in Camillus, N.Y., right outside of Syracuse, at West Genesee HS. In 2007, Steve Bush, then the Wildcats' head coach, implemented a spread-option offense with a mobile quarterback. It was very similar to the formation the Miami Dolphins would run a year later when Bush became an assistant coach with the Dolphins. Bush cannot take full credit for bringing the Wildcat to Miami. The Dolphins also had, as another assistant, David Lee, who ran a similar offense as the offensive coordinator at Arkansas a year earlier. However, Bush did add his input and expertise based on the system he ran at West Genesee.

Mid-Line Triple Option

For years, the double slot Flexbone teams dominated defenses with the inside veer triple option. Defenses began to respond to the play by quickly having the Free Safety fly to the line of scrimmage to help defend the play. The "Slotbone" teams needed a way to impede this tactic. The answer was the midline triple option. Offenses began to put a slot back in, what they call, "Twirl" motion. Meaning the slot starts in motion in one direction and, on the snap of the ball turns back and blocks the first defender outside the pitch read. This misdirection action freezes the free safety because he does not know if the play is going to be the veer triple option in the direction of the motion or the Midline Veer triple back to the other side. The free safety must sit and wait to see which play develops. The advantage goes back to the offense. The fullback dives straight ahead over the center. The quarterback has the same reads as the inside veer triple option. He will read the tackle (inside the square) to decide to give to the fullback or move to the next read. He will read the end (in the circle) to decide to keep or pitch to slot back. [277] *Figure 312*

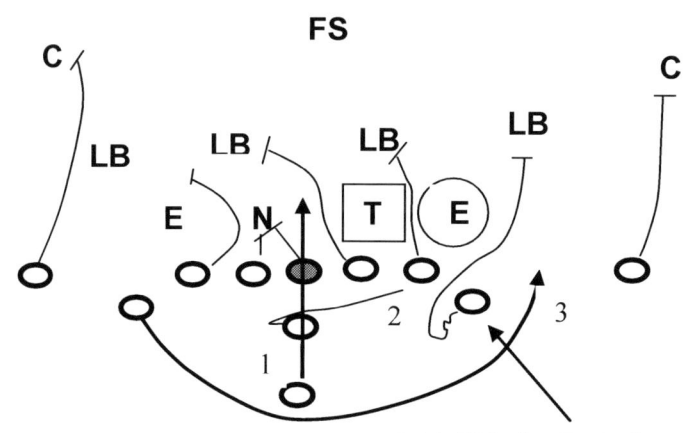

Figure 312 Mid-Line Triple Option

Growth of the One-Back Offense

The offense began to grow in the 1980s and by the mid-1990s, numerous teams were using the "one back" offense. Both Dennis Erickson and Mike Price were instrumental in refining the "one back. Erickson coached at Idaho, Wyoming, Washington State, and Miami, where he won two national championships. Price, who was a boyhood friend of Erickson, took over at Washington State in 1989 when Dennis Erickson went to Miami. Price replaced the tight end with a fourth receiver and produced one of the most prolific offenses in college football. Although Price's attack was not unique, many of the plays from the "one back" were adopted by other offense and are worth mentioning. *Figure 313-317* below:

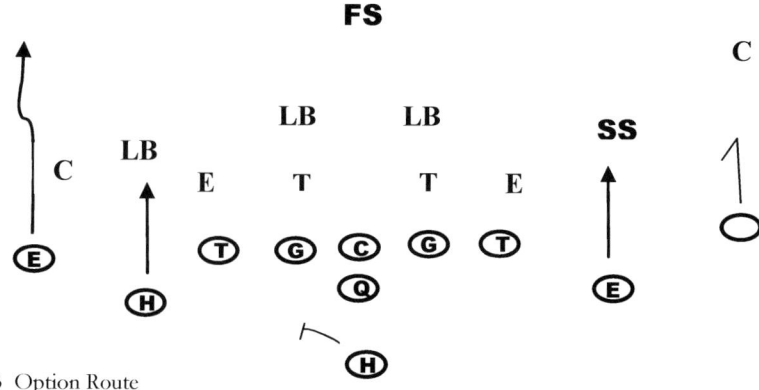

Figure 313 Option Route

Above is a simple option route. If the cornerback played tight and close to the line of scrimmage, as shown on the left side of the formation, the receiver would burst by him and run a deep fade. If the cornerback played loose and away from the line of scrimmage, as shown on the right side of the formation, the receiver would run a five-yard hitch route.

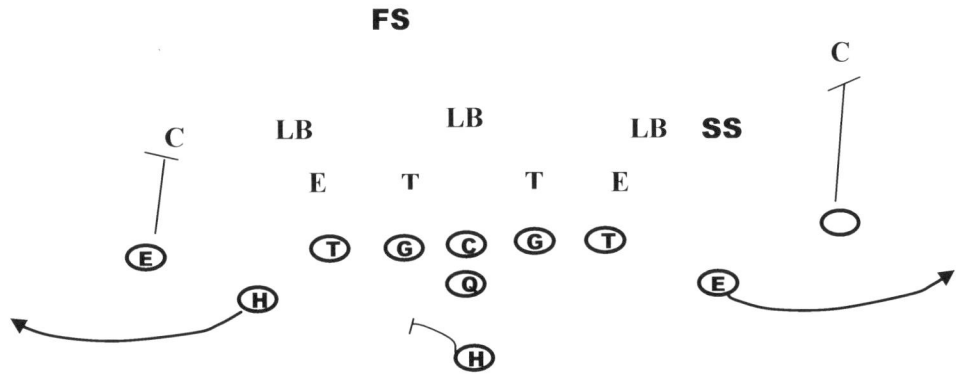

Figure 314 Bubble Screen

If the defense lined up with two safeties, we know that the quarterback would audible to a run. However, after a short time, the defense knew this also and they sometimes would cheat the outside linebackers in to help with the run defense. This brought about the "Bubble Screen" as shown above. In the example above, the quarterback will pick the best matchup and quickly throw the Bubble Screen to that side.

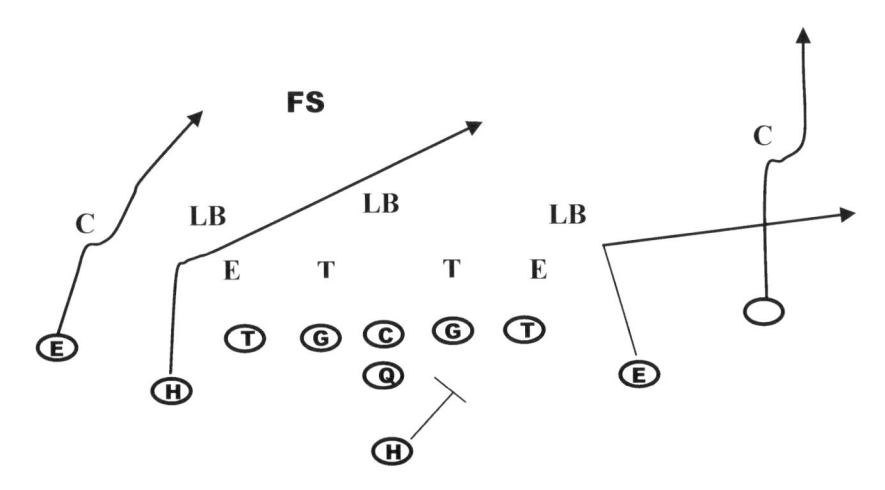

Figure 315 Deep Crossing Route

Another popular concept adapted from the West Coast offense was the deep crossing route, above. The quarterback would look first to the flat route being run by the right inside receiver. Secondly, he would look at the deep crossing route being run by the left inside receiver who is running away from the linebacker on his side. Usually, that deep cross placed a faster receiver on a slower linebacker.

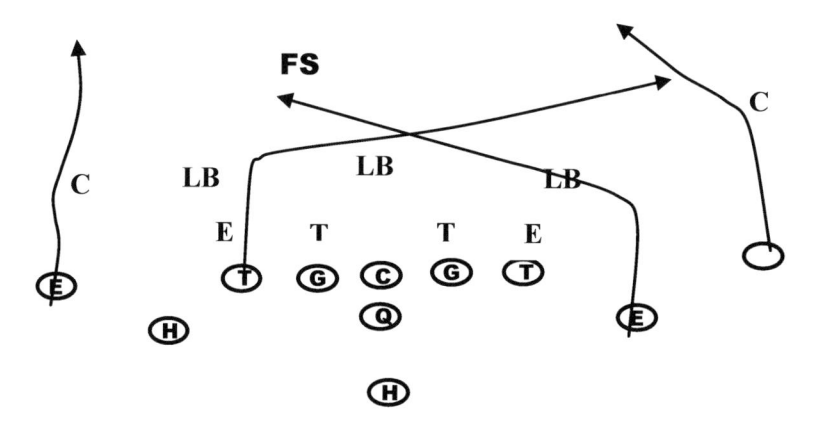

Figure 316   Shallow Cross

The shallow cross was another play that is still a part of many offenses. The quarterback would "peek" at the deep routes quickly to see if the "home run" throw was there. He would then focus on the crossing routes. The right inside receiver (in this example) would run a crossing route that would bring him slightly over the pursuing linebackers. This is called a "rub." The left inside receiver would run just under the first crosser. This tight exchange between the two receivers made it difficult for defenders to follow the shallow cross.

Another possibility versus a cheating defense was to run an option route by the inside receivers. (Not shown) If the defense was playing man-to-man on the receiver, he would make his break on the defender's leverage. If the defender was inside, the receiver broke out. If the defender was outside, the receiver broke inside. If the defense was playing zone, the receiver would break out and settle in a void between two defenders. This was a fundamental concept of the old Run & Shoot.

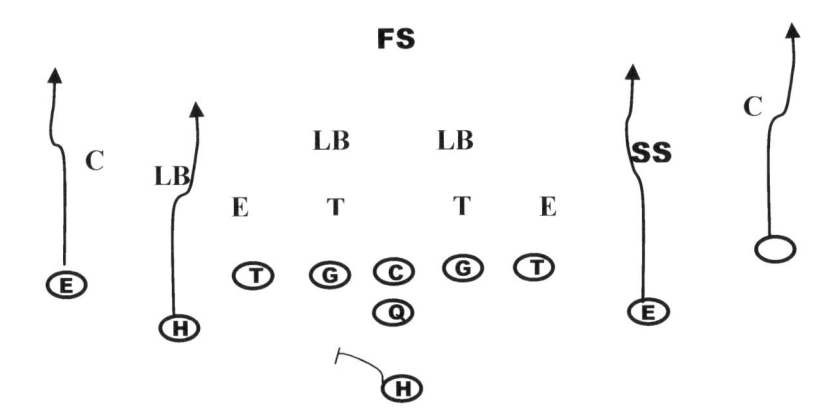

Figure 317 Four Vertical

Another design that is in every playbook today was to run all four receivers on four vertical routes, above. Versus a 3-Deep zone defense, this placed four receivers against three defenders. Versus a man-to-man defense, the quarterback would choose the best matchup.

---

[267] Wyche, Steve, *Zone-blitz masterminds to scheme for Super Bowl supremacy*, : NFL.com, Jan. 30, 2011, http://www.nfl.com/superbowl/story/09000d5d81dfd5b9/article/zoneblitz-masterminds-to-scheme-for-super-bowl-supremacy

[268] Stoltz, Jeremy. *The Zone Blitz*. BearReport.com, posted Apr 19,2007

[269] *Veer explained*. - Coach Hugh Wyatt's Double Wing Football .., http://www.coachwyatt.com/veerexplained.html (accessed October 21, 2015).

[270] Belichick, Steve. *Football Scouting Methods*. Mansfield Centre, Ct., Martino Publishing Co., 1962.

[271] Jaworski, Ron, Greg Cosell, David Plaut, *The Games That Changed the Game; The Evolution of the NFL IN Seven Sundays*, (New York, NY, Ballantine Books, 2010), p.

[272] http://smartfootball.com/offense/*dana-holgorsens-brand-of-the-west-virginia-airraid-offense*#sthash.tqdZJRMc.dgbL.mJk7.dpbs Retrieved 04.17.2014

[273] Wyatt, Hugh http://www.doublewingsymposium.com/dws_new/articles/WILDCAT%20ARTICLE.pdf. Downloaded 9/13/2014.

[274] Wilson, David. *Drawing from history: Origins of wildcat offense remain unsure, but effect on football is clear*
The Daily Orange - The Independent Student Newspaper of Syracuse, NY. Nov. 27, 2012. http://dailyorange.com/?s=wildcat

[275] Wilson, David. *Drawing from history: Origins of wildcat offense remain unsure, but effect on football is clear*

[276] http://ft003386.fusetalkcommunity.com/forum/messageview.aspx?catid=13&threadid=15511&messid=72849&parentid=72839&FTVAR_FORUMVIEWTMP=Br

[277] Coles, Rick. *Midline Triple Option*, American Football Coaches Association Summer Manual, 2008. p. 14,15

CHAPTER FIFTEEN

A New Game

In NCAA history, a quarterback has thrown for at least, 4,000 yards 79 times in a season; 65 of them have come since 2000. [278]

"The Spread Offense"

"It's a natural progression that started back in 1934 when the rules committee shrunk the ball by an inch to make passing easier," 83-year-old Dan Jenkins, the official National Football Foundation historian, explained in an e-mail. "Players are bigger and faster, arms are stronger, high schools throw more today – defense, sadly, is becoming a thing of the past. A great many rules changes have encouraged this, the thinking being that fans have smaller attention spans. Today, young people want instant success and luxury – and more touchdowns." [279]

We have to point out that, while many refer to the Spread Offense as the offense of the twenty-first century, much of the innovation and development began long before that. As we have written in previous sections, the spread had its origin almost 100 years ago. We have talked about the Idaho Spread around 1907. Bezdek ran the spread at Arkansas and Penn State before 1910. Also, around the same time, there was Warner's Double Wing and Warner's "C" formation. Morrison had a Spread at SMU in the 1920s. The Spread Punt was popular in the 1930s. The Triple Wing was the empty set in the 30s. Dutch Myers used the Spread at TCU starting in the 1930s and it became the rage in the 40s. George Halas's Chicago Bears ran a type of spread in the 1940s. The Dennis Erickson/Mike Price, one back offense of the 1970s, is often thought of as the actual forerunner of the modern spread. Navy, Air Force, and Georgia Southern were all running the Spread Option in the 70s. We cannot forget Steve Spurrier's Fun and Gun at Florida in the 80s. Finally, Hal Mumme's Air Raid was in its infancy in the 1990s. All of the above were precursors to the Spread Offense that would dominate the game at the beginning of the twenty-first century.

Early versions of the spread were limited in what they did, but that has changed dramatically. In the late 1990s when the spread was first taking hold, there was the "Purdue spread" that was dominated by the pass and there was the "Northwestern spread" that concentrated on the run.

Today there are almost as many different Spread Offenses as there are teams running spread formations. If the Tight end lines up removed from the line, we call it a spread offense. If a team lines up with mostly four wide-outs, we call it a spread offense. If the quarterback lines up in a shotgun, we call it a spread offense. If a team runs the zone read scheme, we call it a spread offense. There is the "Hurry up, no huddle" spread. Fifteen years ago, we called any formation that lined up with a single back, a spread formation.

You can see that just saying a team is running a spread offense will tell you little about the type of offense the team is indeed running. Auburn defensive coordinator Ellis Johnson says, "It's to the point now where the three or four teams we play a year that line up in two tight ends and a fullback are harder to prepare for. That sometimes confuses players now more than the spread does, because most teams have three and four wideouts just like we do." [280]

At its core, spread formations attempt to stretch the defense and put "playmakers" in space, giving them room to make plays. It initially developed as an underdog tactic of sorts. It was a way to spread out and irritate defenses that were more talented and, hopefully, force some mistakes. However, there is a certain level of tactical superiority to the idea, and it was not long before many of the most talented teams in the country began to employ more and more spread tactics.

If a defense pulls defenders from the inside to cover the spread receivers, the offense will run the ball inside. All attacks attempt to force the defense to spread out and there are a variety of schemes people use to accomplish this. There are the spread offenses of Georgia Tech under Paul Johnson and the Navy offense used by Ken Niumatalolo that spread the field to open up their running game. At the other extreme might be the Air Raid teams that take wide line splits to stretch the defense and slow the pass rush. When the defense is spread, it allows for an inside run game and crossing pass routes. There are the "spread to run" teams typified by Urban Meyer at Ohio State, Dana Holgorsen at West Virginia, or Rich Rodriguez at Arizona. They want to run the ball but are more than willing to throw the ball if the defense stays "in the box" to stop the run.

It is interesting to note that many of the spread's successes have begun at the high school level. High school coaches across the nation have made use of some version of this format with great success. Some of the more notable innovators at the high school level have become major college coaches. There is Art Briles at Stephenville High School in Texas who moved on to Houston and is now the Head Coach at Baylor. Also, there is Gus Malzahn at Springdale High School in Arkansas who became the offensive coordinator at both Arkansas and Auburn and is now the head coach at Auburn. Long time, high school coaches Todd Dodge at Southlake

Carroll High School and Marble Falls High School in Texas and Rush Propst at Hoover High School in Alabama were both spread pioneers. Propst's success was aided by Tony Franklin, who became the offensive coordinator at the University of California at Berkley. In Kentucky, there is renowned coach Dale Mueller at Highlands High School. Mueller has been developing spread principles since 1995. We certainly cannot forget Rusty Russell, a high school coach at the Masonic Home and School for Orphaned Boys in Fort Worth Texas. He is often given credit for the birth of the spread, in 1927. [281]

Spread Option Offense

Most credit Rich Rodriguez, while at Glenville State and West Virginia, and Bill Snyder the Head Coach at Kansas State with the development of the Spread Option.

The year was 1991 and Rich Rodriguez, in his second season as Glenville State's coach, was searching for an offense that would keep defenses off-balance.

An unexpected epiphany came during practice when quarterback Jed Drenning bobbled a handoff, gathered himself and made a split-second decision to run after seeing the defensive end pinch to the inside.

"He said he saw the end coming in, kept it and ran for 15 or 20 yards. So I told him, 'Yeah, we were going to put that in next week,'" Rodriguez said with a laugh. "Then I thought: We may be onto something here." [282]

Credit must also be given to Urban Meyer, while at Bowling Green University, Utah, Florida, and now Ohio State who did much for the advancement of spread option football. Meyer led Florida to the National Championship using the spread option.

Meyer's approach to the offense can be summed up below.

"1. One high: Equal numbers, you can run the ball and be OK. You are equal.

2. Two high: You are plus one. Run the ball, because they outnumber you in the passing game. They can double your receivers.

3. No deep: Can you run the ball (meaning just a hand off)? No, they took the extra defender and put him in the box. Now there are two answers: You run option, or you throw it. And if you throw it, you better have a better receiver out there than their defensive back (and that's usually the case).

"The offense is always correct and should always outnumber the defense. The idea is to run their plays and this philosophy in succession and drive defenses crazy. That is the Spread Option Offense. How you draw up the plays, the blocking assignments, and the formations do not really matter. Meyer's Spread is able to run the exact same play out of multiple formations. Whereas other spread attacks run multiple plays from the exact same formation.

"Meyer's Spread is unique in that you can do both. At the end of the day, it boils down to the fact that the players on the offensive side of the ball are better, faster, stronger athletes and should always win the numbers game. The spread belief, at all levels of football, is the offensive players are better skilled and faster. You should always have an advantage. Unless you play recreational or small school football, where everyone plays both ways." [283]

Oregon's Chip Kelly, who met Rodriguez in 1999 when Kelly was the offensive coordinator New Hampshire, and Rodriguez was the Coordinator at Clemson, has been a major contributor to the offense. Oregon's most significant contribution to the spread is perhaps the speed at which they run their offense. Kelly moved to the NFL as coach of the Philadelphia Eagles in 2013. He is now with the San Francisco 49ers.

An article in American Football Monthly states, "What actually sets the team (Oregon) apart, however, from other high-powered offenses, is the pace at which they operate. Don't blink, they'll be gone. Need a breather for your defense late in the game? Forget it. Think you can control the Ducks by limiting their time-of-possession? Think again. Week after week, they've steamrolled opponents with a lightning-quick offense that emphasizes the run and keeps defenses off-balance by calling and running plays faster than anyone". [284]

The coaching staff stresses preparation to focus on tempo. "The play-calling is sometimes instantaneous and premeditated," said Helfrich. "We already know what we're going to do next. Similar to most teams, we script the first eight-to-ten runs and the first eight-to-ten passes in an ordinary situation. Obviously, if it's third-and-short or third-and-long, we'll adjust." As always, the emphasis is on establishing tempo. "Initially, we're probably not as heavy, in terms of what we do, just because we really want to push the pace and reinforce that tempo is Mission Number One," said Helfrich. (At the time Oregon's Offensive Coordinator and now Head Coach)

One result of that up-tempo pace has been the introduction of signal boards that are displayed on the sideline to send in plays to the offense in the no-huddle. There are six different boards at Oregon. There are four images on each, and they are used about a quarter of the time, according to Gary Campbell, Oregon's Running Backs Coach. "We had to devise signals, number systems, and tags to get our players on the same page," he explained. "They look to the sideline and will recognize the formation, the play, and the snap count."

The signs, as anyone who has seen the Ducks' sideline on television can attest, are unique. Images that appeared on the signs this year include ESPN personalities, wild animals, maps of U.S. States, a battleship, Shaquille O'Neal and the Burger King king. They do not mean anything to opposing coaches or players, and they keep defenses guessing. They are readily visible from the sidelines and they reduce the confusion that can sometimes arise when using hand signals. "Our players know when to combine images or use just one," said Campbell.

To Helfrich, the signs have been a big part of simplifying communication. "The picture boards have been huge," he said. "We tried to take the best stuff of everyone, the Tulsa/Auburn system with the flip cards. We just tried to find a combination of that to fit our system with pictures and words rather than numbers. The communication has evolved to visual communication. And our players are getting better at it. With the picture boards, one picture tells the whole story. That's been a big deal because guys are visual. Guys see a picture that means something to their position and then they go." [285]

Despite the broad alignment, the spread option is a run-first scheme that requires a quarterback that is comfortable carrying the ball. There must also be an offensive line that can pull and trap. Also, it demands receivers that can hold their blocks. At its core, it is misdirection football, making it effectively the old triple option. The exception being that it utilizes spread sets. [286] The quarterback must be able to read the defensive end and determine whether he is collapsing down the line to tackle the running back or playing up field containment. The quarterback must decide the proper play to make with the ball.

Much of what Rodriguez does is based on the old BYU offense. "We beat BYU in a bowl game and Lavell [Edwards] was the head coach, Norm Chow, the offensive coordinator. So after the contest, they said, "Would you come over and talk some football with us? I'm thinking are you kidding me? This is Norm Chow and Lavell Edwards, the passing gurus. I said I'll do it on one condition. You have to give me some of your information, too. You have to teach me what you're doing. Norm and I have been friends since that time. It was a great trip." [287]

Although his offense is run first, Rodriguez believes that one of the most important aspects of the Spread Offense is still the quick passing game.

The Zone Read is a primary play used by, almost, all Spread formation teams. The early Zone Read play is run as shown below. The line will block as they normally do on any zone play. The quarterback primarily "reads" (views the actions) the defensive end (the left E in the figure below). If the defensive end remains outside or charges up the field (B in the figure below), the quarterback will hand the ball to the running back and the zone play will be run. If the defensive end crashes down hard inside in an attempt to tackle the ball carrier if he cuts back (A in the figure below), the quarterback will keep the ball and attack outside. The Inverted Veer play, the Mid-Line, and the Triple from the spread are all plays that find their origin in the Zone Read.
Figure 318

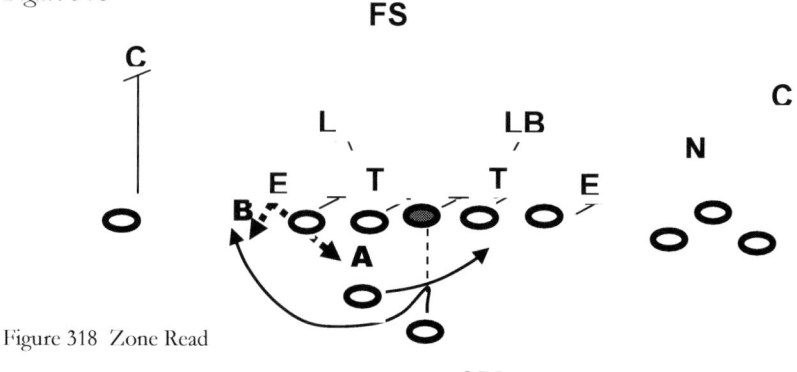

Figure 318 Zone Read

Probably the most frequently seen adjustment of the Zone Read is the **Midline Read**. The zone principles that apply to the Zone Read are also present with the Midline. However, instead of the quarterback "reading" the defensive end, he will "read" the B gap player (defender in the guard-tackle gap), most often the defensive tackle.

With the mid-line read, the linemen still have zone rules. The difference here is who the quarterback will "read". Instead of optioning the defensive end, the quarterback is reading an interior lineman

There are two apparent reasons for the development of the Midline Read. Firstly, the defender being optioned is a defensive tackle who, compared with the defensive end, may be the more difficult defender to be blocked. Secondly, with the frequent use of the "scrape" maneuver by the linebacker, the Midline attacks the exact area that is being vacated by the linebacker. This "scrape" maneuver by the defense has the end slanting hard inside to give the quarterback a "keep" read while the inside linebacker on that side loops to the outside to be in a position to attack the quarterback as he keeps the ball. If the defensive tackle protects the B gap by staying outside (A in the figure below), the quarterback will give the ball to the running back. If the defensive tackle crashes down in an attempt to tackle the running back, the quarterback will keep the ball and attack the area the defensive tackle has vacated. *Figure 319*

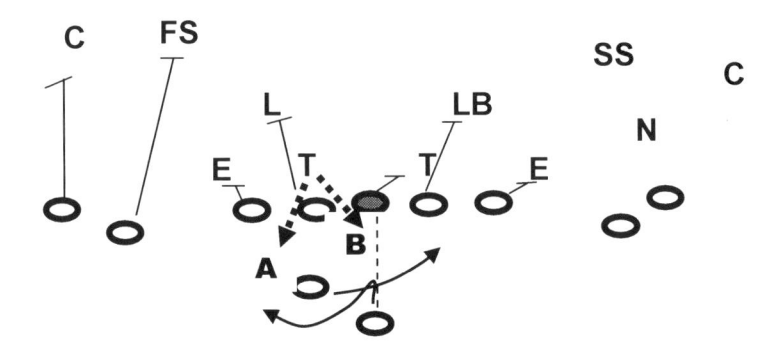

Figure 319 Midline

The **Inverted Veer** has become increasingly popular with the Spread teams. One of the first things to note on the Inverted Veer play is that both the running back and the quarterback are attacking the same side of the defense. If the defensive end stays wide and plays the running back (A in the figure below) the quarterback will keep the ball and follow the pulling guard through the void left by the defensive end playing wide. If the defensive end crashes down (B in the figure below), the quarterback will give the ball to the running back to attack the edge of the defense. *See Figure 320*

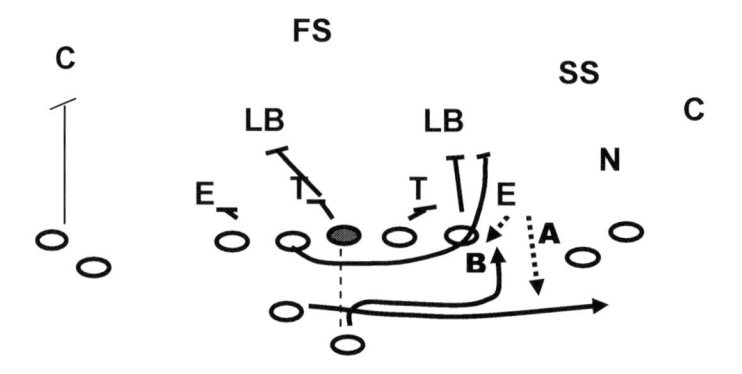

Figure 320 The Inverted Veer   The blocking on this play, with the guard pulling, can resemble the Power play run by many teams today.

The Air Raid Offense:

This version of the spread is heavily dependent on both the quarterback and coaches being able to call the right play at the line of scrimmage based on how the defense sets up.[288]

The roots of the Air Raid offense can be traced all the way back to LaVell Edwards, the Head Coach of Brigham Young University, in the 1960s and 70s. The BYU attack was discussed earlier.

Although the Air Raid differs with each team, the draw is a base run for all of them. The Air Raid differs from what Edwards did in several ways. The Air Raid as a spread offense puts an emphasis on a wide receiver screen, and it is a no-huddle offense. Another difference is that the Air Raid always aligns the Tight End or Y receiver to the right and the Split End or X receiver to the left. They never leave their respective side of the field. The reasons; coaches feel that they can run their no-huddle offense more efficiently if they do not flip-flop the receivers. It keeps the offense simple, and it allows for extra reps for the players during practice.

Mumme's Air Raid: As a high school coach at Copperas Cove High School, Texas, Hal Mumme devised, what most considered, an unorthodox pass-oriented offense. He took his offense to Iowa Wesleyan College in 1989, moved on to Valdosta State University in 1992, and achieved a record of 40-17-1 using his unconventional scheme. "When we really began to set ourselves apart as different from Edwards was adding the shotgun, and then from there the no-huddle," Mumme said. "There weren't many if any teams running a no-huddle offense at that time."[289] "We knew we were changing the game, we just weren't sure if anybody else was going to change with us,"- Hal Mumme[290]

When he was hired by the University of Kentucky in 1997, the offense came into the national spotlight.

Mike Leach, who was Mumme's offensive coordinator at both Valdosta State and Kentucky, has had much success with the offense as the coordinator at The University of Oklahoma and Head Coach at Texas Tech. In 2012, Leach became the head coach at Washington State. Sonny Dykes and Tony Franklin both worked with Leach on Mumme's staff at Kentucky. However, there have been some others who, in recent years, have contributed to the development of the Air Raid. Nevertheless, "Hal was really one of the trailblazers for throwing the ball," says Art Briles, whose Baylor teams are always one of the offensive leaders every year. "Without question, Hal was instrumental in the game being what it is today."

The Air Raid alignment is a shotgun formation with four wide receivers and one running back. The formations are a variation of both the "run and shoot" offense and LaVell Edwards' BYU offense. They usually align with two outside receivers and two inside slot receivers. The attack also makes great use of the trips formations that have three wide receivers on one side of the field and a single receiver on the other side.

The system makes extensive use of the pass. The Air Raid has copied Bill Walsh and his West Coast offense (similar to Edward's BYU offense) in using the short pass as part of the running game, hoping the receiver will turn the short pass into a long gain after the catch. Unlike most offenses that attempt to keep a balance between the run and the pass, the Air Raid may throw the ball more than 70% of the time.

Coaches who run the Air Raid claim that one important part of the offense, that is often overlooked, is their practice routine. As mentioned earlier, the simplicity and the fact that the receivers always align on the same side of the field allow for maximum repetitions in practice. The methods are different in other ways also. They do not stretch at the beginning of practice. The players go into football-related drills immediately.

Another important aspect of the alignment is the split of the offensive linemen. Most spread teams bunch the offensive line together but in the Air Raid offense, the line splits might be as much as a full yard between players. Admittedly, this allows easier blitz lanes, but it also forces the defensive ends and defensive tackles to have to run further to sack the quarterback. The quick, short passes are then able to offset any blitz that may come.

No play is identified more with the Air Raid than the "Mesh" concept, which was directly taken from the old BYU offense. The name of the play refers to the two receivers, Y, and X, who run shallow crosses in opposite directions. The rule is that the Y "sets the depth of the mesh," meaning he works to about six yards deep while it is X's job to come directly underneath him. On the practice field, they begin by touching hands as they run by — to ensure there is no space between them. It is, at its core, a "rub" route, known more derisively by defensive players and coaches as a "pick" play. It is not illegal because the receivers do not actually seek to pick (purposely stop) defenders but instead they simply get on their paths and run by each other, forcing defenders to go around them. Meanwhile, the running backs both check-release — meaning they look for potential blitzes and then release quickly into the flats. [291]

The key innovation from Mumme on the play was to change Z's route from a post, which is what it was in the old BYU system, to a corner route. This transforms the play into a triangle read on the front side. The triangle read being, the Corner, X on the shallow and F in the flat. This creates both a high/low and a horizontal stretch on a zone defense. Further, the corner route has some ability to adjust: against man defenses and in the red zone, it was a true corner route run at 45 degrees and to the pylon and thrown with an arc. Against a soft corner, the receiver bent it flat underneath the dropping defender, so it becomes more of an out route. The theory was for the quarterback and receiver to find the "open grass."[292]

The following diagrams below will show the evolution of the Air Raid
Figures 321-324

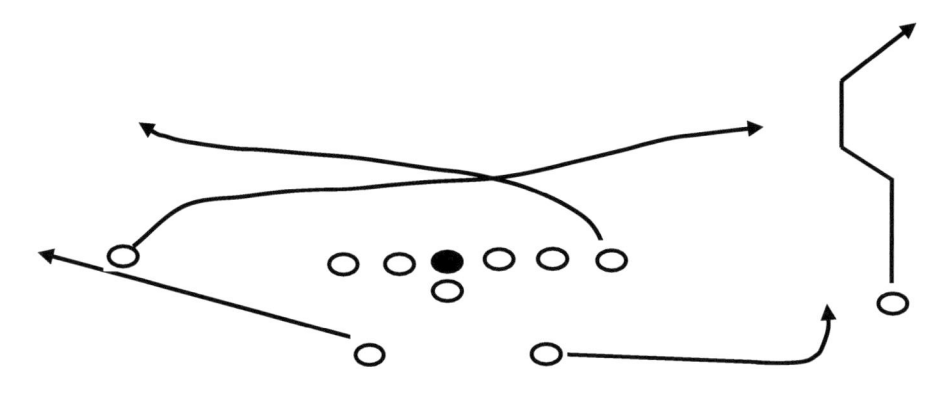

Figure 321 The Mesh from Kentucky '92

Behind only the Mesh concept, the Y-Cross is the route most people think of as classic Air Raid. While back then the offense did not feature many vertical, over-the-top types of routes, Y-Cross was the main "big play" producer for them. The Air Raiders called this Y-Cross, but Sid Gillman used to call it simply what it was: weakside flood.

This route concept came directly from BYU. LaVell Edwards considered it one of their best passes. Moreover, Mumme ripped it off verbatim. The only difference was the increased freedom he gave the X receiver to get deep.[293]

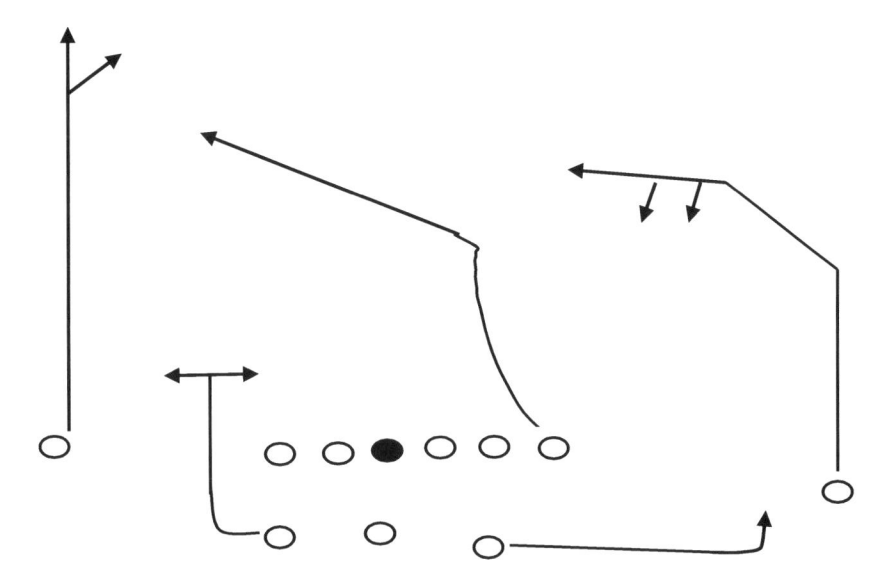

Figure 322 Y-Cross from Kentucky 1998

Four Verticals Route; One cannot be a four wide receiver team without running a four vertical play. Mumme transformed four verticals into a read-on-the-run-find-the-open-spot wherever they are. Receivers were free to break their route off if they found open space along their route. Therefore, while the play was known as four verticals, the instruction was, in fact, "Stay in your vertical lane, but then get open." With this play as its new centerpiece, Leach's offense really exploded.[294]

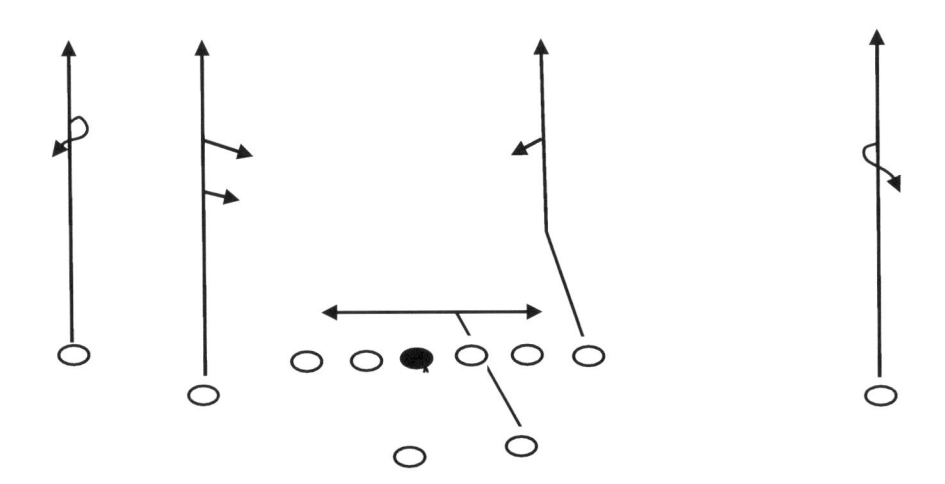

Figure 323 Mumme/Leach Air Raid: All Verticals

The H-Wheel is a somewhat offbeat play developed out of a few BYU routes. One was the desire to run the curl/wheel combination. The wheel route was especially of use given that the H in the Air Raid moved to the flat so often. The wheel was a beautiful change-up. BYU had a play Norm Chow called "Y-Option" or "Y-Choice." Although it was changed a little, this is just one of the examples of a play that began with BYU, changed a little, and became part of the Air Raid offense. In 1997 at Kentucky, Mumme's preferred way of calling the play was actually from trips, shown below, with the Z receiver on the left in-between the X and H. [295] *Figure 324*

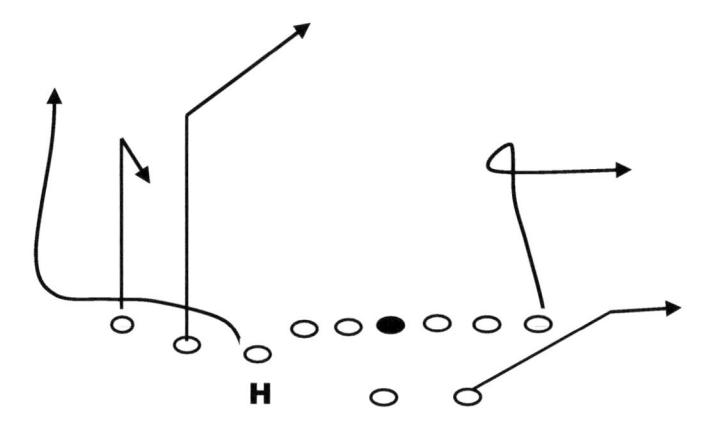

Figure 324 Mumme/Leach Air Raid: 93 H-Wheel

Dana Holgorsen's "Air Raid" Offense: Dana Holgorsen was the offensive coordinator at Texas Tech, Houston, and Oklahoma State before becoming head coach at West Virginia. He has made some significant changes to the basic Air Raid offense that distinguishes it from the original Hal Mumme/Mike Leach Air Raid.

While Mike Leach's Air Raid offense utilizes four wide receivers with a single running back on nearly all plays, Holgorsen will often use two backs in the backfield in addition to the quarterback. Holgorsen's "Diamond" backfield has a single running back behind a shotgun quarterback and two backs on either side of the quarterback. In using this alignment, Holgorsen is attempting to force the defense to defend the inside against power running while allowing individual matchups on the outside. Whereas the Mumme/Leach version of the Air Raid emphasizes short, crossing patterns with receivers running in various directions, the Holgorsen version uses more vertical pass routes; more backs in the backfield, more play-action passes, and pass patterns that look very similar at the start. It makes it difficult for the defense to quickly get a "read" on the play.

Holgorsen also uses "early motion" where one of the running backs, who aligns next to the quarterback in the Diamond, will sprint straight across the formation toward the sideline just before the snap. This motion may cross directly in front of the quarterback. The motion intends to upset the defense's keys. If the defense does not react to the motion, the quarterback may throw a screen pass to the motion back.

Holgorsen has organized his Air Raid into a logical attack that sets it apart from the other Air Raid offshoots. One significant addition is the "packaged plays," where two seemingly unrelated plays are combined in a single play to place stress on a lone defender. He is combining a short hook pass with the offensive line blocking a draw play. In the diagram below the play may develop as a draw to the running back or a short hook to the inside receiver in the "trips" (3 receivers) setup. The circled linebacker may react to cover the inside receiver running the hook or may respond to attack the draw of the running back. He cannot do both. Making this play harder to defend is the fact that the offensive linemen are allowed to get three yards downfield on pass plays. It is not illegal. Consequently, the linebacker cannot get an actual run/pass read. Holgorsen (and now others) combine quick passes and other runs, screens and runs, screens and quick passes, and a host of other combinations. "Packaging Plays" has become an attractive enhancement to help with offensive play calling. *Figure 325*

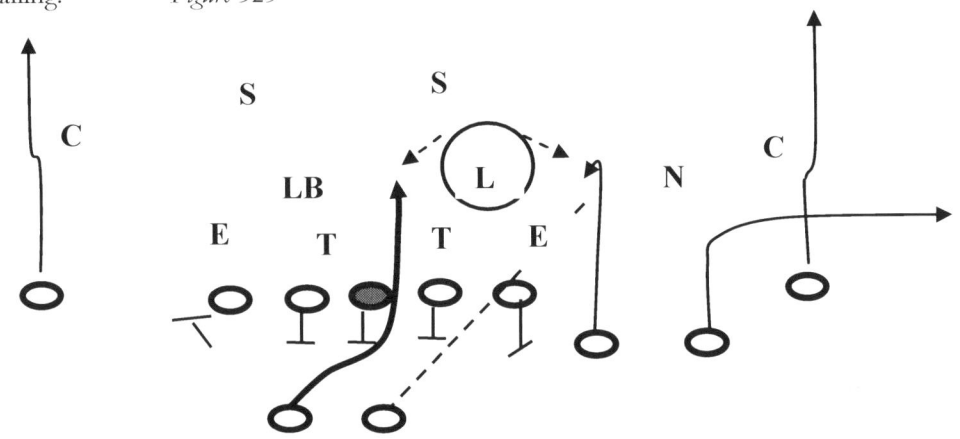

Figure 325 Holgorsen's "packaged play", Draw or Short Hook

The Diamond Formation: Although there may have been others who dabbled in it, Dana Holgorsen is given credit for bringing the Diamond to the attention of offensive coaches while he was the offensive coordinator at Oklahoma State). Holgorsen brought the offense with him when he became the Head Coach at West Virginia. *Figure 326*

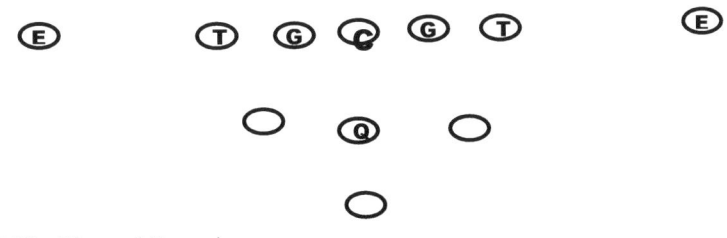

Figure 326 The Diamond Formation

What does the Diamond do for the offense that other spread formations do not? The distinct advantage of the Diamond is in the run game. An offense can run any number of powerful running plays. It is essentially a three-back offense that forces the defense to show their alignment. It allows the quarterback to audible away from the defensive strength with some power runs. With three backs in the backfield, the offense is ideal for running misdirection plays making it difficult to read what the offense is doing. The use of motion forces the defense to widen and remove defenders from the box. The passing advantage lies in the fact that with nine people aligned inside the box between the tackles, defenses must stack the inside with an eight-man front. It leaves the defensive backs one-on-one with the wide receivers.

Below are three classic plays from the Diamond Formation. See *Figures 327-329*

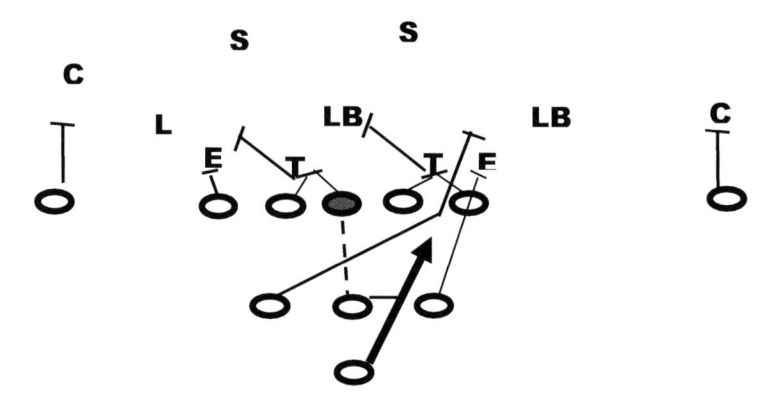

Figure 327 The Power Play from the Diamond Formation

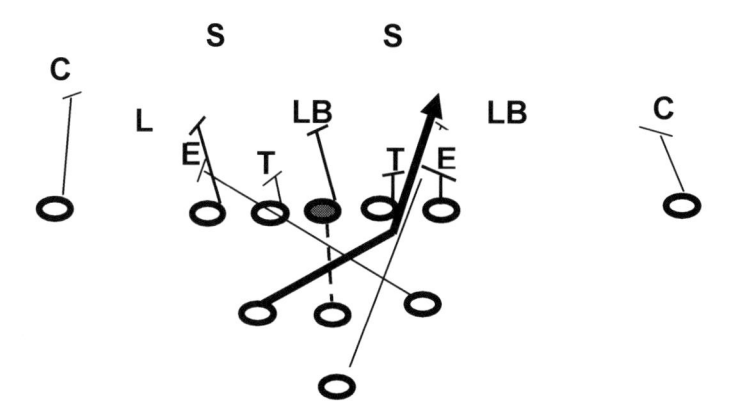

Figure 328 The Misdirection Play from the Diamond Formation

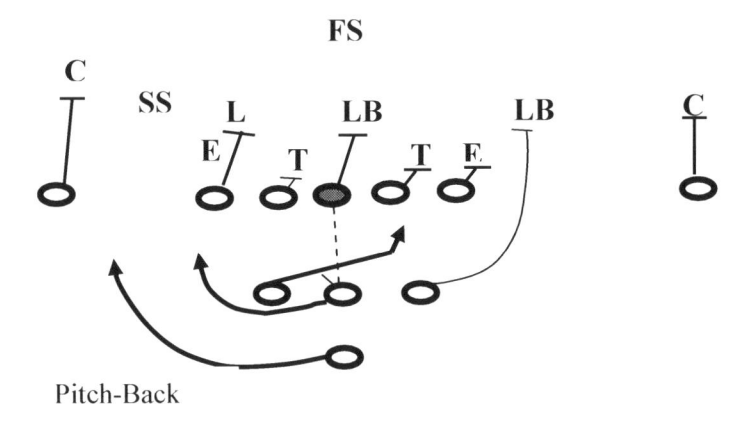

Figure 329 The Lead Zone Option from the Diamond. Note the addition of a pitch-back on this play

The Tony Franklin System: Tony Franklin began his career as a high school coach in 1979. In 1997, he was hired by Hal Mumme to coach running backs at Kentucky. When Mike Leach left for Oklahoma, Franklin was named the offensive coordinator for the 2000 season.

Like everything about the Air Raid, Franklin's story is unusual, even by football standards. After the 2000 season, Tony Franklin resigned from Kentucky. He was out of football. He went on to write a book about his experiences while at Kentucky. Rush Probst, the coach at Hoover HS (AL), offered him a job consulting. Probst wanted to install the Air Raid offense at Hoover. Franklin took advantage of the opportunity as a consultant in establishing the Air Raid. Hoover went on to win a state championship. In addition, Franklin began consulting for some other schools. He refined his presentation of the offense and began charging for his materials. He created the Tony Franklin System and began selling the Air Raid Offense. Among other things, he developed drill tapes, installations guides, game plans. Probably most significant was that he provided a direct line for answering questions about making adjustments to the offense. Although Mumme and Mike Leach developed the initial offense, Tony Franklin sold the whole package to any coach willing to pay for his materials. Tony Franklin Systems of disseminating information may have done as much for the evolution of the game as any other event in the last 15 years. Others have followed his lead, most notably Noel Mazzone with his Nzone System.

Gus Malzahn

Malzahn began his coaching career in 1991 as the defensive coordinator at Hughes High School in Arkansas. He became the head coach the next year.

Lacking experience and searching for an offensive system, Malzahn ran across "Tubby" Raymond's, *The Delaware Wing-T: An Order of Football*.

As indicated earlier, the brilliance of the Wing-T system is that it is not solely a collection of plays, but it is a philosophy of how to attack a defense with a sequence of plays. Starting with David Nelson and continuing through Raymond, the "Delaware", as it is known, is a sequence of plays that fit together to attack a defense. The next play is determined by how the defense has chosen to stop the previous plays.

Although Malzahn began by running the Delaware Wing-T just as it is illustrated in Raymond's book, he was soon experimenting with integrating it with an up-tempo spread formation. Although his offense has advanced beyond the Wing-T, the Delaware Wing-T influences Malzahn's current offense significantly. He uses much motion and deception by the running backs.

Malzahn's Auburn running game relies heavily on power running schemes. Although these schemes are not new to the game, Malzahn has adjusted some of the concepts so that they appear new. He also makes extensive use of the H-Back; often using motion with this back. *Figure 330*

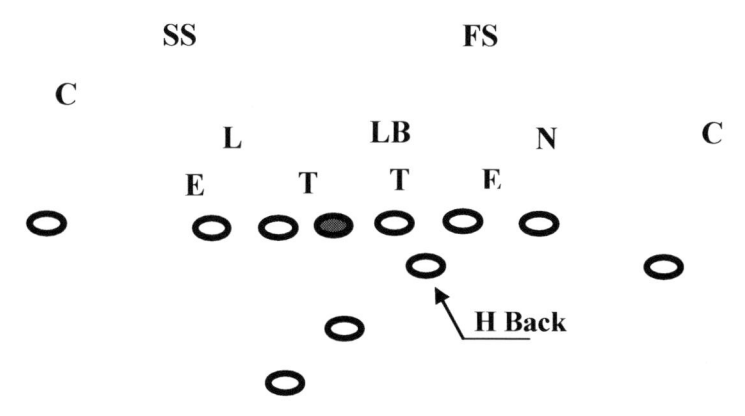

Figure 330 Malzahn's Basic Formation

Malzahn's version of the basic zone read is straightforward. The backside defensive end is intentionally unblocked. The quarterback reads him to determine whether to hand the ball to the running back (attacking away from that defensive end) or take the ball around the defensive end himself. Today it is common for the defensive end to be taught to crash and pursue the running back while the backside linebacker is prepared to scrape outside the defensive end and attack the quarterback. This is referred to as a scrape exchange. With so many defensive coordinators teaching the exchange technique, offensive coaches have adjusted with different looks, motions, H-backs as blockers, and as mentioned earlier, even changing the play to read the defensive tackle instead of the End.

If a defensive back cheats in to stop the quarterback from running the ball, there is no one to cover the split end. The quarterback can throw a quick high-percentage pass to his receiver. Notice, how Malzahn fakes the bubble screen to the slot receiver to prevent the secondary from rotating. *Figure 331*

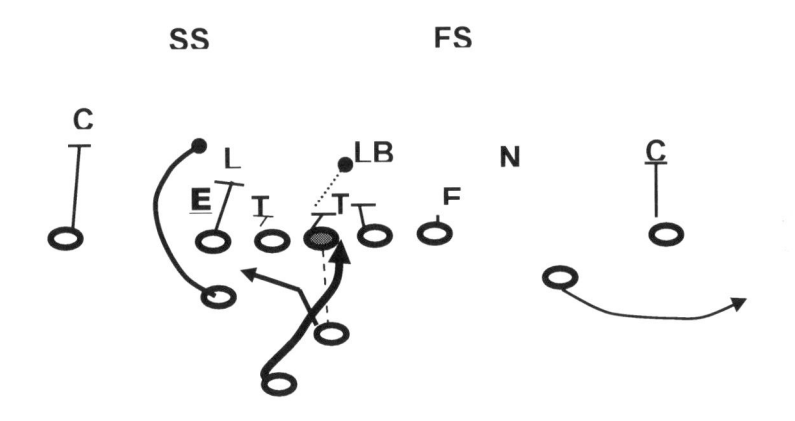

Figure 331 Gus Malzahn's Read Zone using the H-Back

The Counter/Counter-Trey (trap) is a tried and true power misdirection running play popularized by the Redskins under Joe Gibbs. Gibbs, at times, pulled both the backside guard and the tackle to lead the play. Notice Malzahn is using his Guard and his H-back to lead the ball carrier. *Figure 332*

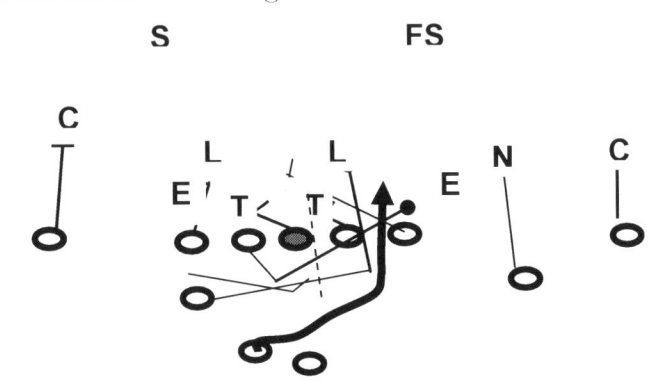

Figure 332 Malzahn's Counter

A throwback to the traditional Wing-T, Malzahn continues to run the trap. Figure 333

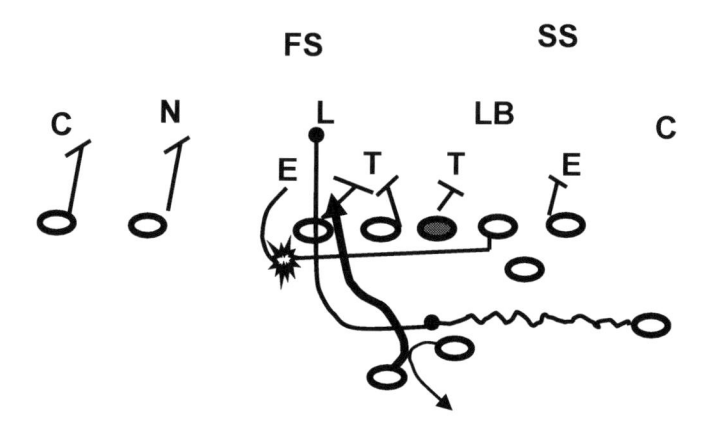

Figure 333 The Auburn Trap

One adaptation of Auburn's buck sweep play is shown below. *Figure 334*
Note the use of the H-Back in motion before the snap allowing him to get out in front of the ball carrier.

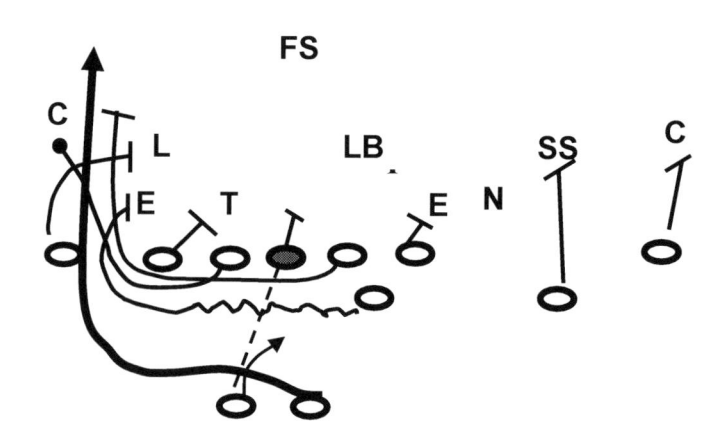

Figure 334 The Auburn Buck Sweep

Although it certainly is not unique to the Malzahn offense, and can be found in almost all of today's offensive playbooks, the "Smash" route is an integral part of his pass game.

Before the snap, the quarterback attempts to determine which is the best side to make the throw. He will then attack the play of the cornerback (C). If the corner tries to stay shallow and play the Stop route of the outside receiver, the quarterback will throw the flag route to the inside receiver. If the Corner takes more than 3 steps back, it is assumed he is playing the flag and there will be no defender to get under the stop route. *Figure 335*

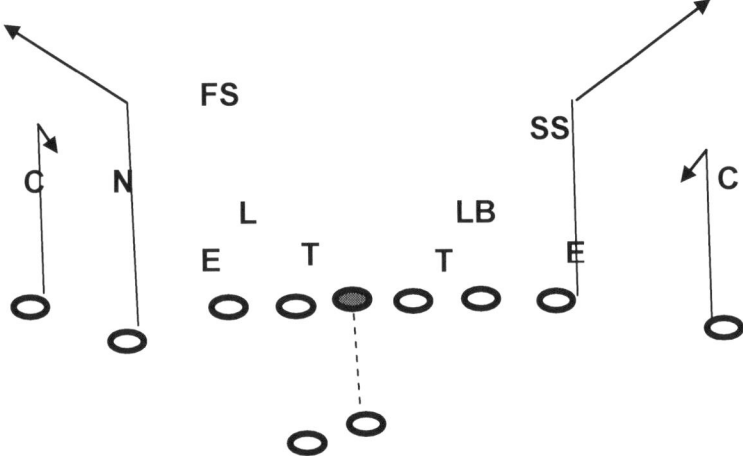

Figure 335 The Smash Route

Art Briles: Baylor

"We do not try to go to the body to set up the knockout shot," Briles said at a recent coaching clinic. "We try to score on every snap." [296]

As mentioned early in this chapter, Art Briles is one of those innovative high school coaches who has served to change the game of football. He led the way for wide-open spread attacks first as head coach at Hamlin High School (Texas) and later at Stephenville High School. He was winning games with a wide-open gunslinger attack back in the 1980s and 1990s, arguably, long before the spread formation became famous.

Although when one takes a quick look at Baylor, they might appear to be just another spread offense team, a closer look shows there are several unique aspects of the Briles approach. The first thing that jumps out at you is the splits of the receivers. While most teams align their wide receivers on or near the numbers, Baylor may place theirs right on the sideline. See *Figure 336*

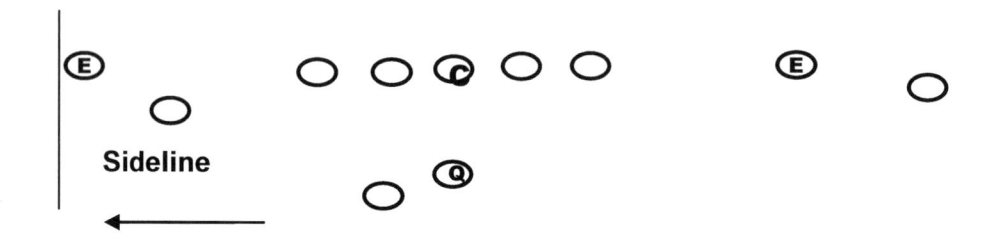

Figure 336 Baylor Offensive Alignment

The consequence for the defense is that it becomes difficult to play any kind of basic pass defense. Most teams rely on some sort of hybrid or split coverage. Either way, with the splits as wide as they are, defenders are on an island. It is difficult for the cornerbacks to get help from their safeties; especially versus play action passes. The second aspect of the Baylor offense that makes them different from other spread teams is that while most spread offenses rely on the zone run for their rushing attack, Baylor does not. Briles' influence by Bill Yeoman, who he played for at Houston, has led him to rely on a variety of offensive schemes.

One of the biggest things that differentiate Baylor from others is the tempo at which they play. "The biggest thing in the success of our offense is the tempo at which we played," explained Briles at a recent clinic. "I want to be the fastest team in America as far as the number of times we snap the ball. People do not pay money to come to a game and watch a slowdown offense. If they go to the restroom, I want them to come back and say, 'What happened while I was gone?' They will miss something if they leave the game. When we have the ball, we will do something with it. You only get 12 possessions a game, and we want to get our money's worth." [297]

Defending the Spread Formations

No two coaches approach defensive preparation the same.

There are those who look at the field in terms of its dimensions. Where is the ball on the field? How close (or far) is the offense from the goal line? How much width of the field will the offense use? These coaches espouse the proverbial "bend but don't break" defense. Do not allow the big play. Make the offense earn their points. This approach to defense is often considered the passive approach. Coaches who promote this form of defense will be quick to point out that there is nothing "passive" about it.

Then there is the "tactical" approach to defense. What is the down? What is the distance? How much time is on the clock? How does their defensive system matchup with the offensive system? Who are their "big play" players? How does the defense assure that their playmakers are matched against the offense's playmakers? Most defenses structured in this manner are considered a "balanced" approach to defense, not too passive and not too aggressive.

Thirdly, there is the theoretical approach to defense. These coaches rely mainly on their study of the opponent with the theory that there is a weakness in every offensive structure. They attempt to find that weakness and develop defensive schemes to take advantage of that weakness. Coaches who use this approach may be passive, balanced, or aggressive but it is most often associated with an aggressive approach to defense.

The whole thing goes back to our earlier discussion. Because team A defeats team B and B defeats team C, it is not a foregone conclusion that team A will beat team C.

The result of the Spread Option offenses that combine the different option reads by the quarterback and an effective vertical passing game is that the defense is left with little room for error. Mental errors or missed tackles have dire consequences when the defense is spread out and players are isolated. The defensive team had better have 11 players who are enthusiastic about pursuing and tackling. Speed is essential.

Bob Shoop, when he was Penn State's Defensive Coordinator, said,"You often divide a defense into three categories, Cornerbacks, the Middle players:(Mike linebacker and defensive tackles], and the Alley players [ends, outside linebackers, and safeties]. With the alley players, it's like going to a Cold Stone Creamery: it's, all the same, guy, just in different sizes. Maybe the Mike and the tackles are the only guys who don't run faster than a 4.8. Everyone else is an athlete." [298]

With perhaps the exception of the old Tampa 2 defense, every defensive structure has to have cornerbacks who can cover on the pass as well as come up and stop the run.

Perhaps the Achilles heel of the Spread Option offense is the need for an athletic, intelligent, and quick reacting quarterback. If the defense can show some different looks on who has option responsibility and who has pure pass responsibility, there is an opportunity to confuse and confound the offense.

There are several ways for the defense to create bewilderment for the quarterback. Breaking it down to its most basic approach, there can be the following.

The defense can play "Cloud Coverage". This defensive structure allows the safety to concentrate on pass coverage and the cornerback, to have responsibility for the run first. This scheme is most sound only when there is one receiver on that side and, of course, a Cornerback, who can tackle in the open field. *See Figure 337*

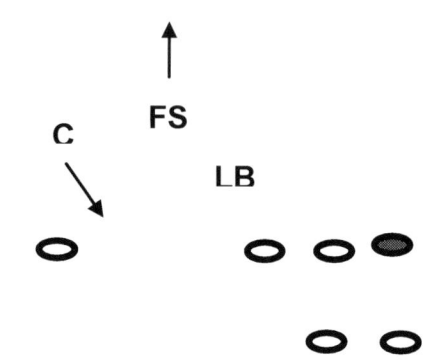

Figure 337 Cloud Coverage

The second option the defense might play is "Buzz Coverage". The cornerback and the safety will both have pass first responsibility. The outside linebacker will handle the run first. This coverage is typical when there are two wide receivers on the side of the call. The caution for the defense here is that because the linebacker has run responsibility at the perimeter of the play, you may be weakening the defense inside the box. *Figure 338*

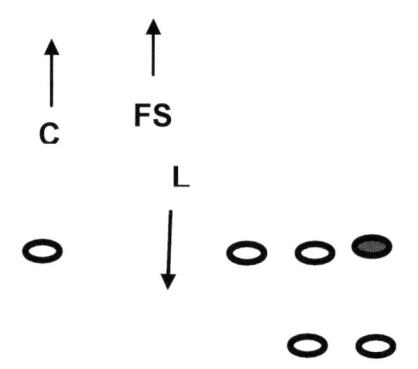

Figure 338 Buzz Coverage

A possible third changeup that might be used by the defense is called, "Sky Coverage." The cornerback will have pass first responsibility, and the safety will have the responsibility of the run. *Figure 339*

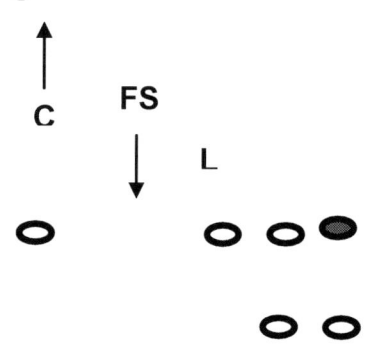

Figure 339 Sky Coverage

Another possibility to confuse the offense is for the defense to play Cover 3 with "pattern matching." This defensive adjustment allows the defense to place 8 defenders on or near the line of scrimmage. Because the Nickel (N) and Strong Safety (SS) are both near the line of scrimmage, they are in a good position to play the run. This defense also places two defenders (N and SS) to play the flat areas. It is significant because it frees the linebackers from a responsibility that they are not physically equipped to do and are not in a proper position on the field to get to quickly. It is called pattern matching because the defender's reaction to the play will be predicated on what the man in front of them does. The difficult aspect of this defensive response is the complexity and coordination of the pattern-match principles. *Figure 340*

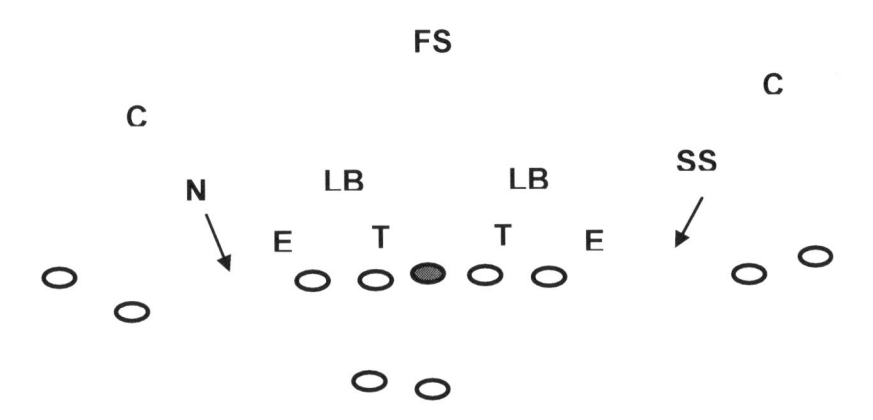

Figure 340 Cover 3: Pattern Matching

A fifth defensive response to the Spread Option offense is preparing a sound option defense combined with a good blitz package. Perhaps the best combination is a defense with an effective blitz scheme with either a cover 3 defense (3 deep defenders) and quarters coverage (4 deep defenders).

Defenses are responding to the spread formations with "Split Coverages." Many coaches feel that, against the spread formation teams, a defense cannot just line up in a basic coverage. Coaches now defend the spread teams by using hybrid coverages, playing one type of coverage to one side of the formation and another to the other side of the formation. Although "Split Coverages" have been used for some years, it is more prevalent today. An example is shown below.[299] *See Figure 341*

Figure 341 Split Coverage

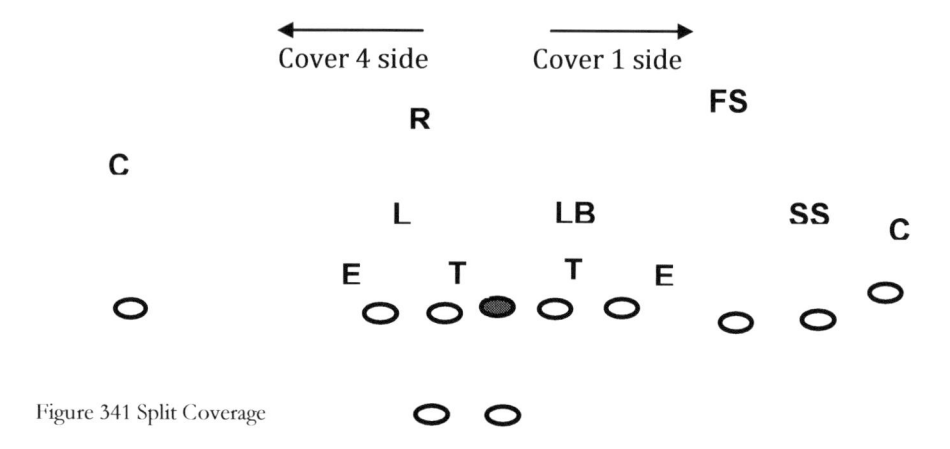

4-2-5 Defense

The use of the spread formation has led to new defensive tactics. The old established defenses most often play with four or five defensive linemen, but with the proliferation of the spread that has changed. Going back to Jimmy Johnson at Oklahoma State and Miami, defensive coaches have been looking for faster and more athletic defenders who can cover the field. The 3-3-5-Stack defense popularized by Joe Lee Dunn is being used extensively versus the spread. On the other hand, Gary Patterson at Texas Christian University has produced a remarkably successful defense. Using four defensive linemen, two linebackers, and five defensive backs, the defense has proven to be very successful versus the spread.

Gary Patterson's statement on the purpose of the 4-2-5 defense. "In this day and age of college football, offenses have become very explosive and complex in the number of formations and plays used in a game. To combat this problem, defenses must have enough flexibility in their scheme to limit offenses in their play selection, but be simple enough to be good at what they do. During a game, we must look like we do a lot but only do enough to take away what offenses do best. This leads me to our philosophy of, "Multiplicity but Simplicity." With every good idea, there has to be a sense of purpose to stand behind it. The purpose of the 4-2 front, five spoke secondary is to give less talented defensive units the flexibility to compete. There is no more helpless feeling than to play "bend but don't break" defense, have the opposition turn up the level of play, and have no answer to it." [300]

Using the 4-2-5, defensive teams have the flexibility to move one or both of the safeties near the line of scrimmage and give the front six defenders help with the running game. The defensive line and linebacker will, also shift and blitz often to confuse the pass protection. In the secondary, Patterson will divide the field in half with each half making defensive calls separately. It is akin to the split coverage previously discussed. "The one thing that we always look at is, can the young man run?'" Defensive Coordinator Dick Bumpas said. "And if he can, then that's a good basis to start for a lot of positions."[301]

Figure 342 shows the 4-2-5 defense indicating the base front and each of the two secondary groups that will work together in their coverage.

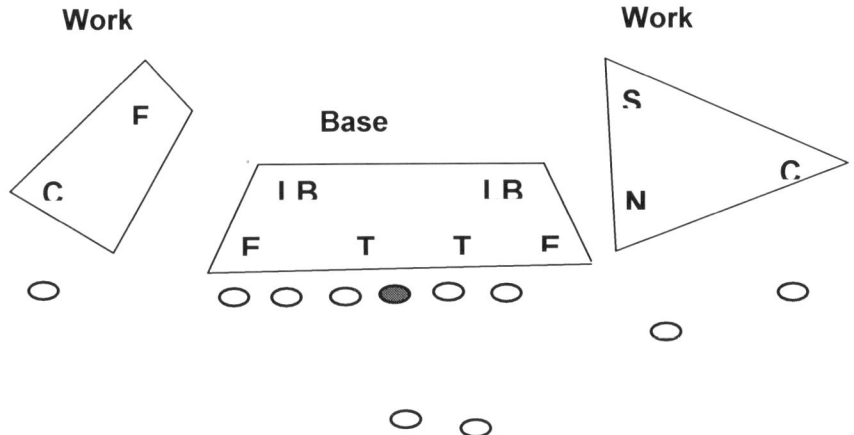

Figure 342 4-2-5 Defensive Divisions

Offensive Response to Spread Defenses

The aggressive response to the defenses that attempt to stop the Spread with "Cloud Coverage" is "The Pop Pass" where the quarterback pulls the ball from the running back, makes it look like he will run, and then pulls up and throws a pass to the wide receiver. There are different versions of this pass to attack the other defenses used to attempt to stop the Spread Option. *Figure 343*

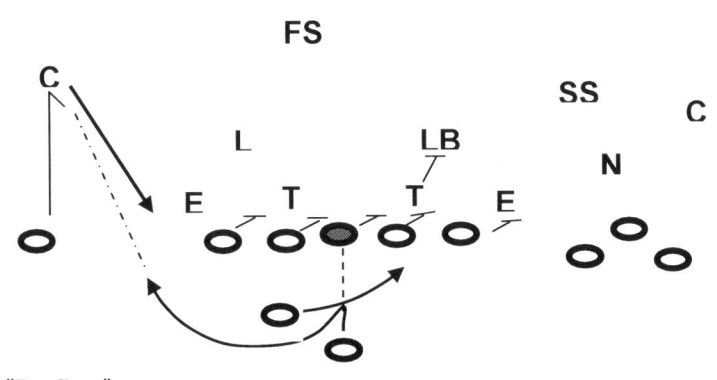

Figure 343 The "Pop Pass."

Adding a pitch back with a third option to the Zone Read play was only a matter of time. The first read by the quarterback is the same as the Zone Read. If the defensive end sits and stays outside, the quarterback will give the ball to the running back and run the Zone play. However, if the defensive end crashes, the quarterback will pull the ball and continue to run his option route. Now, with the addition of a pitch back the quarterback will go on and option the next defender (R in the figure below). If R attacks the quarterback, he will toss the ball to the pitch back on his outside for a long gain. If R plays the pitch back, the quarterback will keep the ball. This is especially effective versus the "scrape stunt" between the defensive end and linebacker. *Figure 344*

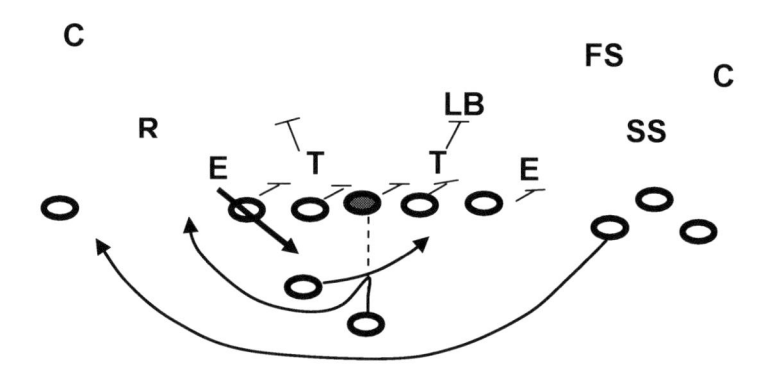

Figure 344 Triple Option off the Zone Read play

Most Spread teams do not have two running backs in the backfield. Consequently, it was always necessary to have a man in motion to become the pitch back. To some extent, this is a tip-off for the defense. Now, some teams use a balanced formation, faking the Bubble Screen and using that receiver in the pitch phase of the play. It is consistent with the initial purpose of the offense, which was to get the ball in the hands of your "playmaker" out in space. *Figure 345*

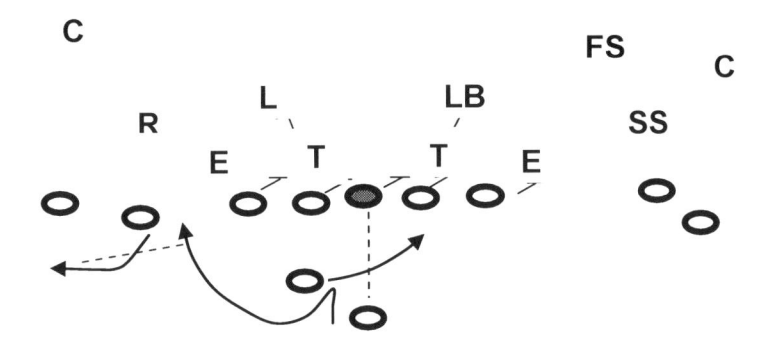

Figure 345 Triple Option using a Bubble Screen fake and using the receiver as the pitch-back

Some teams have even experimented with creating a **Quadruple Option** based on the Zone Read play. They will align with two wide receivers on the same side of the formation that the quarterback will make his zone read. The two receivers will create a high/low read on the cornerback. They will place a corner in a position where he will have to decide to go deep with the outside receiver or play the flat on the inside receiver. The cornerback will get no help from the outside linebacker because the quarterback occupies him. The quarterback will make the same read on the defensive end that he makes on the zone read. However, at this point, he can keep the ball and run, or he can find the open receiver on the high/low read of the cornerback.[302]

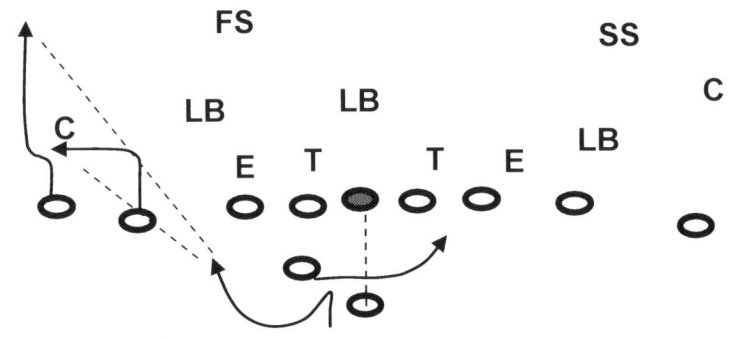

Figure 346

Figure 346 The Quadruple Option

---

[278] *Why Nick Saban and college football are afraid of Hal Mumme.* (n.d.). Retrieved from http://espn.go.com/espn/feature/story/_/id/11547946/why-nick-saban-college-footb

[279] Jacobs, Barry, *Spread Offenses Take Control of College Football.*, NewsObserver.com, Sept. 5, 2013

[280] Van Valkenburg, Kevin, *Yoda of the Air Raid Offense, He Is,*. ESPN the Magazine, September 19, 2014

[281] Dent, Jim, *Twelve Mighty Orphans: The Inspiring True Story of the Mighty Mites Who Ruled Texas Football*, New York, St. Martins Press, 2007.

"Spread traces its roots to Depression-era Texas high school football". ESPN. 2009-07-20. http://sports.espn.go.com/highschool/rise/football/news/story?id=4339959. Retrieved Sept. 14, 2013

[282] Zenor, John. *Created out of a mistake, zone read offenses still hard to stop more than 20 years later*. Published September 25, 2014. Associated Press. http://www.foxnews.com/sports/2014/09/25/created-out-mistake-zone-read-offenses-still-hard-to-stop-more-than-20-years/

[283] Alo, Mohammed. *Urban Meyer's Spread Option Offense*. The Football Times. www.FootballTimes.org/Article.asp?

[284] Zetterberg, Bjorn and David Purdum, Flying Ducks – *Oregon's Prolific Fast-Paced Offense Presents Monumental Challenges to Defenses*. American Football Monthly, Dec. 2010.

[285] Zetterberg, Bjorn and David Purdum, Flying Ducks – *Oregon's Prolific Fast-Paced Offense Presents Monumental Challenges to Defenses*. American Football Monthly, Dec. 2010.

[286] *Rich Rodriguez Talks Offensive Philosophy*. http://espn.go.com/blog/ncfnation/post/_/id/63734/rich-rodriguez-talks-offensive-philosophy, 8/15/2012

[287] *Rich Rodriguez Talks Offensive Philosophy*. http://espn.go.com/blog/ncfnation/post/_/id/63734/rich-rodriguez-talks-offensive-philosophy, 8/15/2012

[288] *Spread offense* - Wikipedia, the free encyclopedia, http://en.wikipedia.org/wiki/Spread_offense (accessed September 12, 2015).

[289] Robarts, Kyle, *Origins of Mumme's Air Raid Offense*, McMurry Sports Information. Updated: September 9, 2010, http://bigcountryhomepage.com/fulltext?nxd_id=290075 02 27 12 retreived.

[290] Van Valkenburg, Kevin, *Yoda of the Air Raidd Offense, He Is.*, . ESPN the Magazine, September 19, 2014

[291] Chris Brown's Air Raid opus at Smart Football, http://smartfootball.com/offense/the-*air-raid-offense-history-evolution-weirdnes* (accessed September 16, 2015).

[292] Chris, The Air Raid Offense; History, Evolution, Weirdness - From Mumme to Leach to Franklin to Holgorsenn and Beyond, Smart Football, July 9, 2012, http://smartfootball.com

[293] Chris, The Air Raid Offense; History, Evolution, Weirdness - From Mumme to Leach to Franklin to Holgorsenn and Beyond, Smart Football, July 9, 2012, http://smartfootball.com

[294] Chris Brown's Air Raid opus at Smart Football, http://smartfootball.com/offense/the-air-raid-offense-history-evolution-weirdnes (accessed September 17, 2015).

[295] Brown, Chris, The Air Raid Offense; History, Evolution, Weirdness - From Mumme to Leach to Franklin to Holgorsenn and Beyond, Smart Football, July 9, 2012, http://smartfootball.com

[296] Brown, Chris. *How Art Briles Potent Offense Made Baylor Nation Title Contender*. Smart Football, Oct. 22, 2013 http://grantland.com/features/chris-brown-how-art-briles-potent-offense-made-baylor-national-title-contender/

[297] Brown, Chris. *How Art Briles Potent Offense Made Baylor Nation Title Contender*. Smart Football, Oct. 22, 2013 http://grantland.com/features/chris-brown-how-art-briles-potent-offense-made-baylor-national-title-contender/

[298] : *"Evolving the option: The pop pass and the future of football ..."*. 26 Jul. 2015 <http://www.sbnation.com/*college-football*/2014/8/20/6044003/read-option-pass-play>.

[299] X & O Labs, a research company for coaches. *Split Coverage Concepts vs. Spread Formations*, Research Report 110105.

[300] Patterson, Gary. *Multiplicity But Simplicity: Why the 4-2-5 Defense*, AFCA Summer Manual, 1997.

[301] Boyd, Ian. *How TCU's defense works, and how it stops up-tempo offense*, http://www.sbnation.com/college-football/2014/6/30/5818160/tcu-football-defense-strategy-formations-xs-os-gary-patterson, June 30, 2014.

[302] Brown, Chris, *The zone-read, gun triple-option . . . and the quadruple-option?*, Smart Football, Aug 17, 2009. http://smartfootball.com/run-game/the-zone-read-gun-triple-option-and-the-quadruple-option#more-85

CHAPTER SIXTEEN

Into the Twenty-first Century

Hurry Up No Huddle.
Perhaps the greatest influence Gus Malzahn has made in the game is his use of the "up tempo - no huddle offense."

Only a handful of coaches in the country come to mind when you think of the establishment of the no-huddle philosophy, and without a doubt, Malzahn is near the top of that list. If he did not pull the trigger on it, Chip Kelly, Mark Helfrich, Kliff Kingsbury, Art Briles, or Mike Leach might have beaten him to the punch. Gus Malzahn's 2003 book *"The Hurry-Up, No-Huddle: An Offensive Philosophy."* is the definitive text on the subject.[303]

So significantly tied to the hurry up offense, Malzahn's corporation, HUNH, LLC applied for a trademark of the phrase 'hurry-up no huddle" in 2013.[304] However, Malzahn is quick to point to Chip Kelly's University of Oregon offense as a leader in the use of the hurry up no huddle.

Malzahn's no-huddle scheme, which he began developing when he was a high school coach in Arkansas, features unbalanced lines, quick-hitting running backs, and constant motion. The pace can be frenetic. The intent is to confuse the defense into making mistakes. The offense works well with a pass-oriented approach or a dominate run scheme.

Why do teams use the hurry up no huddle? The obvious outcome of the quick snap is that there are more plays run during the game thereby lengthening the game. The offense gets to set the tempo of the game. The speed of the game is increased by snapping the ball quickly. That quick snap takes the defense out of their comfort zone, making adjustments difficult and tenuous. The defense is worn down, both physically and mentally, making it difficult for them to focus. When the offense comes to the line of scrimmage, there is still enough time on the play clock for the coach on the sideline to change the play after seeing how the defense is aligning. Finally, it is hard to simulate the hurry up offense in practice.

One of the keys to the success of the no-huddle is how the plays are conveyed to the offensive players. We indicated earlier Oregon's method of communicating their plays. Auburn uses several different signals that include hand motions, numbers, colors, and large cards featuring four images. States Malzahn "We've been doing this for quite a while as far as the signals and trying to disguise things and all that. We feel like we got a foolproof system." [305]

Most teams using the hurry up no huddle offense presently use some different tempos to confuse further and frustrate defenses.

Auburn appears to have two or three different "speeds" that they use to get the ball snapped quickly

1. Huddle – The offense huddles one to two yards from the line of scrimmage. The play is called, the team breaks the huddle quickly, and the ball is snapped before the defense is set. Why? Because the huddle is so close to the line, the linemen merely turn around step up, and they are in place. The skill players rush out. They get lined up as quickly as possible. The deception is that the defense sees the offense huddling up and feels they can catch their breath. Then, the offense breaks the huddle and snaps it almost as fast as if they were skipping the huddle altogether

2. Quick snap - The offense goes no-huddle but without trying to speed everything up. Simply aligning on the line of scrimmage without a huddle creates personnel and matchup problems for the defense. Therefore, it is not necessary to go at break-neck speed every play or every series.

3. High-speed - This is when the offense truly gets it cranked up. They sprint to the line, make the call and get the ball snapped as quickly as possible. [306]

Offenses are playing at such a fast pace the defensive players do not even have time to look at the scoreboard to figure out the down and distance. Defenses do not have time to organize themselves let alone make substitutions. "You can't get in the huddle anymore." Colorado coach Mike MacIntyre said. "You're seeing defenses holding up cards, just to let kids know it's second-and-5 or thired-and-2. You get up and trying to find your way back and the ball is being snapped, and you don't even know what down it is sometimes." [307]

Defending the No-huddle

When asked about how much college football has changed since the advent of the hurry up no huddle offense, the highly respected coach of the University of Alabama, Nick Saban, who has been coaching in some capacity since 1972 made the following comment. "To me, this is as much as I've ever seen the game change over the last three or four years because it's a huge advantage. It is a huge advantage to play offense that way. [308]

"To combat the no-huddle, you have to adjust your system so there's not a lot of terminology, that you have quick calls that can get in the game quickly, players can get lined up, get focused on what they need to do to execute," Saban said. "I think that last year just about everybody went no-huddle against us. I think we actually got better as the year went on in defending it." [309]

There are several essential ingredients for coaches in creating a defense to combat the Hurry-up no-huddle offense. 1. Find versatile defenders who can handle different assignments. 2. Substitute freely, but not necessarily by the situation. 3. Teach defensive players to make and react to calls on the fly. 4. Unearth players who can tackle in the open field.

Defenses have been forced to search for a "hybrid" player; one that can be physical and stop the run but also has the speed to get into pass defense. The rate at which the ball is snapped after the previous play makes it tough for a defense to make substitutions. It is hard to get additional defensive backs on the field on third and long. Much of the up-tempo offense is predicated on the number of defenders in "the box" (an area that stretches approximately from offensive tackle to offensive tackle).

"No one is talking about this, but look for more fake injuries by the defense," ESPN analyst Kirk Herbstreit said. "I've talked to defensive coaches. These guys are actually practicing faking injuries in practice. There's nothing in the rule book at this point that states defenses can't fake injuries," Herbstreit said. "I promise you, in some big game after some crucial second down that sets up a third down, they're going down. It's going to be embarrassing. It's going to be so fake. Nothing prevents it other than being unethical." [310]

David Gibbs, Defensive Coordinator at Texas Tech on defending the no-huddle, "We have a system in place. We have a scheme, and I'm a big believer in if you just coach your kids to do what they're supposed to do, that seven out of 10 times they're going to be fine. No matter how good the other team is, you're going to be OK.

"But the problem is, you try to force things. You cannot dictate, in my mind, on defense anymore, unless you're better than the offense. Which, nowadays, is Alabama, with all their NFL defensive players, are they better than Ohio State? Are they better?

"So, therefore, you better learn how to survive, and you better learn how to take the ball away. The old bend-but-don't-break (philosophy), it's more alive now in college football than ever, but when I watch defensive schemes, I don't see that mindset. I see them being aggressive and I see them playing bump man all the time even though there's no way in the world in college football now the corners are as good as the wide receivers. With all the 7-on-7 going on in high school and all the throwing and catching that those guys do and all the great skills guys. Growing up, do they want to play wide receiver or do they want to play defensive back?"

It would be wrong to suggest that any one defensive scheme or group of systems is the answer to stopping the hurry-up-no-huddle offense. We will speak of one approach that is being used. Keep in mind these are just some examples. They are not THE answer, but it will provide a look at what teams are doing versus the spread. The first defense shown below is a 4-2-5 nickel defense with quarter coverage and press corners. Most people using this approach will move the Nickel to several different alignments. Shown below are three different coverages. *Figures 347-349*

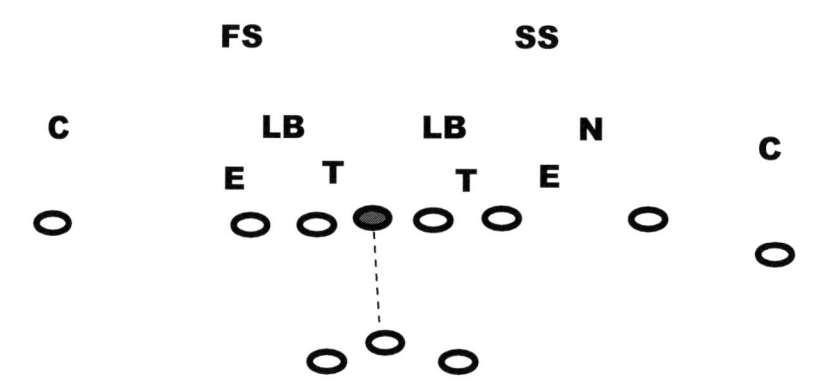

Figure 347 Cover 2

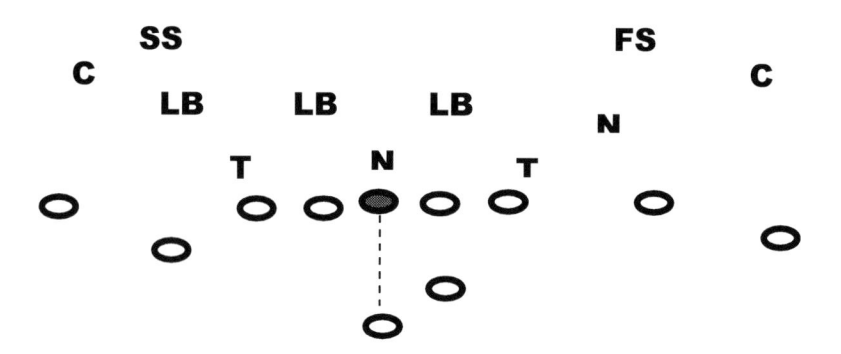

Figure 348 Cover 4

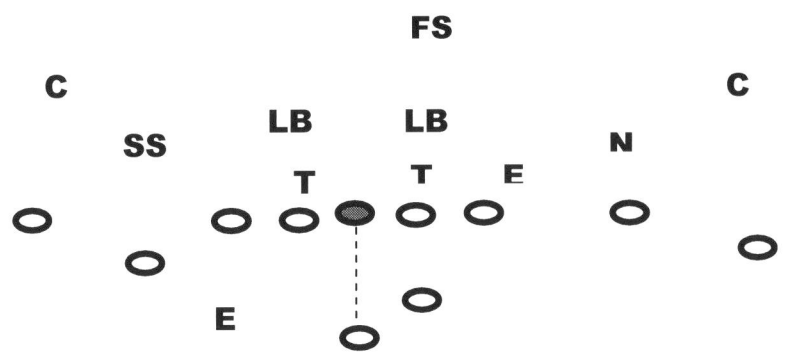

Figure 349 Cover 3

Bunch Formations

As Coaches Andrew Coverdale and Dan Robinson have pointed out, the Bunch Attack uses carefully tightened receiver splits. They attempt to create havoc in several ways. They create space on outside routes. Can attack the backside of the formation quickly against defensive overloads toward the Bunch. They can generate separation versus man defenders through natural rubs. They attack zones using flood and trail methods. They will also create problems by delaying pattern reads through the proximity of the Bunched receivers. [311]

There are two traditional strategies for an offense to handle tight pass coverage. Receivers can be bunched together and then release from the line of scrimmage. It makes it difficult for the pass defenders to cover them tightly. The bunch formations are great to free a favorite receiver from being covered by the defenses best defender.

The second method to handle tight pass coverage is the use of motion. There is nothing new about motion, but it remains an excellent means of freeing a receiver from tight coverage. Return motion is especially effective.

Below we have shown two routes from two typical "Bunch" formations. The Crack-Arc screen gets the ball to the perimeter of the defense quickly. The widest receiver will crack block the second defender to the inside. The middle receiver will be catching the ball. He must gain depth into the backfield as he runs his screen route. The inside receiver will arc block and attack the outermost defender and lead the screen. *Figure 350*

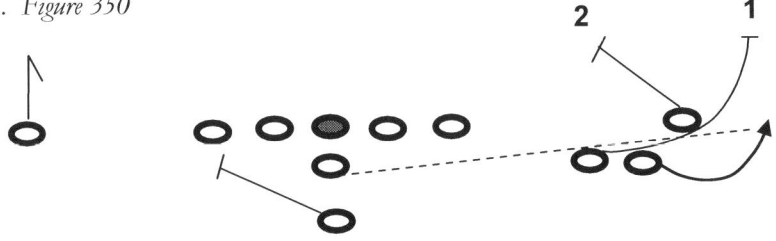

Figure 350 The Crack-Arc Screen

The "Spacing Route" is another familiar bunch route. The widest receiver runs a 6-yard hitch route. The 2nd receiver in from the outside will run a "spot" route. He runs 6 yards deep, plants his foot, and turns back to the quarterback. The 3rd receiver from the outside will run an "Arrow" route. He will run a straight line aiming for a point four yards deep as he gets to the sideline. The backside receiver runs a three-step slant route. If the quarterback feels that his pre-snap read shows the slant to be open, he will throw the backside slant. If the quarterback senses a blitz, he will immediately throw the "arrow" route. If neither of those scenarios is present, the quarterback will read from the inside out. He will look first to the "spot" route, then to the "hitch" route. *Figure 351*

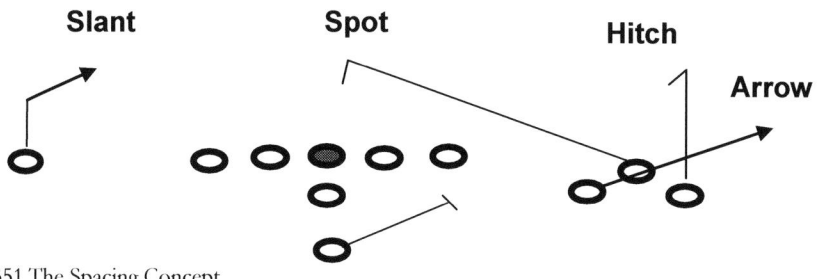

Figure 351 The Spacing Concept

Packaging and Hybrid Plays

Earlier we mentioned Dana Holgorsen's "package" plays. Many offenses are now sending their teams to the line of scrimmage with two (or more) plays that may be run, depending on how the defense lines up. Offenses may package two run plays together; a run and a pass play, or two pass plays. This is just another way of calling an audible. Many of the spread teams will line up, allow their coaches to assess the defensive alignment, and only then decide on what play to be run.

Another form of this same concept is creating "hybrid Plays". According to Gabe Fertitta, offensive Coordinator, Catholic High School, Baton Rouge, (LA), These are plays that have multiple options on the same play. Fertitta first implemented this system while Head Coach of Bay St. Louis, MS

> "Almost all offensive coaches already do this to some extent. But for our team, we set out to create a system of these plays that involved *pre-snap reads* (gifts), *post-snap reads*, and in some cases, using an *option game* following the post-snap read." [312]

In an article in American Football Monthly, Mike Leach Head Coach of Washington State had the following comment when asked what defenses gives his spread the most trouble.

Leach: "Truthfully, not too many. My thinking is this - our success is based on our execution, not our scheme. Fundamentally, our package must cause the defenses problems. It's their job to stop us. We want to be able to attack the whole field and utilize every skill position. Their job is to force us to squander a quarter or a half of the field, which in turn gives them less to defend. That's not our philosophy. I don't really care what they do. It's up to us to be able to utilize and identify what it is that they are doing. If we can do that, then we are able to use their weaknesses against them." [313]

Chris Ault and the Pistol Offense

The Pistol Offense was the creation of Chris Ault and his staff at the University of Nevada. In 2004, they began using the Pistol as a way to run their power running game from a spread formation. It is a cross between the shotgun and one-back offense. Ault never liked running out of the shotgun because there was not enough north/south running (running straight the defense). Ault designed the Pistol, which features a shorter shotgun alignment. The quarterback lines up four yards behind the center. That is somewhat closer than the shotgun alignment. Ault placed the tailback directly behind the quarterback instead of at his side. To Ault, the success of the Pistol is in its flexibility *Figures 352-354*. "I came up with the name because a pistol fires straight ahead; it's one bullet straight ahead," he said. "We still want to run the ball north-south." [314] "Everybody thinks the pistol is just a read, but the pistol is a formation," he said. "And from that formation, if you're a power offense, you can run the power. If you're a counter offense, you can run the counter. It's not just a read offense. I think the read offers another dimension to it, but it's really a versatile formation." [315] Jim Mastro, the Nevada running backs coach, when speaking of Ault offers, "He's changed the landscape of college football today." [316]

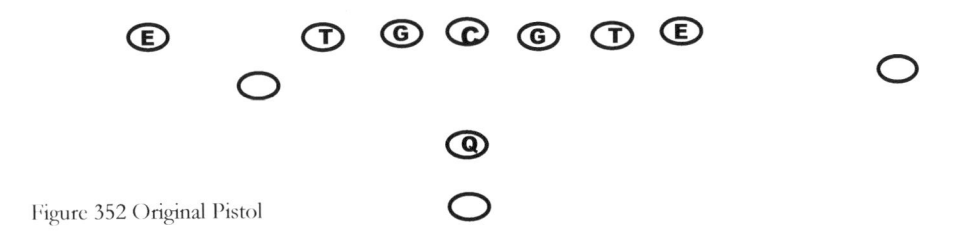

Figure 352 Original Pistol

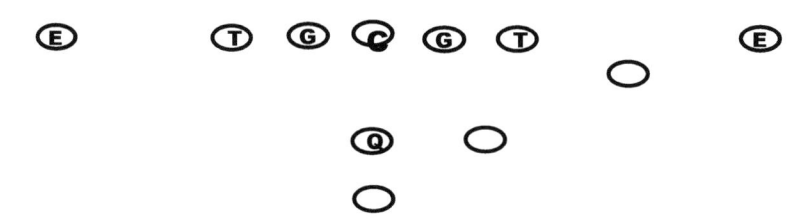

Figure 353 Pistol with Double Split Slot Adjustment

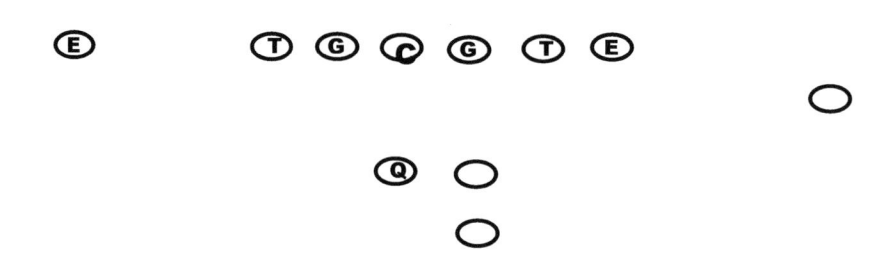

Figure 354 Pistol with Off-Set & Tight End/ Flanker

  The Pistol offense is, perhaps, the fastest growing offense that we have seen in recent years. Chris Ault and his staff have been very open in providing information regarding the technical aspects of the Pistol.

  Another attractive aspect of the Pistol is its multiplicity. The quarterback is closer to the line of scrimmage than he is in a typical shotgun providing him a quicker read. With the quarterback upright and the running back aligned directly behind him, it is difficult for the defense to see him. Also, just like the I formation, the running back can go either way. It is unlike the typical shotgun formation where the defense can align away from the running back because he has to cross paths with the quarterback to run the inside zone. [317]

  Chris Ault is also given credit for creating the "jailbreak screen" that is a part of so many of today offenses. [318] *Figure 355*

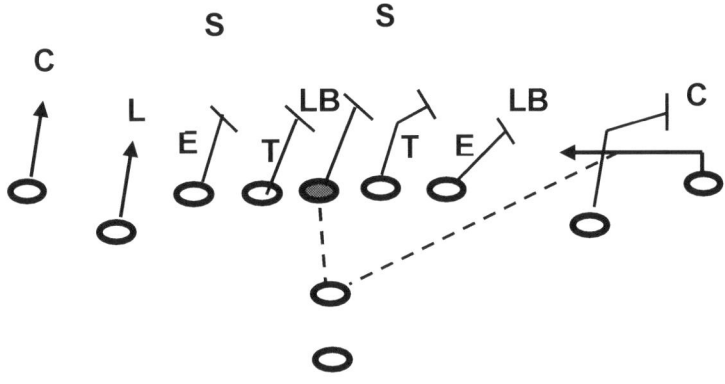

Figure 355 Chris Ault's "Jailbreak Screen."

The Flexbone Option

The Flexbone, as was discussed earlier, is run from a spread formation and stems from the triple option of the wishbone.

Possibly the rarest version of the option is the one used by Paul Johnson's Georgia Tech Yellow Jackets, Ken Niumatalolo Navy Midshipmen, and Jeff Monken at Army. Unlike most spread offenses, the Flexbone offense places the quarterback under center. They will usually align with two wide receivers, two slotbacks (known as A-Backs) and a fullback (known as a B-Back). They will often use motion by the slotbacks to create a numbers advantage. The offense will have more players at the point of attack than the defense will have on the play side. Georgia Tech's offense consistently ranks near the top in college football in both rushing yards and plays over 20 yards. Despite not often throwing enough to qualify for NCAA official statistics, Georgia Tech's offense also ranks high in Passing Efficiency due to its high yards per attempt.

"I know everyone's excited about the up-tempo concepts of today's passing game," says Ken Niumatalolo of Navy, "And everyone loves the idea of keeping defenses off-balance, confused and spreading them out. But for our team, with the type of athletes we possess, the goal of winning the time-of-possession statistic and limiting the number of times that the other team's offense steps onto the field has consistently yielded positive results." [319]

Below are three simple plays from the Flexbone.

The triple option. The quarterback will ride the B-back into and line and will "read" defender 1. If defender 1 does not attack the B-back, the quarterback will give the B-back the ball. If the defender closes down on the B-back, the quarterback will pull the ball and continue to his second read, 2. If the second read attacks the quarterback, the quarterback will pitch the ball to the motioning A-back. If 2 stays outside and plays the A-back, the quarterback will keep the ball and run up the alley. *Figure 356*

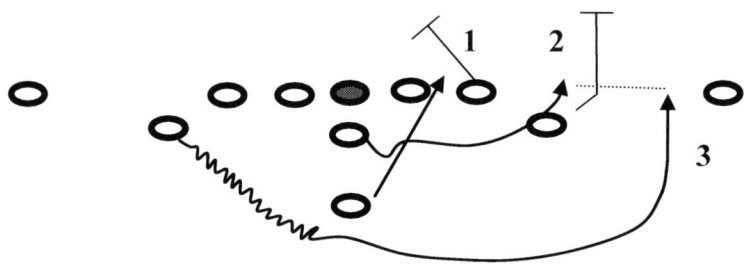

Figure 356 Flexbone Triple Option

Counter Option: When defenses begin to rotate or shift with the motion the flexbone teams will have the A-back start in motion one way and quickly reverse direction and run the option back away from the motion. *Figure 357*

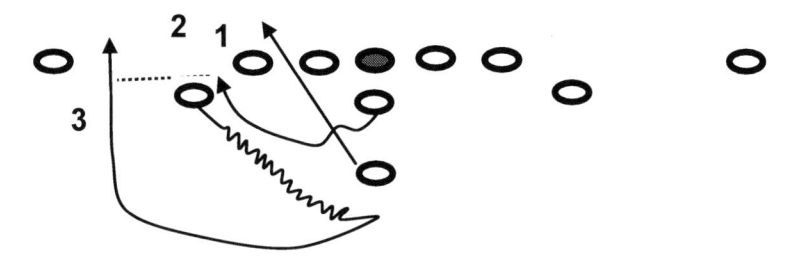

Figure 357 Flexbone Counter Option

The Midline Option: Note: This play should not be confused with the Midline Option that was discussed in the section on the spread option offense. The defensive tackle to the side of the play will be the "read" key. If the tackle crashes down on the B-Back, the quarterback keeps the ball and runs through the void left by the tackle. If the defensive tackle plays the quarterback, the quarterback will give the ball to the B-back for a long gain. *See Figure 358*

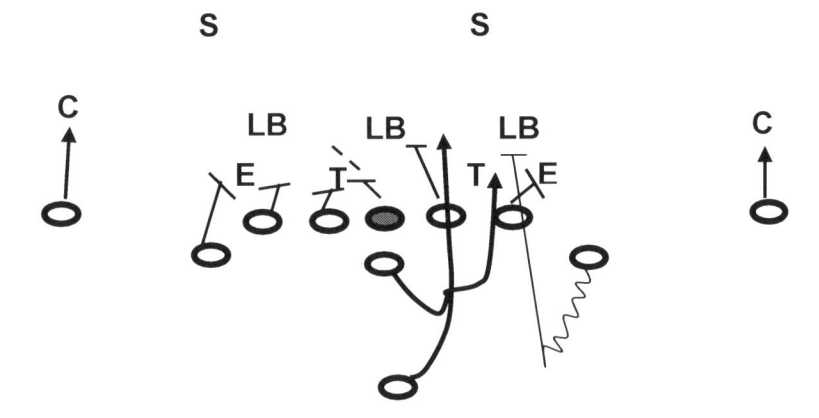

Figure 358 Flexbone Midline Option

Spread-Flex

Very similar to the Flexbone, a slightly different offense has emerged. Called the Spread-Flex, the offense combines elements of the Flex-bone and the Spread offense. There have been several small colleges, as well as Air Force, that successfully use this offense. Teams that have employed the concept use an abundance of pre-snap shifts and motion. They attempt to get the ball out to their wide receivers. It creates confusion and allows the offensive team to establish mismatches for the defense. Envision having to create a defensive game plan for Georgia Tech (run oriented, triple option) and Washington State (Mike Leach and his pass-happy offense) on the same field and the same date.

Triple Shoot

Manny Matsakis is considered the father of the Triple Shoot Offense. He introduced the concept while coaching at Hofstra University in New York. He then took it with him to Emporia State University (KS). However, it was when he moved on to the University of Wyoming that people began to notice the offense. He served as the Head Coach at Bethany College in 2013 and 2014. In 2015, he brought his Triple Shoot offense to Widner University as their Offensive Coordinator.

The Triple Shoot finds its roots in three different offenses that have been discussed previously. It is derived from the Run & Shoot, Wing-T, and the old 1930s and 40s Spread Formation of "Dutch" Meyers. It features a no-huddle system that spreads the field with four receivers and a single back. It utilizes a system approach to offense such as that used in the Wing-T and to some degree the Run and Shoot. Just as "Tiger" Ellison numbered the defenders in his Run & Shoot offense, Matsakis identifies defenders on how they align to his four-receiver offense. The pre-ordered alignment of the defense determines the blocking assignments. The Triple Shoot uses route adjustments by the receivers after the play has begun, much like the Run & Shoot.

The run offense has several series but relies generally on the Belly series of the Wing-T. Additionally, they will run the Veer, Zone, Option, Reverse, and the Pop-Out run that many people refer to as the Jet Sweep or Fly Sweep. Below is the Matsakis Pop Out sweep. *Figure 359*

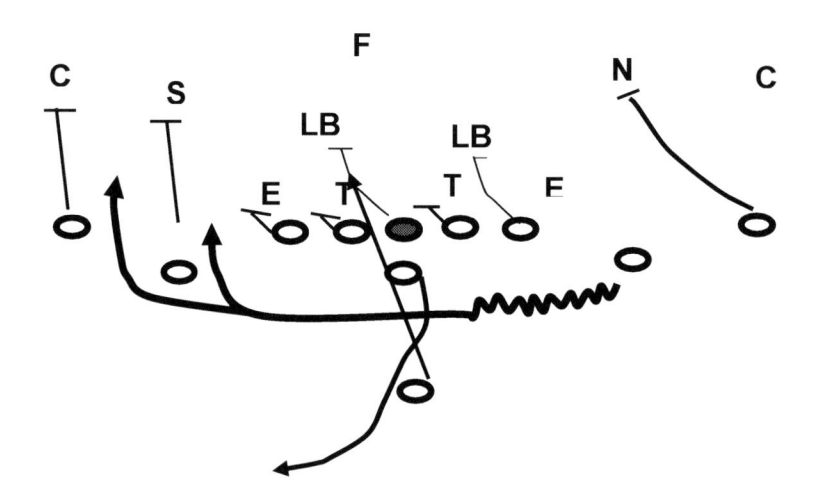

Figure 359 Triple Shoot Pop-Out sweep

Figures 360, 361 show two of the Triple Shoot play action passes. When running the Even Wheel, the quarterback will look to throw the ball to the Post first, then to the Wheel running up the boundary. As has become common today, often the Wheel is thrown to the back shoulder of the receiver.

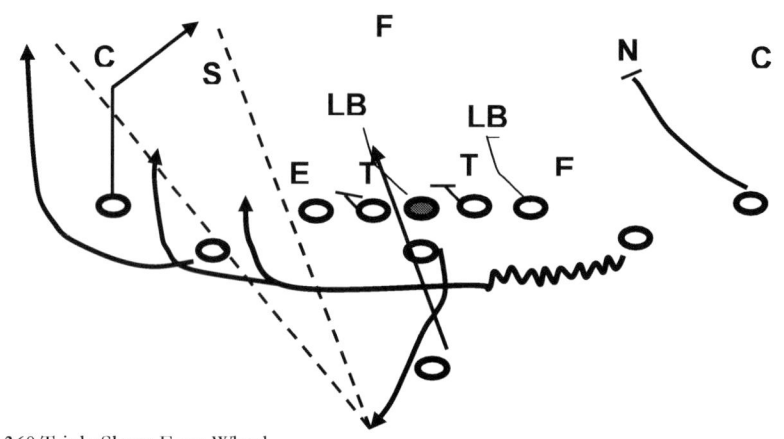

Figure 360 Triple Shoot Even Wheel

The Load Switch Route is run with a fake of the Pop Out sweep. The quarterback will look backside to the Stretch Route, which is running up inside the back side hash mark. In the example shown, the two front side receivers will run the Switch combination. The outside receiver is responsible for reading the deep zone defender, the free safety (F). If the free safety attacks the Pop-Out sweep, the receiver will run the skinny post. If the Free Safety does not react to the sweep but stays deep in pass coverage, the receiver will break off his route underneath the safety. [320]

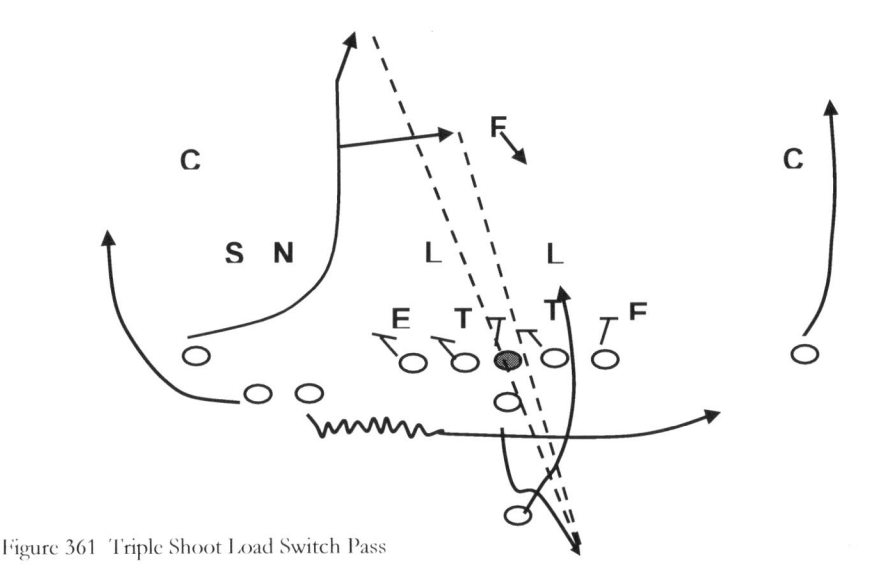

Figure 361 Triple Shoot Load Switch Pass

Revisiting the 1970s Big Ten Offenses

Everyone is spreading the field with their offense and attempting to get playmakers in space to make athletic plays. As noted earlier, defenses have gotten faster, more agile, and smaller. There has developed a small group of coaches who are combating that defensive adjustment by playing bigger, stronger players on offense. They are running attacks very similar to those that were in vogue in the Big Ten during the Carter administration.

Led by John Harbaugh of the Baltimore Ravens and Jim Harbaugh, now at Michigan, some teams have returned to power football.

"What the Harbaughs have brought back to the NFL is what the Big Ten used to be like," said Glen Mason, a former University of Minnesota coach. "They are running basic off-tackle plays, 'power' plays that have been around since the year of the flood, and an NFL defense doesn't have any idea how to stop it. They aren't prepared for old-school football." [321]

Commenting on the evolution, John Harbaugh stated, "New England is running an inside dive that is about as Woody Hayes as you can get. They put four blockers on two inside guys and dive the ball. That's three yards and a cloud of dust, and that's Bill Belichick running it."[322]

The Spin Offense

The Spin is the innovative offense devised by Dale Weiner at Catholic HS, Baton Rouge, LA. It uses a balanced set with two split ends and two slot backs. The quarterback aligns in a shotgun and executes a spin on every play. The fullback aligns 2' in front of the quarterback offset over one of the two guards. The slots align in a position that allows one of them to go in motion on every play. The offense relies on misdirection and closely resembles the traditional Wing-T and the Single Wing Spinner series. Weiner's offense blends a mixture of sweeps, counters, screens, and a heavy dose of play action passes. Below are several classic Spin plays.[323] *Figures 362-365*

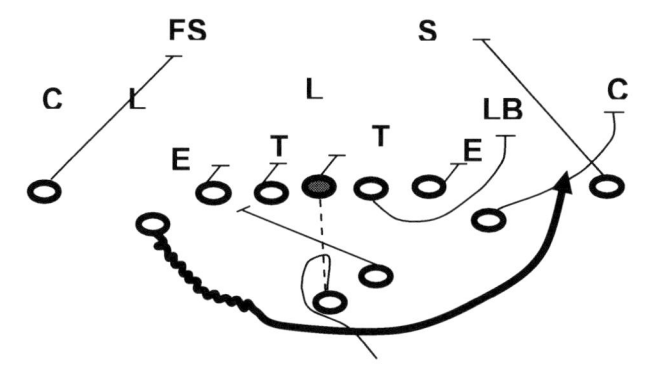

Figure 362 The Spin Sweep

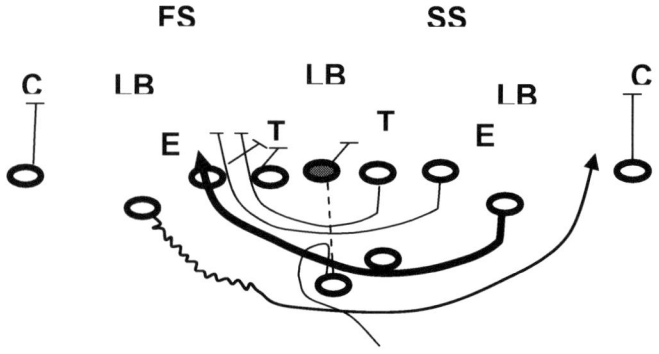

Figure 363 The Spin Counter Sweep

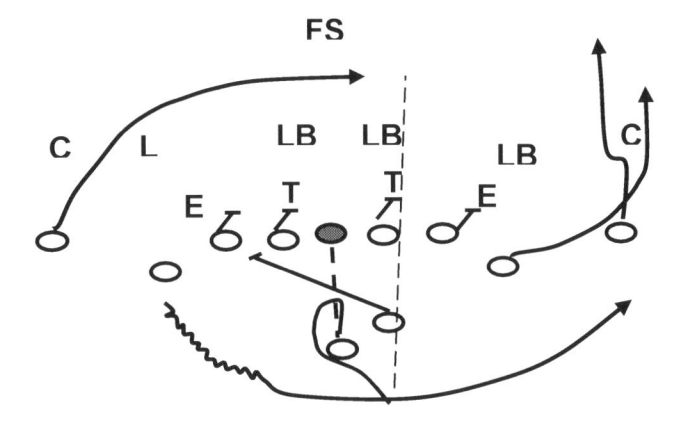

Figure 364 Spin Offense Play Action Pass

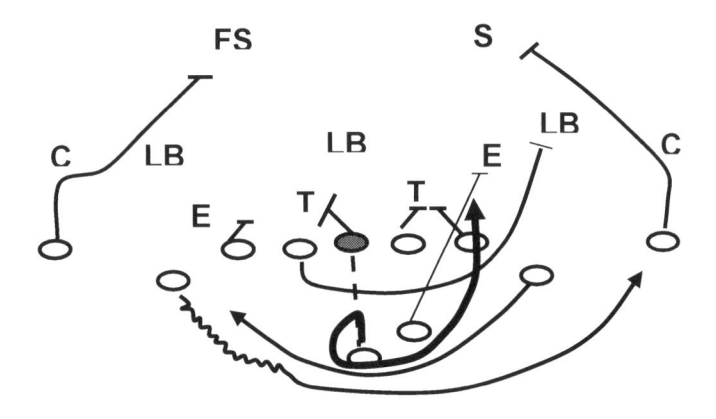

Figure 365 Spin Offense Quarterback Power

Willamette Fly Offense

Although there are several versions of the Fly, the one most associated with the phrase Fly Offense is the one used by Mark Speckman at Willamette University (OR). The organization is rather unique. It is a systems approach to offense.

Speckman's discussion of the offense; "I have participated in many spirited discussions about how many plays our team should have. I believe that the best system is easy for your team to execute and hard for the opponent to stop. In teaching our offense, we try and stay away from the idea of plays. Instead, we use three different styles of teaching our run offense." For the linemen, there are words to describe whom to block. There are about eight rules. The receivers have concepts to follow; of which there are three. The backs learn the path they will follow for that play. [324]

"This system creates a lot of variation. By 'mixing and matching' back paths and blocking rules, you can quickly amass a wide variety of plays. I have found that coaches and players do not always feel comfortable with new plays but have great comfort with 'wrinkles' described with 'day one' terminology." [325]

The trademark play of the Fly Formation, the Fly Sweep is shown below.
Figure 366

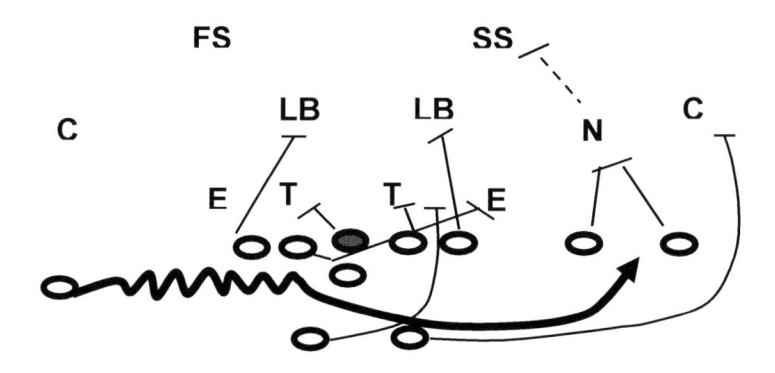

Figure 366 The Fly Sweep

Wild Bunch

The Wild Bunch formation is the invention of Coach Ted Seay. Seay was originally a Wing-T disciple. He also spent several years running the Run & Shoot along with aspects of the Triple Option offense. However, searching for a more comprehensive passing attack, Seay combined the concepts espoused by Andrew Coverdale and Dan Robinson in their 1997 book, *The Bunch Attack: Using Compressed Formations in the Passing Game*. We have discussed the advantages of the Bunch formations earlier in this chapter. Seay added the Fly Sweep from Willamette's Fly formation. Also, he later incorporated the Rocket Sweep series. He assembled these many aspects into a single offense. In creating his Wild Bunch formation, Seay flexed his Tight End (Y) but did not place him as wide as a standard wide receiver. He is in a position about 6 yards from his offensive tackle. The split is near a position that, at one time, was called a "nasty" split. *Figures 367-369*

Figure 367 Wild Bunch Formation

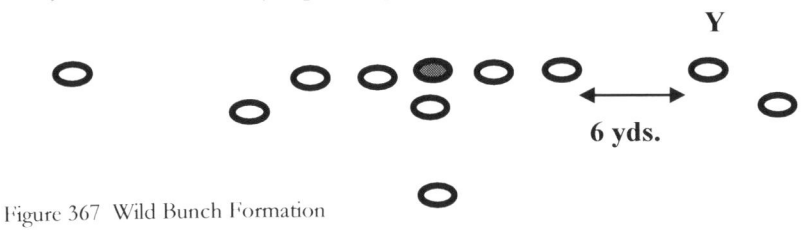

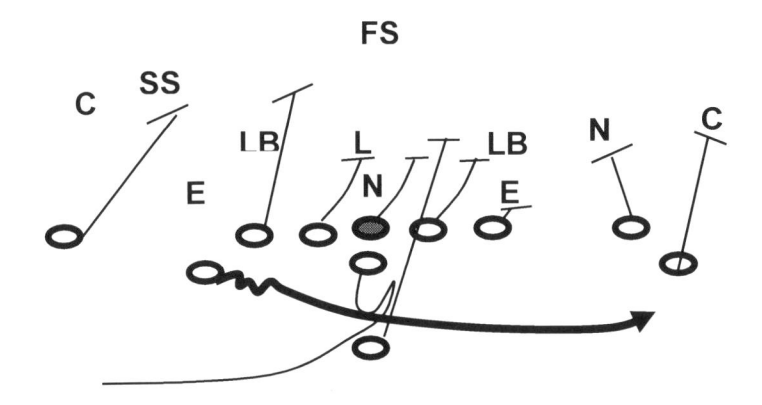

Figure 368 Wild Bunch Fly Sweep

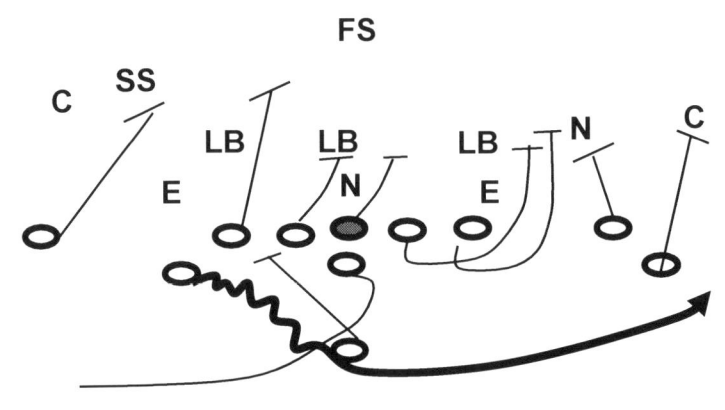

Figure 369 Wild Bunch Rocket Sweep

Tsunami Offense

The Tsunami is the creation of Leon Feliciano, the head football coach at Tomales (CA) High School. The offense employs the concepts of the Double Wing. It is a run-first, power formation. The fullback is near the line of scrimmage behind the offensive tackle. He is in an advantageous position to get to his blocking assignment quicker. The remaining back is aligned slightly deeper than the fullback is and behind the offensive guard. It places him in a position to follow the fullback. The primary Tsunami formation is below. [326] It looks very similar to some of "Pop" Warner's Ends Back Formation from around 1908.

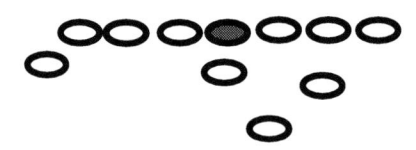

Figure 370

Figure 370 Tsunami Formation

The Tsunami Toss play, which is the primary power play of the formation, is shown below. Note the enormous blocking power that is amassed at the point of attack. *Figure 371*

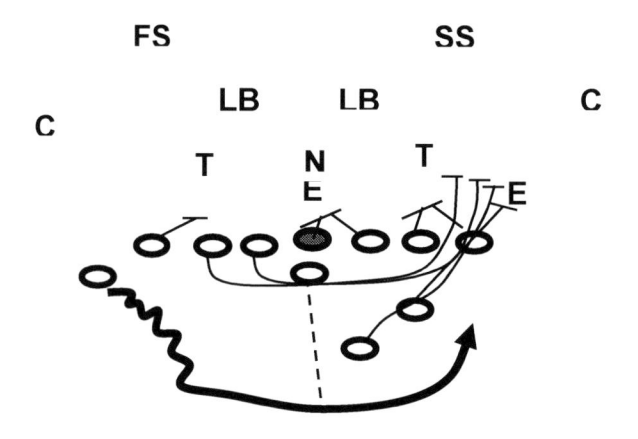

Figure 371 Tsunami Offense Toss

Double Wing

As discussed earlier, the original Double Wing was the creation of "Pop" Warner. Warner popularized numerous formations in the early part of the twentieth century, one of which was a Double Wing. Warner thought of his Double Wing as a passing formation.

The modern Double Wing came into being sometime in the mid-1980s as a power offense. One of the first to employ the formation was Don Markham at Bloomington (CA) High School. By the late 1990s, there were several teams in both California and Oregon using some form of the Double Wing. Jerry Vallotton wrote a book on the formation in 1997, *The Toss*. He produced a revised edition of the book in 2009. Hugh Wyatt, a strong proponent of the Double Wing, and Markham discussed and compared each of their versions of the formation on more than a few occasions. Wyatt produced a video series, The Wyatt Dynamics. Wyatt is an old Wing-T coach and used many of the principles of that formation in his offense, especially creating double-team blocks at the point of attack. Markham's version contains much more of the down block principles.

There is no single Double Wing formation. Some teams choose to take no splits between the offensive linemen Some Double Wing teams use a balanced line and other prefer an unbalanced line similar to Warner's. Many of the advocates of the Double Wing formation have adopted the direct snap, resembling Warner's formation. Below are several of the signature plays of the Double Wing.   *Figures 372-374*

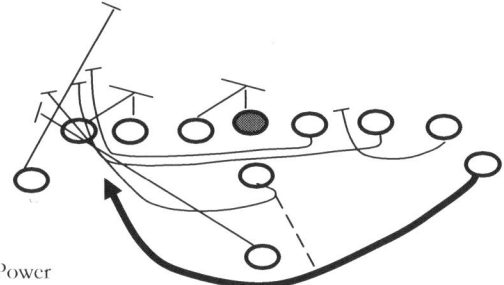

Figure 372 Double Wing Power

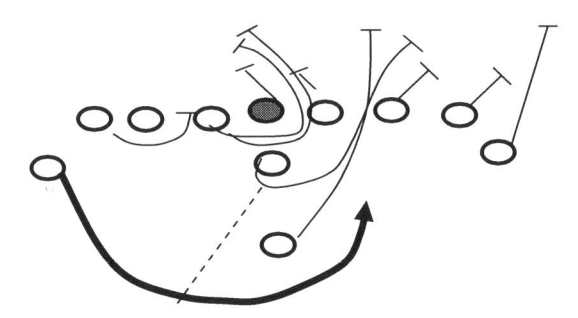

Figure 373 Double Wing Iso (isolation play)

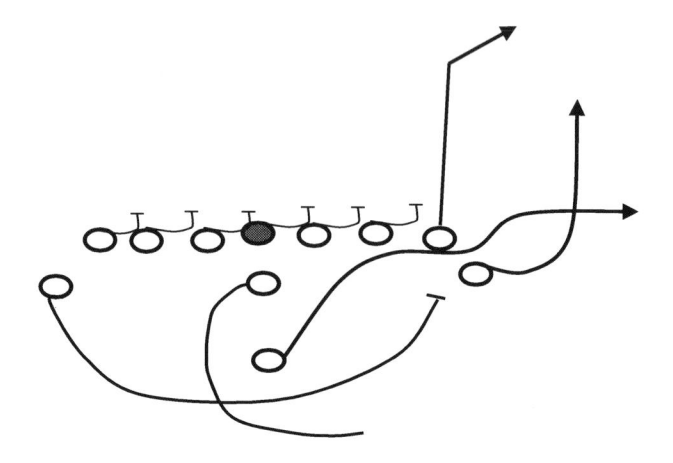

Figure 374 Double Wing Keep Pass

The A11 Offense

Created in 2007 by two Piedmont HS (CA) coaches, Kurt Bryan (Head Coach) and Steve Humphries (Offensive Coordinator), the A11 generated controversy right from the start. Bryan and Humphries used a loophole in the rules regarding scrimmage kicks. In 2007, players participating in a "scrimmage Kick" formation were exempt from the numbers requirement. It allowed all players, even those with the numbers 50 - 79, to be eligible pass receivers. As long as the player receiving the snap aligned 7 yards or more behind the line of scrimmage, the formation was determined to be a "scrimmage kick" formation. Bryan and Humphries used the formation as an every down formation. Using a type of spread formation with all players spread across the field, players could become eligible receivers by stepping up to the line of scrimmage, by stepping back a yard from the line of scrimmage, or by going in motion. Many of the formations also placed two backs in the backfield either of whom could receive the snap. Not knowing which back will receive the snap places added pressure on the defense. Who will receive the snap? Will he pitch or hand the ball off to the other back? Will he pass the ball? Defenses could not determine, until just before the A11 snapped the ball, which the eligible receivers would be. It was calculated that the possible number of formations using this format exceeded 16,000.

Coach Dan Kenilvort of Sir Francis Drake High School concocted the most successful defense against the original A11. Kenilvort had only two players in a position to rush the quarterback and placed the remaining nine defenders in a line stretching the width of the field. Each of the nine was in a position to defend if the offensive players in front of them became one of the eligible receivers. Kenilvort held Piedmont to 7 points.

In February 2009, the National Federation of State High School Associations rules committee voted 46–2 to close the loophole allowing the linemen-free formations featured in the A-11.

In the 2009 season, the creators of the A11 introduced a modified version of the formation. Ineligible numbered "anchors", creating a 3-man offensive line, now flank the center. Like any ineligible receiver, the anchors can neither receive forward passes nor advance downfield before a forward pass is thrown across the line of scrimmage. They may catch lateral and backward passes, take handoffs, advance downfield before a screen pass to an eligible receiver, or even throw the ball if it is handed or pitched back to them. Two other players spread out along the line of scrimmage must also wear number 50-79 that automatically make them ineligible. [327]

After Bill Belichick and the New England Patriots used a strategy with a similar concept as the A11 during the 2014 season. The NFL imposed an additional rule to discourage teams from placing players with eligible numbers at an ineligible position.

Mike Leach, the highly regarded inventive coach at Washington State, had this to say regarding Bryan and Humphries creation, "They really have some good ideas that I think ought to be looked at." [328] Below we have shown several formations being used currently that are similar to the A11. *Figures 375-380*

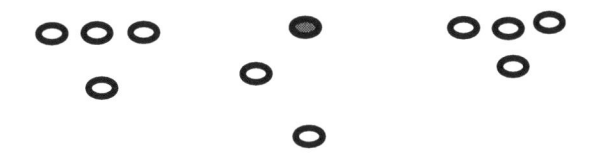

Figure 375 Used by the University of Southern California vs. Hawaii

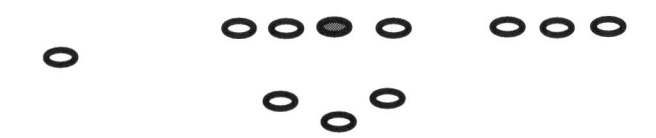

Figure 376 Used by Miami (FL) vs. Ohio State

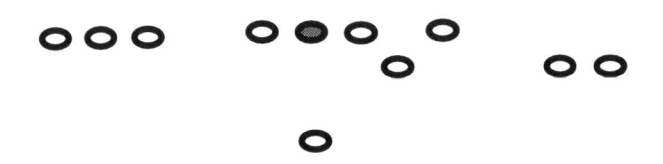

Figure 377 Used by Auburn vs. Mississippi State

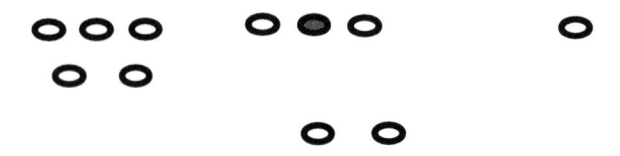

Figure 378 Used by Auburn vs. Mississippi State

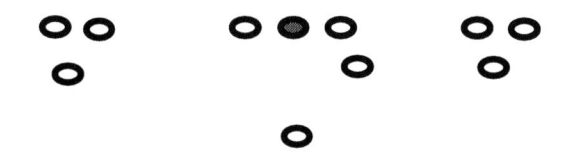

Figure 379 Used by The Philadelphia Eagles vs. the New Orleans Saints

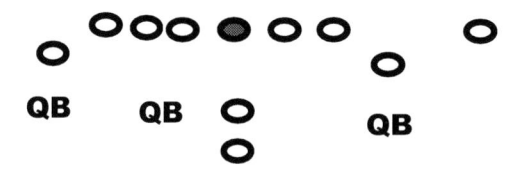

Figure 380 Princeton 3 Quarterback System vs. Cornell

The Evolving Tight End

Until the mid-1980s, the position of Tight End in the offense had one of two possibilities. There were the Tight Ends who were excellent blockers and served as a third glorified tackle. They were players who were solid blockers but, in most cases, less than capable receivers. Then there were the Tight Ends who were receivers. These players were too big or too slow to be "true" wide receivers. They were players who were excellent receivers but, in most cases, less than adequate blockers.

As discussed earlier, Don Coryell and Joe Gibbs of the NFLs Chargers took an exceptional Tight End, Kellen Winslow, and began to move him around. They could place Winslow in a position to be a primary blocker at the point of attack, and they could place him in a slot position and utilize his receiving talents. A new kind of Tight End was born.

With the popularity of the Tampa 2 Defense, the "hybrid" Tight End became a valuable commodity. In recent years, the flexible Tight End concept has grown significantly. By referring to the section on Air Coryell in Chapter 13, you can see how the Tight End can become an integral part of the modern day offense.

The second manner that the Tight End play is evolving is the use of two and even three Tight Ends on the field at the same time. The concept was, of course, used first by the old Washington Redskins offense. Coaches have discovered that a good way to give defenses an extra challenge to prepare for is to move the Tight Ends around to generate different formations. It creates distinct problems for the defense in the run game, but it also plays a significant role in the passing game. Offenses attempt to line a fast Tight End on a large, and presumably slower, linebacker. They can place a large Tight End on a smaller defensive back. With this, offensive coaches have now found another way to create personnel problems for the defense.

With many defensive coaches using "hybrid" alignments, the Tight End provides a way for the offense to create balance in the pass protection.

Firstly, the "cover two" system on defense is still very popular. It is one of the better systems designed to counter the widespread "West Coast Offense." However, the Tight End position (because of his alignment next to the tackle, and his physical build) ends up in the dangerous "seam", where the cover-two is weakest. By the time an opposing defender gets to the Tight End, he has already taken a couple of steps. In addition, is a physical mismatch for the likely swift safeties trying to bring him down.[329]

Second, teams have discovered that there is a host of "smoke and mirror" adjustments that can be made with a Tight End. Line him up next to the Right Tackle and defenses do not know if he is going to block or be a receiver, etc.

Now when a defensive coordinator sees the offense bring in two wide receivers and one Tight End, he is likely to use a base defense. However, maybe he should have brought in a third Cornerback because many teams now line up the Tight End in the slot! If the defensive coordinator calls a Nickel defense (three Cornerbacks), for the subsequent formation, the quarterback may just audible to a run, and the Tight End will position himself to become a run blocker. In other words, a top-notch Tight End almost guarantees a mismatch. That is until a defensive mastermind develops a new formation or a new Linebacker archetype.

Third, the recent move by many teams to return to the old 3-4 creates an exceptional opportunity for Tight Ends. The danger with the 3-4 is picking up the blitz. With a two Tight End set, the blockers are already up to the line and facing each outside linebacker - threat neutralized. However, with two Tight End sets we quadruple the number of disguised packages the team has available on offense, and with motions, we create a much-enhanced playbook.[330]

An example of one of the many possibilities of resourceful three Tight End formations that create problems for the defense is shown below. The run possibilities are obvious. However, from this alignment the offense can motion to create passing mismatches that create headaches for the defense. *See Figure 381*

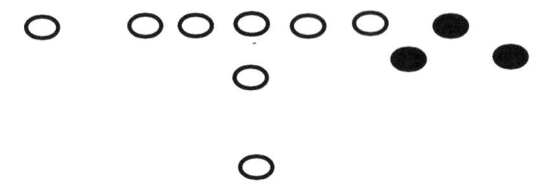

Figure 381 Three Tight End Formation

Big Nickel Defense

The Big Nickel defense was created in the 1990s by Fritz Shurmur of the Green Bay Packers, but it has made a comeback and gained universal popularity in the Twenty-First Century. Shurmur substituted an extra safety that had many of the characteristics of a linebacker. This defender can be a cover defender on passes, be used as a Blitzer, or provide excellent support against the run. *Figure 382*

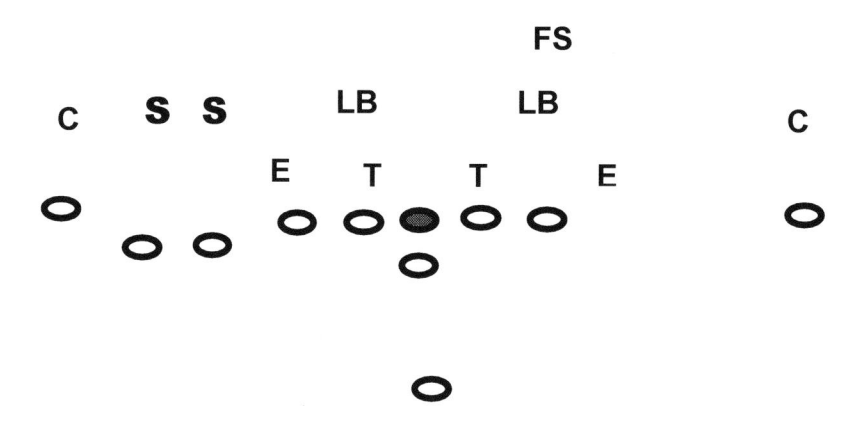

Figure 382 Example of the Big Nickel Defense (two Strong Safeties S)

The Use of Technology in the game

In the Chapter on Field Tactics in his 1894 book, *Scientific and Practical Treatise on American Football*, Alonzo Stagg suggests several ways to keep accurate information on both your team and your opponents. [331]

As early as 1913 Herbert Reed, in his book *Football for Player and Public*, addressed the need to have a system to evaluate each of his opponents - to discuss their style of play, their tendencies, strategy, and tactics. [332]

Percy Houghton, in considering a coach's greatest task stated. "His greatest task, however, lies in sorting data relative to offensive and defensive methods which he has accumulated from time to time from various sources of information." [333]

Paul Brown, who in the late 1940s and 1950s, was creating playbooks for his players to study, probably made the first real use of technology. Brown also made extensive use of film to evaluate his team's performance and to study his opponents. So, although, there has been a technology explosion in the last ten years, coaches have always attempted to, not only, learn more about their team and their opponents but to become more efficient by using the best "technology" available at the time.

There is a never-ending list of products using technology in today's game of football. Among others things, technologyy is being utilized in the recruitment of players, tracking the progress of individual players, game preparation, game use, and post game analysis. Coaches have been making judgments about all of the above aspects of the game for years. However, in many cases, the study has been subjective, open to bias, and, in many cases, emotional.

In **recruiting,** the social media has been used for some years. Coaches have software that allows them to follow the recruit and keep track of their strengths and weaknesses as an athlete, a student, and a person.

However, the University of Michigan has brought virtual reality into the process. In explaining their use of virtual reality in recruiting, assistant coach Jay Harbaugh says, "For the first time in collegiate athletics virtual reality will be used for recruiting.

"It's immersive and really captures the emotion, where you didn't feel as much like a spectator. So to be that program and that university that is setting the bar high is something that is exciting for everybody." [334]

Recruits are given a set of goggles that give them a glimpse of their experience as a Michigan athlete. They can watch themselves putting on their Michigan uniform and running out of the tunnel and into the stadium with thousands of cheering fans.

Coaches can track the progress of players after creating personal programs for ensuring maximum growth. GPS chips are placed on players shoulder pads that will track all of the player's on-the-field movements.

"The goal," Tennessee head coach Butch Jones said last fall, "is to optimize everything else coaches do – to help their players peak on Saturday. 'You build a portfolio of data on each player so over a period of time you can tell when they're wearing down, do they need an extra rest, do they need a day off, all those things.' 'The most important thing is what you do throughout the week to get them ready to perform at their peak, at their optimal level, come game day.'"

"'We're using them for the first time," Mark Richt told the Times Free Press. 'What it's doing is giving us an idea about the volume of running — how much distance are these guys traveling and what speed are they traveling and how often do they hit at maximum speeds?

"You learn a lot about the volume of work that they're doing. We're still learning how to use them and how to use the data to help us because we really don't have anything to compare it to. " [335]

Many types of technology have been used for years in **game preparation**. However, that process has reached new levels. Playbooks have been put on mobile devices so that players can take them wherever they go. Practice video is placed on mobile devices so that both players and coaches can take them home to view. Coaches can make changes in plays or formations and players have them, almost, instantly. Virtual reality is being used in the classroom so that players can view potential game scenarios and learn how to react to them. It is especially beneficial because it used to be that, with the limited repetitions in practice, not all the possible scenarios could be covered. Backup players now have the benefit of seeing how the action will develop. Possibly the most important aspect of all is the fact that the possibilities of injury are significantly reduced. Coaches and their information technology people can analyze hundreds of different aspects of their performance as well as of their opponents' tendencies.

Dartmouth University is experimenting with the development of a "Mobile Virtual Player". The idea is the remote control dummy will absorb some of the hits that would normally be put on players. [336]

Use of technology **during games** has exploded since the high school rule change in 2013. The rule, which was adopted by the National Federation of State High School Associations, reads, "The committee has expanded use of communication devices to allow, coaches, players and nonplayers to use any form of available communication technology during authorized conferences outside the 9-yard marks, on the sidelines and during the halftime intermission period."

They can now use video to break down what is happening on the field. They can note and make adjustments on the sideline that previously were only achieved in the video room. It is only the beginning.

Finally, **post-game** applications include software that allows coaches to examine video of the previous game, make notes and coaching points for individual units or individual players and distribute the information digitally. The team is better prepared for discussions in the meeting rooms before the next practice or contest. Coaches can now hold spontaneous conversations with each other or with players using video footage and statistics that are available with the touch of a finger.

Having made the case for the use of developing technologies in the game let us end this section with a quote from Alabama Coach, Nick Saban**.** "We use a lot of stats, but this game is not that complicated. The team that wins usually blocks the best tackles the best and takes care of the ball the best." [337]

The St. Louis Rams have the youngest team in the NFL. Like most workplaces, the Rams were inundated with employees whose habits were vastly different from those of their bosses. As Coach Jeff Fisher put it, "Our players learn new." [338] Les Snead, the General Manager of the Rams, concluded by saying, "The next frontier in football is understanding the mind and figuring out how you can test and teach." [339]

303 Malzahn, Gus. *The Hurry-Up, No-Huddle: An Offensive Philosophy* Paperback – Monterey;, CA: Coaches Choice.January 1, 2003

304 Hinnen, Jerry, Report: *Gus Malzahn seeks to trademark "Hurry Up No Huddle"*. CBS.com., Nov. 22, 2013

305 James Crepea, Auburn Athority, *Gus Malzahn: Auburn has 'foolproof system' for signalling plays??*, Montgomery Advertiser A Gannnett Co., 10:23 a.m. CDT September 30, 2014

306 *modernizing the wing-t* - NFL HSPD, http://www.nflhspd.com/coaches-corner/article/modernizing-the-wing-t/ (accessed September 18, 2015).

307 http://sports.espn.go.com/college-football/story/_/id/13554358/*college-football-coaches-dissect-demise-defense*

308 Hunt, Vasha Vhunt@al.com, Nick Saban says football has changed 'as much as it ever has' since spread of no-huddle

309 Hunt, Vasha Vhunt@al.com Nick Saban has prepared in the offseason for more tempo and questions whether no-huddle offenses are what's best for football.

310 Solomon, John, *The no-huddle craze: College football defenses play catch-up and even practice fake injuries* http://muckrack.com/link/jgb1/the-no-huddle-craze-college-football-defenses-play-catch-up-and-even-practice-fake-injuries updated August 27, 2013

311 Coverdale, Andrew, Dan Robinson. *The Bunch Attack: Using Compressed Formations in the Passing Game*, Coaches Choice Books: Champaign, IL, 1997

312 Fertitta, Gabe, Successfully Using Hybrid Plays In Spread Offenses, AFCA Weekly, July 14, 2015.

313 Snyder, John Allen. *Slowing Down the Spread*, American Football Monthly, Aug/Sept. 2012.

314 Thamel, Pete, *Trading the Shotgun for the Pistol*. Sports Illustrated, Oct. 10, 2010.

315 McDonald, Jerry, *Colin Kaepernick's college coach to his pupil: 'Just awesome'* San Jose Mercury News. Jan. 14, 2013. http://www.mercurynews.com/sports/ci_22373815/colin-kaepernicks-college-coach-his-pupil-just-awesome

316 Thamel, Pete, *Trading the Shotgun for the Pistol*. Sports Illustrated Oct. 10, 2010.

317 http://www.football-offense.com/*what-is-the-pistol-offense/*

318 Thamel, Pete, *Trading the Shotgun for the Pistol*. Sports Illustrated Oct. 10, 2010

319 Podoll, Mike. *Option for Success*, AFCA Magazine, July-August 2015. p. 12.

320 Brown, Chris. *Triple Shoot Part 2 - Run game and play-action*, Smart Football, May 13, 2009.

321 Clark, Kevin. *Hot New Thing in the NFL: Ancient Big Ten Offenses*, Wall Street Journal, Sept 30, 2013.

322 Clark, Kevin. *Hot New Thing in the NFL: Ancient Big Ten Offenses*, Wall Street Journal, Sept 30, 2013.

323 Kucher, Mike.*The Spin: The Greatest Offense You've Never Heard Of*, American Football Monthly, Dec. 2006.

324 Speckman, Mark. *The Basics of the Williamette Offense*, 2004 AFCA Summer Manual, p. 24.

325 Speckman, Mark. *The Basics of the Williamette Offense*, 2004 AFCA Summer Manual, p. 25

326 Feliciano, Leon. The *Tsunami Offense*, , leon.feliciano@shorelineunified.org

327 *A-11 offense* - Wikipedia, the free encyclopedia, http://en.wikipedia.org/wiki/A-11_offense (accessed October 24, 2015).

328 Levin, Josh. *Could This Offense Revolutionize Football?*, NY Times Sports Magazine., November 1, 2008, http://www.nytimes.com/2008/11/02/sports/playmagazine/112rd.html?_r=0

329 *Three Tight End Offensive Formation magic 3* - FootballTimes, http://footballtimes.org/Printer.asp?ID=218 (accessed October 25, 2015).

330 *Three Tight End Offensive Formation magic 3* - FootballTimes, http://footballtimes.org/Article.asp?ID=218 (accessed October 24, 2015).

331 Stagg, Alonzo, & Henry L. Williams. *Scientific and Practical Treatise on American Football*. D. Appleton & Co., New York, NY. 1894. p. 233.

332 Reed, Herbert. *Football for Player and Public*, Frederick A Stokes Co., New York, NY. 1913. p 208-220

[333] Houghton, Percy. *Football and How to Watch it*. Marshall Jones Co., Boston, 1922. p. 95

[334] Samuels, Doug. Video: *How Michigan is scoring recruits using virtual reality*, Aug 4, 2015, Footballscoop.com.

[335] Bernett, Zach. *How some SEC staffs are using GPS to practice more efficiently* ; Aug. 12, 2015, http://footballscoop.com/news/how-some-sec-staffs-are-using-gps-to-practice-more-efficiently/

[336] Samuels, Doug. To Make Practices Safer, Dartmouth paired with Engineers to Make a Mobile Virtual Player." Aug. 21, 2015. http://footballscoop.com/news/to-make-practices-safer-dartmouth-paired-with-engineers-to-make-a-mobile-virtual-player/

[337] Solomon, Jon. *SEC, Big Ten coaches weigh in: pros, cons of advanced stats in football*, Aug. 5, 2015. http://www.cbssports.com/collegefootball/writer/jon-solomon/25260483/sec-big-ten-coaches-weigh-in-pros-cons-of-advanced-stat

[338] Clark, Kevin. *How the Rams Built a Laaboratory for Millennials*. The Wall Street Journal, Sept. 14, 2015. http://www.wsj.com/articles/how-the-rams-built-a-laboratory-for-millennials-1442257224

[339] Clark, Kevin. *How the Rams Built a Laaboratory for Millennials*. The Wall Street Journal, Sept. 14, 2015. http://www.wsj.com/articles/how-the-rams-built-a-laboratory-for-millennials-1442257224

Index

3-3-5, 257, 258, 293
4-3 "Over, 203, 204
4-3 defense, 191, 193, 194, 202, 203, 205, 243, 257
4-3 Under Front, 204
4-4-1-2 Rover, 162
46 defense, 245, 246
5 Man Line Defenses, 133
5-2 defense, 176, 197, 221, 222
5-2 Monster, 222
5-3-2-1, 92, 93, 118, 164
5-3-3, 133, 134, 135, 161, 163, 192
5-4-2, 133, 135, 150, 155
6-1-4 Defense. *See* Defense
6-2 Spot defense, 108
6-2-2-1, 43, 109
6-2-2-1 Defense. *Defense, defense*
6-3-2, 138, 155
7 Box, 22
7 Diamond, 36
7-2-2, 19, 22, 109, 140, 155
7-3-1 Defense. Defense
7-Diamond defense., 176
8-2-1 Defense, 58, 140, 141
8-3, 141
A11 Offense, 317
A-Formation, 71, 75, 114
Air Force, 199, 215, 247, 271, 308
Air Raid offense, 277, 278, 281, 284
Alabama, 130, 170, 175, 176, 199, 200, 273, 284, 299, 300, 323
Allen, 229, 260, 324
Allison Danzig, 3, 15, 20
Amherst, 4

Ancient Games, 1
Arkansas, 64, 85, 169, 188, 222, 257, 266, 271, 272, 285, 298
Army, 64, 71, 82, 87, 102, 111, 118, 126, 168, 170, 176, 188, 193, 194, 201, 306
Arnsparger, 212, 218, 219, 231, 252
Auburn, 40, 272, 274, 285, 287, 298, 299, 318, 319, 324
Ault, 304, 305, 306
Australian Rules football, 3
B" Formation, 80
Baltimore Ravens, 310
Baughan, 260
Bay City Wing-T, 247
Baylor, 145, 272, 278, 288, 289, 297
Belichick, 258, 260, 270, 311
Bellard, 198, 199, 212, 213
Bennie Owen, 90
Bible, 1, 111, 119, 138, 148, 160, 169, 236
Bierman, 49, 98, 99, 109, 132, 148, 164, 165, 170
Big Nickel defense, 321
Big Ten Conference, 39
Billick,, 266
Blaik, 168, 170, 188, 193, 201
Bloody Monday, 4
Bob Higgins, 79
Boston Game, 5, 6, 7
Boston Latin, 5
Boxing the Tackle, 18
Bridges, 145
Brigham Young University, 235, 277
Briles, 272, 278, 288, 289, 297

Broken bone, 199, 213
Brown, 4, 5, 69, 76, 118, 131, 150, 190, 191, 192, 210, 211, 227, 297, 324
Broyles, 188
Bryan, 317, 318
Bryant, 170, 175, 177, 178, 194, 199
Bubble Screen, 268, 295, 296
Buck Lateral, 76, 125
Bullough, 220, 221
Bumpas, 294
Bunch" formations, 302
Bush, 266
Button Hook Pass, 65
Buzz Coverage, 291
C" Formation, 81
Caesar, 2
Camp, 8, 9, 10, 12, 13, 14, 15, 19, 28, 29, 30, 31, 32, 41, 48
Canada, 3, 5, 7
Capers, 252, 254
Cardwell, 164
Carlisle, 70, 71
Carlisle Formation. *Single Wing*
Carson, 216, 254
Cason, 198
Chicago, 23, 39, 65, 92, 100, 103, 107, 117, 120, 121, 149, 150, 157, 229, 245, 271
Chicago Bears, 229
Chow, 235, 237, 240, 241, 275, 281
Cincinnati Bengals, 240, 249, 251
Claiborne., 224
Clemson,, 274
Cleveland Browns, 190, 260
Close" Formation, 67
Cloud Coverage, 290, 291, 294
Colgate, 71, 93, 108, 118
Collier, 218, 234, 260
Columbia, 6, 9, 127, 170

Concessionary Rules, 7, 9
Corbin,, 23
Cornell, 6, 39, 63, 65, 66, 70, 79, 115, 130, 141, 169, 319
Coryell, 182, 208, 209, 210, 211, 212, 227, 232, 234, 240, 319, 320
Counter Trey, 228, 239
Coverdale, 302, 313, 324
Cower, 253
Crisler, 125, 126, 141, 148, 164, 165, 168, 170, 188
Criss-Cross Play, 45, 46
Cup" Defense, 87
DaGrosa, 3, 87, 110, 160, 169
Dallas Cowboys, 106, 195, 205, 243, 249
Dallas Shift. *See* Shift
Danzig, 14, 15, 23, 28, 30, 31, 41, 52, 58, 59, 76, 82, 83, 110, 115, 117, 119, 127, 141, 148, 169, 194
Dartmouth, 4, 14, 63, 103, 169, 323
Davis, 14, 16, 30, 41, 208, 210, 211
Dawson, 200, 212
Defending the Notre Dame Shift. *Shift*
Defense, 22, 36, 37, 38, 43, 44, 52, 53, 73, 86, 87, 88, 89, 92, 93, 106, 108, 109, 110, 118, 120, 127, 137, 138, 139, 140, 141, 146, 150, 160, 162, 163, 174, 175, 177, 179, 180, 182, 191, 192, 193, 200, 202, 205, 206, 212, 216, 218, 219, 221, 222, 223, 224, 225,환227, 229, 231, 243, 245, 246, 251, 254, 255, 257, 293, 297, 320, 321
Defensive Alignments, 171
Defensive Numbering System, 175
Deland, 24, 27
Delaware, 188, 189, 190, 247, 285
DeLeone, 230
Diamond Formation, 282, 283
Dietzel, 188

Dime Alignment, 251
Dodd, 164, 169, 170
Dodge, 8, 9, 272
Dooley, 225
Dorchester High School, 5
Dorias, 65, 103, 106
Double Invert, 223, 224
Double Pass, 69
Double Split, 186, 187, 190
Double Wing, 20, 70, 75, 76, 78, 80, 89, 118, 121, 130, 131, 135, 139, 158, 167, 195, 215, 270, 271, 315, 316, 317
Dungy, 205, 254, 255
Dunn, 257, 258, 293
Dykes, 278
Eagle Defense, 150
Edwards, 235, 236, 240, 241, 275, 277, 278, 279
Ellison, 207, 208, 212, 227, 308
Elway, 227
Ends Back, 20, 21, 22, 23
Ends In, 37, 58
English, 2, 3, 5, 7, 25, 28
Episkyros, 1
Erdelatz, 170
Erickson, 228, 267, 271
Eton, 2, 7
Eugene Baker, 8
Evashevski, 170, 188
Fairbanks, 199, 213, 218, 220, 221
Fangio, 252
Faurot, 140, 147, 148, 151, 154, 156, 157, 158, 169
Fertitta, 304, 324
Fielding H. Yost, 58
First Defense for Passing Game, 86
First International Game, 7
Five Man Line, 117
Five Yard Rule, 12

Five-spoke defense, 174
Flex Defense. *See* Defense
Flexbone, 247, 248, 251, 266, 306, 307, 308
Flexbone Option. *See* Option
Flexible T, 215, 231
Fly Offense, 313
Flying Interference, 35
Flying Wedge, 24, 26, 27, 28, 30
Fontes, 208
Forward pass, 1, 19, 22, 26, 28, 44, 54, 61, 63, 64, 65, 66, 69, 84, 87, 89, 90, 92, 102, 318
Four Vertical, 270
four-spoke defense, 174
Four-Spoke Secondary, 120
Franklin, 273, 278, 284, 297
Free substitution, 167, 168
Freeze Option, 230
Freshmen Eligibility Rules, 39
Fry, 249
Fun and Gun, 261, 271
Gaelic Football, 3
Gailey, 250, 251
Gap 8 Defense, 141
Gap Control, 221
Geise, 224
George Woodruff, 18, 28
Georgia Southern, 248, 271
Georgia Tech, 86, 112, 170, 199, 248, 272, 306, 308
Gerrit Smith, 5
Gibbs, 209, 232, 235, 238, 239, 240, 286, 300, 319
Gillman, 208, 210, 211, 212, 227, 240, 241, 243, 279
Grant, 240
Greek, 1
Green Bay Packers, 200, 321

Grounding Rule, 112
Guards Back, 22, 34, 35, 36, 43, 44
Gus Malzahn, 272, 285, 286, 298, 324
H" back, 238
Halas, 120, 121, 149, 157, 271
Harbaugh, 310, 311, 322
Harlow, 93, 94, 130, 160, 161, 182
Harpastron, 1
Harvard, 4, 5, 6, 7, 8, 9, 10, 11, 14, 23, 24, 25, 26, 27, 29, 39, 48, 51, 53, 54, 60, 64, 66, 69, 70, 82, 92, 93, 94, 103, 117, 118, 130, 160, 161, 182
Haughton, 66, 67, 68, 69, 92
Hayes, 170, 213, 311
Heffelfinger, 18
Heisman, 26, 40, 59, 63, 86, 97, 112, 115
Helfrich., 274
Hickey, 195, 196, 261
Hidden Ball Trick, 40
Holgorsen, 272, 281, 282
Holmgren, 240
Houston Veer, 197, 198
Howard Jones, 99, 100, 102
Huddle, 1, 19, 41, 100, 141, 158, 159, 161, 193, 249, 250, 251, 274, 277, 298, 299, 308, 324
Humphries, 317, 318
Hurry Up" Yost, 54, 149
hybrid defense, 260
hybrid Plays, 304
I- formation, 168, 182, 185, 196, 208, 213, 256
Idaho, 66, 228, 267, 271
Idaho Spread Formation, 66
Illinois, 39, 50, 64, 65, 85, 94, 97, 101, 102, 110, *Shift*
Intercollegiate Athletics Association, 60
Intercollegiate Football Association, 9, 10, 28, 29

Inverted Veer, 275, 276, 277
Iowa Shift. *Shift*
Johnson, 243, 244, 245, 248, 272, 293, 306
Jones, 83, 99, 100, 120, 121, 122, 179, 180, 194, 208, 251, 322
Jotham Potter, 8
Kansas City Chiefs, 203, 211, 218, 235
Ken Keuffel', 164
Kentucky, 170, 273, 277, 278, 279, 280, 281, 284
Kiffin, 205, 255
Knoll, 254
Lafayette College, 41
Landry, 106, 192, 195, 203, 205, 207, 212, 249
Leach, 278, 280, 281, 284, 297, 298, 304, 308, 318
Leahy, 157, 158, 182, 183
LeBeau, 252, 254
Lee,, 266
Lehigh, 16
Levy, 250
Line of scrimmage, 11, 12, 13, 14, 20, 23, 27, 29
Little, 100, 127, 148, 170
Littlefield, 133
Lock Step Shift. *Shift*
Lombardi, 194, 200, 201, 202, 205, 212, 234
London Football Association, 3, 6
Lonesome End, 193, 194
Loose" Formation, 68
Maine, 188, 200
Markham, 316
Martin, 215, 231
Maryland I, 183, 185
Mass Plays, 19
Massasoit House, 9, 10

McCarty, 256
McGill University, 7
McKay, 196, 208
Meyer, 118, 142, 144, 148, 272, 273, 297
Miami Dolphins, 266
Miami., 228, 252, 266, 267
Michigan, 3, 9, 39, 40, 54, 59, 90, 109, 115, 125, 126, 149, 164, 165, 167, 168, 169, 170, 188, 222, 223, 247, 249, 310, 322
Michigan Angle, 222
Michigan State, 164
Mid-Line, 266, 267
Midline Read, 276
Mid-Line Triple Option. *See* Option
Midline Veer, 266
Minnesota, 31, 39, 42, 49, 50, 63, 65, 98, 99, 100, 103, 112, 115, 125, 132, 133, 164, 165, 170, 246, 254, 266, 310
Minnesota Shift. *Shifts*
Mississippi State, 199, 213, 257, 258, 319
Moffat, 41
Monken, 306
Mora,, 252
Morrison, 111, 112, 117, 133, 271
Motion, 42, 43, 115, 239
Mousetrap" Play, 69
Mudd, 235
Mueller, 273
Mumme, 271, 277, 278, 279, 280, 281, 284, 296, 297
Munn, 164, 165, 166, 167, 169
Naming of the Positions, 13
Naval Academy, 29, 82
Navy,, 170, 199, 258, 271, 306
NCAA, 39, 54, 60, 187, 188, 194, 213, 216, 235, 271, 306
Neale, 150, 190, 191, 192, 193, 246
Nebraska I, 214, 248

Nelson, 15, 30, 59, 61, 63, 64, 82, 83, 110, 188, 189, 285
Neumeier, 227
neutral zone, 13
New York Giants, 192, 194, 205, 260
Neyland, 170, 176, 177, 178
Nickel Defense, 229
Niumatalolo, 272, 306
No huddle, 249, 250, 272, 298, 299, 301
Noll, 210, 216
Normal" Formation, 142
Northwestern, 39, 48, 272
Notre Dame, 50, 64, 86, 87, 100, 102, 103, 104, 105, 106, 112, 113, 114, 117, 128, 129, 130, 131, 149, 150, 155, 157, 158, 168, 182, 183, 188, 200, 225, 247
Notre Dame Shift. *Shift*
Oakland Raiders, 211, 216, 235
Odd Front, 203
Ohio State, 92, 93, 97, 117, 147, 170, 213, 240, 249, 272, 273, 300, 318
Oklahoma, 90, 92, 151, 158, 159, 169, 170, 179, 199, 213, 218, 243, 278, 281, 282, 284, 293
Old Division Football, 4, 14
Olivadotti, 221, 231
One back" offense, 228, 267
One-gap 3-4, 220
Oneida Football Club, 5
Onside kick, 29, 61
Open Formation, 67, 105
Option, III, 158, 185, 196, 197, 198, 199, 212, 213, 230, 238, 243, 247, 248, 250, 251, 261, 266, 267, 270, 271, 273, 281, 284, 290, 292, 294, 295, 296, 297, 306, 307, 308, 309, 313, 324
Oregon, 208, 274, 297, 298, 316
Osborne, 249, 251, 256
Over-shifted, 38, 73, 163, 176

Owen, 90, 92, 192, 193
Parke Davis, 12, 15, 18, 24, 25
Parseghian, 188, 200, 225, 247
Pasqualoni, 230
Paterno, 225
Pattern Matching, 292
Patterson, 293, 297
Penn, 16, 18, 22, 28, 29, 31, 32, 34, 35, 36, 39, 41, 43, 52, 63, 64, 79, 85, 86, 93, 141, 225, 271, 290
Penn Charter School, 31
Pennsylvania Defense, 57, 107, 108
Percy Haughton, 66, 70, 83, 117
Perles, 216
Philadelphia Eagles, 150, 229, 246, 274, 319
Phillips, 175, 176, 218, 220, 221
Pistol Offense, 304
Pittsburgh Steelers, 216, 252, 253, 254
Pop Pass, 294
Power-O, 228
Princeton, 4, 5, 6, 8, 9, 10, 11, 12, 16, 17, 18, 20, 23, 24, 25, 27, 29, 34, 39, 41, 48, 53, 60, 63, 98, 115, 118, 125, 126, 164, 165, 169, 170, 319
Propst, 273
Pulling Guard, 19
Punt, Pass, and a Prayer, 94
Purdue, 39, 272
Quarterback Sweep, 53
Raymond, 188, 189, 190, 285
Regular Defense, 56, 57
Regular Formation, 69, 70
Revolving Tandem, 41
Richt, 272, 273, 297, 302, 322
Robber coverage, 263
Robert Zuppke, 50, 85, 94, 110
Robinson, 188, 302, 313, 324
Rockne, 50, 65, 86, 87, 102, 103, 104, 105, 106, 110, 112, 114, 119, 128, 129, 148, 149, 168
Rodriguez, 272, 273, 274, 275, 297
Rogers, 199, 212
Romans, 1, 2
Roosevelt, 53, 60, 82
Roxbury High School, 5
Royal,, 198
Rugby, 1, 2, 3, 6, 7, 9, 10, 13, 30
Rugby School. *See* Rugby
Rules Convention, 13
Run and Shoot,, 207
Run to Daylight, 202
Russell,, 273
Rutgers, 5, 6
Rutigliano, 218
Ryan, 245, 246, 251, 266
Schembechler,, 222
Scouting, 258, 270
Scovil,, 235
Screen Pass, 65
Screwballistics, 160
scrimmage rule, 11
scrummage, 8, 10
Seven Diamond, 18, 37, 71, 118
Seven Man Line, 36
Shakespeare, 2
Shaughnessy, 120, 121, 122, 149, 150, 154, 170, 229
Shift, 38, 42, 43, 47, 48, 49, 50, 51, 56, 58, 86, 97, 98, 99, 100, 101, 102, 103, 105, 106, 107, 112, 130, 132, 133, 207
*Shift*ft.
Shifts, 38, 42, 135
Short Punt, 40, 115, 116, 117, 139, 158
Shotgun., 195
Shrove Tuesday, 2
Shula, 218
Shurmur, 260, 321

Single Tackle Back, 32
Single Wing, 70, 71, 72, 73, 74, 76, 78, 79, 88, 102, 108, 115, 118, 121, 122, 126, 127, 130, 131, 135, 139, 155, 158, 160, 164, 165, 166, 183, 188, 195, 200, 216
Six Man Line, 81, 82, 135, 136
Sky Coverage, 291, 292
Smith, 30, 82, 183, 199, 212, 245, 249, 251, 254
SMU, 111, 271
Snavely, 79, 107, 130, 141
Snyder, 157, 266, 273, 324
Soccer, 1, 2, 3, 6, 7, 12, 14
Solem, 164, 167
South Carolina, 224, 258
Speckman, 313, 324
Spin Offense, 311, 312
spinner series, 79, 165
Split "T, 151, 154, 157, 158, 161, 164, 179, 196
Split Coverage, 293, 297
Split Cross Play, 45
Split Play, 44
Split-6, 224, 225
Spread Formation, 87, 106, 111, 112, 131, 142, 148, 156, 261, 308
Spread Offense, 111, 227, 271, 275
Spread Option. *See* Option
Spread Punt, 107, 271
Spread-Flex, 308
Springfield, Massachusetts, 20
Spurrier, 261, 262, 263, 271
Stagg, 8, 17, 19, 20, 22, 23, 26, 27, 29, 30, 31, 35, 38, 40, 41, 42, 43, 44, 45, 46, 47, 50, 51, 52, 53, 59, 64, 65, 69, 70, 79, 86, 92, 97, 100, 103, 106, 107, 108, 112, 115, 120, 150, 207, 321
Standing T" Formation, 147

Stanford, 82, 83, 110, 117, 127, 170, 228
Stanford,, 149
Stram, 203, 204, 218
Strong, 76, 215, 222, 236, 242, 253, 258, 292, 321
Stunt 4-3, 216
Swing Formations, 69
Switzer, 198, 212, 213, 231, 243, 247, 251
Syracuse, 112, 165, 167, 230, 266, 270
Tackles Back, 31, 32, 36
Tackling Rule, 13
Tally, 266
Tampa-2, 205, 254, 255, 256
Tarkenton, 240
Tatum, 151, 158, 218
Teague, 216
technology, 258, 322, 323
Tennessee,, 170
Texas, 92, 111, 115, 131, 133, 170, 175, 176, 198, 200, 272, 277, 278, 281, 288, 293, 296, 297, 300
Texas Christian University, 131
T-Formation, 11, 19, 54, 103, 104, 105, 120, 147, 149, 150, 187
The 5-2 Monster, 222
Three Tight End Formation, 321
Tight Six, 137
Trafford, 25
Triangle concept, 242, 243
triangle read, 243, 279
Triple Shoot, 308, 309, 310, 324
Triple Wing, 131, 271
triple-option, 199, 247, 248, 297
Tsu Chu, 1
Tsunami Offense, 315, 324
Tufts, 7, 14
Turtleback, 23
Two-platoon, 126, 196

Two-point conversion, 194
Umbrella Defense. *See* Defense
Unbalanced Line, 50, 131, 216
University of California, 273
University of Illinois, 41, 101, 121, 133
University of Mississippi, 257
University of Pennsylvania. *Penn*
University of Southern California, 99, 196, 257, 318
Urban Meyer. *See* Meyer
V Trick, 16, 17
Valatton, 316
veer, 156, 197, 198, 247, 256, 266
Veer blocking, 156
Villanova, 266
Virginia, 9, 82, 168, 182, 272, 273, 281, 282
Walsh, 12, 15, 208, 209, 236, 240, 241, 245, 255, 278
Walter Camp, 8, 9, 10, 11, 13, 18, 19, 25, 28, 30, 32, 41, 51, 54, 84
Warner, 20, 47, 50, 63, 64, 69, 70, 71, 72, 75, 78, 80, 81, 83, 89, 97, 110, 112, 113, 114, 117, 118, 120, 127, 150, 265, 271, 315, 316
Warren,, 235
Washington and Lee, 9
Washington Redskins, 209, 228, 238
Washington State, 228, 267, 278, 304, 308, 318
Wedge, 2, 16, 17, 18, 19, 23, 24, 25, 26, 27, 28, 29, 31, 35, 41, 54, 70, 171
West Coast offense, 208, 209, 236, 240, 241, 255, 256, 269, 278

Western Maryland, 93
Whoa Back, 47
Wichita State University, 230
Wide" Formation, 68
Widenhofer, 216
Wilce, 92, 93, 110, 117, 148
Wild Bunch formation, 313
Wildcat offense, 265
Wilkinson, 151, 158, 169, 170, 179, 180, 181, 194
Willamette University, 313
Williams, 30, 31, 32, 39, 49, 59, 63, 98, 112, 229
Wing-T, 188, 189, 215, 247, 285, 287, 308, 311, 313, 316
Winslow, 232, 234, 319
Wisconsin, 39, 49
Wishbone, 198, 199, 213, 247, 248, 256, 306
Woodruff, 28, 34, 35, 36, 37, 39, 41
Wyatt, 265, 266, 270, 316
Wyche, 234, 249, 251, 270
Wyoming, 228, 267, 308
Yale, 4, 5, 6, 7, 8, 9, 10, 11, 12, 13, 14, 16, 17, 18, 19, 23, 24, 25, 26, 27, 29
Yeoman, 196, 197, 198, 289
Yost, 3, 32, 40, 54, 56, 57, 58, 59, 81, 82, 90, 149
Z Formation, 70, 71, *SSingle Wing*
Zone Blitz, 251, 252, 253, 254, 258, 270
Zone block, 234, 235
Zone Read, 275, 276, 295, 296
Zuppke, 41, 65, 85, 86, 87, 94, 101, 110

Frank Francisco *is a veteran of forty-three years of coaching football. With a love of the game, studying the development of the sport has been a lifelong endeavor. Having begun his career coaching high school freshmen tailbacks in the Single Wing and ending it coaching college quarterbacks in the Spread Formation, he is exceptionally qualified to write about the evolution of the game. He is the father of two grown sons and he and his wife Joyce spend summers in the rolling hills of Pennsylvania and winters in Florida.*